Drafting Successful Access and Benefit-sharing Contracts

Legal Studies on Access and Benefit-sharing

Series Editors

Elisa Morgera
Matthias Buck
Elsa Tsioumani

VOLUME 5

The titles published in this series are listed at *brill.com/labs*

Drafting Successful Access and Benefit-sharing Contracts

By

Tomme Rosanne Young
Morten Walløe Tvedt

TUTA SUB AEGIDE PALLAS · 1683 ·

BRILL
NIJHOFF

LEIDEN | BOSTON

The Library of Congress Cataloging-in-Publication Data is available online at http://catalog.loc.gov
LC record available at http://lccn.loc.gov/2017042221

Typeface for the Latin, Greek, and Cyrillic scripts: "Brill". See and download: brill.com/brill-typeface.

ISSN 2213-493X
ISBN 978-90-04-35656-6 (hardback)
ISBN 978-90-04-35657-3 (e-book)

This book is printed on acid-free paper and produced in a sustainable manner.

Printed by Printforce, the Netherlands

Contents

Preface IX

1 ABS and Contracts 1
- 1.1 The Contractual Challenge of ABS 2
- 1.2 Methodology: The Legal and Factual Analysis Undertaken for This Book 12
- 1.3 Getting a Handle on the ABS Concept 19
- 1.4 Purpose and Organization of This Book 20

2 Drafting Functional ABS Contracts: How Contracts Can Achieve Reasonable ABS Objectives 22
- 2.1 Addressing the Ambiguity of ABS with the Specificity of Contact Law 23
- 2.2 Basic Contract Concepts – How Contracts Function 33
- 2.3 The Sources of Law for Interpretation and Drafting of ABS Contracts 40

3 Planning and Negotiating the Contract 52
- 3.1 Preparing to Establish a Contractual Relationship 53
- 3.2 Mapping the "Optimal ABS Contract" from the Negotiator's Perspective 53
- 3.3 Negotiating Strategy 60
- 3.4 From Strategy to Binding Contract – Identifying the Specific Situation of the Current Negotiation and Coordinating it with the Strategy 63
- 3.5 The First Steps in the Negotiation 71
- 3.6 CAVEAT: The Illusionary Two-step Contractual Approach 74

4 "Make Sure You Contract with the Right Parties": Addressing the Challenges of Contracts with Companies and other Entities 80
- 4.1 An Example: What It Means to "Contract with the Right Parties" 82
- 4.2 "Legal Personality" – Basic Criteria for Legally Binding Any Entity 87
- 4.3 Ability to Perform: Addressing the Nature and Stability of Corporate Entities 95
- 4.4 Contracting with the Right Individuals – Legally Recognized Capacity and other Issues 96
- 4.5 Legal Authority to Act on Behalf of a Party 101
- 4.6 Including and Properly Binding All Necessary Parties 106

5 **"Be Specific and Concrete": The Subject Matter (Res), Functional Clauses and Objective of the Contract** 113
5.1 Contractual Precision – Ambiguity Kills Contracts 115
5.2 The Operative Provisions / What Does the Contract Do? 116
5.3 What is Transferred? – The Need for Precision about the *Res* 118
5.4 Obligation/Action Clauses: The Duties and Expectations of the Parties 123
5.5 Triggering Contractual Rights and Duties 138
5.6 "Objective" or "Purpose" Clauses 143
5.7 Change of Use or Intent 146

6 **"Manage and Address Major Risks": The Third-party Transfer Challenge** 157
6.1 The Transfer of Genetic Resources, ATK or Preliminary Research Results to Third Parties 158
6.2 Laws and Consequences Regarding Transfers of Resources and Rights 161
6.3 Assessing the Parties' Options Regarding Third-party Transfer 164
6.4 Key Legal Elements of a Transfer Clause 167
6.5 Advice on Drafting Provisions Addressing Third-party Transfer 175
6.6 Special Third-party Transfer Risks 191

7 **"Know the Possibilities and Limitations of Contract Law": Contract Validity, Equity and Enforceability** 197
7.1 Valid or Void – What Makes Your Document a Contract? 197
7.2 Basic Concepts and Principles of Contractual Functionality 198
7.3 Drafting Issues of Validity for ABS Contracts 206
7.4 Effect of Contract Invalidation 222
7.5 Valid but Unenforceable – What Can be Done with "Soft" Obligations? 223
7.6 Contract Classification Issues 224
7.7 Industry Standards 226

8 **"Expect the Best; Plan for the Worst": Contract Provisions that Improve Enforceability and Address Contract Amendment** 229
8.1 Why Not Wait until Enforcement Is Needed? Addressing Enforceability in the Text 230
8.2 Types of Legal Remedies Available and How the Contract Can Affect Them 232

8.3 Enforcement-related Provisions in ABS Contracts 241
8.4 Practical and Procedural Elements Relating to Enforcement of ABS Contracts 254
8.5 Arbitration and Mediation Clauses 262
8.6 Parties that Are Not Parties: Other Persons or Entities that Might Seek Enforcement 263

9 **"Protect Contractual Expectations to Minimize the Need for Litigation": Guarantees, Incentives, and Other Security Arrangements** 268
9.1 The Advantage and Disadvantage of Non-judicial Remedies 269
9.2 The Contractual Balance and the Role of Non-judicial Remedies 270
9.3 How Non-judicial Remedies Function 270
9.4 Non-judicial Remedy Mechanisms for Use in ABS Contracts 276
9.5 How ABS Contractual and Legislative Requirements Can Enhance Future Remedial Options 284
9.6 Avoiding the Draconian – "Reasonable and Streamlined" Mechanisms 290

10 **"Avoid Making Legal Assumptions": The Perils of Relying on a "Governing Law" Clause and/or "Private International Law"** 293
10.1 The "Governing Law" Clauses 294
10.2 "Private International Law" – A Misunderstood Concept 297
10.3 The Basic Questions Considered by "Private International Law" 299
10.4 International Commercial Law 300
10.5 Impacts of PIL and International Commercial Law on ABS Contracts 316

11 **Contract-related Provisions of ABS Regime Instruments** 321
11.1 Contracts as Tools of the ABS Regime 322
11.2 Components of the ABS Regime 323
11.3 Global ABS Regime Instruments Addressing ABS Contracts – The Broadest View 324
11.4 Caveat: Other International Instruments and Regimes of Potential Importance to ABS Contracts and Their Parties 328
11.5 Specific Provisions Directly Relevant to Drafting ABS Contracts 332

12 The Risks and Benefits of Shortcuts: Models, Forms, Guidelines and Existing-contract Examples 364
12.1 The Desire for "Model Contracts," "Model Clauses" and Other Examples in ABS 364
12.2 Types of Models and Examples and Their Associated Risks 370
12.3 Finding the Best Model, Form or Example for Your Needs 376
12.4 Future Developments 384

13 Conclusion 389
13.1 Contracts and ABS 390
13.2 The ABS Challenges and the Seven Rules of Contracts 394
13.3 The Quest for Shortcuts 396
13.4 Making ABS a Functional and Effective Tool for the Future 396

Resources Cited 399
Index 413

Preface

"Drafting Successful Access and Benefit-sharing Contracts" builds on the fact that the international negotiations in Access and Benefit Sharing are (at least mostly) over, so now the time has come to accept that the Nagoya Protocol and the binding obligation in the Convention on Biological Diversity are what we have got, and move forward and find the best ways to use them effectively. The time is now to create and use practical tools that will work to develop and implement a functional ABS system at every level. The ABS Contract is one of those tools. ABS Contracts are, at base, contracts bound by contract law. There may not be much formal "ABS law" that deals with ABS contracts as yet, but the principles of contract law are very detailed and well established in every country.

Most ABS contracts are "international contracts" (contracts in which at least one key element is found in more than one country). After hundreds of years of legal development in addressing international contracts, there is still no uniform global contract law. As a new area of contract law comes into being, it is common for special rules and practice within that area to develop on a contract-by-contract basis. This process may happen quickly or slowly, depending on many factors, including

(a) How many contracts are written per year in that area;
(b) How much information becomes public regarding the contracts as they are written;
(c) Whether and how those contracts require official interpretation (arbitration, renegotiation, litigation) that is known publicly; and
(d) How many of those contracts have been completed to the satisfaction of all parties.

At present, there are few ABS contracts in existence and still fewer that have been completed. Public information is limited, especially regarding the resolution of conflicts or enforcement. This book uses the authors' experience in the negotiation of ABS related contracts and their in-depth knowledge related to natural resource contracts in general, supplemented by research in contract legal issues around the world, both at national and international levels.

On the basis of that foundation, "Drafting Successful Access and Benefit-sharing Contracts" provides the reader with a strong foundation of the manner in which the most basic aspects of contract law should be applied to the drafting of ABS contracts. The authors realize that new ABS contracts are arising daily, and that over the next few years it is likely that some aspects of ABS contracts will become recognized standards for the development of ABS contracts. The principles expressed in this book, will continue to provide a basic underpinning enabling negotiators, drafters, parties, arbitrators and judges to interpret the application of those new standards, as well as to help in the development of this new and important contractual area.

The research behind this monography has been possible by grants from the Norwegian Research Council through two research projects: Biotechnology in Agriculture and Aquaculture – Effects of Intellectual Property Rights in the Food Production Chain (project number 220630/O70) and Exploring Legal Framework for Marine Bioprospecting and Innovation (project number 208543). It has also been supported by the ABS Capacity Development Initiative, and is written with a view to the needs of strengthening capacity to negotiate and draft better contracts.

We want to thank everyone who have attended trainings and consultations, and sharpened your understanding of ABS and the role of contracts during the last decades.

The Fridtjof Nansen Institute, Polhøgda
June 2017

CHAPTER 1

ABS and Contracts

From the earliest stages in the process of negotiating the CBD and endeavouring to implement Access and Benefit Sharing ("ABS"), the Parties had strongly agreed that private law (contracts) would operate to resolve the twin ABS challenges of enabling reasonable access to genetic resources and providing fair and equitable sharing of benefits arising from their use.[1] Reliance on these claims during the first 24 years following adoption of the Convention on Biological Diversity ("CBD")[2] has inevitably demonstrated that contracts alone did not turn ABS into a well-functioning innovative financial mechanism. In order to make a functional contractual mechanism, there is a need to develop a better understanding of contractual drafting in the area of ABS.

In addition, in the early years, the inclusion of this overwhelmingly financial element in an environmental convention was often justified by stating that ABS would provide an economic incentive for biodiversity conservation.[3]

---

1 Early discussions and commentators did not cite any authority for their contractual presumption, stating that it is "inherent in the language of CBD Article 15." See, Bonn Guidelines, Art. 59; COP 5 Decision V/26; COP 6 Decision VI/24; COP 7 Decision VII/19; see also the various Reports of the International Negotiating Committee (INC) and International Committee for the CBD (ICCBD), 1992. See also Glowka, 1998, at 8; Laird, 1993; Reid *et al.*, 1993; and Ten Kate and Laird, *et al.*, 1999. Notably, although many of these authors were lawyers, they did not include any direct discussion of contractual or legal issues, presumably assuming any detailed analysis unnecessary. At the time of adoption of the CBD, however, numerous professional law news magazines and journal articles decried the fact that although ABS negotiators were assuming that contract law would govern ABS, they had apparently not noticed that it was currently impossible under the most basic contract law of most countries.

2 Adopted 5 June 1992, UNTS vol. 1760, p. 79, entry into force 29 December 1993. ABS is directly discussed in Article 15 of the CBD. Its benefit-sharing component is specifically identified in Article 1 as one of the objectives of the Convention. In addition, several definitions ("biological resources," "country of origin of genetic resources," "country providing genetic resources," "genetic material," "genetic resources" and "technology") in Article 2 and provisions relating to the use and protection of indigenous and traditional knowledge relating to genetic resources in Articles 10(c) and 8(j) are frequently discussed in connection with ABS, particularly following the 2010 adoption of the Nagoya Protocol.

3 Ten Kate and Wells, 2001. See also Glowka (undated). Many commentators described ABS as a "great bargain," in which the conservation efforts of genetic resource providers were supposed to be compensated by receipt of a share of value-creation from the utilization of genetic resources.

 | DOI 10.1163/9789004356573_002

Experience to date has shown disappointing results in this area as well. The great question for today, in the wake of the CBD's 2010 Nagoya Protocol on Access and Benefit Sharing ("NP"),[4] is whether countries, users, providers and others can turn these disappointments into successes through which ABS is able to contribute substantially to the conservation and sustainability of ecosystems and species, by promoting widespread recognition and sharing of an alternative economic value of biodiversity.

If the ABS framework is to become functional, it must be functional within the global commercial system. In effect it must create a commercial mechanism for genetic resources supported by reasonable and effective incentives (both legal and practical) that encourage both users and providers to comply. This book explores how contracts can be used as a tool towards achievement of this goal.

This chapter begins with a brief examination of the need for and objectives of this book, followed by a discussion of the primary contractual conceptual issues that are most relevant to the particular challenges of contract law and practice when applied to ABS. It ends with a brief discussion of the authors' methodology in preparation of this book.

1.1 The Contractual Challenge of ABS

Contracts constitute a key area of ABS development. The ability of ABS contracts to be properly implemented using contract law and principles will be a key to the success of the entire ABS regime. The Nagoya Protocol negotiations made it very clear that the Parties would not retreat from their original reliance on private contracts and related instruments as the primary vehicles for implementing ABS, and indeed that they were also going to apply that mechanism to all transactions relating to the use of "traditional knowledge associated with genetic resources" (Associated Traditional Knowledge or ATK). The CBD and NP are, however, very unspecific about the commercial and contractual aspects of ABS. Perhaps the reason for this is the omnipresence of contracts in modern life. In some form, contracts and commerce permeate virtually all human life around the world (even in the most remote indigenous communities). It is understandable that these negotiators, under intensive pressure to resolve numerous highly controversial technical and sustainability questions by a fast-approaching deadline, would assume that their statements, decisions and Protocol provisions about contractual/commercial implementation would be sufficient to address their needs, and that by turning ABS implementation over

4 Adopted in 2010, the NP entered into force 12 October 2014.

to contract law, they had avoided the need to negotiate the details of the ABS implementation system.

1.1.1 *Why a Book on Contracts in ABS?*

Unfortunately, especially when applied to trans-national/international contracts,[5] the system of contractual and commercial law is not as clear or simple as many ABS negotiators assumed or had been told. To fully understand the nature of the ABS challenge with regard to contracts, it is necessary to begin by looking at the types of contracts for which international law is well established.

The concept of legally binding contracts is quite ancient, with references to their use dating back more than 4,000 years.[6] Consequently, there have been millions of examples of the traditional types of contracts, such as contracts for sale, service/employment contracts, banking and investment instruments, land grants, easements, insurance, licenses, *etc.* Over the centuries, a great many of these have been brought into public courts and arbitrations to resolve disputes. As a result the details of their functionality as contracts is relatively clear.

In more recent years, however, it has become necessary to apply the basic principles of contract law in many new situations. For example, in the past century, it has been necessary to develop the ability to apply some or all of the mechanisms used in conventional contracts to issues such as the use of airwaves for radio and television transmission, software development and licensing, internet sales and the development, identification, gene-mapping and use of micro-organisms. In each of these examples, modern contract practice has, over a period of decades, found ways in which contractual mechanisms can apply, and come to agreements on some standards applicable in each. All of these types of contracts are still developing.

> "TRANS-NATIONAL" OR "INTERNATIONAL CONTRACT"
>
> a contract in which one or more of the "elements of the contract" (as defined below) happens in or involves a second country.

5 See box. It has proven unexpectedly difficult to determine which contracts are "international" and which are domestic. Indeed, the lack of consensus on this issue has been one major source of global inability to develop a body of international contract law. The above definition we have selected is a simplification of the definition of "international contract" found in the 1980 Rome Convention on the Law Applicable to Contractual Obligations (OJ C 27, 26.1.1998, pp. 34–46) which is the most complete of the various attempts to adopt a body of international contract law. The Rome Convention has only 12 Parties, all European countries.

6 There are examples of contractual laws in the Code of Hammurabi (Babylon, c. 1772 BCE) and other ancient legal texts. The Old Testament, the Koran, and many other ancient texts include descriptions of various contractual relationships.

Even with conventional types of contracts, the law of contracts is not entirely clear or predictable. There are still situations in which the parties may disagree over a contractual point and must resolve their differences in court. Where the contract involves new contractual mechanisms developed to address new needs, the system is even less predictable, and still developing. The need to apply contract principles to new and different situations and subject matter necessitates the development of new solutions; while the fact that it still involves the application of contract law imposes the obligation to ensure that these new solutions do not break down the centuries-old practices and principles applicable to more traditional contracts. This raises new challenges and uncertainties for those attempting to use contract in these new ways.

As discussed in greater detail in this book, especially in ¶ 1.1.2, Chapter 2 and Chapter 5, *infra,* uncertainty is the enemy of functional contracts. Where the facts, requirements and benefits under the contract are not clearly established in a manner that allows them to be concretely applied to all future situations, a contract may face serious difficulties in implementation and enforcement. This book proposes to examine the reasons that the law governing conventional contracts is not easily applied to contracts addressing new concepts such as genetic resources, ATK and access and benefit-sharing.

Another area in which innovation is still rapid and prediction is less easy is international contracts. Even though all countries have (their own, sometimes very different) principles of contract law, the manner in which the law applies to a particular contract that has international components[7] is still far from predictable – the international nature of any contract makes its drafting, implementation and enforcement much more difficult.

Consider for example, the contract for the sale of goods – one of the most typical examples of a "conventional contract." Sale of goods contracts are generally thought of as relatively easily governed by domestic law. Several basic principles, such as the need for concrete specificity (model, quality, quantity

7 *I.e.,* where one or more of the following comes from or is found in more than one country: *all parties (considering their nationality and location); the* res *(right, action or property that is the subject of the contract (e.g., genetic resources or* ATK*)); the location in which any activities described in a contract occur; the country under whose law a legal action (lawsuit or arbitration) to enforce or interpret the contract is brought, the location to which all or any part of the* res *is transported;* etc. Note: this definition is based on the definition that was agreed in the negotiation of the 1980 Rome Convention on the Law Applicable to Contractual Obligations. Unfortunately, owing to other factors, that convention never entered into force. In 2008, the European Parliament and Council adopted Regulation (EC) No 593/2008 of the on the law applicable to contractual obligations, which it claims replaces and modifies the Rome Convention and makes it an EU (Rome I) regulation. The regulation does not use the term "international contracts."

and a fixed price) seem virtually universal. Despite the consensus, the parties to a trans-national sale of goods contract, face some uncertainties, both contractual land jurisdictional.

In negotiating international sale of goods contracts and most types of conventional contracts, the parties rely on the large body of practical experience and jurisprudence at the national and international level, and even an international agreement. Unlike most international contracts, international contracts for the sale of goods are discussed in an international agreement, United Nations Convention on Contracts for the International Sale of Goods (CISG), which has entered into force.[8] Unfortunately, as detailed in Chapter 10, *infra*, there is very little agreement among countries on international contractual issues. As a result, the first challenge for any party seeking to rely on the CISG is to determine whether the subject matter of the contract falls within the limited scope of that agreement.

Even conventional contracts become extremely complex when they operate in the trans-national arena, and the challenges for contracts addressing new technologies are multiplied still more. This book will focus on the ABS contract, which is clearly a novel situation for contract law, having been created in the latter years of the 20th century and substantially re-agreed as recently as 2010.

Added to that, as explained in Chapter 10, there is no generally accepted body of binding international contract law. There is also no international court with jurisdiction over international contract disputes. Instead all contracts involving any private individual are governed and enforced under national contractual and commercial law, which varies *greatly* from country to country. For all of these reasons, it is difficult to be confident that any international contract (even a conventional one) will be legally valid, or that its obligations and payment terms will be binding.

> "ELEMENTS OF A CONTRACT"
>
> for purposes of determining whether a contract has elements from two or more countries, the "elements of a contract" include the following: *all parties* (considering their nationality and location); *the res* (right, action or property that is the subject of the contract, as discussed in Chapter 4); *the location in which any activities described in a contract occur; the country under whose law a legal action may be brought, the location to which all or any part of the res is transported; etc.*

8 The CISG and other international instruments on contract issues are discussed in more detail in Chapter 10, *infra*.

ABS is clearly not a conventional type of contract. It's basic legal concept is less than 40 years old. In many essential ways, it is completely unlike any of the conventional contract categories. For example, it merges commercial objectives with environmental and social-welfare objectives, which is by itself a difficult task in a contract. In addition, the resources accessed pursuant to an ABS contract may often be unknown or undescribed, and the expected outcome or result of the actions taken and obligations imposed under the ABS contract may be highly uncertain. There are also serious unanswered questions regarding ownership or rights of disposition of the *res* in an ABS contract *and* the *res* itself is ambiguously described and understood. Often, the parties' respective duties under an ABS contract are unclear and ambiguous. It may often be nearly impossible to determine when a contractual duty has been triggered or violated, unless a considerable care has been taken in crafting the wording and procedures of the contract.

ABS contracts also share numerous additional challenges with many other types of less conventional contracts. For example, their validity may often depend on government approval that is outside of the control of any party. Indeed there may be numerous other statutory requirements that can affect whether the ABS contract is valid.

As a result of their novelty, ABS relationships have proven difficult or impossible to address contractually up to now, even at the domestic level. When users and providers have attempted to use contract law as a tool for ABS implementation, their efforts have often led only to legal and functional obstacles that have often prevented ABS enforcement or even consensual implementation.

It has long been obvious to commercial and legal experts and practitioners that the ABS system must eventually address and resolve a number of commercial and contractual matters.[9] If it does not do so, that system cannot function effectively and many provisions in ABS contracts and other documentation will not be enforceable. Simply put, unless the contracts and other instruments are carefully created and consider and comply with a range of very detailed contract law issues, contractual and commercial law and practice will prevent or hinder benefit-sharing, rather than enabling, promoting or supporting it.

This book is intended help to fill a gap in ABS discussions – to examine specifically how the practice of contract development and implementation can support rather than impede the fulfillment of the objectives of CBD Article 15 and the Nagoya Protocol. Specifically, it describes the most important of the challenges that must be confronted in creating ABS contracts, and makes some

9 For a detailed discussion of these issues, see Tvedt and Young, 2007. A discussion of critical deficiencies regarding contracts is also found in Young 2007 ("Applying Contract Law to ABS").

suggestions for negotiators seeking to ensure that their ABS contract is legally valid and enforceable.

1.1.2 *"Our ABS Contracts Are Based on TRUST and RELATIONSHIPS, So Why Should We Care About Contract LAW?"*

The most common questions when contract law was mentioned in the ABS negotiations are very simple – Why not just rely on our mutual trust and/or our existing relationship with the other party? Why should we worry about the details of contract law? These questions arise because the law (when viewed as a system of courts, police and legal penalties) is seen as a very sharp tool. Most people (in all countries) do not want to consider their contract as the first step in a process that will end with lawsuits, judgments and penalties. Moreover, it is known that lawsuits often harm the existing relationship among the parties – and in nearly all types of contracts, the parties desire that their relationship that should continue and produce future contracts and additional benefits. Often, critics assume that, the presence of lawyers and complex contracts increases the risk of legal action, noncompliance with the contract, and damage to the relationships. They presume that those risks will disappear if the lawyers and contracts are not a part of the transaction. In the ABS negotiations, such critics said, informally, "In our country, people do not go to court very often. ABS contracts should function without a court and without all this talk about what is 'binding or enforceable.' "[10]

Although that statement was entirely true, the speakers were ignoring the basic fact underlying the entire system of commercial/contract law in all countries: All parties to a contract prefer not to go to court. In fact, the underlying reason that contract law exists is to make it easier for contract parties to avoid going to court. If the parties to a contract have written down their agreement, it is less likely that they will have differing opinions on what was agreed, and thus fewer disputes. The use of written contracts is intended to help the parties avoid disagreements, misunderstandings and the need to litigate. If the contract is well written, it may achieve this goal. The entire global system of commerce would break down if contractual implementation only happened

10 These statements were frequently focused on the United States, which is often perceived by others to be an extremely litigious system. In fact, however, it is a country whose 321 million people (as of February 1, 2014, per http://countrymeters.info/en/United_States_of_America_%28USA%29/) engage in hundreds of millions of contracts (at least) every year. The fact that tens of thousands of contracts (less than 0.01% of the total) are litigated every year indicates in fact that the US's very elaborate system of commercial law (among other factors) is functioning to help prevent the need for contract litigation.

through the courts. One emphasis of this book is to help ABS contracts to achieve clarity.

To explain this more clearly, it is useful to think about the most common contracts in each of our lives – such as contracts for buying/selling a product or property, lending or borrowing money, or doing work for hire. For all of us, these contracts are familiar. The other parties are usually people from our own community, state, province, and very often friends, colleagues, neighbors, or family members. Our contracts are with people or companies that we have done business with before; or who have been recommended by one of the above-mentioned people. Regardless of contract law, when we enter into an agreement with such a person (to sell him a car, to lend him some money, or to do a day's work in exchange for pay), that agreement may be effective for three essential reasons: first, our relationship with and/or trust of this person or the person who recommended him; second, the fact that both parties are from the same culture, country/community, industry and/or society, and have similar or identical views of what a contract is and/or what each can and should expect; and third, the fact that all parties are aware of the consequences to themselves if they violate the contractual relationship. Because of these three intertwined factors, in many aspects of our everyday lives, we may not need to have any written contract at all (or at most a page or two of writing). But without these three factors, it is very difficult for even a simple (written or oral) contract to operate properly.

There is a lack of these three factors (relationship of trust, shared cultural context and societal consequences) in most ABS contracts, and the ways in which a properly written contract can fill in these gaps are explained in detail in throughout this book. Often, in the ABS context, NONE of the three essential factors are present. A contractual relationship that lacks these factors can go forward only by finding contractual ways to replace them. Thus, legal enforceability can create a relationship/reputation element that the contract's parties will respect. Equally, an enforceable contract can ensure that the parties share the same (or at least similar) expectations of what will happen under the contract. It can also ensure that all parties have a clear understanding of the consequences that will arise if the contract is violated or terminated. Where these three factors do not exist, as in ABS, because the issue is not yet fully addressed by contract law and because the parties are from different countries, they can be developed either at the level of the individual contract, by writing them into a detailed contract that both parties understand; or at the national or international level, by developing *and obtaining legal acceptance of* standards for ABS contracts that are internationally recognized.

With regard to the latter option (the development of standards), there has been a lot of experience in the past 50 years with formal processes, and a long history before that, in which standards were developed more informally, over a long time.[11] As further discussed in Chapter 12, standard development may happen in two ways. The first of these is legislative. At the national level, countries may directly adopt and implement statutory standards for ABS contracts Internationally, especially once such legislative standards have been adopted by a large number of countries, the recognition of the need to harmonize them internationally may prompt a variety of international efforts, from formal systems under the International Organization for Standardization (ISO) or under the CBD to guidance and other assistance to countries in ensuring that national standards are harmonized.[12] In particular, such acts needs to specifically determining how and to what extent one country can and should recognize apply and enforce another country's ABS legislation.

Second, standardization may happen judicially. Where the judicial system (or a specific court, arbitration body or designated official) is tasked with interpreting and enforcing ABS contracts, the decisions made by these bodies will eventually influence contractual negotiations. As national contract practices themselves begin to change, the courts will recognize and further clarify these "judicially recognized industry standards." As international bodies are called to address contractual disagreements, or more likely to address their enforcement.[13] These processes may be helped along if they are supported by the creation of a judiciary at a supranational level, as has happened in other (potentially related) fields, including investment agreements and patent enforcement.

Returning to the three basic components of a contract based on trust, we can see many ways in which ABS contracts are not able to use them, and must find contractual legal provisions to fill in the gap. With regard to the first element (past and ongoing relationship), for example, the traditional approach is

11 Both nationally and international standards and certifications systems have developed to enable the adoption of formally accepted standards in a wide range of industrial and commercial situations. Most recently, these systems have been used as means of integrating social welfare factors (dubbed "corporate social responsibility.") For a detailed discussion, see Young, 2004.

12 In general, the concept of "harmonized" legislation means that although countries strive for interoperability, they are each free to be adapt their provisions to their country's own legal, social, cultural and geographic particularities.

13 The enforcement of commercial judgments is one of the few areas in which countries both inside and international law outside the EU have been able to agree on international principles applied to private commercial challenges. See, Chapter 10, *infra*.

clearly not sufficient, even though, up to now, most ABS contracts have been negotiated between a provider/community/provider-country and an individual (researcher or other). As discussed in detail in Chapter 4, this individual may claim that he is negotiating on behalf of a larger company or corporation. He may even give assurances that, if he should, in the future, transfer the genetic resources or ATK to another person or company, he will ensure that the transferee will be bound by the contract. Although the provider may know this individual well, he may not have any knowledge of the company, nor can he have any certainty about some unknown future transferee. The provider must call for or take measures to address this uncertainty (*see* Chapter 4, *infra*). Another factor that relates to personal relationships is reputation. In most local transactions, the parties know that their future transactions would suffer, if they get a bad reputation by violating one contract. Large companies may have the same concern, especially where they have a long-term interest in creating durable "supply chains" for future procurement. In ABS, however, it is often the case that the amount of material that must be collected by the user is relatively small. Hence, most users will not need to rely on longer-term relationships.

In addition, as discussed in Chapter 5, many other factors that are not known to the other parties may impact a company's incentive to participate in an ABS contract. For example, in some countries, the law forbids any company with shareholders from taking actions which negatively impact those shareholders' best interests. In other words, the company cannot give away any of its assets unless authorized by formally adopted corporate policies (sometimes called "corporate social responsibility" policies). If a company is not obligated under a contract to pay money or other benefits, then it may be in violation of those principles if it should decide to make any payment without an obligation. All of these factors may diminish the provider's ability to rely on personal or institutional relationships to ensure ABS compliance. Even where the relationship exists and is strong, however, it is only one of three factors that must be linked into the contract.

As detailed in Chapter 5, in ABS contracts, the second ("expectations") factor is more likely to be the source of contractual problems than a means of avoiding them, even when all elements of the contract occur within a single community. The parties to any contract often interpret the agreement differently with respect to issues that were not specifically mentioned in their original discussion and/or simple written contract. For example, a contract between a woodcutter and the owner of the forest giving each one-half of the value of each tree that the woodcutter will cut and sell may yield different views on what the parties meant by "value," especially if there is a shift in circumstances between agreeing on the contract and making the payment. The forest owner may expect half the appraised value of the tree, while the harvester may offer only half of the price paid by the sawmill, after deduction of harvesting costs. Additionally, the owner may expect payment immediately, but the harvester may expect to pay at the end of the year. Where the contract is international, there are also issues regarding currency, exchange rate, risk of loss in transport and many other issues. While a more detailed contract could not eliminate all differences in expectations, it could clarify many points in advance.

The third factor (consequences) is also critical in order for contracts to function. As noted above, where the parties do business within a single community, their reputations within that community for fair dealings are very important. Thus, when a contractual issue becomes a problem, they have a strong incentive to meet and work it out, so that they will not get the reputation of taking advantage of those they contract with, or of always going to court. Where the parties are from different communities, however, the consequences may be different. A party from outside the community may not be motivated to avoid a bad reputation within the community, if he does not plan to return for future deals. Consider for example, a foreign buyer who comes into Community X and enters into a contract to buy one farmer's entire annual harvest of beans, but changes his mind when the market price for beans drops, deciding to buy wheat from a farmer in Community Y instead. If he does not have any future plans for more deals in Community X, that buyer may not treat the bean farmer fairly, because he does not have a commercial reason to care whether his actions would negatively affect his reputation in Community X. In such a case, the only way to ensure that the buyer behaves fairly may be through the existence and enforcement of an effective and binding contract. In most cases, the existence of the contract alone may be enough to inspire him to act appropriately – making it unnecessary to bring any kind of enforcement action. The contract's existence motivates that buyer to make a serious effort to work things out non-judicially.

All of these factors can be injected into transboundary contracts between commercial/industrial entities and providers by developing shared understanding through contractual clarity and the development of internationally accepted legal standards. The overall objectives of this book are to help those negotiating and drafting ABS contracts, by increasing their understanding of what makes those contracts more effective and to give them an idea of the specific contractual tools and mechanisms that they can use to address particular concerns. In this way, it is hoped that they can increase the likelihood that the contract will be found legally valid and binding under the existing law in any user, transferee or other country. In addition, it will help to increase the understanding of the ways in which commercial contract law applies to this rather specific area, and may eventually contribute to the formal or informal development of standards or models for ABS contracts. Like the contracts mechanism itself, the book's goal is to attempt to ensure that all parties' expectations and awareness of consequences are as similar as possible and that they are written clearly so that all parties have a shared understanding of exactly what is required and how binding those requirements are. If the parties to a contract have such a shared understanding, it will normally not be necessary to formally "enforce" the contract – they will have a predictable level of incentive to resolve any difficulties informally.

1.2 Methodology: The Legal and Factual Analysis Undertaken for This Book

As noted above, the greatest challenges for negotiators and drafters of ABS contracts arise from two realities: First, the "ABS community" (users, providers, governmental officials and contract negotiators) generally has an incomplete understanding of the legal and practical issues that govern international contracts. As a result, they may sometimes adopt MAT and other ABS documents that are legally invalid in the user's or arbitrator's country, or would not be enforceable against the user. After the document is signed and taken back to the user's home office, the fact that it contains no legally binding provisions may lead that user to ignore it. By contrast, the provider, not being conscious about this legal situation, has a different set of expectations. Second, some particular aspects and elements of ABS contracts render them markedly different from other contracts and increase the possibility that an ABS contract could be declared invalid.

Although a number of scholars and other authors have made some attempt to address the role of contracts for ABS,[14] none has attempted to address these basic challenges. For many years following adoption of the CBD, despite only

14 Three of the earliest of these works, written by large expert groups – The Crucible Group, 1994, The Crucible II Group, 2000, and The Crucible II Group, 2001, attempted to address some of the legal challenges of ABS – aimed at spelling out a number of formulations for countries to choose from whether collectively or nationally, to address what they perceived as primarily a problem of intellectual property rights development and their integration into ABS. Another notable early effort was undertaken by a consortium lead by World Resources International, documenting its project for the pre-CBD creation of a benefit-sharing arrangement between Costa Rica and the pharmaceutical giant Merck. Reid, *et al.*, 1993. Other writers focused on the Philippines early effort to develop national ABS legislation, a process which included a large number of international "experts" (participants in the negotiation of CBD Article 15), but was later damned with faint praise, when one of these experts described the entire process by saying "Well, its an experiment."

modest results and a relatively low rate of benefit compared to the costs of setting it up, the Costa Rican system[15] has often been described as a template for all developing countries seeking to obtain or maximize ABS benefits. Unfortunately, in addition to the high cost and technological demand, a number of other factors indicate that the Costa Rican approach to ABS probably cannot be replicated successfully.[16] More recently, a few projects have focused on the development ABS experience by fostering the direct negotiation of individual ABS and TK-related benefit-sharing arrangements between specific users and individual or community providers. In many cases, such negotiations led only to impasse, at most they resulted in an instrument that relies on voluntary compliance by a user that is not bound to act.[17] Finally, as noted in ¶¶ 1.1.1 and 1.1.2, *supra*, many of those primarily involved in the negotiations have come to the paradoxical conclusion that legal analysis is not productive and that their attempts to require a binding and functional ABS contract are the cause of the non-functionality that continues to inhibit efforts to put the ABS regime in place.

The authors' aims in this book are to identify some of the key factors that prevent ABS contracts from functioning; to create a more amplified understanding of the issues and obstacles to be addressed in ABS contracts and MAT; and to maximize their validity and enforceability, with particular attention to issues that should be addressed in developing model contracts, model provisions, and national measures relating to ABS contracts and MAT. To do so, this book explores the relevant legal situation under the national contractual, commercial and procedural law in a selection of country jurisdictions, as well as the specific issues of international treaties and so-called "private international law" as applied to ABS contracts.

This book attempts to avoid the errors and omissions of previous discussions of ABS contracts, in three ways. First, rather than making generalizations regarding commercial law and prognostications about the "probable" issues raised by ABS contracts, it is based on intensive efforts to research the commercial, contractual and procedural law around the world that may pose challenges for ABS contracts and their implementation and enforcement. We have engaged in significant research into these issues across a range of countries, and have undertaken more detailed investigations in several countries in which we have lived or worked.[18]

---

15 Described in detail in Reid, *et al.*, 1993, and later in Cabrera, 2009

16 See, Cabrera and Lopez, 2007.

17 See examples from Latin America, cited in Ruiz Mueller, 2015.

18 As explained and mentioned many times throughout this book, the most important challenge of writing a book on contracts for use in transactions in many countries arises

Second, this book does not presume that all ABS contracts are similar, or that all users or all providers have similar goals. Instead it considers the impact of a variety of factors, including not only sectoral issues, but also the motivations of various types of users and the particular concerns of various levels of provider-side negotiators.

Third, this book is emphatically NOT intended as a set of case studies and does not propose to base any of its recommendations on one or two specific experiences. The authors do recognize the value and importance of promoting understanding of the individual ABS contracts and negotiations that have occurred to date, to the extent that they can be known. Experiences can contribute to the understanding to the means by which certain legal, commercial and political objectives can be promoted. They provide a basis for the authors' analysis of certain issues and proposals for contractual solutions to particular ABS challenges. In this book we have attempted to rely on such experiences in many ways. First, we have studied available legal cases directly involving specific ABS contracts that have been agreed and publicly discussed, as well as all documents that have been proffered as "model ABS contracts." In addition, we have been involved in or advised the negotiation of numerous ABS arrangements and contracts for the extraction and/or use of natural and biological resources. We have based particular discussions of legal challenges and negotiation/drafting issues on our personal experience in these situations. Third, this book provides these discussions in the context of our background of general academic knowledge and practical hard-law experience, to provide real hard-law solutions for ABS – contract development.

1.2.1 *Sources (Treatises and other Formal Writing)*

We must also note that literature and written resources on ABS are both too few and too numerous. Although there are literally thousands of legal treatises and guides to contract law, there have been only a very few books or pamphlets on ABS contracts. Available books and pamphlets are generally divisible into four groups: (i) in-depth discussions focused on a single example of an ABS contract;[19] (ii) in-depth discussions focused on a single body of ABS model

---

because each country has its own unique principles of contract law. Although many of these principles are similar from country to country, no two countries' contract law seem to be completely identical. Accordingly, in every effort to apply the lessons of this book to the process of drafting an effective ABS contract, it will be necessary to undertake specific research into the contractual laws and principles of all countries in which any party, any resource or any ABS activities may occur.

19 The most detailed and complete example of this category is Andersen and Winge, 2012, discussing the details of Ethiopia's experiences with the Teff Agreement. Other examples are generally found in papers and pamphlets presented at CBD meetings. We have

contracts;[20] (iii) in-depth discussions of a single specialized legal issue as it is expected to arise in ABS contracts;[21] and (iv) general discussions of the application of contract principles to ABS transactions.[22] Although all of these types of sources have informed the writing of this book, relatively little direct scholarship on the basic questions of the law and practice of ABS contract drafting could actually be gleaned from any of them.

In addition, particularly in the case of discussions that focused on a single contract or a single body of models, such writings often include statements and conclusions that the authors did not find that were correct. The empirical approach to any study (coming to general conclusions on the basis of specific examples) is always perilous when one has only one example to build conclusions on. If a particular paragraph was not a basis for controversy in the one experience, it is probably inappropriate to conclude that it should be

reviewed many of these and spoken with many people who have been involved in ABS contract negotiations that we were not a part of, and have additionally used our own ABS contract experience, as well as our experience with natural resource contracts, commercial contracts, technology licenses, *etc.*

20 A variety of users and countries have adopted "forms" and other model instruments and written detailed descriptions of how these models will function. One of the most prominent of these was circulated by the Government of Australia, after it adopted its two-level ABS permitting process. See, *e.g., Australian Government Response to* [*CBD Secretariat*] *Notification 2011–216, Access to Genetic Resources and Benefit-sharing*. Unfortunately, these descriptions are written at a time when there has been little or no actual use of the model, and as such, they function as advertisements of the models, without any details regarding whether they function effectively and/or in what situations they are or are not effective.

21 In general, these publications address the topic of "intellectual property" (IP) law, as it applies to ABS. As noted throughout this book, intellectual property law often bears a particular relevance to the ABS process when GR or ATK has been accessed and studied and found to have commercial or other value. To the extent that IP law must be addressed, it is important to obtain a detailed analysis of those principles. Unfortunately, IP law is both specialized and complex. Hence, a complete treatise or guidance on how to apply IP law in the course of an ABS transaction would be as long as this book – much longer than any of the pamphlets and articles published up to now. They are supported by the database of ABS contracts, maintained by WIPO (http://www.wipo.int/tk/en/databases/contracts/), which includes many examples of "downstream" IP contracts – *e.g.,* contracts addressing the ownership of patents, or licensing their use by others.

22 Prior to the publication of the current volume, the only other example of this type of treatise is Young and Bhatti, 2009, which attempted to present the current status of ABS law and experience with regard to contracts, at a time before the NP, when relatively little direct experience had been made public.

used in all contracts. Similarly, if a contractual problem developed over a particular paragraph, it is usually false to assume that a revision that solves that particular problematic aspect would make the provision or the contract work in future

As a consequence, the authors have been forced to rely on career-long experience in the negotiation, drafting and implementation of literally hundreds of contracts (including many ABS contracts in more recent years). On this basis, this book identifies contractual/legal challenges and the legal approaches that can be used to solve them in the context of ABS transactions, also discussing the special problems that arise wherever the parties to a contract use someone else's contract as a template.

1.2.2 *Legal Issues Covered*

In selecting the legal issues to be covered by this book, the authors were keenly aware that the basic laws related to contract negotiation, documentation, implementation and enforcement at national level fill many volumes in the legal literature of every developed country and in many developing countries. Similarly, the special added challenges arising from the narrow concept of "private international law" (or "choice of law") comprise one or more very thick volumes of national and international legal analysis. The same can be said of most of the key international treaty provisions relating to contractual law, commercial law and enforcement. Virtually all of these are potentially relevant to ABS contracts and MAT.

Realizing that it will not be possible to include full discussions of even a significant fraction of the relevant contractual, commercial and procedural issues that might be relevant to a particular ABS negotiation or to the development of model contracts or provisions, the authors have focused on a selection of some of the contractual issues that are of particular concern in ABS contracts. Special attention is given to the question of what will happen if the contract is violated or if there is some dispute about it. These issues include, for example:

- The factors that cause a contract to be recognized as legally valid and enforceable (in general, as well as in ABS) (Chapter 2);
- An approach to the development of a strategy for the negotiation of a legally effective ABS contract (Chapter 3);
- Key questions regarding the parties, such as the issue of "legal personality" of companies and other entities, and making sure that the contract is actually binding on them (Chapter 4);
- How to draft certain key provisions of the contract so concretely that they are legally recognized as "enforceable" (Chapter 5);

- The effect of third-party transfers (Chapter 6);
- Primary legal issues affecting contractual validity and enforceability (Chapter 7);
- The availability of legal remedies (Chapter 8);
- Guarantees that the contract will be performed and other specific concerns (Chapter 9); and
- The actual impact of the choice of governing law and of concepts like "private international law" and "international commercial law" (Chapter 10).

In most of these discussions, (*e.g.*, contractual validity) the issues presented are matters that are of critical concern in all international contracts, but raise special concerns in the ABS context. Other issues (*e.g.*, legal personality and property ownership) are matters that are easily addressed in conventional contract negotiations, but can be both vital and nearly impossibly challenging in ABS contracts. In this book, the authors have attempted to isolate the first level of obstacles to contractual functionality and legal certainty as regards ABS contracts and MAT. A contract that successfully surpasses these obstacles, although not necessarily free of challenges, is well on the way to effective, functional ABS performance. The authors cannot aim to eliminate all legal problems that might prevent enforcement of an ABS contract or MAT, but are attempting to avoid the possibility that the contract or MAT will be instantly ignored by a commercial party, or "tossed out of court" due to basic insufficiencies.

1.2.3 *Traditional Knowledge Associated with Genetic Resources*

As a practical matter, the Nagoya Protocol's inclusion of specific expanded obligations relating to the utilization of "traditional knowledge associated with genetic resources within the scope of the Convention"[23] (herein "associated traditional knowledge" or "ATK") is a source of significant additional confusion and complexity in the ABS discussion. The concept of ABS as applied to the "access to and utilization of genetic resources" is already extremely challenging from a legal perspective, in light of the nature of genetic resources and the ABS framework's rather novel objectives. The addition of similar access rights and benefit-sharing obligations relating to the utilization of ATK – effectively as a form of collectively-held restricted knowledge – is extremely daunting for

23 Neither the concept of "traditional knowledge associated with genetic resources within the scope of the Convention" nor that of "utilization of traditional knowledge" are defined in the CBD or NP, and there is insufficient detail on these concepts in any of the provisions of either document to enable one to draw inferences regarding the legal meaning and scope of these terms. See, Morgera and Tsioumani, 2014.

purposes of legislative and/or contractual implementation. Moreover, unlike the CBD's ABS provisions in Article 15, which are directed to international situations (as noted above), all references to ATK and traditional knowledge in the CBD and the NP are focused on domestic issues. Thus, although international transactions involving ATK are certainly covered in the NP, the Protocol's most intensive obligations relating to ATK are those imposed on governments with regard to "indigenous and local communities"[24] within their borders.

For purposes of contract development, while ABS contracts and transactions regarding GR have been relatively few, there have been enough of them to form a basis for the suggestion of an initial list of model provisions and other analysis. By contrast, there are far fewer available examples of successful or partially successful contracts for access to and use of ATK, and a much more extensive list of open issues and ambiguities in the NP.

For these reasons, the primary focus of this book will be on contracting for access to and utilization of GR. For each separate discussion on an ABS issue or contractual concern related to GR, however, it will identify additional concerns that may need to be addressed when the transaction is focused on ATK.

1.2.4 *Target Readership*

One of the most significant challenges of preparing a publication on a legal topic for an audience of non-lawyers is the need to be accurate without being overly detailed and confusing. Often, writers attempting to meet the needs of ABS participants have, consciously or unconsciously, made incorrect statements by oversimplifying their description of key ABS contractual issues. At the same time, it is a common failure of lawyers to focus long discussions on small details of law, thereby confusing the reader seeking a basic understanding. Striking a balance between these two extremes is a difficult task.

There is a wealth of comprehensive research underlying this book, including detailed investigations of national laws (as noted above) on ABS as well as those on contracts, property, commerce, trade and contractual enforcement.

---

24 At this writing, the use of the term "indigenous and local community" is again being debated in the CBD framework. The CBD's longstanding Ad-hoc Working Group on Article 8(j) has again proposed that the CBD instead use the phrase "Indigenous Peoples and Local Communities," as recommended by the UN Permanent Forum on Indigenous Issues (UNPFII.) See UNEP/CBD/WG8J/8/INF/10/Add.1. Given the unlikelihood that the CBD will be amended for purpose of changing this phrase alone, the authors have opted to use the specific term used in the Convention, but do so with no intent to comment on or detract from the UNPFII's concerns.

The authors, although finding it fascinating themselves, realize that this book is targeted at individuals, communities, companies, researchers, government officials and agencies that have little or no interest in the details of commercial/contractual law or contract enforcement. For this reason, we have attempted to restrain our fascination with them, and are instead providing in this book the outcomes of that research – conclusions about legal issues that may arise in the negotiation, drafting and enforcement of ABS contracts and MAT, and possible approaches for addressing those issues. Our statements are supported by footnotes to the particular laws and analyses that support our conclusions. Lawyers seeking more detailed analyses of particular issues are welcome to contact either or both of us.

1.3 Getting a Handle on the ABS Concept

In writing this book, the authors have assumed that those attempting to negotiate, draft, implement or enforce ABS contracts will already have as clear as possible an idea of what ABS means, including how it was developed and how it is perceived internationally and domestically. For those that do not, however, it is strongly recommended that, before delving into the details of ABS contracts, you should get some basic understanding of ABS, both as originally created (under Article 15 of the CBD) and as more currently perceived, following the adoption of the NP. Some of these issues are also addressed in Chapter 11 of this book. For those seeking a more detailed understanding, the authors recommend the other publications in this series,[25] as well as some other books and analyses that have been published.[26]

Unfortunately, as you will discover in the course of that research, the ABS concept contains many ambiguities, and its interpretation varies greatly from country-to-country and from ABS contract-to-ABS contract. Nearly all commentaries on ABS, no matter how unbiased they attempt to be, are influenced by the views of their authors and sponsoring organizations. Thus, ABS is not a

25 See particularly, Morgera, *et al*, 2014, and Jacui, 2015.

26 Among the other such resources in the field are Ahrén, *et al.*, 2012 and Young, 2009c. With regard to the ABS aspects of the International Treaty on Food and Agriculture, two resources are Schloen, *et al.*, 2011. and Moore, and Timowsky, 2005. The authors note that, contrary to current popular thought, the accuracy and quality of these publications should not be inferred from their date. The older publications are included in the footnotes of this book primarily owing to the authors' belief that they impart a clearer and more accurate picture of the ABS concept.

topic that can be easily summarized in a way that would not detract from the legal accuracy that is the intention of this book. To the extent that a particular ABS element is relevant to one of the discussions in Chapters 2 through 13, that element will be explained in a way that will support the book's discussion.

1.4 Purpose and Organization of This Book

This book is intended to provide persons negotiating ABS contracts with a basic understanding of the role of contracts in the process. It focuses on the questions of what the parties to a contract can and cannot do in negotiating and drafting, in order to promote and guide implementation, and to protect its parties in the event of contractual violations. It identifies and addresses some of the critical issues that have most frequently been sources of difficulty in the negotiation and implementation of contracts and provides some guidance on how to address them.

It will begin with a brief introduction to the legal principles underlying contracts and commercial law, and a general discussion of the manner in which one can approach the negotiation and drafting of a carefully crafted contract as a tool for protecting the parties against misunderstanding violation and various other unpleasant surprises (Chapter 2). It will then turn to seven of the most essential primary principles of contractual drafting and their specialized application in ABS situations. These principles will be examined in the context of seven basic rules of contractual negotiation and drafting:

- "MAKE SURE YOU CONTRACT WITH THE RIGHT PARTIES"
  (Chapter 4) Focusing on the challenges of contracts with companies and other entities discussing the challenges of legal personality, responsibility and legally recognized ability to enter into contracts.
- "BE SPECIFIC AND CONCRETE"
  (Chapter 5) Discussing the challenges of unambiguous agreement on the precise subject matter (*res*) and objective of the contract.
- "MANAGE AND ADDRESS MAJOR RISKS"
  (Chapter 6) Focusing on the challenge of post-access transfers of genetic resources and traditional knowledge, as one of the unique risks that pose a significant risk to completion of ABS contracts.
- "KNOW THE POSSIBILITIES AND LIMITATIONS OF CONTRACT LAW"
  (Chapter 7) Discussing the factors of ABS contracts that affect their legal effectiveness – validity, enforceability and equitable outcome.

- "EXPECT THE BEST; PLAN FOR THE WORST"
  (Chapter 8) Focusing on the questions that affect contractual enforceability, how they can prevent the need for enforcement action, and how the ABS contract draftsman can address them.
- "PROTECT CONTRACTUAL RIGHTS/EXPECTATIONS":
  (Chapter 9) Focusing on the rational use of guarantees and other tools to help ensure that both parties behave in a contractually responsible manner and are protected against the other party's financial irresponsibility.
- "AVOID MISTAKEN LEGAL ASSUMPTIONS "
  (Chapter 10) Focusing on the Perils of relying on a "Governing Law" clause, or concepts of "Private International Law" or "international commercial law" as a means of avoiding the need to address the risks of ABS contracts.

Following these discussions, the book will provides some critical background about the role of international ABS instruments (Chapter 11). It will then (Chapter 12) turn to the often-raised suggestion that "model contracts" and/or "model provisions" should be adopted, providing an analysis of the legal and practical challenges that arise in the preparation of model legal instruments and how those challenges arise in and are multiplied by the ABS regime; ending with some cautious suggestions regarding the manner in which model contracts can be effectively developed and used.

This book is written as a response to the growing desire of countries for assistance with the negotiating and drafting of ABS contracts, as noted by requests to the ABS Capacity Building Initiative, to the Fridtjof Nansen Institute and to Tomme Young. Many of these requests are seeking "quick-fixes" and/or ready-made contracts. As explained in this book, however, it is difficult to relay on such simple "one-size-fits-all" contractual tools, if one wants to ensure that a particular contract in a particular situation will be functional and thus actually create binding benefit-sharing obligations and legally certain access. To this end, the book tries to provide sample language (not guaranteed, but providing an example of language that has worked in various contracts) and other directly useful advice and tips for contract negotiators and draftsmen, while also providing enough background information and legal explanation to help them understand why it is important to address these issues concretely in writing.

CHAPTER 2

Drafting Functional ABS Contracts: How Contracts Can Achieve Reasonable ABS Objectives

The practical negotiation and drafting of effective contracts is the subject of many complex and detailed books. One could spend many years becoming proficient in contractual practice, even in a single country (and, as noted below, each country's national contract law and principles may differ from all others). The authors have devoted a significant portion of their professional careers to gaining sufficient understanding of international contractual and commercial practice, and do not expect their readers to be willing or able to do the same. This chapter seeks to provide the reader with sufficient introduction to the basic concepts of contract/commercial law in general to enable effective use of Chapters 3 through 9. It focuses on providing a general introduction to the challenges arising when one seeks to apply contractual principles to transactions in the ABS regime, emphasizing key questions affecting contractual functionality.

Perhaps the most important objective of this chapter however, is to introduce the reader to the single most important lesson this book hopes to teach:

THE PRIMARY LESSON OF ABS CONTRACTS

An "ABS contract" that does not meet all contractual requirements has no chance of enforcement. Such a contract may become little more than a daydream that has been committed to paper. Even if the parties to the negotiations appear to be in accord at the time, their circumstances and goals may change. They agree to a binding contract so that all parties know what to do when things change. The legal status of the contract, as explained below, will make all the difference.

When commercial enterprises must face new financial and other challenges, they make decisions based on the obligations they owe. If an obligation is contained in an enforceable contract, it will carry more weight than a "daydream on paper." Responsibilities under a binding contract may withstand other pressures, such as the need to cut unnecessary costs. The fact that a contract is binding and could be

 | DOI 10.1163/9789004356573_003

enforced will operate to encourage a commercial enterprise to implement it and resolve problems by consensus (without the need for enforcement action). A document that is not binding will face a different fate – it will essentially disappear, unfulfilled.

Unfortunately, current national and international ABS laws and treaties provide virtually no legal support for creation of a binding agreement in the ABS context. An ABS agreement can meet every element of these instruments and still fail because it is not a binding contract.

It is essential for the process of negotiation and drafting of an ABS contract to focus on making it a binding contract. This is entirely separate from the process of compliance with relevant ABS legislation and principles. When you negotiate, you should focus on making a **legally binding contract.**

This chapter will begin by explaining the above lesson in more detail (Part 2.1). It will then provide a basic outline of the way that contracts function (Part 2.2). It closes with an examination of the multiple sources of relevant law (international law, national law, regulations, guidelines, policies, practices and models in a variety of legal areas) and some of the implications of that multiplicity (Part 2.3).

2.1 Addressing the Ambiguity of ABS with the Specificity of Contact Law

It is important to realize that a discussion of "ABS and contract law" is an effort find harmony in a blend of two difficult and contradictory concepts. Conceptually, ABS is extremely ambiguous, and its components have not been concretely specified. Its vagueness and legal uncertainties leave countries with wide discretion for its implementation. By contrast, contract law is a tool designed to enable implementation of numerous business, service and financial relationships and commitments. As such, it requires concrete, unambiguous concepts and provisions in order to function.

The following discussion begins with an examination the ambiguities that must be addressed in order to reconcile ABS with contract law. It follows with a discussion of the contract law factors that would normally cause ABS contracts to be found "unenforceable." It ends with a brief synopsis of the combination of the two.

2.1.1 *The Ambiguity of* ABS

ABS is a new concept originally negotiated as a political (not a legal) concept. As such it is, by definition, ambiguous.[27] Even where national law implementing ABS is unambiguous, unanswered questions about which country's laws apply to a particular ABS situation may prevent its application.

In an ABS transaction, although all parties want to give/receive a fair share of the benefits arising from utilization of genetic resources and/or ATK – in exchange for giving/receiving access to those resources, they may have different ideas about the meaning of key elements like "ATK," "genetic resource," "access," or "utilization." The basic inability of the CBD and NP definitions to support effective legal contracts and their enforcement has been addressed in numerous publications.[28] These ambiguities and other factors have been used by many countries as their justification for their inability to adopt user measures or for the adoption of measures that do not ensure enforcement of the provider country's ABS requirements.

This book will not repeat that body of work or go into detail to document these ambiguities. Instead we will simply note that, although the CBD and/or the NP contain purported "definitions" of some terms,[29] those definitions are "policy" definitions, and not sufficient to concretize them as contract-law concepts. It is relatively simple to determine whether a policy definition is sufficient to support contractual implementation. When a contract is intended to address a particular specimen, species or element of traditional knowledge

27 In recent international environmental negotiations, the Parties have taken strongly opposed positions, with little willingness to seek true compromises. In order to create a document that all Parties will agree to adopt, the negotiating delegations frankly admit that their goal is "creative ambiguity." Specifically, they attempt to find a form of words that will accommodate the concepts of all sides without forcing those concepts to change. The resulting ambiguity is only legally problematic where the concept must be implemented in a situation that involves governments, communities, institutions or persons from or in more than one country.

28 Schei and Tvedt, 2010, explored the different notions in the understanding of "genetic resources" in different international organization. The authors have explored the differences between ABS, patents and contracts and found that the greatest degree of ambiguity involved in all three areas, arises from the fact that ABS has not been concretely agreed as a legal concept.

29 See CBD Article 2, for "definitions" of "genetic resources," "genetic material," "biological resources," "biotechnology" "country of origin of genetic resources," "country providing genetic resources," and "*in situ* conditions," all of which are relevant to the ABS issue, although few are legally specific enough to be enforced in a court; and NP Article 2 for "definitions" of "utilization of genetic resources," "derivative," and a repetition of the CBD definition of

or a particular action (specimen collection, other access, utilization, *etc.*), the parties should focus on ensuring that the contractual description and/or definition gives concrete information, so that an external analyst (including a judge or arbitrator) can determine precisely what material, knowledge or action is within or outside the scope of the contract. The definitions in the CBD and NP do not support that level of certainty.

For example, the ABS concept applies to "access to genetic resources or ATK," without defining what actions or decisions constitute access, or what it means and includes when it speaks of ATK. Its definitions of "genetic resources," "derivatives" and "utilization" do not make it clear whether or not a particular specimen is a genetic resource, or whether a particular activity is "utilization." When you buy a car, your contract would not be sufficient if it defined the *res* only as an unspecified "transport device." In order for the contract to be valid it would specify the precise identifying numbers and other information. Even a contract with a "finder" would be as specific as possible about the make, model, year, color and other factors that are important to the buyer. An ABS contract that refers only to "genetic resources" or "ATK" is similar. It must be specific enough that all parties agree about what is included. To date, however, neither the NP nor national laws have resolved the doubts about what those terms mean. For example, the NP negotiations attempted to clarify the meaning of the term "utilization of genetic resources." The negotiations led to a definition that is not concrete.[30] To understand the extend of this ambiguity, a fruitful exercise is to examine that definition and attempt to use it to create a concrete list of specific actions that are clearly included within it.

2.1.2 *Contract Law's Intolerance for Ambiguity*

In stark contrast to the international ABS instruments, contract law is built on specificity and concreteness, and indeed cannot function without it.

"biotechnology." (The NP also incorporates all definitions from the CBD. It is unclear even to those present at all deliberations why the biotechnology definition was repeated).

30 NP Article 2(c) defines "Utilization of genetic resources" as follows: "to conduct research and development on the genetic and/or biochemical composition of genetic resources, including through the application of biotechnology as defined in Article 2 of the Convention." This is not actually a definition of contractual specificity, but rather an indication of the Parties agreement regarding the outer limits of activities that may be included in national law governing the ABS concept. In ¶ 2.1.3, *infra*, we present a number of questions that cannot be answered if a contract merely states that the user may utilize genetic resources, and gives or relies on the definition from NP Article 2(c) to provide the meaning of that term.

A contract that says, "I will give you some apples tomorrow in exchange for some money" is not specific enough to be enforced. If the seller says that the amount of paid is not enough, the buyer may respond that the seller did not provide enough apples. The contract's terms do not help these parties resolve their disagreement. Even a judge looking at it will say that the contract was not specific enough to enable him/her to decide. Normally, in that case the judge will refuse to hear the case at all. At most, if one party has taken the apples, but not paid for them, the judge may give a judgment for the provider, applying some other law as a basis for valuing the apples.

The situation is even worse where the *res* of the contract (the specific item that is changing hands) or the actions to be taken under the contract are less clear. For example if A promises to give B a check for $100 today, in exchange for B's promise to give A a "surprise" tomorrow, has the contract been violated if A's check bounced and B's "surprise" was an empty box?

Where a contract is interpreted by a court, we sometimes see two approaches. In most countries, the "rule of law" approach applies: Contracts are interpreted relatively strictly, considering both the specific language of the contract and any specific relevant law or legal principle that of the particular country.[31] This is all the more challenging in international contracts, since every country's minimum standards for contracts, and the principles for their interpretation are different. For the parties, failure to meet these minimum standards could mean that the contract is invalid. The object of the rule of law is to reduce the number of lawsuits, by giving the parties advance knowledge of how the law would resolve their claim. Where there is a body of law, accepted standards, principles and experience, the parties to a contract can relatively easily predict how a court or arbitrator will interpret and apply their contract. They can know in advance if there are areas of uncertainty about which the court's decision cannot be predicted. This level of specificity and certainty increases the likelihood that contractual parties can resolve their problems by consensus. As a result they are less likely to need to file a court case or arbitration.

A few countries still describe their judicial and arbitration systems as "flexible" – meaning that their courts and arbitrators will weigh the equities instead of applying the laws, standards, principles and previous decisions strictly. In these countries, there remains a possibility that a court might choose to enforce a contract that would normally be considered legally insufficient, citing goals of fairness, equity or social responsibility. Unfortunately, the net result

31 The complex legal challenges relating to "Governing Law" and the relevant concepts and misconceptions regarding Private International Law are discussed in detail in Chapter 10 of this book.

of this approach is that few commercial enterprises will be willing to enter into contracts involving that country. When the winning party seeks to enforce such a judgment in another country (where the losing party's home office, operations or substantial assets are located), that second country's courts may hold that the original judgment cannot be enforced within the second country.[32] So long as ABS contracts remain legally ambiguous, this same fate will apply to them.

2.1.3 *Combining ABS and Contract Law: Applying an Ambiguity-intolerant System to a Highly Ambiguous Concept*

In essence, the ABS regime, as adopted, challenges its Parties, to find a way to make it work. The primary task before them is to resolve ambiguities, enabling ABS to be implemented through ambiguity-intolerant contract law. Until countries can meet this challenge, individually and collectively, ABS will remain contractually non-functional.

Consider, for example, an ABS contract by which A grants to B the right of "access" to A's genetic resources, in exchange for B's promise to provide a share of the benefits arising from utilization of those genetic resources. Over the following months, B collects samples of wild plants, and also purchases grains, legumes, succulents and fruit in local markets. He returns home and engages in plant breeding using germplasm of the collected plants, but he also plants some of the grains, legumes, fruits and succulents in his garden, and squeezes juice from other fruits and succulents. Which, if any, of the various biological items is also a "genetic resource"? Was he "accessing a genetic resource" when he bought it on a local market? Was it "utilization" to plant seeds in his backyard? What about when he squeezed them for juice? The parties' agreement on these matters must be concrete. None of these questions could be answered by applying the NP or any provisions of currently existing national ABS legislation. Lacking national or international law on these points, however, the parties to a well written contract could resolve them with binding effect by agreement, at least for purposes of their own contract. To do this, they need to find the rules and principles that guide the negotiation and drafting and apply them to the making of an ABS contract.

Before they can rely on national law or international guidance, that law or guidance must, at least, answer the following questions (and many others):

---

32 A number of reasons may be given, including allegations that the original court failed to apply the strict rule of law. These possibilities are discussed in greater detail in Chapters 4, 8 and 10.

- Is every biological material a "genetic resource"? If so, must every purchase or sale of a biological material obtain PIC, MAT and an ABS contract? If not, what is the clear standard on which to determine whether a particular substance is a genetic resource?
- If the market purchase of grains, fruits, legumes and succulents is "access to genetic resources," does this mean that ABS applies to every purchase/sale of any biological material? If not, how to we restate a concrete rule to distinguish purchases that are ABS from those that are not?
- If he is "utilizing genetic resources" when he squeezes juice from the fruits and succulents, does this mean that all purchase of agricultural crops for consumption is governed by ABS? If not, what is the concrete standard for determining which actions are "utilization" and which are not?

Only a few countries have codified their national answers to this type of questions, and those answers are not the same. Similarly, the texts of the international ABS instruments do not resolve these questions in a uniform manner. As a result, in drafting a contract for access to and utilization of genetic resource and/or ATK, it would be a major mistake to assume that ABS terminology has a clear and agreed meaning.

One example of an area of concern is "prior informed consent."[33] Although it is used in ABS discussions to refer to a specific procedure to be adopted in the law of each provider country, that term has a very specific legal meaning in other areas of law. A court may apply it in a way that is very different from what the negotiators of the NP and CBD expect, and this difference may be problematic for the parties to ABS contracts.

---

33 The concept of "consent" arises in a great many legal situations, from sexual relations to hazardous chemicals to land-use and zoning. It has long been applied in tort law governing "acceptance or assumption of risk" ("*Volenti non fit iniuria*.") The principle has been fully recognized for far more than a century. See, *e.g.* Pollock (1886), at p. 354. The phrase "prior informed consent" is generally used in all of these contexts, however, it has appeared as a reference to a specific legally mandated process in the medical world, where patients and scientific test subjects are required sign a document indicating that they are aware of the risks when they agree to the relevant medical procedure. Although the concept of PIC was prominent in Article 15 of the CBD, courts examining an ABS contract containing this term could easily misinterpret that phrase, believing that the parties were merely referring to the established body of contract law. Since the NP negotiations, some participants have sought to alter the PIC concept, in the context of ABS contracts involving indigenous peoples. They have proposed substituting the term "free prior informed consent" or "FPIC." See Jonas and Shrumm, 2013. This terminology change is intended to align work under ABS with the FPIC concepts promoted in other sectors.

Even among experts who have been actively involved in ABS since its inception, terms like "access," "benefit-sharing," "genetic resources," "traditional knowledge," "derivative," "utilization," "provider," "user" still have multiple meanings, with no accepted legally sufficient definition. If parties to an ABS contract use any of these terms without more specific definition, or if they simply restate the ambiguous language of the CBD or NP definitions, their contract will be so ambiguous that it becomes legally unenforceable. A party may find that the contract means something very different from what he intended. Other concepts in the NP, including "mutually agreed terms"[34] and "legally authorized holder"[35] can cause an ABS contract to be interpreted in a way that the parties did not intend, unless they are clearly explained.

Most courts would dismiss a case seeking interpretation or enforcement of a contract based on these terms, because contract law is "ambiguity-intolerant." If a court should agree to interpret these terms, it is virtually impossible to predict the outcome. The unpredictability is enhanced by the fact that the court that is interpreting and/or enforcing the contract will most often be a court in a user country, which may apply its own principles in applying the law of the provider country.[36]

To enable a contract to be enforced (whether by consent or by a court or arbitrator), it is absolutely essential to eliminate ambiguity regarding the essential components of the contract. Many of the most important ways in which ABS ambiguity has caused ABS contracts to be non-functional are addressed in greater detail in Chapters 3 through 9.

34 "Mutual agreement" is another principle that had a very different meaning under basic contract law, long before ABS existed. See Chapter 7. A court might apply these principles to any clause of the contract that uses the phrase "mutually agreed terms," even if the contract parties only intended to refer to national ABS legislation on MAT.

35 As detailed in numerous legal analyses, the question of which person or community is legally considered the owner or holder of any *res* is a topic that has been addressed in law for thousands of years. It has not been clarified in ABS practice, and few countries have addressed the ownership of GR or ATK in any clarifying law. Unfortunately, the identification and rights of holders and owners of various types of property is critical to the validity of any contract. Hence, this too could be a major source of ambiguity.

36 Following the adoption of the NP, many developed country negotiators made it clear that, in their view, all ABS legislation, even legislation governing users, must be adopted by the provider country. It is not clear what this means, given that in other situations, these countries have not allowed foreign countries to regulate the actions of their citizens when on home soil. See, *e.g.*, Natural Justice, 2013.

2.1.4 *Making it Work – Contractual Enforceability in* ABS

In the course of examining the contractually important elements of the ABS instruments, it is important for all readers to recall that ABS is, at base, a very unusual hybrid that seeks to use a private, market tool and its desirable commercial benefits to achieve globally agreed objectives of environment conservation, local and improvement of developing country and indigenous livelihoods. This plurality of objectives was clearly recognized in the CBD negotiations, which directly acknowledged that "substantial investments are required to conserve biological diversity and that there is the expectation of a broad range of environmental, economic and social benefits from those investments"[37] and viewed ABS as one example of such investments. It is clear then, that ABS must operate through binding contracts. As in all other commercial contracts, the knowledge that the ABS contract is enforceable is a key element motivating its parties to implement the contract, even if their situation changes, and to seek consensus solutions, in the event that problems need to be resolved.

> TIP
>
> As a practical matter, one should approach the ABS transaction on two concurrent tracks:
>
> - TRACK 1: Negotiate and draft the contract governing the actions of all parties to the ABS transaction, *focusing on ensuring that it is a binding contract under all relevant concepts contractual and commercial law, and avoiding the reliance on or use of* ABS *concepts and terminology.*
> - TRACK 2: Determine if the transaction is governed by national ABS legislation and comply with all procedures mandated under that legislation (PIC, MAT, permit, certificate, reporting, monitoring, checkpoints, *etc.*)
>
> Where there is any conflict between these two tracks, that conflict should be resolved using contractual principles, with an eye to contractual enforceability.
>
> This approach seeks to ensure that, if the contract is enforced or its enforceability analyzed, the parties, courts or arbitrators will apply the principles, standards and legislation applicable to all contracts. This will increase the predictability of the contract's results.

37 CBD, Eighteenth Preambular clause.

Although this entire book is focused on helping the reader achieve a concretely contractual approach, the following discussion focuses on how to maximize legal recognition and enforceability of a contract. Since national ABS laws are diverse and many have not been applied or even adopted, this book cannot go into detail on the specific requirements of particular national provisions. It can and will address the challenge faced by all international contracts, of attempting to ensure that the contract assigns all relevant requirements in a concrete and enforceable way. Writing a good ABS contract is also not dependent on the legislation of the provider country and can be done even for a country without any clear ABS act. The following is a brief summary of the challenges faced and addressed in applying the above approach:

> It is important to avoid relying on ABS definitions, principles and legislation as the basis of the contract. It is clear, however, that the parties to the contract will have to concurrently take action under "track 2"; the parties will have to make sure that their transaction complies with all relevant laws governing transactions involving genetic resources and ATK.

How is this done without using ABS terminology and concepts in the contract? The question is answered most easily by comparing two approaches to a provision that assigns responsibility for compliance with PIC and MAT: In the past, some contracts have relied on ABS terminology, providing only that "the user will obtain prior informed consent and negotiate mutually agreed terms." This language is composed almost entirely of ABS phrases that are legally ambiguous, and not contractually specific. If a controversy should arise over national legislative compliance, the contract will provide no help or direction to enable the parties to resolve the controversy.

A better approach would be for the ABS contract to avoid reliance on ABS terminology. The parties should instead agree on a more concrete and specific instruction, which states, for example, which party takes primary responsibility for compliance with legislative requirements, what the duties of the other party might be, and about what happens if there is a problem in fulfilling those duties:

Example: *Party X will take all actions required pursuant to* [here specify the relevant legislation, or, if there is no legislation, insert the words *"the requirements imposed by Z [the responsible agency]"*] *to ensure that this transaction receives "prior informed consent (PIC)" and properly negotiates* *"mutually agreed terms (MAT)" as the quoted terms are interpreted by that* [legislation or agency]. *Party Y will take all reasonable actions to support Party X in this activity. If after all reasonable options and efforts have been attempted, it is not possible to successfully conclude the PIC and MAT process, then* [insert all acceptable options, *i.e.:*

- *"this contract will terminate and no part of the res will be transferred or otherwise used in the manner described in this contract"* and/or
- *"the parties may apply to the* [*responsible agency*], *to submit the matter to the Global Multilateral Benefit-sharing Mechanism* [*if it exists*]*"* and/or
- *"the parties may, if they mutually agree to do so, seek the assistance of an international mediator or ombudsman to help them complete the process."*[38]]

Although this example language is longer and contains more words, it has the advantage of being contractually specific. If a question about national ABS compliance were to arise, any party, court or arbitrator could relatively easily determine whether the parties had complied.[39] As noted, where the parties can predict with a relatively high level of certainty whether the provision will be enforced and how it will be interpreted in any given situation, they are much more likely to resolve any problems by consensus.

Contractual experience and contract principles have developed over many centuries, and been honed by the courts into standard practices. As a result, many common types of contracts in long-standing areas of commercial practice can use short provisions and undefined terms, with confidence that the court will interpret them consistently. The day will come when ABS contracts may operate in this way, however, at present, that day has not arrived. More experience with ABS contracts is needed, before courts, arbitrators and parties have a shared understanding of ABS terms and concepts. Until then, the parties to ABS contracts must focus on clearly delineating their agreement, so that there is no doubt about what is required of each party.

---

38 Note: the contract might also clarify who shall pay the costs of the mediator/ombudsman and how he or she will be selected.

39 The only uncertainty is the use of the term "reasonable," however this term is used so often in contractual law and practice that courts and lawyers have a relatively clear understanding of what it means.

In the context of ABS, the greatest threat to the enforceability of ABS contracts arises from a misunderstanding regarding the definitions of terms. Common examples of vagueness in ABS contracts relate to the amount or nature of the *res* and the need for specificity regarding payment. Both of these particular challenges are discussed in Chapter 5 of this book.

Many non-lawyers and others with limited experience in international commercial practice share a misunderstanding that any agreed international policy definition is sufficient to eliminate vagueness. They assume that a contract based on these definitions will be binding on companies and persons. In commercial law and practice,[40] however, only a definition that is "objectively specific" (able to be determined on the basis of objective information and evidence) can overcome the argument that a particular contractual term is too vague or ambiguous to enforce. Regardless of where it is found, a definition or term that fails this test is not enforceable.

2.2 Basic Contract Concepts – How Contracts Function

In order to understand this book's discussions and to be able to contribute to making ABS work, the reader will need to understand the nature of contracts and the basic factors that affect their legal status. These issues are discussed in detail in Chapter 7. The following sections only note some key points that help explain why it is essential to apply the rules set out in this book.

2.2.1 *What is a Contract?*

As explained in Chapter 7, there are many kinds of agreements, but only a few of them are "contracts." At base, a contract is simply an agreement under which one person commits to a particular action[41] in exchange for a reciprocal commitment from the other party.[42] Contract law first determines whether these commitments are a valid contract, and second, whether the overall agreement can be legally interpreted, implemented and, if necessary, enforced.

---

40 This sentence also applies to legislation, however, this book's focus excludes legislative issues. The authors hope to develop a guide to legislation that fosters the functionality of ABS and ABS Contracts, however, that work has not yet been funded.

41 To do something, refrain from doing something, grant some intangible right or preference, provide specific goods or commit to provide specific services.

42 For an example of this concept as applied to the offer/acceptance model, See UNIDROIT Principles 2010, §§2.1.1–2.1.22. An example of how this works in legislation is found in Witkin, 2005, at Vol. 1, § 202.

If a contract exists, it may not be "enforceable" if it is not sufficiently concrete. At the same time, the lack of concreteness in a contract increases the likelihood that parties will disagree about what the contract requires, which will in turn increase the likelihood that enforcement will be needed.

The idea underlying the parties' use of a contract is that it will serve as a self-standing legal document regulating fully their relationship with regard to its subject matter. To accomplish this, its text must address all aspects of that relationship. As discussed in Chapter 5, if any essential element of a contract is left out, there are many potential undesirable outcomes, including invalidation of the contract or interpretation/implementation of the contract in a way that the parties didn't intend.

Over the course of the negotiation of the Nagoya Protocol, controversy sometimes arose over the use of adjective such as "valid," "binding," "legally certain," "functional" and "enforceable," when used to describe contracts. These terms quantify the legal status and enforceability of a contract. They are explained in detail in Chapter 7.

As noted above, where there is a legal certainty regarding ABS contract enforcement, a user company or entity that has signed an ABS contract may cite its financial duty to its employees and shareholders in deciding not to take an action or make a payment, as specified in a potentially unenforceable contract. If it should decide this, then the provider may be forced to either give up its expectation of payment or sue the user in court. In ABS terms, this would mean that, as a result of legal uncertainty, the ABS contract/system is "non-functional." In order to avoid this terrible outcome, at the time of negotiation, the provider is strongly advised to take all steps and undertake all research necessary to maximize his certainty that the benefit-sharing and other key elements of the ABS contract will be fully enforceable.

2.2.2 *The Objectives of Contract Negotiation and Drafting*

In negotiating and drafting a contract, the parties and their advisors have three key objectives: First, their primary goal is to eliminate the possibility of future misunderstandings regarding their various mutual commitments, as much as possible. Learned counsel, John Price, described this objective as "attempting to provide insurance against a lawsuit."[43] The more specific and detailed the contract is regarding its overall purpose and the rights and obligations of its parties, the more likely that the parties will be able to go forward without mix ups.

43 Price, 1982.

Second, but equally important, is the goal of creating an instrument that is legally recognized as a valid and enforceable contract in every jurisdiction in which it is likely to be applied. In most domestic contracts, which are negotiated, implemented and enforced within a single country, this question is relatively straightforward. In ABS, however, contracts are typically "international contracts." As a result, a valid and effective ABS contract must combine two elements: ensuring that the contract meets the legal requirements for validity and enforceability, and making sure that these conclusions will be reached in every country in which the contract may eventually be applied.

Third, but also essential, is to address (including through provisions that address remedies) the gaps in the three traditional transactional elements described in this book at ¶ 1.1: relationship of trust, shared culture/perspectives and recognized consequences. Where you do not have a pre-existing relationship of trust with the other parties to the contract, it will be important to address that gap in the contract. The primary tools of "contractually created trust" are legally enforceable guarantees, warrantees, indemnities and other security and assurance provisions, where properly applied (see Chapters 8 and 9). Similarly, where the parties are from different cultural circumstances, it may be necessary to include provisions addressing issues that would not need to be mentioned in a local contract.[44] Finally, in many ABS contracts, some of the conventional consequences of breach that operate as major incentives for contract fulfilment in the local community (*e.g.*, loss of reputation or future commercial relationships in the community) are not relevant to a foreign user or researcher/collector. To address this gap, the contract may need to adopt more comprehensive motivational incentive mechanisms and appropriate contractual consequences to encourage compliance if the parties' situations should change in future.

These three objectives are all integral elements of the contractual negotiation and drafting process and of the discussions of specific principles of contractual drafting as discussed in Chapters 4 through 10 below.

2.2.3 *How and Why Contracts Function*

As detailed in Chapter 7, it is possible, especially at the local level to form a contract by "handshake agreement" – mutual oral promises by two individuals

44 Such provisions will need to be concrete – to reflect the fact that interpretation, implementation and enforcement will normally involve decision makers from outside the local community, who need to be absolutely clear about what they must do. Once again, it is not enough to say, "comply with community standards" or "traditional law." The agreement needs to identify what actions, payments, *etc.*, are required under those standards

sealed by shaking hands, relying on each party's "word of honor" to do what is promised. Where the contract is intended to address larger matters, or extend beyond local neighborhoods, however, it must function on the basis of legal validity and enforceability, even where neither party wants or expects to have to rely on courts or arbitrators to ensure performance. In turn, legal validity and enforceability depend on a level of concreteness and certainty that makes any other outcome impossible. Even before applying the primary rules of ABS contract negotiation, it is important to consider several essential components, without which, it is basically impossible to apply the contract mechanism.

At present, ABS contracts face significant challenges involving two key essential prerequisites of contract functionality. First, ABS depends on both parties' certainty and clarification of one party's of unique ownership or rights in the *res*. Second, however, although ABS contract functionality will become simple over time, that simplification arises through streamlining, based on the development of a shared understanding of all of the details of ABS contracts. At present, ABS contracts are a very new kind of contractual instrument, and are only in the earliest stages of the streamlining process. The following sections discuss these two aspects of ABS contracts and how they should impact negotiation and drafting.

2.2.4 *Who is Authorized to Grant or Dispose of Genetic Resources or ATK?*

One of the most important elements of any contract is the assurance that the parties who are granting rights and taking on obligations are authorized to do so. In former years, it was common for tricksters to attempt to defraud someone by offering to sell him property that the trickster did not own and had no intention of obtaining.[45] Before a contract can be negotiated, it is essential to know who is legally authorized to sell or otherwise dispose of the property or other right that is the *res* under the contract.

This is connected to the buyer's need to know whether the right being granted is "exclusive" – that is, if the buyer acquires X from the seller, it is essential to know whether some other buyer may also buy X, whether from this seller or someone else.

---

and law, and specify them in detail. Many elements and examples of this need for concreteness are discussed in Chapter 5.

45 This is known in the US as "offering to sell the Brooklyn Bridge." A more sophisticated modern version is sometimes called "the Producers," based on a famous play, in which two individuals sell shares in a new play. By opening night they have sold shares worth more than 1000%. When the investors all seek their share in the profits, they discover that each share is nearly worthless – that a 10% interest is effectively worth less than 1%.

Most contracts depend on the certainty that the buyer/user will live up to his contractual commitments. If the contract's party is not able to take the required actions, it may create a loophole enabling one or more of the parties to walk away without performing. These issues are discussed in more detail in Chapter 4.

Challenges related to ownership of and/or authority over genetic resources and ATK are particularly important in the context of ABS contracts, where the user seeks to acquire an interest in the species that may lead it to seek a patent on particular genetic information or invention based thereon. Given that patent law is based on exclusivity, most users would wish to that their patent protects the particular genetic information entirely, regardless of source. Under ABS, however, each country's sovereign right over genetic information[46] is based on whether that information is found in their country. If the same genetic information is found in more than one country, each such country is legally able to grant access to it. This means no country or provider[47] can grant an exclusive right to that information. It can grant exclusive rights to the samples collected in that country, but cannot control who acquires or uses information from samples collected in other countries. Even greater complexities arise where a country has not adopted legislation clarifying who owns or is authorized to grant access to genetic resources, or where that legislation does not address the most critical issues in a legally specific way.[48]

---

46 This point also applies to each community's right over ATK. ATK issues are more complex, however, given that the same knowledge is often shared among many communities, and that, in some cases a single individual holds the knowledge as a part of his or her role in the community, even though many believe that the knowledge belongs to the community. The NP notes that "it is the right of indigenous and local communities to identify the rightful holders of their traditional knowledge associated with genetic resources, within their communities." NP, 23rd Preambular Clause.

47 In a few countries, the law devolves the right/authorization to grant access to genetic resources to an individual or community on whose property the genetic resource is collected. This increases the non-exclusivity problem, as the same resource may be found on property of literally hundreds of persons. It adds a further complication, because each country has many different categories of property, each with different types of ownership. It is possible, for example that one person owns the land, but a different person owns the trees, crops or animals on the land.

48 This book does not discuss legislative issues. Although many articles have been written on the particular regulatory provisions that each NP Party is obligated to adopt, relatively few have addressed the legislative needs created by the contractual elements of ABS, given

The relationship between the non-exclusivity of the grant of access to GR or ATK, and the attempts to use patents to control innovation based on those GR or ATK is among the many issues that were not resolved in the NP. At this writing, the NP Parties are discussing the possible creation of a Global Multilateral Benefit-sharing Mechanism, which may help resolve some of these questions, although not resolving questions related to patents.[49]

2.2.5 *Streamlining the Process*

In every country, the sheer number of oral and written contracts has not only led to the creation of detailed law, but has also eventually resulted in a high level similarity within contracts of certain specified types and sectors. Most contracts therefore do not resort to the courts or arbitrators. As discussed in Chapter 12, when a particular contract term or practice is successful, it is imitated in other such contracts. Eventually, the courts in that country may recognize nationally accepted "**standard commercial/industrial practices**" in that particular industry or type of contract. Once the relevant court has recognized a standard practice in an industry, then that practice will govern contracts within that industry, unless the particular contract clearly adopts a different practice.

> "**standard commercial/industrial practices**": Practices of a particular industry or commercial segment in a country that are so common within that group that the courts of that country have come to recognize them as universal, and to apply them to contracts in that industry or segment, unless the contract specifies otherwise.

As a result, once legal standards have come to be recognized for a particular type of contract, the contracts of that type can become much shorter. So long as a contract in that industry has been drafted carefully and well in accordance with such standards, it can be written relatively simply. The parties need only address a particular standard area where they want to deviate from the standard terms or practices.

In addition, where the particular industry is frequently addressed in international contracts, the collected body

---

that such legislation is necessitated for functional reasons, rather than by express provision in the NP. The NP's only reference to this concept arises in Articles 5.2 and 6.2, where it appears to limit the rights of indigenous communities with regard to genetic resources to situations in which they "have the *established right* to grant access to such resources." (*Emphasis added*).

49 NP, Art. 10. The status (and in future the results) of current discussions of this mechanism can be found online at https://www.cbd.int/abs/benefitsharing-whatdone.shtml.

of nationally accepted standards may gradually merge into internationally accepted standards, through a combination of contractual practice (many international contracts incorporating the standard) and formal interpretation by courts and arbitrators.[50]

At present, however, ABS is a very new concept. Few commercial and contractual ABS practices have evolved or been publicized. Indeed, where particular contracts have been touted as pioneer efforts in the development of ABS practice, they have often met with failure.[51] As a result, there are virtually no accepted standards of ABS commercial and contractual practice. For this reason, as noted above, reliance on ABS principles alone will produce an instrument that is too ambiguous to be legally recognized or considered enforceable in most countries' legal systems. It is essential, in contracting for access to and utilization of genetic resources and/or ATK, to make special efforts to minimize the number of issues that could be used to challenge or invalidate that contract, at least until such time as the field of ABS contract law achieves a level of certainty, that enables parties to predict how any court might come down on primary questions of contract validity and enforceability.

Over time, the challenges of ABS will almost certainly be met by changes and developments in many aspects of ABS contractual practices. Based on the examples in other relatively new types of contracts that developed over the past century (radio and TV broadcasting/air rights; the software industry; database development; the exchange of microorganisms; *etc.*), new types of contracts mechanisms, escrow systems, guarantee programs and transferrable permits are among the options that might come to be internationally accepted using recognized standards that most national legal systems recognize as valid. At present, ABS contracts will need to be relatively long, as the parties and their lawyers struggle to find provisions that protect all parties and clarify

50 When a particular industry or commercial segment's contractual practices have received "standard practice" recognition in many countries, efforts are made to ensure that they are interpreted similarly by all countries. Unfortunately, the processes for legal recognition of a standard practice vary from country to country, and are often unpredictable. For this reason, international non-profit standards organizations, such as the International Standards Organization (ISO), ASTM International (an engineering standards body that developed from the American Society for Testing and Materials) and similar bodies seek to create uniform non-biased standards that can be applied in various industries, and are often legally recognized as international standards. Given that ABS contracts involve technical and scientific, as well as legal, issues, these organizations' ongoing work by these bodies might provide some idea of how international ABS standards could eventually be formalized.

51 See, *e.g.*, the Teff Agreement in Ethiopia (Andersen and Winge, 2012, discussed in more detail in Chapters 4 and 5).

their rights and expectations. In the future, however, their initial solutions will certainly be refined and standardized by laws, court decisions and common practice. As a result ABS contracts will evolve, allowing them to rely on the experiences of past contracts, which will come to be seen as "industry standards."

2.2.6 *Planning and Writing a Contract that is FUNCTIONAL*

This book gives significant attention to the importance of clear, concrete and detailed statements of who the parties are, what the contract will transfer (the *res*), and what obligations and rights each party takes on under the contract, and numerous provisions affecting the transfer and enforceability of those obligations and the security of the parties' expectations. In this book, these principles are expressed in the form of seven basic rules, which are restated here for emphasis:

- "MAKE SURE YOU CONTRACT WITH THE RIGHT PARTIES" (Chapter 4)
- "BE SPECIFIC AND CONCRETE"(Chapter 5)
- "MANAGE AND ADDRESS MAJOR RISKS" (Chapter 6)
- "KNOW THE POSSIBILITIES AND LIMITATIONS OF CONTRACT LAW" (Chapter 7)
- "EXPECT THE BEST; PLAN FOR THE WORST"(Chapter 8)
- "PROTECT CONTRACTUAL RIGHTS/EXPECTATIONS" (Chapter 9)
- "AVOID MISTAKEN LEGAL ASSUMPTIONS" (Chapter 10)

The most important part of the process of creation/negotiation of any contract, however is the step that comes before any of these rules are applied: planning. It is absolutely essential that the parties carefully and unambiguously map out what the contract will achieve overall and a step-by-step analysis of how it will do this. Once such a plan is concrete, it is a relatively easy task to specify what each party must do and what rights it has under the contract. Without such a plan, the drafting process will narrowly focus on piecing together a number of individual clauses. In that process, it is difficult to avoid creating loopholes and inconsistencies or overlooking essential elements and motivational mechanisms.

2.3 The Sources of Law for Interpretation and Drafting of ABS Contracts

In considering the legal aspects of contract negotiation and drafting, it is important to recall that "contract law" comes from a variety of sources. The first source is historical; contracts have been addressed under formal legal principles for thousands of years.[52] The formal basis of historical contract law may be either in legislation or in court decisions, depending on the manner in which a country's legal system functions. The historical source of contract law is based on primary principles, as those principles are interpreted in the country in which the law is being consulted.

In addition, in nearly all countries, some type of national contract legislation is adopted to address common problems encountered in contractual negotiations, interpretation, implementation and enforcement. In many countries, this legislation is collected into an extensive body of commercial law, or a formal "commercial code."[53] This type of legislation is typically adopted to protect certain persons who agree to contracts that might otherwise be found to be "incomplete" and ruled unenforceable. Of course, the extent to which the provider of genetic resources will find himself able to utilize contract law to resolve ABS contract challenges will vary among countries, particularly those that do not operate on the basis of a commercial code, as discussed below.

Another important source of contractual law is previous practice. This source affects contracts in three ways. First, each party to a contract develops future contracts on the basis of past experiences and transactions, if the parties are clear in their negotiations regarding the reasons for their actions, then those reasons may form a part of the interpretation of the contract. Second, in many legal systems, the law keeps a record of the result of court cases that interpret particular contract provisions and obligations. This "precedent" approach allows subsequent contract parties to know what kinds of provisions are upheld and how specific terminology has been interpreted. They can model their future negotiations on the basis of past transactions of others. Third, as discussed in ¶ 2.2.5, *supra*, over time the legal profession and each industry that uses contracts begin to develop standards that can sometimes shorten and streamline contract practice. Some such standards apply to all contracts, while others are specific to a particular area or industry. As noted, however,

52 In Mesopotamia, the code of Hammurabi, for example, included numerous provisions relating to particular types of contractual relationships. It was adopted and used nearly 2800 years ago.

53 See, *e.g.*, the Uniform Commercial Code in the United States. This document has been the model for various US states, which have adopted their own commercial and/or contractual codes. Even where a state's code does not have a provision on a particular topic, courts and parties in that state frequently rely on the UCC's provisions in interpreting contracts.

these sources develop over time. ABS has a relatively short legal history, so the only previous practices that apply to ABS contracts are contract practices that apply to all contracts.

The third main source of contract law is the contract itself. Each party that negotiates a contract is, in effect, writing the specific rules and requirements that will govern all future actions under the contract, so long as the contract is in compliance with, the basic principles of contract. When a contract addresses a point on which there is no historical or experiential source, the terms of that contract will be the primary (or only) sources of law to address that point.

This brings us to the two competing misunderstandings with regard to the law of contracts. The first is that, through national legislation, any contract-related challenge faced by a particular contractual regime can be solved legislatively. The false assumption is that national legislation automatically supersedes the contractual rights and provisions of individual contracts.

The second misunderstanding is the converse of the first. Many persons without experience in contractual practice assume that the parties can overcome any obstacle, including legal challenges or conflicts, by adopting an express contractual provision saying so.

Both of these views are manifestly false. Although, it is possible to use national legislation to adjust the manner in which contracts are authorized, negotiated, drafted, executed, interpreted or enforced, there are serious limitations to whether and how legislation can be used to alter or overturn existing rules of contract law. Efforts to adopt such legislation are carefully scrutinized because, if the legislation is effective in changing contract law, there is a possibility that such a change could open up an unintended loophole in all contracts. This could have devastating impact on commercial practices well beyond the intended coverage of a new and specific law.

Similarly, although the parties to a contract can agree on provisions that alter some aspects of the legal interpretation of their rights, duties and intentions, there are a large number of legal factors and obstacles that cannot be overcome by express contractual provision. For example, the parties cannot avoid problems relating to the joinder of parties (Chapter 4) by simply saying that the parties to the contract have the legally recognized right and ability to enter into the contract. Similarly a declaration that a contract is concrete, valid or enforceable will not prevent a court from deciding that it is ambiguous, invalid or unenforceable (Chapters 5, 7 and 8).

Where a contract is or could become an "international contract," as defined in Chapter 1, a fifth source of law relevant to such a contract may in limited situations arise out of international conventions and treaties (Chapters 10 and 11). Other key sources include model legislation, agreed guidelines and standards (Chapter 12).

In many ABS negotiations, the parties may misunderstand the role of national ABS legislation. Like almost all other parts of the international ABS regime, this issue is extremely ambiguous. For example, the CBD and NP are agreements among sovereign States and are only binding, if and to the extent they constitute commitments of those States, regarding what the States will do or refrain from doing in the future. Despite this fact, the majority of the provisions in both the CBD and the NP are focused on the actions of individuals, communities and other entities, who are not signatories of or in any way bound by either instrument.[54]

To date there has been little or no formal legal experience with the actual judicial or arbitral interpretation of ABS contracts,[55] and few ABS contracts have been made public in other ways. As a result, at present there are three primary sources of ABS law, that might impact contracts: the text of the contract, (rarely) national legislation on ABS, and (even more rarely) international treaties within the ABS regime. The following sections discuss the latter two sources.

2.3.1 *The Basic Role of National ABS Legislation*

The most important challenges of the ABS regime arise from two facts:

- ABS is specifically intended to be implemented by individual contracts between providers and users and that there is no internationally agreed body of contractual laws. Every contract must be governed by a specified country's national law and practices.
- Every time a contract dispute is submitted for judicial or arbitral arbitration, the law of the country in which that proceeding is held will apply to many key issues (such as whether the contract is valid, binding and/or

54 There are at least two types of legislative provisions in the NP: One type specifies the States' commitments to take "legislative, administrative or other measures." The other focuses on an agreed outcome, and calls on the States to take action to achieve it. A few of these provisions can impact contract drafting, implementation and enforcement. For this reason, as noted elsewhere, the draftsman of an ABS contract should be well aware of the contents of ALL national and international requirements related to ABS. In that sense, all ABS provisions relate to contracts, however this section focuses only on those that address the form and content of the ABS contract, or have been mistakenly understood to do so.

55 Young, 2006. Although described in the media as cases involving the rights of holders and/or providers of genetic resources or traditional knowledge, virtually all cases that have been filed or decided alleging the misappropriation or misuse of genetic resources or ATK have been filed under patent law, and do not formally include any allegations relating to ABS.

> enforceable). As discussed in detail in Chapter 6, this means that persons negotiating and drafting ABS contracts, must either attempt to create a contract that is fully valid, binding and enforceable in every possible country, or attempt to prevent or control the transfer of the genetic resource, ATK and/or the rights and obligations under the contract.

Given the fact that few countries have adopted complete national ABS regimes, however, coupled with the fact that every national ABS regime is different, much of the discussion of national ABS legislation, it is not possible to provide many useful examples from national ABS legislation showing how some countries are addressing these challenges.

The role of national ABS legislation is even more complex by virtue of the fact that ABS is a transnational concept – enforcement of contracts adopted under the provider country's law will normally increase in complexity after the users, collectors, genetic resources and ATK have been taken or transferred out of the provider country. The greatest challenge for national ABS legislation and individual ABS contracts is finding a way to ensure their enforceability under the legal processes of the user or transferee country – a country that may not recognize the provider country's ABS legislation as something it is legally obliged (or even able) to enforce.

For purposes of this Chapter, however, the national-law orientation of ABS contracts has another important consequence: it means that, at best, national ABS legislation can have only a limited impact on the negotiation and drafting of ABS contracts. This is true for a simple reason; each country's laws apply only to persons and activities within its jurisdiction, and in limited situations to that country's citizens and vessels when they are located in areas beyond national jurisdiction. Although it is possible in some cases for Country X to bring an action against a foreign national for violation of Country X's laws, such an action is often very difficult, expensive and unsatisfying, when brought in some other country. A contract made in Country X, however, may often (usually) be enforced or arbitrated in the locality of the breaching parties or their relevant assets. Unless the plaintiff in such an action can demonstrate that the provisions of Country X's ABS legislation are both legally enforceable and a part of the contract, an arbitrator or court may not consider it in making its decision.

For this reason, it is usually better to interpret national ABS legislation as creating a regulatory framework governing activities within the country, and/or governing ABS contracts that are entirely domestic within that country. The NP provisions mandating, recommending or permitting particular national legislative action are primarily designed to guide the regulatory oversight process – the administration of genetic resource and ATK at various governmental levels.

As a result, national ABS laws generally include many detailed regulatory requirements and processes, but very little specific guidance regarding the ABS contract between user and provider.[56] As noted in ¶ 2.1, *supra*, the parties to an ABS contract will need to comply with these national regulations (and all other relevant national laws) in the same way that *all* contract parties are required to comply with *all* applicable national laws when they implement their contract.

2.3.2 *The Role of National ABS Legislation Called for under the CBD and NP as a Source of Law Governing ABS Contracts*

Another potential source of law on ABS contracts is found in the CBD and NP's provisions requiring or enabling national legislation to implement ABS. Some people, even ABS experts, may be surprised to discover that very little of the contents of the CBD or NP considers or addresses the concept, content or implementation of ABS contracts. The countries that are Parties to the NP and CBD were primarily interested in determining with some precision exactly what *governments* were required and/or allowed to do in establishing and implementing the ABS regime, rather than detailing what the parties to ABS contracts can or should do.

In Chapter 11, this book discusses the various ways in which the States' various requirements under the NP and CBD influence contract drafting, interpretation, implementation and enforcement.[57] The following summary focuses only on the question of how the NP and CBD fit in among the other sources of law governing ABS contracts.

---

56 At present, there are relatively few examples of national ABS legislation that is currently in operation. Part of this regulatory inaction may be the result of concerns about trying to determine whether the NP has changed national obligations. As noted above, neither the NP nor pre-NP national ABS law addressed ABS contractual law issues, directly or indirectly.

57 The NP contains one clause which offers direct guidance to contract parties – Article 18, which relates to the controversial issue of "compliance." Although its mandate is not expressed clearly, clause 18.1 is nearly detailed enough to provide guidance for the negotiation and drafting of ABS contracts in one key area: dispute resolution. Its scope is limited to NP Art. 6.3(g) (general call for the adoption of national legislative guidance on MAT) and NP Art 7 (general call for legislative measures governing access to ATK), but it does specifically require parties to "*encourage*" persons negotiating ABS contracts to include provisions addressing the following points: "The jurisdiction to which they will subject any dispute resolution processes; the applicable law; and/or options for alternative dispute resolution, such as mediation or arbitration." The use of the "and/or" in this clause underscores the fact that it is not a mandatory provision, although of course States may make such clauses mandatory.

(a) NP/CBD Non-mandatory Provisions and other Guidance to States

Although the NP provides few direct discussions of States' legislative mandate with regard to the contents of ABS Contracts, it makes it clear that the States may address a great many other contractual elements within their national ABS legislation. The primary contractual impact of the NP's mention of these matters is the clear implication that ABS contracts (whether with governments, communities, institutions or individuals) must be influenced by, and may be regulated by national law. To some extent, the ABS contract must be negotiated with awareness of the ABS law in all relevant countries (countries of the user, provider and possible transferees or middlemen).

In general, most national ABS laws addressing contracts will be useful to indicate issues that must be addressed, but can be adjusted by contractual provisions. Specifically, such laws will be equal to the contents of the contract, in the eyes of an interpreting court or arbitrator. In some cases, however, national law may specify matters that cannot be negated by a contract provision. For example, if national law specifies how to determine who owns (or has the established right to grant access to) genetic resources or ATK, then the ownership/established-right issue cannot be satisfied by a contractual provision stating that the parties agree that X is authorized to negotiate on behalf of the providers.

(b) Impact of the Lack of National ABS Legislation

Where a country has not formally adopted national ABS legislation, some have suggested that the negotiation of an ABS contract in that should not be governed by that country's law, but should be considered to be governed only by the principles of the CBD and NP.[58] This issue was raised in the NP negotiations with specific proposals that were controversial and eventually not included. Consequently, answer to the question of what law governs an ABS contract remains as it has always been. The CBD declared that genetic resources were sovereign matters to be addressed by each country according to its own choices.[59] This means that national legislative choices must control with regard to genetic resources and ATK within the country.

One possible legislative choice is to determine that the country's existing national laws on contracts, property, natural resources, *etc.*, are sufficient, and no law or regulation specifically titled "ABS" is necessary. This option is not recommended, because it promotes uncertainty, but it is clearly a legal choice. The implication is that, if parties seek to negotiate an ABS contract in a country

58 Also discussed in Chapter 11.

59 CBD, Articles 3 and 15.1.

that does not have specific ABS legislation, they will be permitted to ignore the provider country's national law. In fact, however, the opposite is true. They must do more legal work, to determine what other national laws, policies and instruments may apply.

One specific way in which the NP adds to confusion over this issue is found in the first and third clauses of Article 6. Article 6.1, which reasserts that each country has sovereign rights over natural resources, including genetic resources, stating that "access to genetic resources for their utilization shall be subject to the prior informed consent of the Party providing such resources that is the country of origin of such resources or a Party that has acquired the genetic resources in accordance with the Convention, *unless otherwise determined by that Party*." (*emphasis added*). This clause places the obligation to make a clear waiver determination on countries that waive PIC. Confusingly, however, Article 6.3, places specific requirements on "each party requiring prior informed consent" (in other words on countries that have not made any determination and are not required to do so). Specifically, it requires these States to

> take the necessary legislative, administrative or policy measures, as appropriate, to (a) Provide for legal certainty, clarity and transparency of their domestic access and benefit-sharing legislation or regulatory requirements; (b) Provide for fair and non-arbitrary rules and procedures on accessing genetic resources; (c) Provide information on how to apply for prior informed consent; (d) Provide for a clear and transparent written decision by a competent national authority, in a cost-effective manner and within a reasonable period of time; (e) Provide for the issuance at the time of access of a permit or its equivalent as evidence of the decision to grant prior informed consent and of the establishment of mutually agreed terms, and notify the Access and Benefit-sharing Clearing-House accordingly; (f) Where applicable, and subject to domestic legislation, set out criteria and/or processes for obtaining prior informed consent or approval and involvement of indigenous and local communities for access to genetic resources; and (g) Establish clear rules and procedures for requiring and establishing mutually agreed terms [...]

This example of poor treaty drafting creates a legal conundrum for ABS contract negotiators. Few ABS parties have adopted legislation.[60] It is not clear

---

60 Currently (as of May 2016), only 43 countries have posted any information in the legislative measures component of the ABS Clearinghouse, 22 of these are EU members and other European countries which have posted only the EU Regulation on ABS, without any

if any of the currently existing nation legislation fully meets all of the above requirements. If a State has not directly waived PIC, it must be considered to require PIC. It would be legally dangerous to assume that, because a State has not adopted ABS legislation, that one may enter into a contract for genetic resources (which are clearly subject to the State's sovereign right). The fact that a country is one of the majority of countries that have not adopted national ABS legislation will not affect the country's sovereign right to its genetic resources, nor its right to adopt legislation specifying how and with whom one negotiates for access to ATK. There is only one legally tenable conclusion where a country requires PIC, but has not adopted the above described provisions. The parties proposing an ABS Contract in that country should contact the appropriate authorities to determine what needs to be done.

(c) User Measures

From the perspective of those negotiating and drafting ABS Contracts, the current state of uncertainty regarding "user measures" (legislation in the country with jurisdiction over the user or transferee of genetic resources accessed in another country) presents the greatest and most uncertain challenges. Throughout the history of the ABS concept, there have been two primary areas of controversy: the problems of enforcement of ABS Contracts and the role of provider-country legislation in the country of the user, transferee, arbitrator, or other party. These controversies are integrated, particularly because some user countries have suggested that the provider country must bear all responsibility for adopting legislation on ABS enforcement. Unfortunately, most enforcement actions need to happen in a country in which the user operates and/or has substantial assets. In many ABS situations, that will not be the provider country.

These issues are further examined in Chapter 7 of this book. Here, it is necessary only to note that the NP includes specific mandates regarding the enforcement of ABS contracts and provider-country ABS requirements in the country of the user, transferee or other party.

(d) Other National Law Affecting ABS Contracts

One of the factors that has been frequently overlooked in discussions of ABS Contracts up to now is the fact that, like all contracts, they must comply with a very broad range of national laws on non-ABS topics. In every country, there

national legislation implementing that Regulation. This leaves only 21 countries that have posted national ABS legislation in the ABS Clearinghouse. Only 13 of the latter group have posted specific legislation on ABS (the others have posted general biodiversity legislation, which mentions ABS or alludes to the CBD in general).

are many bodies of law (in addition to the country's contract/commercial law) that address or impact one or more elements that may be covered in a contract. A perfectly drafted ABS contract that complies with all of the national legislative and administrative ABS requirements will still not be functional or effective if it violates other laws of the country where the contract is to be enforced.

No two countries have identical national contract law. In addition, each country's (often unwritten) "standard practices" regarding contracts may also differ from country to country. Most important, the validity and enforcement of an ABS contract will often be determined on the basis of a great many categories of national law including the following:

- General environmental and sustainability law;
- Social-welfare law and laws protecting the poor and indigenous persons and communities;
- Property law;
- Administrative law – especially, the rights and duties of provider countries and of providers;
- Laws (and related diplomatic practices) governing trans-frontier movement of goods, customs and communication between national officials of different countries to address these matters;
- Domestic trade law, and domestic legislation addressing international trade;
- Transboundary legal action: availability of national and international courts and tribunals to address misappropriation and most actions for misuse of genetic resources, particular in cases involving a user under the country's jurisdiction that is utilizing genetic resources or ATK from another country;
- National law implementing public international law and applying it to actions and agencies in the country; and
- National laws addressing the rights and duties of persons and entities under the State's jurisdiction, with regard to matters involving international enforcement – including enforcement of foreign or international judgments and awards granted in foreign or international arbitration, mediation, and conciliation.

For example, national property law, and other bodies of law that govern the rights of the parties and others with regard to the *res* can have a significant impact on ABS, even if it does not specifically mention genetic resources or ATK.[61] Although frequently misunderstood, for example property law varies widely

61 As detailed in Young and Bhatti, 2007, the common practice of analysing genetic resource issues by assuming genetic resources will be governed by the provisions of a country's land law is legally unjustified and leads to inappropriate conclusions.

from country to country, with significant differences on a question critical to ABS – the category of property or right that applies to genetic resources and/or ATK (and transfers of those rights and resources).

National legislation on property and other types of *res* varies greatly. Virtually all of the following categories are addressed in national legislation in a way that applies specific rules for determining and regulation of the rights of owners and holders, and addressing the requirements imposed on transfers specifically is included in each type of property. In every country, the variety of rules affecting property and contracts include different provisions and practices, depending on whether the *res* of the contract is governed by the legal frameworks on land and other immobile property; movable property; government or nationally owned property (including national trust); intellectual property; other types of intangible property or rights; or un-ownable property. All countries have laws addressing all of these in some form. Each of these categories may be is subject to different rules. One of the most important legal issues that must be studied in connection with the negotiation and drafting of an ABS contract is to determine where GR and ATK fit within the national framework – to which type regulatory/contractual category does it belong? This answer varies from country to country. If one negotiates and drafts the contract based on the assumption that GR are governed by the rules governing transactions in land, then there is a good chance that the contract will be invalid under the laws of the provider country itself. Many other complications arise out of this basic concern, as discussed in Chapter 7, *infra*.

2.3.3 *The Role of Treaties as Sources of Law Governing International Contracts*

It is sometimes stated that International law of contracts provides a basic source of law governing ABS contracts. Some discussions also refer to "private international law," without realizing that it is not international law at all.[62] It sometimes surprises people to discover, as discussed in more detail in Chapter 10 of this book, that there is no body of "international contract law." Many participants and advisors in the NP negotiations were apparently unaware that most international treaties addressing contractual issues and enforcement of judgments are legally inapplicable to ABS, and even if applied, they do not

62 As explained in Chapter 10, "private international law" is a term that refers only to the national laws and principles that a national court will apply when deciding a case involving a contract with foreign elements (a contract in which parties, properties, activities and/or other interested are in (or governed by the laws of) more than one country).

address the issues of greatest concern with regard to the legal certainty and functionality of ABS contracts.

Chapter 10 explains in some detail the reasons that there are so few elements and situations for which international treaties addressing commercial and contractual issues may be a source of law for ABS contracts. The impact of international law on ABS contracts may change if international negotiations in the future, regarding issues such as certification, enforcement, compliance, standards and model instruments are successful. Until then it is important to remember that treaties within the ABS framework have very little impact on ABS contracts and their implementation.[63] Given that international law on contracts is not binding on the parties to an ABS contract, it is important that the contract should not rely on international law in any way. Every contract should be able to address any international law doubts that may arise.

63 See, *e.g.*, Art 7 of the SMTA adopted under the ITPGR, which provides: "The applicable law shall be General Principles of Law, including the UNIDROIT Principles of International Commercial Contracts 2004, the objectives and the relevant provisions of the Treaty, and, when necessary for interpretation, the decisions of the Governing Body." As noted in Chapter 10, there is no international body of "general principles of law" and the UNIDROIT principles do not address many key elements of the SMTA. For these and many other reasons, any court or arbitrator receiving a case calling for enforcement or interpretation of the SMTA would find it very difficult to interpret this "governing law clause," and might either declare it invalid or decide that it is inapplicable. Thus, unfortunately, the SMTA does not provide a useful model for most ABS contracts seeking to achieve legal certainty and contractual enforceability. Note: UNIDROIT has adopted two new versions of the UNIDROIT Principles (in 2010 and 2016), since the SMTA was adopted. It will be important to use the correct version. Art 7 of the SMTA leaves open the question of which version of the UNIDROIT Principles it refers to.

CHAPTER 3

Planning and Negotiating the Contract

This book's primary focus is the creation and drafting of ABS contracts. In general, this is a legal issue, and most of these discussions affect negotiation by giving the negotiators an idea of the specific content requirements of the contract. Although every negotiation is unique, these legal principles are generally applicable to all ABS contracts. In ABS contracts, especially at the point of negotiation, one of the most important challenges relates to the parties' uncertainty, both regarding the nature of their relationship and their reasonable expectations regarding what the contract will produce for them. The unpredictability of the research and development process – how the genetic resources in nature become the product or process in the market is a critical factor affecting the success of any ABS contract.

The contract is the most critical step that the parties can take to minimize this uncertainty and unpredictability. In this connection, the authors are aware of certain factors, legal approaches and issues that are directly relevant and directly applicable to most pre-negotiation and negotiation processes. Although these matters are not precisely legal in nature, we cannot resist sharing these aspects of their experience in ABS contract negotiations, by providing a specific example of one practical approach that can be used to maximize the effectiveness of the contractual negotiating process.

Within the contract negotiations, the first step is to stop emphasizing the uncertainties of ABS; instead choosing to recognize that the best way to achieve ABS success is to work around them building a legal and practical relationship that enables all parties to know what to expect and to implement the contract properly. This chapter presents a methodology by which the provider can prepare to negotiate effectively, to achieve a functional, implementable contract. The authors' objective is to suggest the practical tools that may enable each party to negotiate and build a good contractual text. Several of the topics mentioned in this Chapter, are more comprehensively addressed in later chapters from a technical legal perspective.

Section 3.1 introduces the nature of the various parties' optimum contracts and strategic approaches, and the reasons it is important for each party to make a strategic plan for establishing a contractual relationship. Section 3.2 discusses the mapping of the party's "optimal" contractual relationship, giving a view of the manner in which the issues most critical to that party would be addressed in the "best-case scenario," as viewed from that party's perspective. Section 3.3 discusses how that party uses the "optimal-contract map" to

 | DOI 10.1163/9789004356573_004

develop its own negotiating strategy. Section 3.4 looks into the way that information from and about the user can be integrated with the optimal contract map and negotiating strategy and how these three tools can be used in the negotiation process. Finally Section 3.5 examines the impact of this mapping and drafting approach on the legal discussions contained in Chapters 4–9.

3.1 Preparing to Establish a Contractual Relationship

Every contract negotiation is, by definition, a classic example of a "give and take" situation, with each party trying to minimize what it is required to give and to maximize what it may take. Obviously, each party is very keen to know what each of the other parties hopes to obtain through the negotiations and why. Insight of this type is very useful to each negotiator, enabling him/her to know where he will be able to "give," and where he has the best opportunities to "take." For the same reasons, however, each party wishes to maintain the confidentiality of much information regarding his/her own motivations and psychology with regard to the transaction.

This informational gap is often misunderstood. Some ABS parties may often expect the other parties to disclose all of their confidential information and motivations in the course of the negotiations. As discussed in ¶ 3.4, however, this expectation may lead negotiators to place too much reliance on the statements that are made to them by the other parties.

The law and standard negotiating practices compel the parties to share some kinds of information, but, as discussed in ¶ 3.4, also allow each party to keep many aspects of its plans, intentions and negotiating strategy confidential. Thus, every negotiation is tinged with an element of "gamesmanship," as each party seeks to maximize its own position, often by trying to predict the concerns of the other parties. This chapter presents one approach to the important task of ensuring that one's own motivations and needs are not omitted or incompletely addressed in the course of the negotiating process.

3.2 Mapping the "Optimal ABS Contract" from the Negotiator's Perspective

To be effective any contract must be more than just a loose collection of paragraphs that oblige the parties to take particular actions or grant the parties particular rights. To be functional, a contract is a "building plan," which will guide the parties in constructing their desired edifice – *i.e.*, achieving the contract's objective in a functional, legally valid and durable way. If a building plan randomly includes specific requirements without carefully fitting them into the overall construction concept, it will rarely produce the desired result, and may well produce a pile of rubble.

Viewing a contract as a building plan or road map for their relationship, it is clear that it must be very precise and specific, so that each party's performance can be definitely evaluated on the basis of whether each specific action has satisfied the specific contractual provision. Thus, the most important pre-negotiation step for any contract negotiator is to "plan" the operation of the optimum contract from his perspective – to build a "map" in as much detail as possible describing what he wants the contract to do and how it should do it, identifying each element of the overall plan (all objectives, necessary events and conditions, triggers, key results and interim steps, *etc.*), linking the elements together, determining who is responsible for each element, and specifically identifying the consequences that arise upon the failure of each element.

Over the course of the negotiation, this "map" will be adjusted to address facts and compromises, but the negotiator should still rely on the adjusted map, and should make every effort to re-evaluate every change to it. The "building plan" analogy might be useful in explaining the importance of this step. As noted, if the negotiators add a clause without considering its impact on every other clause in the contract, then that clause might have unintended impacts, leading to a result the negotiator neither expected nor desired. Consider a building plan in which one clause specifies the importance of natural light and calls for large windows and skylights, and a separate clause focuses on landscaping. At some point in the negotiations, to save landscaping and gardening costs, the contract specifies that certain areas need not be landscaped, only covered with gravel. It is almost axiomatic that maintenance of the gravel will result in cracked windows, unless the change is also accompanied by changes in the design or location of the windows and the type of glass.

3.2.1 *Building an "Optimal-contract Map"*

In essence, as shall be discussed in Chapter 5, there are three primary operative components of a contract: its objectives,[64] its identification of the *res*,[65]

---

64 Discussed in more detail in ¶5.2, *infra*. Note that this refers to the "objective clause" of the contract. It does not refer to the parties' individual objectives, whether disclosed to all parties or not, unless included in the contract.

65 As discussed in more detail in¶5.3, *infra*, the *res* is a term that encompasses the particular assets, actions or agreements to refrain from action that are the subject matter of the contract.

and its provisions setting out the parties respective rights and obligations.[66] These three components become meaningful only when the contract also clarifies the various conditions, triggers and other factors that tie them together. The negotiators "map" of the optimum contract is designed on the basis of *his own* perspective. It is designed to ensure that the particular points of concern to that negotiator (and the party he represents) are not overlooked or omitted.

In addition, the other elements of the contract, as discussed in this book are also interlinked with these key factors. Thus the optimal-contract map will need to include critical concerns regarding the identification and binding of parties,[67] the manner in which transfers and changes of intent will be addressed, and critical elements of implementation, enforcement and remedies.[68] The map of each of these should also note how each part of them is linked to all three of those operative components. In an ABS contract, the authors' typical map of the process would start by looking something like this (although usually written in pencil on several sheets of legal-sized paper):

Component 1 Access

Element	Priority/ Importance	Who is responsible?	Other necessary parties	Timing/ confirmation	Expected/ Required/ Possible results	Effect of failure/ Breach
[Access Precondition #1]						
[Access Precondition #2]...						
[Preconditions of Access #X]						
[definition of the resources to be accessed (*res*) #1]						
[definition of the resources to be accessed (*res*) #2]...						

66 Discussed in more detail in ¶5.4, *infra*.

67 Discussed in more detail in Chapter 4, *infra*.

68 Discussed in more detail in Chapters 5, 6, 7. 8 and 9, *infra*.

Component 1: Access (cont.)

Element	Priority/ Importance	Who is responsible?	Other necessary parties	Timing/ confirmation	Expected/ Required/ Possible results	Effect of failure/ Breach
[definition of the resources to be accessed (*res*) #X] [Extent of Grant] [Trigger of Granted Right #1] [Trigger of Granted Right #2]... [Trigger of Granted Right #X] [Access/Collection Requirements] [Access Oversight] [Effect of Post-access violation on access rights] [Further collection & sampling] [*Etc.*]						

Component 2 Utilization

Element	Who is responsible?	Other necessary parties	Timing/ Confirmation	Expected/Required/ Possible results	Effect of failure/ Breach
[Utilization Stage #1]					
[Utilization Stage #2]...					
[Utilization Stage #X]					
[Link from access to utilization #1]					
[Links from access to utilization #2]...					
[Links from access to utilization #X]					
[Utilization Condition #1]					
[Utilization Condition #2]...					
[Utilization Condition #X]					
[Location and nature of utilization activities #1]					
[Location and nature of utilization activities #2]...					
[Location and nature of utilization activities #X]					
[Compliance with legal prerequisites, provider country #1]...					
[Compliance with legal prerequisites, any other country #X]					
[Transfer options, limitations, requirements]					
[Extracts, essences]					
[Patents and other trade protections]					
[*Etc.*]					

Component 3 Benefits, Monitoring/Regulatory elements, Benefit-sharing, Expiration, Termination

Element	Procedure, nature and calculation	Who is involved and how?	Trigger and how to confirm	Timing	Rights on delay or dispute	Effect of failure
[Type of benefit shared #1]						
[Type of bene shared #2]...						
[Type of benefit shared #X]						
[contract expiration – process]						
[Reconciliation: contract expiration – patent rights]						
[Reconciliation: contract expiration – other rights]						
[Reconciliation: termination for cause – process, benefits, patent, other]						
[*Etc.*]						

Open questions

Issue	Points of concern
[Example: Confidentiality]	[Will there be a confidentiality clause? If so, what is covered: species/science/technology only or contract provisions as well? How do failure, breach and/or termination of the other parts of the contract affect the confidentiality clause? What is the consequence of breach of the confidentiality clause?]
[*Etc.*]	

This type of map is a "living document," in the sense that it needs to change and be updated continually throughout the course of the negotiation. As each adjustment is agreed in the negotiations, this "map" enables the party to see whether and how the originally mapped objectives are met or changed, and to examine how those changes affect the rest of the contract. It does this by keeping a record of the interlinkage of the various elements of all components, whether relatively formally (by adding a column headed "interlinkages") or informally (by slowly covering the entire table with arrows, asterisks and other indications of linkage.) Every provision of the ABS contract, and every change to such a provision, should be carefully considered in terms of its position in and impact on the overall contract.

3.2.2 *Who Needs to Create a Map?*

Whether they create an "optimal-contract map" as described above or not, every party should coordinate with its negotiators and advisors to create its own perspective of the objectives that should be met by the contract. The above map "template" is loosely based on the map used by a provider in a recent negotiation; however, any middleman, researcher, collection, user or other party might easily generate its own map – using the same component headings, but listing different elements within each component.

3.2.3 *Making and Using the Map*

In creating your own map, each of the bracketed items would be replaced by clearly stated issues and elements, which are, over the course of the negotiations, constantly refined and annotated. Other elements and even additional components may need to be added to address key objectives or concerns. For example, in some provider countries, long-term multiplication and cultivation of particular native species is a possible (and sometimes required) element of an ABS contract, as is the user's commitment to purchase these outputs. Even where not required, many parties may need or want to include these concepts in a new component in their map. This additional component would clearly be directly linked to all three existing components. In some ways, it would appear relatively easy to add this component, given that agricultural production contracts already exist in virtually all countries and standard and/or model contracts on contract farming already exist. As a result the main legal challenge of integrating contract farming provisions into an ABS contract will be the need to properly link the farming requirements to the other ABS components, without negatively impacting the legal functionality of the agricultural element.

The blank spaces in the above "map" will be all need to be filled in, some immediately and some over time. None of them is a "tick box" – all need to have substantive content. The map may often form the basis for drafting the contract. As noted above, it is also potentially useful to the negotiators of the party, as a relatively concrete indication of their evolving objectives and the extent to which they are achieved.

Each party will engage in this mapping process individually. At the beginning of negotiations, all of the parties' maps may be very different, because each one is influenced by the private (unshared and undisclosed) motivations of the respective parties. Each party will normally wish to keep its map and other negotiation tools confidential. Although a party's maps should not be shared with other parties, all of their respective maps will begin to resemble one another during the course of negotiations. By the final stages, it will be possible for each party to circle one or two items on which the parties are unable to reach agreement. At that point, a party's map can help it to identify ways to resolve differences, while ensuring that it does not unknowingly give up other rights.

3.3 Negotiating Strategy

In general, parties will get a lot of advice from many sources regarding their negotiating strategy. The other chapters of this book, by contrast, focus on the provision of legal advice.

This section will not attempt to give advice on strategy, because each party's strategy is different, and because each party may need a different strategy for each negotiation. Instead, it will focus on the manner in which a strategy should be developed, and suggesting some of the primary legal areas which the strategy developing process should consider.

Once the party has an idea regarding its optimal contract, it must use this information to create the second key confidential tool that it will use in the negotiations – the "negotiating strategy." This process is not only the first use of the map, but also the first test of its correctness and completeness. The following paragraphs provide an overview of the strategy development process, with particular focus on setting priorities and identifying key limits on the negotiations.

3.3.1 *From Optimal-contract Map to Negotiating Strategy*

The process of developing a negotiating strategy is based on the "optimum-contract map," as described above. It is, in effect, the last pre-negotiation step in that process, and the first critical step in utilizing the map. Throughout the development of the strategy, one of the primary tasks will be to identify inter-linkages. If element X is connected to elements J, K and L, then the strategic development process will begin by examining how the element X and its outcomes affect and are affected by J, K and L. Then look at all elements linked to J, K, and L, to determine their impact on other elements, *etc.* Recalling that a contract is legally considered to be an integrated whole, this process will eventually create a web of impacts that may encompass nearly every element in the map.

3.3.2 *Setting Priorities and Strategies*

Once the contract's operative aspects have been mapped, it is a relatively easy process to prioritize particular aspects. This is the heart of the negotiating strategy.

Like the optical-contract map, the negotiating strategy is also a constantly evolving document. Each strategic decision involves rearranging the map elements in order of priority, and considering whether and how the party would potentially be willing to adapt this item, if necessary in order to reach agreement. In some cases this process is simple. Where the payment of money or establishment of valuation is considered, for example, the confidential strategy would involve identifying not only the target amount, but also the minimum amount one would accept (or the maximum amount one would be willing to pay), in case that target amount is not immediately accepted.

Where the priority item is non-monetary, however, it may be more difficult to strategize. Thus, for example, the party may intend to ask for a personal guarantee from the major stockholder or company president. In that case, the strategy process may need to identify other options for achieving the underlying objective of contractual security, and determine which of them is most desirable and which less desirable options would still be acceptable. In addition, the strategy may need to consider whether the acceptance of a less desirable option would affect other components of the map, changing their strategic priority.

Prioritizing is a strategic process in contract negotiations. One does not say simply "our priorities are elements X, Y and Z," but rather (for each priority element) "Our first priority is element X, because through it we will be able to achieve the following priority outcome(s): [identify specific outcomes or results to be achieved with regard to item X.]"

Following the identification of priority elements and outcomes, it is essential to retrace all of the connections identified in the map.

3.3.3 *"Non-negotiable" elements*

Most negotiation-strategy sessions include at least one statement that "element 'Z' is NON-NEGOTIABLE." As a matter of law, however, there is very little in a contract that is actually "non-negotiable."[69] Therefore, if one party's negotiator tells the others that a particular element is "non-negotiable," this is normally interpreted to mean, "if we don't get the particular result we ask for in this element, then there will be no contract." Most contract negotiations involve the investment of a significant amount of time (and often money) by all parties. Thus, all negotiators for the party with a "non-negotiable" demand should intensively discuss that demand before any negotiations begin, to confirm that the particular result is so important that the parties will not enter into the contract without it. Then, that item should be the first to be discussed and fully aired in the earliest stages of the negotiations, so that the party with the non-negotiable demand cannot later be accused of "bad-faith negotiation,"[70] if he eventually terminates the negotiation because the other party did not accept this item.[71]

---

69 It is generally illegal to enter into a contract to violate the law. In addition to liability for the violation, entry into the contract might make all contract parties (including those who took no illegal action themselves) liable as "conspirators."

70 In general, a party is considered to have negotiated in bad faith when he has "enter[ed] into or continue[d] negotiations when intending not to reach an agreement with the other party." UNIDROIT Principles 2010, Article 2.1.15 ("Negotiations in bad faith.") There may be many negative consequences for one who has negotiated in bad faith. Most important of these is potential liability for damages, which may include all "losses caused" to the other party (a concept that may include lost opportunities to contract with others, costs of hiring advisors, *etc.*). Note: as discussed in Chapter 10, below, the UNIDROIT principles are not formally a part of any country's law. They are, however, an attempt by a group of eminent commercial lawyers to crystalize the essence of general commercial principles from around the world. As such, they are a good indication of how some concepts should be viewed. Clearly, before relying on any "general principle," a party should engage in research to determine how a court in the relevant country might view the issue.

71 In that case, the party that terminated the negotiation will not be liable for terminating the negotiation, unless it can be shown that he was "negotiating in bad faith" (*ibid.*) As UNIDROIT 2010, Article 2.1.5(1) notes, "A party is free to negotiate and is not liable for failure to reach an agreement." It is not always clear, from country-to-country, court-to-court or contract-to-contract, what type of evidence is needed in order to prove bad-faith negotiation or which party has the burden of proof. Accordingly, it is strongly urged that all parties disclose their "non-negotiable" points at the beginning of any negotiation.

3.4 From Strategy to Binding Contract – Identifying the Specific Situation of the Current Negotiation and Coordinating it with the Strategy

Once the party has developed his optimal contract map and negotiating strategy, it is useful to develop a third negotiating tool – a specific analysis of the particular nature of the other party's goals and expectations. There are many sources for information relevant to this process: the information that the other party is legally required to provide; the information that the other party provides without mandate, and what is generally known about the particular type of party involved.

In ¶¶ 3.4.1 and 3.4.2, the authors will discuss these three sources, and the manner in which the information should be used. Then, ¶ 3.4.3 will briefly discuss the manner in which a party analysis should be developed and used.

3.4.1 *Legally Required and Non-mandatory Disclosures and Statements*

There are many laws in many countries that attempt to prevent or redress the harms caused when one party intentionally or unintentionally deceives the other or fails to disclose critical information. These laws address concepts such as fraud, misrepresentation, deceit, non-disclosure, coercion, duress, corrupt practices, *etc.*

These laws and practices seek to protect both sides of the transaction, protecting the potentially harmed parties from these harmful practices, but also protecting the other parties from the possibility of being unjustly accused. The primary mechanisms of this double protection are the concepts of "legally required disclosures" (which can lead to liability, if the relevant party fails to provide full and accurate information) and the right to "retain confidential information."

With regard to confidentiality, as noted in ¶ 3.1, the negotiation of a contract involves multiple parties, each of whom has come to its own internal determination of the value of the contract to its own objectives and activities. As discussed in ¶¶ 3.2 and 3.3, each well prepared party has also developed its own analysis of what it is seeking and what its priorities are. The fairness of the negotiation process depends on each party being able to maintain the confidentiality of its private determinations of value, willingness to commit and flexibility.

The full-disclosure element, however, is also critical. There is a very old general rule of commerce called *caveat emptor* ("let the buyer beware"), which states essentially that the party who is obtaining something under a contract has the duty of investigation, to determine whether that "something" actually is what the other party claims that it is. In modern transactions, of course, this is not always possible. In nearly every contract there is some critical fact that is known only to one party. For example, in a contract with a corporation, only the corporation's officers may know all key factors regarding its current financial condition. If a corporation involved in a contract negotiation were nearly bankrupt, the other party would not wish to go forward with the transfer without other substantial assurance. That other party, however, will have no way to access confidential corporate information to determine the corporation's financial status.

This indicates the reason behind a recent change to the *caveat emptor* concept – the need for a balance between confidentiality and full disclosure. Achieving this balance is legally difficult. Although national legal principles and laws on this issue may vary, there are several apparent rules of thumb that might be thought of as universal:[72]

"RULES OF THUMB" FOR PARTIES MAKING OR REFUSING TO MAKE DISCLOSURES IN CONTRACT NEGOTIATIONS

(1) where possible, disclose all facts that are known to you, but not reasonably accessible to the other parties, if they might potentially be relevant to the contract;
(2) when you prefer not to disclose a fact, but Rule (1) requires disclosure, you have only two options – either disclose the fact or terminate the negotiations;
(3) when there is no reason not to disclose a fact; disclose it (this is not a legal requirement, but may help avoid problems);
(4) parties are not required to disclose their negotiating strategies. The concept of "negotiating strategy" is narrow, however; so the party may be obliged to disclose some of the facts underlying that strategy, if Rule (1) applies to them;
(5) each party should ensure that the other parties have access, as necessary to determine any relevant facts not disclosed under Rule (1);

72 At minimum, if a party were to discover that one of these did not apply in a particular country, that party may decide that it does not want to enter into a contract in that country. In general, it is advisable to work with a commercial lawyer in the relevant country. Such an advisor can provide an "opinion letter" in which the lawyer describes the state of the relevant national law and practice.

(6) where a party is asked for information on a matter that he feels is "reasonably accessible to the other parties," that party must either (a) answer the question fully and accurately or (b) tell the asking parties to find the answer for themselves. Most important, in such situations, DO NOT LIE – if you prefer not to disclose, state directly the legal reason that you feel that you are not required to answer.

(7) when making any disclosure (whether under Rule (1) or Rule (3) or otherwise), do not leave anything out, and ensure that your statements are accurate.[73]

Equally important with regard to disclosures, however, is the action of the party receiving or requesting the disclosure. Here, the list of rules of thumb is much shorter:

"RULES OF THUMB" ON RECEIVING DISCLOSURES IN CONTRACTUAL NEGOTIATIONS

(1) Ensure that all disclosures are in writing, and that the person making the disclosure signs it and if necessary indicates his relationship to the party on whose behalf he is making the disclosure;

(2) If a disclosure is not made in writing, write a memorandum of the disclosure in detail, and require the disclosing person to sign it and state his relationship to the party, as above;

(3) If there are documents or other means of confirming the contents of the disclosure, require the disclosing person to provide them, and state their origin and relationship, as above.

These rules coordinate with many of the discussions in Chapters 4 through 9 of this book.

3.4.2 *Common Types of Parties*

One approach in building a party analysis is to focus on the typical categories of each kind of party with whom you are negotiating. Although this process

73 Unintentional non-disclosure and misrepresentation based on lack of knowledge are both actionable, either civilly or criminally, depending on the context of the statement.

is equally recommended to all ABS parties, it is the providers that generally face the most difficulties in analyzing the other parties' perspectives. For this reason, the following discussion focuses on the needs of those negotiating on the provider side of the ABS discussion, discussing a few of the most relevant issues from that perspective and the most common types of users.

Many general assumptions can be identified regarding the needs and objectives of each category of users. Analysis of the particular critical issues for each type of users can be done at a general level learning from experience and deductive methodology. Information on the general nature of the category of user will enable the provider to draw some typical lessons regarding the user, which can be useful in negotiating the specific transaction. Many of the issues addressed in Chapters 4 through 10 may require greater or lesser levels of detail (and possibly additional specific provisions), depending on which category is applicable.

In general, the categorization of users is based on the type of use they intend to make of the genetic resource or ATK. As detailed in other books,[74] the actions of a user after he has removed the genetic resources or ATK from the provider country may be difficult to track, oversee or monitor. In determining how to proceed under your own negotiating strategy, however, it is often useful to understand the types of activities that this category of users is focussing on, as a tool for understanding which issues will be most critical to him in the negotiations and how to propose terms and compromises.

The following sections describe some of the most common types of users. The goal of this discussion is, on the basis of and a brief description of each type, to identify some of the ways that they differ from one another, and how those differences might impact negotiations.

(a) Academic Researchers

Academic and taxonomic researchers, whether nationals of the providing country or from another user country, are sometimes considered "special cases" for purposes of ABS. The argument often presented in the negotiation of the Nagoya Protocol was that taxonomic and academic research should not be covered by the scope of ABS and not require a contract. Although these two categories are often considered together, this analysis considers them separately. This section will discuss academic researchers and the next section will consider taxonomic researchers.

Academic researchers are the group of users that most commonly engage in genetic and ATK research activities in developing countries. In most

74 Tvedt and Young, 2007. See also, Ruiz Mueller and Lapeña, 2008.

developing countries, students pursuing a Masters degree or PhD who have obtained grants to undertake foreign research are a common sight.[75] Depending on national interpretation of ABS terms, most of these researchers could be considered to be governed by ABS principles, and may need to obtain an ABS contract (as well as possibly PIC, MAT and a permit) in order to do their work.

In many cases, such researchers are required under their grant or degree requirements to bring samples of biological material to their home university or granting institution. The student will often have no immediate commercial intentions in conducting his academic research on the biological samples. His primary aim and consequently time horizon will often be limited to successfully finishing his degree requirements. Few students have a clear business plan structured around their degree-oriented research. In ABS, many provider countries push for special treatment for these researchers – even encouraging providers to consider this kind of activity as an unregulated exception from ABS requirements. Complicating this, however, the researcher's home university or granting institution may often have a more long-term idea about the path for a developing a commercial finding based on material researched by its students or faculty. They may intend or set as a criteria for the grant that the researcher's findings will eventually become the property of the university or even the researcher's granting institution or supervisor.

Often, when he enters the country on a time-limited project, an academic researcher may face a conflict between the requirements of his home university or granting institution and the contractual provisions requested or required by the provider. Additionally, his research plan may not include enough time to deal with the sometimes lengthy process of negotiating an ABS contract and related documents.

The commercial success from students work on genetic resources varies. Where the research grant is part of a privately funded research project, there will often be a number of obligations involving the granting institution, potentially also applicable to its relationship with a collaborating commercial entity – a relationship that might not be disclosed or visible to the provider.

Regarding this category of users, the provider should investigate (and the negotiations may need to specially address) any or all of the following probable pathways for genetic resources leaving a country in the hands of this type of user:

---

75 In the discussions leading to the Nagoya Protocol, the issue of academic (and/or "non-commercial") research received a lot of attention. See, *e.g.*, cbd-INF, 2009.

- Research that leads to findings that have commercial potential, calling for further research and commercial development either by that user or by some other user;
- Collected genetic material or ATK that eventually makes its way into the collections of the researcher's home university or granting institution free of longer term contractual obligations or conditions; and
- Genetic material, ATK or research results that are transferred to a third party.

Since these typical situations are visible in the situation of a student taking material abroad, the ABS contract which a student must sign can be designed to these scenarios.

This category of users may raise particular concerns with regard to ensuring that the university and all other involved institutions are properly bound to appropriate obligations (see Chapter 4). These situations may be further complicated, where the researcher is originally from the providing country[76] but, at the time of the negotiation, is engaging in research under the auspices of a foreign university or granting institution.

(b) Taxonomic Collections

The taxonomic collections face many issues and concerns that are very similar to those of academic researchers, as described above. Like academic researchers, they view their activities as non-commercial, and have actively sought a "streamlined option" for obtaining ABS approval for their work in developing countries. Although the NP did not specifically require such an option, it does allow countries to adopt one.[77] It also does not mention taxonomic research specifically, mentioning only "non-commercial research purposes." Given that most taxonomic institutions obtain at least a small amount of funding by

76 In many countries persons who are citizens or established residents of the provider country may be subject to different requirements under ABS law than those from another country. Some countries require the user to establish a kind of residency by forming a partnership or company in the provider country. All of these approaches may make it difficult to identify or regulate the status of a national of the provider country who is in the employ or other relationship with a foreign academic or research institution for purpose of his research in the provider country.

77 At Article 8(a) ("Special considerations"), the NP requires "each Party" to adopt legislation or other measures that "[c]reate conditions to promote and encourage research which contributes to the conservation and sustainable use of biological diversity, particularly in developing countries." This provision includes as one option for meeting this requirement, the development of "simplified measures on access for non-commercial research purposes, taking into account the need to address a change of intent for such research."

providing access to samples of material in their collections, many taxonomic collections are relatively uncertain about whether and how any of the "streamlined option" might apply to them.

From a contractual point of view, granting taxonomic researchers access to genetic resources without a contract could create a loophole in the system. Taxonomic research frequently results in the addition of samples to foreign collections. It may often lead to the discovery of interesting properties, whether by the original taxonomist/collector or by some person who engages in research through the foreign collection. Such discoveries may then lead to new commercial research in a situation that is completely separated from the provider and that does not require further contact with that provider country. This suggests that "streamlining" for taxonomic research should focus on the development of a contractual system or form that shortens the approval time, but does not eliminate the provider country's rights.

(c) Commercial Companies

It is not really possible to summarize all of the different types of companies under a single heading. Companies may vary. There are dozens of different types of multinational conglomerates and dozens of different types of local partnerships, with literally hundreds of other types of company in between. They may be profit-motivated, governmentally created, or non-profit. Most important, as explained in Chapter 4, they are "creations of law." This means that, in order to exist they must comply with the law of the country in which they were formed, and to be recognized in a contract they may be required to meet additional requirements in the provider country.

Another important factor relating to companies is that they may change in many ways, over the life of the contract. A company may merge with or be absorbed into another company or divide into a number of companies. A company that was originally focused on a particular goal or activity may change its focus, in an effort to find a successful niche. Companies often have complex relationships with other companies within their "corporate family," as well.

All of these factors, and many others can potentially affect the provider's negotiation strategy. After the contract is signed a number of unknown or unexpected facts and changes may occur involving a company. Such changes may have a significant impact on the ABS contract. Although principles of commercial law have developed in most countries to address many such corporate changes, those principles have not yet been applied to ABS contracts or genetic resources/ATK. Until the body of commercial law becomes clear with regard to ABS issues, the ABS contract can only be legally functional if it considers all such matters in as much detail as possible.

3.4.3 *Developing and Using a "Party Analysis"*

The most critical question in relation to the development of a "Party Analysis" as a tool for negotiating an ABS contract relates to the sources of the information received. The source determines many elements of the analysis, including the level of reliance on the information contained in the analysis, and the manner in which its various points should impact the contractual negotiations and drafting.

As an initial matter, it is important to discuss reliance on the various types of information received. Depending on the nature of that source, a piece of user-related information may help streamline the drafting of the contract, or only cause the receiving party to call for confirmation. Similarly, where different sources provide conflicting information, an analysis of the sources will determine which one to rely on.

For example, the information given the greatest credibility is information contained in a legally mandatory disclosure from a party, particularly where that disclosure is in writing and the party agrees to include that disclosure as warranted information under the contract.[78] This is strongest, because the party making the disclosure has a strong legal reason to ensure that it is complete and correct. Even as to this source, however, it is advisable to confirm the information.

As to the other primary sources of information, it may be difficult to give credibility to any of them. Where information comes from a party's non-mandatory statement or disclosure, there is a possibility that the party is simply "puffing" (making positive statements with the goal of encouraging the other party to pay a higher price or agree to some other provision). In general, if the statement is not an outright lie, the party will not be held legally responsible. The statement will be seen as "a matter of opinion." Clearly, the other party should not rely very heavily on such a statement. Usually, the best test of whether one can rely on a non-mandatory statement is to ask whether the party making the statement will warrant it in the contract.

Where information comes from a basic analysis of the category of party involved, the strength of your reliance on this information depends on two factors: How strongly can you rely on the other party's statement regarding what type of party he/she is? and, How certain are you regarding whether your analysis of that category of party is up-to-date and accurate?

---

78 See Chapter 9, *infra*. "Warranted information" is generally information that is included in or appended to the contract, the truth of which is the subject of a warrantee by one or more of the parties.

The second critical question is how the party analysis should impact your strategy. In general, it is not advisable to drop an item from the optimum contract map or negotiating strategy on the basis of information regarding the nature of the user or his non-binding statement of his plans regarding how he will use the genetic resource or ATK. It is important to recognize, the value of information, as a tool for addressing certain key challenges. Every contract should still address all of the risks and concerns regarding future contract violations, transfer, change of intent, identification of benefits to be shared, and other ABS conundrums. Where there is a detailed party analysis, however, these general provisions can be supplemented by more specific clauses that make it easier and clearer to comply with the contract in the context of the party's situation. In particular, for example, it may be easier to set clearer benefit-sharing provisions for an academic researcher while retaining broader clauses to address other, unplanned uses. Not only will this encourage the development of academic research contracts, it will also provide an incentive for the parties to keep their activities within the boundaries of academic research. Thus, it is clear that the value of the party analysis should not be underestimated.

3.5 The First Steps in the Negotiation

3.5.1 *Allocating the Task of Preparing the First Draft*

Some parties and commentators have suggested that the party who is responsible for preparation of the first draft has the means of controlling the entire negotiation. Certainly, in many recent ABS negotiations, the party preparing the first draft has been able to impose many of its preferences on the contract, but it is not clear that the party's ability to impose its preferences are in any way tied to its agreement to prepare the first draft. When the party doing the drafting is highly experienced in commercial negotiations and contracts, and the other party is not, there is always a chance that the drafting party may gain the upper hand in the negotiations. However, where an inexperienced party provides the first draft and a highly experienced party reviews it, the results do not significantly change – the highly experienced party is still able to achieve its individual objectives, possibly at the expense of the other party's needs. Where both parties are more equal (whether through previous experience or by being advised by experienced counsel and other negotiators), the allocation of the task of preparation of the first draft will have little impact on the ultimate result.

Although there is no general rule about which party should draft the contract, there are several legal and practical elements that might affect this decision. First, as a practical matter, the party that prepares the draft might find themselves in a defensive position, not only with regard to the clauses that address "priority elements" in his negotiating strategy, but with regard to all other clauses. A common negotiating strategy used by the other party in such instances is to kindle these defensive responses with regard to a great many clauses – a strategy which enables that party to conceal his own priorities within a forest of small, perhaps meaningless negotiating points. In addition, the drafting party may feel honour-bound to retain clauses he has put forward, even when he did not have a particular reason for including them (apart from the fact that he had seen them in other contracts.)

Regardless of who drafts the contract, every issue within it is entirely negotiable by all parties up to the time that the entire contract is finally approved and executed.[79] Parties should be careful, however, in the course of the negotiations, and avoid giving or implying "final approval" to any clause, where a change to another clause might necessitate a change to the finally approved clause. A later insistence on renegotiating a clause on that had previously gotten final approval might, in certain instances, be deemed "bad faith."[80] To avoid this kind of problem, it is useful to constantly reiterate that nothing is finally approved until everything is agreed. This approach enables the parties to effectively engage in the continuous review of their negotiation strategy throughout the negotiations, as recommended above.

3.5.2 *Rules of Contract Construction/Interpretation*

Another complex legal issue also becomes important once the negotiations begin – the concept of "rules of interpretation or construction" that may apply to the terms of the contract. In most countries, there are systems of rules regarding how contracts are interpreted.[81] These rules are used where a contract contains an ambiguity that is not "fatal to the contract" – in other words, an ambiguity that can be resolved by interpretation without declaring the contract null and void.

At the beginning of the contract negotiations, at the time when the parties decide which party will have the task of preparing the first draft, many negotiators become concerned about one or more of these rules. The most common concern at this time is a rule that is recognized in many countries: that, in the event of an ambiguity that cannot be resolved using other rules, the court or arbitrator interpreting the contract will "construe the provision against the

79 See footnote 69, *supra.*

80 See footnotes 70 and 71, *supra.*

81 In some cases, such rules are set out in statutes, in others they are built up through a body of published judicial decisions.

party who drafted it." Many negotiators have expressed concern about this rule, fearing that even where the drafting party simply copies a clause from another source, it will be "construed against him."

This fear, however, is based on a misunderstanding. Many parties and negotiators assume that the initial drafting will be easy, with one party drafting a provision and the other[s] accepting or rejecting it. This is far from true. As noted in Chapter 2, modern contracts are actually exercises in the development of mutual agreement, rather than an offer/acceptance situation. In most modern contracts, the negotiation process includes many revisions between the initial draft and the final. Normally, when one looks at the final draft, it is nearly impossible to track which party suggested which clause and/or how each party's negotiators changed it. In such a situation, it is virtually impossible to construe anything against the drafter, because it is usually impossible to attribute any part of the contract to a particular party.

Even if one party is clearly identified as the drafter, the dreaded result of "construing the clause against the drafter" will only happen if the clause is ambiguous. This underscores the importance of avoiding use of terms and clauses from the CBD and/or NP in your contract, their ambiguity may lead to construction of the clause against you.[82]

3.5.3 *The Danger of "Cut-and-Paste"*

It is often a mistake for the party preparing the first draft to start out by copying provisions taken from a final agreement that has been accepted in another transaction. For one thing, it is important to remember that most ABS

82 As noted in Chapter 2, *supra,* the NP/CBD's language (even its definitions) is too vague and ambiguous to be legally used by a court or arbitrator in interpreting a contract, compelling compliance, or developing a compromise award. The NP negotiators were unable to come to agreement on concrete meanings of most terms and requirements. They opted for "constructive ambiguity" – a term that means adopting phrasing that can support whichever meaning a country desires. While this approach is useful in enabling the States to close the negotiations, and acceptable where it applies to optional or hortatory clauses, or clauses requiring States to take domestic action that is not expected to have any trans-national impact, it is manifestly inappropriate as a means of addressing a contract, particularly one that must be unambiguous, international and implemented under contractual principles.

These comments also apply to the Bonn Guidelines and the ITPGRFA, whose SMTA is also subject to this same problem of ambiguity and vagueness as a previously negotiated compromise, copying the SMTA's provisions may give away much of the drafting party's original position, before the negotiations begin.

This situation is exemplified by the attempts to resolve difficulties under the Teff Agreement, see description in ¶ 4.1, and see Andersen and Winge, 2012.

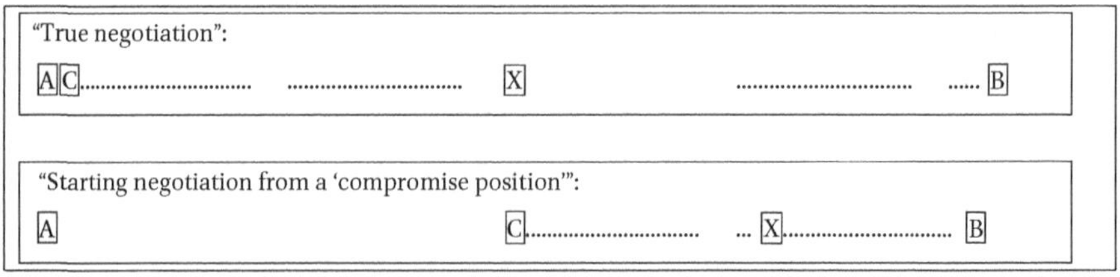

DIAGRAM 1 *Difference between starting from the concluding point of a pre-negotiated contract and starting on original positions.*
Key: A represents is Party A's best desired result; B is Party B's best desired result; C shows the position of the first draft in this spectrum, and X is the eventual compromise achieved.

contracts are so new that one cannot know whether a particular contract will actually turn out to be legally and practically functional. It may, for instance, include a clause or approach that a future party or court will decide is "fatal" to the contract – *i.e.,* that causes the court to declare the contract void. Unless the contract you are copying has already been successfully completed one cannot be certain that the contract is legally valid or functional.

Moreover, even if the contract was successful, there may be many factors in that original contractual relationship that are not applicable to your contract. If the other contract was between parties with a long-standing relationship that both parties hope will continue, then the success of the contract may be more dependent on that relationship than on the written clauses.

The most important reason not to cut-and-paste the provisions of another contract, however, is that by doing so, you are starting the negotiation at a point that was deemed by the former parties to be an "acceptable compromise" between their positions. They were able to agree on a mid-point that gave both parties some part of their original desires. If your negotiations start at that mid-point, there is a chance that the party submitting this "first draft" in your negotiations would be putting himself in a negative position. (See diagram 1) Clearly, it is far better to start from one's actual starting position than to start from the compromise position achieved by a former negotiation, when the other party is starting from his own actual starting position.

3.6 CAVEAT: The Illusionary Two-step Contractual Approach

Before turning to the negotiating and drafting process, it is necessary to debunk a continuing ABS myth – the myth of the two-stage contractual negotiation. In the past, this myth was propounded both in scholarly papers on ABS and in the negotiations themselves. It allowed the scholars and negotiators to ignore a critical ABS obstacle.

3.6.1 *Development of the Purported "Two-stage ABS Contractual Process"*

The two-stage approach was originally suggested as a detour around a problem that arose in the negotiation of Article 15 of the CBD. Negotiations had broken down over the fact that, in general, at the time of the user's initial collection or acquisition of biological samples and/or ATK, neither the user nor the provider has any clear idea whether any of the accessed material/information will yield commercially or scientifically useful results. This led to doubts about whether the commercial approach could work with regard to ABS. These doubts were very problematic, particularly for developed countries that strongly favoured placing the burdens of ABS operation on the private sector and developing/provider countries.

Those early ABS discussions ultimately concluded that the problem could be avoided if ABS negotiations occurred in two phases: First, the user and provider would negotiate the specifics of the collection and initial investigation/analysis processes and a provision that would require the user to return to the negotiating table if and when any of its initial analyses indicated that some specimen could provide a compound with useful properties or some ATK practice could lead to a useful product or scientific discovery. Second, the user and provider would agree on the benefit-sharing and other aspects of the continuing relationship, in that follow-up negotiation. Thus, once bound by this "first stage contract," the parties would come back to the bargaining table to negotiate benefit-sharing, only after they had a better idea of what benefits were available.[83] This approach was strongly supported, primarily by delegates with no understanding of commercial processes.[84] Eventually, it came to be described as the prevailing view of how ABS would work.

3.6.2 *The Fallacies of the Two-stage Negotiation*

This concept underlying the two-step approach is somewhat naive commercially. It assumes, without any basis, that the user will return to renegotiate an obligation to make an additional payment, at a time when there is nothing else

83 This concept is reflected in the CBD, in the fact that it calls for two separate MAT requirements – one for access (CBD Art. 15.4) and one for benefit-sharing (CBD Art. 15. 7.).

84 Although delegates with strong ties to commercial users were also participating in those discussions, those users had no incentive to disabuse the others of their misunderstandings.

that the provider is required to give the user (and nothing the user needs from provider to give it a reason to want to keep the provider's good will.)

In the early days of ABS, however, several ABS contracts were negotiated that specifically included the second-stage renegotiation process.[85] There has been little published information available regarding the success or failure of these contracts; however, the authors have inquired into them personally, learning that such contracts only resulted in benefit where the first stage of the contract required "up-front" payments in some form. It is not clear, however, what this result should be attributed to. It may indicate that the users did not prioritize this research and have still not undertaken of research/analysis on the specimens they obtained. Another possibility is that the research has not produced positive results indicating that the genetic resource or ATK can be used in the development of a product or other benefit. Finally, however, it could indicate that the user has "forgotten" to meet its second-stage responsibilities, or has transferred the genetic resource or ATK to a different user who does not believe himself bound by the ABS contract.

The idea behind this two-step approach is that the user may not wish to make commitments until it has completed the research phase and has some idea of the value of the genetic resource or ATK. Two-step advocates normally wish to encourage researchers to start working by minimizing paperwork and "red tape." They assume that it will be better for both provider and user to wait for results before negotiating the benefit-sharing elements of their relationship. Unfortunately, the benefits of the two-stage approach are one-sided. The user can collect resources and start to work quickly, often with little or no up-front payment or commitment. But he has no motivation to return for the second-stage negotiation. At that point, the user already has the resource, and may view the return to the negotiating table as a cost with no added benefit. Even if the user does come back, however, he will be the only party at the negotiating table that actually knows what the research results are or how valuable they are. He will have no reason to want to share that information with the provider.

The two-stage approach has been incorporated into national ABS legislation of a few countries, the most promoted of these being Australia.[86] In these

85 See, *e.g.*, Reid, *et al.*, 1993. The Government of Australia (one of its strongest proponents), has never relinquished the two-level transaction approach.

86 Environment Protection and Biodiversity Conservation Regulations 2000 (Cth) ("the EPBC Regulations"). These regulations address only the use of resources on "Commonwealth areas," a term that includes only land owned by the Commonwealth (federal government) or a Commonwealth agency, land in specified external territories, Australia's EEZ and OCS and commonwealth reserves, as well as the airspace over these areas. Although the term

countries, the regulatory system is built around the idea that the user will return when he finally has found something of commercial value, before he begins to develop/offer it commercially. There is little indication that these provisions have been functional or effective in developing any benefit-sharing.[87] They are built on "self-reporting" – that is, the user determines whether to designate his use as either "non-commercial," "potentially commercial" or "commercial." If he designates his initial use as non-commercial, the user's activities under it are generally exempt from ABS-related requirements unless or until he returns for the second stage. In theory, if or when the user decides to undertake commercial development, he must return to the agency and enter into a formal ABS agreement. In Australia, sixteen years after the initial date of this law and 10 years after the date of the first permits in the database, the relevant agency has approved 275 initial permits, of which 241 were domestic (permits obtained by Australian nationals, institutions and companies.)[88] Of the 275 permits reported in the database, 271 are designated non-commercial. At least 43 of these permits (including all three "commercial" permits) were issued on the activities Australian governmental institutions.

It is perhaps not unexpected that nearly all permits are non-commercial, given that the regulations give the user the power to designate which type of permit applies.[89] Another encouragement is the fact that there appears to be no negative consequence (or indeed oversight authority) for a user who makes such a declaration. Such a user may later make commercial use of the genetic resources in Australia, so long as he has agreed to come back to the table to negotiate

---

"Commonwealth area" normally includes land held under lease by the Commonwealth or in a Commonwealth agency (including certain islands and national parks), the ABS regulations do not apply to such lands, absent certain contractual provisions in the lease. Thus, resources on most of the land within Australia are not covered by these regulations.

87 In the Australian example, the ABS law adopted in 2000 mandates that certain potential users of resources found on Commonwealth areas (*ibid*) must obtain an initial permit before bioprospecting and research. These regulations govern "access to biological resources," a concept that is set out in the Regulation (*ibid*) at § 8A.03.

88 Confusingly, a later paragraph of the 2011 report to the NP on the Australian system (footnote 90, *infra*) states that a further 190+ permits were granted in National Park areas and other leased lands that are not covered by the regulations (excluded from the term "Commonwealth area" with regard applied to ABS, see footnote 87, *supra.*) It is not clear whether these other users are the source of any of the contracts reported in above, or how the results should be interpreted in light of the fact that most land in Australia is under state or territorial law, and thus outside these regulations.

89 To qualify as non-commercial, the user must sign a form declaration to this effect.

a formal ABS arrangement. Outside of Australia, the "non-commercial" permit-holder is not bound by any contract, and the Australian government will have little or no ability to assert its permit requirements beyond its own borders.

Similarly, the fact that most permits are obtained by domestic users is not surprising for two reasons. First, as noted elsewhere in this book, provider-side legislation is generally nearly unenforceable outside the provider country. As a developed country with an extensive government sector, however, it should be possible for Australia to police its domestic users very well. Second, although it has issued a few non-commercial permits foreign users, Australia views itself as primarily a user country and may be willing to allow those few foreign users to operate without permits, in the hope that other countries will follow the Australian example and adopt user-beneficial two-stage approach.

One of Australia's submissions to the NP negotiations stated without explanation that "There are currently seven access and benefit-sharing contracts completed for organizations engaged in commercial research [on Australian genetic resources]. Four of these are with Australian Public Institutions and three with foreign research organizations. A further contract with an Australian research institution is under consideration."[90] Clearly, one Australian government organization obtained at least one of the domestic ABS contracts in conjunction with its initial permits, since a contract is a prerequisite of the issuance of a commercial permit.[91] The database does not indicate that any other user has obtained a permit for "commercial" or "potentially commercial" uses. This indicates that up to four Australian and three foreign users may have returned to negotiate an ABS contract. Based upon earlier news stories, at least one such contract was with a company[92] that is not listed in the database of initial permit holders. That company's ABS contract was conditioned on its establishing a research facility in Australia. Such conditions are often easier for developed countries to require, and need not depend on vague concepts such as ABS as an inducement.

3.6.3 *Returning for Additional Collection*

Another type of "return clause" that has been found in many pre-NP ABS contracts addressed the user's ability to return to the provider country/community/region, to collect additional samples. It has long been noted that many species

90 Australian Government Response to Notification 2011–216; Access to Genetic Resources and Benefit-sharing; Ref.: SCBD/ABS/VN/SG/74553.

91 Regulations, *supra,* footnote 86, at § 8A.07. It is not clear whether or not a single ABS contract can cover more than one permit, under the Australian system.

92 AstraZenica, a global pharmaceutical company.

display particular genetic properties only when cultivated in their original *situs*. More recently, however, it has been discovered that some genetic-based properties vary for other reasons. For example, the compound epibatidine was found only in in a particular sampling of one population of *Epipedobates anthonyi.* When scientists returned to collect more, the new sampling did not display the target trait.[93]

From a contractual drafting perspective, the possibility that a user will seek to engage in further collection does not suffer from the same problems as the "two-step contract" described in ¶ 3.6.1, *supra*. Indeed, if the user wishes to return to the country and collect more species, this indicates that he has an incentive to negotiate regarding that follow-up collection process. In fact, the user's preference with regard to "re-collection" will be the opposite of his approach to the two-step contract. He will normally want to include specific provisions in the first step contract, which pin down the price to be paid and other requirements to be imposed in the event of a return for "re-collection," for a simple reason: A return to the bargaining table at that point could benefit the provider who will know that the user will only wish to return if his analysis of genetic resource has indicated that it may contain promising compounds or other possible value.

In these discussions, the user may refuse to provide information on those initial results considering them confidential and/or trade secrets, and downplaying their importance. The fact that the user is coming back for more, however, may be important to the provider's negotiating strategy. To prepare for this possibility, the provider may want to ensure that the collection provisions of the contract are strictly limited (in time, geography or number), so that a new contract or amendment will need to be negotiated in the event that the user seeks permission to re-collect.

93 Angerer, 2011. The cryogenically preserved toxin had been collected and studied, but when researchers returned to the same population *in situ*, they could not isolate the same compound.

CHAPTER 4

"Make Sure You Contract with the Right Parties": Addressing the Challenges of Contracts with Companies and other Entities

The most important contractual provisions affecting enforcement and compliance of an ABS contract are those that identify the parties to that contract and determine the extent to which those parties are bound under it. Although, to many non-lawyers, these provisions look simple and are often overlooked, they are extremely important.

Usually, in order for a contract to be valid, it must have at least two parties. Only an entity or person that is named as a party to a contract has enforceable obligations (at least as a point of departure) from that contract. All parties must have "legal personality," in order to be legally bound by a contract. This means that every entity (company, organization, institution, community, agency or country) named in a contract must be legally able to enter into a contract on its own behalf – to bind itself in a manner that the other parties may legally enforce if necessary.

With regard to individual persons, a comparable issue relates to whether the person has the requisite "legally recognized capacity" to enter into a contract (referred to in most English-speaking countries as simply "legal capacity.") Under legally recognized capacity rules, the law must deem that each party can legally be held responsible under a legal instrument, before that person can be bound by a contract. Legally, this includes a set of rules to determine whether the law will uphold a contract involving a particular party.

Both "legal personality" and "legally recognized capacity" are concepts governed by national law. The relevant rules differ greatly from country to country. As discussed in more detail in Chapters 7 and 10, it can be difficult to determine which country's law will decide these issues in any international contract. It may be more challenging in the context of ABS. In general, the law that is applied to a particular contract issue could be the national law of one of the parties; of a court or arbitrator ruling on the contract; or of any person or entity to whom some contractual duty, right or property has been transferred. For every additional country in which the contract will operate or be enforced there is an additional risk that one or more of the contract parties to the contract will be considered as lacking either legal personality or legally recognized capacity.

 | DOI 10.1163/9789004356573_005

If one party to a contract lacks legal personality or legally recognized capacity under the applicable national law, that contract may be completely invalidated. The legal consequence of such invalidity is that the law will not uphold claims for any loss, damage or expectation based on the contract. In negotiating, drafting and implementing any ABS contract, then, the parties should make a significant effort to meet the formal criteria for both legal personality and legally recognized capacity. In doing so, they should attempt to consider the laws on these matters in every country that may play a role.

For ABS contracts, these same issues apply, but may have a different (higher) degree of practical importance. Unlike the majority of contracts, many ABS contracts are "international contracts," involving at least two countries. In most domestic contract negotiations (especially at the most local level), there is no doubt about whether the people and companies involved meet the legal personality and capacity requirements under their domestic law. For that reason, it may not be important to formally address these issues, and they may not even be mentioned in those negotiations. By contrast, in international commercial negotiations in developing countries, it is always important to verify all parties' legal personality and legally recognized capacity as a key element of the negotiations.

To date, however, ABS contract parties have paid little attention to these issues. Their unawareness has the potential to create many serious problems. As noted throughout this book, many of the challenges facing ABS contract implementation arise only after the user already has the genetic resources. At this point, the entire controversy will depend on what happened at the time the contract was signed. If the right actions were taken to create legal relationships between legally valid parties at that point, then the parties will have legal options available to help them resolve their challenge. If not, they are "out of luck."

Questions relating to the identification, status and involvement of parties are tightly interconnected with virtually all other elements of the contract. The determination of which persons and entities are the "right parties" for the agreement needs to be made through a close analysis of the issues discussed in this chapter, integrated with an analysis of the contract's objectives, the *rcs*, the nature of the parties' obligations, and the future possible actions of the parties (Chapters 5 and 6.)

This chapter focuses on the participation of companies and other types of entities as parties to ABS contracts. It discusses the following issues:

- Legal personality (¶ 4.2),
- Ability to perform assigned contractual obligations (¶ 4.3)

- Legally recognized capacity and responsibility to meet contractual commitments (and a brief discussion of the impact of the contract on third parties) (¶ 4.4);
- The question of whether representatives acting for the parties are legally authorized (¶ 4.5); and
- An inquiry into the question of whether all "necessary" parties have been included in the contract and what consequences attend failure to include the party able to take the required action (¶ 4.6).

It will begin (¶ 4.1), however, with a brief example, drawn from the Teff Agreement, of the manner in which the issues discussed in this chapter contributed to the failure of an ABS contract.

4.1 An Example: What It Means to "Contract with the Right Parties"

To many non-lawyers, contractual provisions relating to personality, capacity, responsibility and authority may appear to be either very simple or as something that can be ignored (sometimes called "boilerplate,"[94]) because it appears to be such a simple issue. In international contracts such as ABS, however, provisions identifying and binding the parties to the contract are extremely important. Indeed, the failure of some parties to address this issue has already prevented ABS enforcement/compliance in more than one recent case.

One example of the importance of these issues is the 2004 Teff Agreement between Ethiopia (two designated entities) as provider and a Dutch company as user. This contract was originally intended and publicized as "one of the most advanced agreements for the fair and equitable sharing of benefits of its time ... [and] a pilot case for the implementation of the Convention on Biological Diversity in terms of access and benefit-sharing."[95] Expectations that this contract would mark a great advance down the path to ABS functionality ended in 2009, however, with the bankruptcy of the Dutch company

94 The term "boilerplate" is generally used to refer to contract clauses that are inserted, in order to "satisfy the lawyers" – that is, contract clauses that address complex legal things. Often, one party will encourage the others to ignore such a clause, saying "its just boilerplate" and implying that this type of clause is the same in all contracts, and that the "normal" (non-lawyer) negotiators need not discuss it at all. Unfortunately, in ABS contracts, there is no such thing as "boilerplate" – all clauses are important and must be negotiated. Often a so-called boilerplate clause that has been ignored in the negotiations will have devastating impact in the event of a breach of contract, or other difference of opinion among the parties.

95 Andersen and Winge, 2012, at p. v.

that was named as the user under the contract. This bankruptcy effectively terminated the contract, even though the utilization of the genetic resource continued in the hands of companies and individuals related to the bankrupt company and the owners of the bankrupt company. By the time of the termination of the contract due to the bankruptcy, the genetic resources were already in the hands of shareholders or other persons and other related companies in the Netherlands. On paper, the bankruptcy did not formally terminate the contract. All the contract actually did was make it virtually impossible for Ethiopia to enforce it. Although many factors and reasons contributed to this result,[96] the contract's failure to clearly identify and verify the parties and their ability to perform was the most important.

As executed, the Teff Agreement listed the following parties: the Institute of Biodiversity Conservation (the provider) and a Dutch company called Health and Performance Food International (HPFI) (the user), as well as the Ethiopian Agricultural Research Organization. These entities and their legal status were not discussed. The contract merely named them and listed their addresses.

As a legally formed Dutch company, the user company HPFI (the only user company designated as a party to the contract[97]) clearly had "legal personality," *i.e.* it was legally able to enter into contracts. It was, however, wholly owned by two holding companies, each of which was wholly owned by the same two specific individuals. These two persons acted on behalf of HPFI throughout the negotiations. In addition, the individuals that owned the two holding companies also owned other companies that were active in plant breeding, but were not named as a party to the ABS contract.[98] Neither the two holding companies, nor the individuals that owned them were identified and

96 It is often noted that the Teff users were apparently not intending to comply with ABS requirements, from the beginning. If so, the clarification and adjustment of the identified parties would not necessarily have produced actual benefit-sharing, but it might have forced the users to take more recognizably ill-intended measures to evade their responsibilities, and thus might have improved the providers' litigation prospects.

97 Interestingly, the contract separately bound two Ethiopian entities, presumably with the goal of ensuring that HPFI would never face the converse problem in its dealings with the providers.

98 In the address listed for HLPI, the contract provides a clue to this relationship – it gives an e-mail address that includes the company name, "soilandcrop." Soil&Crop was owned by the same individuals throught their holding companies and was interested in doing plant breeding on teff. Hindsight suggests that, at a minimum, the negotiations should have included in-depth investigations of all relevant entities, and either included them all or addressed their relationship to the contract. The failure to do so contributed to the providers' inability to enforce the contract.

bound as parties to the ABS contract.[99] The contract did not discuss any questions involving HPFI's relation with other individuals and entities in any way. Under Dutch law, however, all of these other entities and persons are deemed separate from HPFI, and are not responsible for its liabilities and obligations. This placed a double legal barrier between the true owners of HPFI's assets and the duty to share benefits with the providers.[100] Thus, the persons and companies receiving and utilizing the genetic resources were not bound by the contract.

HPFI was later declared bankrupt by its owners. At the time of the bankruptcy, it was discovered that patents and plant breeders' rights with regard to Teff, had been obtained in the name of other HPFI-related entities that were not parties to the Teff Agreement. These companies were utilizing Teff genetic resources accessed under the Teff Agreement, without any contractual obligation to the Government of Ethiopia and other named providers.

When it became necessary for Ethiopia to enforce the Teff Agreement, HPFI declared bankruptcy. Ethiopia then made two important discoveries: (i) the individuals involved in HPFI had taken all valuable assets, including its Teff patents, out of the corporation;[101] and (ii) the individuals that had been acting on behalf of HPFI had reportedly "lost commitment" to the contract.[102] In other words, they were neither motivated nor obliged to comply. The valuable rights that were the basis of their commitments had migrated into the possession of other companies (companies with the same directors, but which were not party to the Teff Agreement.)[103]

For purposes of this chapter, the primary lesson of this example, is that the Teff Agreement failed, at least in part because it did not sufficiently bind all of

99 The company registering the plant variety protection rights on three varieties of teff was Soil&Crop, which was not a party to the Teff Agreement. Later other affiliated companies have appeared selling teff in European markets.

100 As a formally created limited company, HPFI operated as a legal barrier, preventing Ethiopia from seeking enforcement from the two holding companies (also limited companies.) Those holding companies, in turn, operated as legal barriers protecting the persons that owned them. Although acting on behalf of HPFI, those persons allegedly held no personal responsibility under the contract.

101 Some months before the owners themselves declared HPFI bankrupt, the Teff flour patent was transferred to another company, in which the same persons had all beneficial/financial interests. Andersen and Winge, 2012.

102 Andersen and Winge, 2012, at p. 112.

103 Some of the possible contractual options that might have been useful in avoiding these challenges are discussed in Chapter 9.

the necessary parties.[104] If the parties had engaged in the basic research, discussions, guarantees and documentation necessary to ensure that the contract bound the right parties, they might have been in a better position to implement and enforce their contract, when things began to go wrong.

In this connection, it should be remembered that ABS contracts are very different from conventional sourcing contracts, particularly in terms of the parties' motivations. In conventional sourcing contracts, the primary force motivating both parties throughout the contract's implementation is maintaining their legal relationship. The seller hopes to sell next year's harvest to the buyer, and the buyer wants to develop a reliable continuing supply. If there is a legal flaw in the manner in which such a contract binds the parties, those parties are often likely to ignore it. Unfortunately, most ABS contracts do not provide strong practical motivations for post-access user compliance.[105] Hence, it is essential to strengthen the parties' legal motivation through the terms of the contract.

In the Teff Agreement, although the users were motivated to obtain the contract, for a variety of reasons[106] their later commitment to comply was weak or non-existant. This lack of commitment, combined with the fact that the benefits of the contract were not held by HPFI, led to HPFI's bankruptcy and the other actions that caused the contract to fail.[107] The other companies and

104 Rather clearly, where a corporate entity that is party to a contract becomes bankrupt, and the persons with legal interests in that entity are willing to remove its assets, rather than use them to satisfy the entity's debtors, there are many other problems beyond failure to include the necessary parties. If the individuals and other entities holding interests in HPFI had been formally bound by the Teff Agreement, they might still have evaded their obligation, however a more carefully drafted contract could have improved Ethiopia's chance of successful implementation, and that starts with identifying and binding all parties with the authority and ability to take the actions called for under the contract.

105 As noted in ¶¶ 1.1 and 2.2, the commercial world functions on mutual benefit and non-compelled motivations. Contracts and their power are only a small part of the process, necessary to ensure that all parties agree on what they must do, and know what will happen if they fail to meet those obligations. If one party is not continuously motivated to maintain a strong and beneficial commercial relationship, then the contract's provisions must be *extremely* strong (often called "iron-clad"). Even iron-clad provisions on enforcement may not be sufficient to encourage a recalcitrant party to comply and meet its contractual obligations. The strongest clauses may not be able to overcome that party's opposition, in the event that it is necessary to seek enforcement.

106 The combined list of reasons put forward for the Teff Agreement and its failure are set out in Andersen and Winge, 2012, at pp. 110–113.

107 There are legal questions about what happened, however it is clear that HPFI filed bankruptcy and that the individual owners of its two holding companies transferred all

individuals were not bound, and thus had no primary motivation to fulfill the ABS contract.

The lesson from the Teff Agreement: This chapter discusses three essential steps: the *selection* of the specific parties to a contract, the *verification* of those parties' legal status (that they have legal personality and legally recognized capacity to enter into a contract) and *confirmation* that the parties identified comprise all of the necessary parties to the contract. These efforts will have an enormous impact on the success of a contract. The provider needs to know the corporate structure including the structure of the user to take informed decisions on how to design the parties to the contract. Although proper negotiation and drafting of these aspects of the Teff Agreement would not necessarily have protected Ethiopia if HPFI's directors had intended to defraud the providers, they could well have produced a better motivation if the parties had focused on their legal obligations and potential liability.

Sadly, another lesson from the Teff experience is that no matter how much appearance of goodwill exists at the time of the negotiation, the parties should not count on it to continue throughout the contract's implementation. Goodwill often fades. Commercial companies with nothing more to gain from an agreement will often lose interest in completing it.

Certainly, in contracts involving long-term relationships, where the parties are wellknown to each other and have a motivation to maintain their good relationship, a "gentlemen's agreement" may be enough.[108] As noted in Chapters 1 and 2, however, where the parties lack that ongoing level of commitment and motivation to comply with the contract; they must rely more heavily on the creation of a precise and concrete legally instrument, not only to help the parties know precisely what is required, but also to motivate them to comply.[109] Proper selection and qualification of parties is a key determinant both of these

valuable assets to different entities that they owned – effectively circumventing the contract. *Ibid.* In light of the fact that their rights were uncertain, and protracted legislation in a European court would have been expensive, Ethiopia and the other providers did not attempt to bring a lawsuit against the "successor corporations" and the director and manager. Even if such an action were successful, its costs might have equaled or exceeded the sums awarded by the court or arbitrator.

108 In many negotiations, the authors have been told of a legal contract that lacked all of the factors discussed in this book, but was functionally successful. Clearly, if all parties strongly want the contract to succeed according to its terms throughout the entire life of the contract, it will succeed. The reason the authors recommend negotiating a clear, precise and enforceable contract is simple – at the time of the negotiations, one cannot predict whether a party's motivation will disappear before the contract ends.

109 As discussed in ¶ 1.1, the authors do not mean to suggest that only litigation can ensure enforcement. In the example set out in ¶ 4.1, however, if HPFI had determined that its

factors. Ensuring that the proper parties are legally bound helps to strengthen the binding nature of the contract. This will also shore up the motivation of contract parties, if situational changes might otherwise prompt them to renounce their commitments.

4.2 "Legal Personality" – Basic Criteria for Legally Binding Any Entity

Roughly defined, the term "legal personality" may be said to refer to the question of whether an entity or community is legally empowered to may take certain actions in its own name. For this purpose, the term "entity" refers to a company, organization, institution, university, agency or State. The same kinds of questions determine whether a community may enter into a legal instrument, as a unit, and what this means for the individuals within that community.

When will an entity or community be considered to hold (and allowed to assert) contractual rights? For individual human beings, legal personality is indisputable. The individual's rights to enter into a contract depend solely on whether he has "legally recognized capacity" to do so (see ¶ 4.3, *infra*). Entities, communities and other groupings of people, however, must meet different criteria, if they wish to assert a recognized, singular legal personality – to enter into contracts and take other actions as an entity, rather than acting in the names of the individual members. If an entity with recognized legal personality enters into a contract, only that entity will be responsible for the contractual commitments. Its individual members will not be separately responsible.

Legal personality is necessary whenever an entity seeks in its own name to enter into a contract, incur debts and own property. Other rights and obligations available to an entity that has legal personality, include the rights to bring a lawsuit, the possibility of being sued, and the obligation to pay taxes.

The following sections focus on legal personality in general and its particular application to ABS, after which it offers some contractual suggestions about how to address legal personality in an ABS contract negotiation.

4.2.1 *Criteria for Legal Personality and Consequences Where it Does Not Exist*

An entity or community is really just a collection of people. Where it has legal personality and enters into a contract, however, only that entity (and not the

contractual obligations were clear and that Ethiopia could and would enforce them if necessary, then HPFI and its affiliates might well have opted to either comply with the contract or seek a negotiated compromise.

individual people) will be responsible for compliance or non-compliance.[110] The people who comprise the entity or community (its members, shareholders, partners, *etc.*) are to some degree "shielded" by the entity's legal personality, so that they can rarely be held liable for their role in the entity's actions or omissions.[111] On the other side of the issue, if the entity does not have legal personality, then some other individuals, often including the person(s) claiming to negotiate on behalf of the entity, may be held personally liable for any contract violation, even by other persons acting on behalf of the failed entity.[112]

For this reason, in most international commercial contracts, legal personality issues are considered critical and usually addressed in great detail. This is clearly necessary to protect the rights of all parties to the contract. To date, however, little or no attention has been given to legal personality issues in ABS contracts. An entity's legal personality is a complex matter. As further explained in ¶ 4.2.3, *infra,* it is not an issue that can be addressed by simply including a clause in the contract. In order to protect themselves with regard to legal personality issues, contract negotiators must do their own work – identifying all the relevant parties and verifying their legal personality and other factors early in the negotiation process, to ensure that all necessary parties are formally bound by the contract.

4.2.2 *Establishing Legal Personality*

(a) In General

Domestic rules regulating legal personality are sometimes very ambiguous and may vary greatly. There may even be significant differences in these rules among subnational jurisdictions in federated countries. In all countries, various types of legal entities (companies, institutions, communities, *etc.*) must meet specific requirements (sometimes specifying the entity's level of capitalization, requiring the establishment of a bank account or posting a bond and other actions), in order to have "legal personality" – that is, in order to enter into a contract as an entity. Every company is necessarily created under a legal system that requires certain types of formative documents, registration and sometimes various proofs of responsibility.[113] In some countries, the law imposes different rules for the formal recognition of smaller entities.

110 Unless the contract imposes separate liability on the individuals or other entities involved.

111 See generally, Park, 2009.

112 See discussion in ¶ 4.5, *infra.*

113 A formally recognized company receives that status under national or subnational law, which normally requires certain types of formative documents, registration and sometimes various proofs of responsibility. The country or subnational jurisdiction will

In a contract, the lack of legal personality may have two possible outcomes. It may invalidate all or part of the contract or it may significantly alter the parties' contractual rights. By contrast, if an entity has legal personality, then only that entity, and not its employees or investors, will be bound and/or liable under the contract. An entity with legal personality can be sued (for performance or for damages) in connection with any contract it has entered into. In addition, however, it's legal personality provides a "corporate shield" or "veil" for the company's owners. Those who enter into a contract with the company will normally have no legal right to "pierce" the corporate veil and seek a remedy from the investors, in the event that the corporation cannot comply with the contract. In the event of a breach of the contract by that company's owners, directors, managers, employees or representatives, the other party's only contractual remedy may be a claim against the company – not the offending employee or representative. In some cases, even where a company's investors violate the contract, they too may be protected from contractual responsibility.[114] These protections may make the use of a company with legal personality desirable, as a way of avoiding responsibility, in case the contract does not produce the desired result.

The laws determining whether a company has legal personality are intended to ensure that any company has sufficient capital available to meet is obligations. By doing this, the lawmakers hope to encourage individuals to invest in companies, by limiting their risk.

In many countries, there are many different types of corporate entities, each subject to different rules regarding formation and legal personality.[115] The persons forming the companies select among these options, on the basis of many

normally maintain some kind of list of entities and/or provide approval or certificates that demonstrate its status. In most countries, a variety of other types of entities that lack legal personality may exist, without such proofs. See, *e.g.*, Cornell University, Legal Information Institute database; Singh, 2015; Davies, 2008. Gen Goto, 2013; Arlt, *et al.*, 2002.

Some examples of the breadth of corporate and company registration requirements can be found online. In the United States, for example, corporate law is set at the level of individual states and protectorates, meaning that there are 52 different bodies of corporate law, as well as certain federal laws that address corporate issues in the context of securities (selling shares in corporations and other bodies), bankruptcy, and anti-monopoly regulation. (See Cornell University database.).

114 Depending on the nature of the violation, the investors' may be liable for fraud or some other tort, however, as noted in Chapter 8, it is far more difficult to obtain and enforce a transboundary tort judgment than a transboundary contract.

115 For example, in the US state of California, the primary types of legal entity that have legal personality include "corporation," "limited liability company," "non-profit corporation," "partnership," "limited partnership" and certain unincorporated associations operating

different factors (cost, taxation, liability, insurability, *etc.*), all of which affect the specific characteristics of the company's legal personality. In any contract involving a company, the parties must be fully apprised of the type of legal personality involved, and how that type affects their transaction.[116] For example, corporations are often "affiliated" (including, "parent-subsidiary" or "mother-daughter" relationships.) It may not be enough to name only one of the related companies, especially, if the structure is used to compartmentalize liability.

In the Teff example (¶ 4.1, *supra*), the user claimed that the contract was directly binding only on the single corporation that signed the contract, and not on its directors, managers, employees, shareholders, related corporations, *etc.* The parties could not afford to bring an action disputing this claim. This example underscores the importance of making sure that the right parties are bound by the contract, as discussed in detail in ¶ 4.6, *infra*.

(b) Institutions and Universities

Institutions of various types (universities, hospitals, research institutions, charities, aid organizations, *etc.*) are also "entities" for purposes of establishing legal personality.[117] There are some key differences between this type of entity and most commercial entities. For example, many institutions do not limit or oversee the instruments that are signed in the field by researchers and other employees, either because the institution or agency is protected against liability by law, or because it relies on the benign nature of its objectives/motivations and the fact that it is not a profit-driven entity to insulate it from lawsuits. These bodies' legal personality issues are often obscured, in light of the fact that the persons entering into contracts on behalf of such entities are frequently researchers or aid workers, unaware of the relevant legal issues.

---

pursuant to a legal name filing (sometimes called a "dba," which stands for "doing business as.") California Corporations Code.

116 These rules become increasingly complex, where companies create "subsidiaries" (sometimes called "daughters companies"). Many additional rules may apply in an attempt to ensure that these companies are not used as ways of avoiding corporate financial obligations. Unfortunately, one consequence of this complexity is that it may be prohibitively expensive for an aggrieved contract party to bring an action claiming that a company related to another contract party should be held liable for obligations of that party.

117 See, *e.g.*, California Corporations Code §§ 2500–10841, which sets out the (very different) rules and requirements necessary in order for a public, charitable, religious, heath or other institution to have recognized legal personality. Similarly, depending on the national law being applied (see Chapter 10), it is not clear whether a partnership will be considered as a separate entity for these purposes. If not, then the partners and directors may be directly liable for the actions of the partnership.

In some countries, certain types of institutions are governed by systems that are very different from those used by commercial entities. In particular, it is often very difficult and time consuming to obtain approval or ratification from persons authorized to bind the institution, with regard to a contract negotiated by a lower-level person in the institution. In all contracts with institutions, it is important to be aware that there is a significant difference between these institutions and other entities and individuals, in terms of what motivates them to enter into a contract and how and why certain provisions are included.

(c) Governmental Entities

Governmental entities may pose unexpected legal personality challenges that must be addressed during contract negotiations. National public administrative law or constitutional law can include different rules regarding these entities' rights and ability to enter into contracts. In Norwegian administrative public law, for example, the extent to which an administrative organ can bind itself and the government is an unclear question of law. Other countries' rules on these issues may be very different.[118]

In ABS contracts, many types of government bodies may be "users." Some of these – universities, genebanks, and botanical gardens, for example – might normally be governed by the principles set out in 4.2.2(a) and (b), above. When these bodies are governmental entities, however, additional inquiry will be necessary to determine if their governmental status raises additional issues.

It is also common for government agencies or departments to be designated as "providers" in some countries. Even though they are governmental institutions, the parties negotiating the ABS contract cannot take it for granted that they have legal personality or are otherwise able to enter into contracts.[119]

(d) Communities

With regard to providers, significant, complex and (sometimes) ambiguous restrictions may apply when considering to the legal personality of communities. Actions taken on behalf of a community affect the rights and personal lives of all local residents. The community needs to represent them all.

118 In the US, for example, federal government agencies are bound by a wide range of laws that limit or alter their rights to enter into contracts in various situations. See, *e.g.*, Feldman *et al.*, 2011. At the state level, each US state has adopted its own laws and regulations governing contracts entered into by governmental entities.

119 As noted in ¶ 4.3, *infra*, even the persons representing a corporate or governmental entity may not be fully aware of the extent of their power to bind the entity or of the entity's ability to enter into a contract at all.

Where a community seeks to enter into a contract, that community may be required to meet certain legal standards designed to clarify which persons may act on the community's behalf and in what situations, in order for that community's decisions and contracts to have legal force outside of the community setting. These rules are necessary to ensure that one or a few members of the community do not enter into contracts claiming to act on behalf of the community, but taking unfair benefits for themselves. National legal frameworks often specifically explain how a community may gain legal personality (by qualifying as a township or municipality), but often these rules do not apply to rural or indigenous communities. Even when they do apply, those communities may find it difficult to comply with them. (In that case measures are needed to ensure that any person(s) that claim to be acting on behalf of the community are actually authorized by the community to do so.)

It is similarly necessary in virtually all countries for the law (or in some cases the community members, acting collectively) to specifically determine which resources (especially genetic resources and ATK) belong to the community as a whole, and which belong to particular individuals.[120] In a growing number of countries, a specific procedure or legal record is required, to set out the powers and duties of community representatives (or in some cases the government), to specify the obligations of community members under a contract signed by community leaders, and to clarify the dividing line between community resources and the individual resources of particular community members or families.

4.2.3 *Examples and Suggestions: ABS Contract Provisions on Legal Personality*

The issue of legal personality is very basic. This means that the parties' failure to properly address legal personality can have a dramatic impact on all aspects of their contract. If a party does not have legal personality, then the contract may be invalid or its impact may be very different from what the parties intended. The final determination of this issue may depend on the laws and

120 For example, in many communities, traditional medical, local varieties, or cultural knowledge is held only by one or more individuals (shamans or other designated persons.) Their title might be hereditary, leading some to believe that they individually hold the established right of a provider of the knowledge. If the knowledge is part of the community's traditions, however, many communities may disagree, claiming that the knowledge is community-owned. Before entering into an ABS arrangement with an individual making a claim that he has the established rights of a provider, it may be critical to engage in more intensive investigation.

courts of one or more other countries – not only the provider's country, but also the user's country, the country whose courts or arbitrators might interpret the contract, and perhaps also a "transferee country" that was not a part of the original transaction.

The most effective way to confirm any entity's legal personality is through research before the contract is signed. It is not sufficient to simply ask one party to give assurances about the local law or the law of his home country.[121] Rather, to confirm another party's legal personality, it is normally necessary to obtain or confirm a legally verified statement or certificate from an independent source in the party's home country. One must also determine conclusively that the party's legal personality is recognized by the country in which the transaction is going forward.

If a negotiator does not have time, money or incentive to obtain formal verification with regard to the legal status of an entity in the negotiations, it may be possible to insert a clause that will give recourse against the specific individual who claims to be acting on behalf of that entity. This protection is not strong or complete, but it is potentially better than nothing:

SAMPLE: PROVISION ON LEGAL PERSONALITY

Regarding the legal personality of an entity (Party X) that is proposing to enter into a contract, the contract could include both of the following clauses:

- *Party X, and all persons executing this Agreement on behalf of Party X, individually and collectively state under penalty of perjury and fraud that Party X is a* [choose one: *corporation, partnership, company, government agency, community*] *that is fully legally recognized under the national law of the country under which it is governed and is legally able to enter into and be bound by contracts and other legal instruments both in that country and in the country in which this Agreement is*

121 If those assurances are not correct, that will not affect the rights of the parties under the contract. In other words, if one party formally, but falsely assures the other (even in a contractual clause) that all parties have legal personality and contractual capacity under the laws of the country, the contract may still be unable to bind the entity involved. It may be possible to invalidate the contract, but the rights connected to it, and the rights to take action on the false statement are doubtful and difficult, particularly where the assurance related to a legal issue that other parties could have verified for themselves.

entered. In support of this statement, they attach to this Agreement a copy of all legal instruments necessary to attain that status, and individually and collectively state under penalty of perjury and fraud that these instruments are in full force and fully compliant with all relevant law.

- *Party X and all persons executing this Agreement on behalf of Party X hereby individually and collectively* <u>*guarantee and warrant*</u> *the truth of the statement made in the preceding clause. This guarantee is separately stated in this instrument, in the expectation that, if this Agreement or any part of it were invalidated for any reason (including the legal status of Party X and persons executing this Agreement on behalf of Party X), this guarantee shall survive and may be legally asserted.*

This provision does not *ensure* that Party X has legal personality, nor does it *ensure* that Party X or the individuals executing the contract for Party X will be bound. It assures *only* that:

(i) if any of the documents or assurances in the clause are ultimately found to be untrue, the other party will have a claim against Party X (a fraud/misrepresentation claim), which cannot be defeated simply by stating that the contract is invalid;
(ii) If a claim is made, both Party X and any person negotiating on its behalf may also be sued under the guarantee/warranty clause and possibly required to pay some level of damages, depending on the other terms of the contract; and
(iii) if the guaranteed statement is untrue, the individual(s) signing on behalf of Party X can be held individually liable for the false claim. Even if those individuals do not have sufficient economic worth to bear the costs of compliance with the contract, they will potentially be subject to legal claims for the fraud or misrepresentation. As such, individuals who plan to remain in the provider country may have an added incentive to ensure that these statements are true and that the proper documents are provided.

The clause will not, however, enable the other party to enforce the contract against Party X, if Party X lacks legal personality, if the persons negotiating the contract for Party X are not authorized to do so, and/or if those persons do not have "legally recognized capacity to enter into a contract," as briefly mentioned in ¶ 4.6.1.

4.3 Ability to Perform: Addressing the Nature and Stability of Corporate Entities

Connected to the assessment of a potential party's legal personality, it is also important to undertake a more practical investigation into the entity's nature and stability. In many ABS contracts, one or more of the parties is a "start-up" company – a recently formed company whose owners and operators are taking the initial steps in building an enterprise around their "new idea." This is expected, in light of the fact that genetic research and development, and the manufacture and sale of products based on genetic resources and ATK are still relatively new ideas and technologies. Providers who are negotiating with a start up frequently find themselves in the difficult situation exemplified in the Teff Agreement (¶ 4.1, *supra.*) That is, they are pressured to rely on the start-up company's self-description in deciding whether that company has the assets necessary to meet their commitments under the contract.

In domestic contract law, many countries have adopted measures and principles to protect parties against the possibility that such a company will (intentionally or not) ultimately be unable to meet its obligations.[122] Unfortunately, these laws are normally in the form of standards of financial responsibility, which only apply to give another party a legal remedy that can be exercised by going to court after the start-up company has failed to meet its obligations. As demonstrated by the Teff Agreement, many factors of cost, uncertainty, distance and complexity will often operate to prevent the provider in an ABS agreement from undertaking a law suit against a defaulting user, so these legal protections are not particularly useful.[123]

Rather than relying on national legal principles, then, parties considering an ABS contract with a start-up company (or any company on which they have insufficient confirmed information) should take the time to review the "actual capacity" of the company to meet the expectations of the contract. This is a very important type of pre-contract investigation, and should not simply rely on the statements made by the negotiators representing the start-up company.

---

122 The concept of bankruptcy and related financial laws is very complex, and only briefly mentioned in this book in ¶ 6.6. As noted in text, it is not very useful for the parties to rely on bankruptcy laws, since those laws normally do not mandate full payment of the bankrupt parties' debts, and since the only way to use them will be to participate in a legal action in the country in which the bankruptcy is filed.

123 In the Teff case (see ¶ 4.1, *supra,*) that country was the Netherlands, and it was considered too expensive to assert the provider's rights in that country's courts, even though the provider had a strong case against the bankrupt user and its related persons and entities.

This research will directly affect two critical steps that must be taken in the course of the negotiation:

- The determination whether all necessary parties have been formally and sufficiently bound by the contract (discussed in ¶ 4.5, *infra*); and
- The inclusion of contractual tools for protecting the parties in ways that may not require litigation, *i.e.*, third-party guarantees and similar provisions (discussed in Chapter 9, *infra*.)

Other key challenges with regard to contracts with new and/or unknown companies are addressed in connection with the possibility that some of this user's rights, obligations or the *res* itself will be transferred to a different person or entity, whether within or outside the countries involved in the ABS contract (Chapter 6, *infra*.)

4.4 Contracting with the Right Individuals – Legally Recognized Capacity and other Issues

To this point, our discussion of the rule "Make sure you contract with the right parties" has focused on the special issues regarding how to properly address the inclusion of companies and other corporate and institutional entities as parties to a contract. There are, however, many other critical elements of this rule, which are primarily relevant where one or more individuals are parties to a contract. These issues too may have a direct impact on whether an ABS contract is legally valid and enforceable. As very briefly outlined below, these include (1) the laws governing "legally recognized capacity to enter into a contract" (including the special rules governing contracts with members of "protected classes,") and (2) the issues raised by the concept of "third-party beneficiaries." All of these issues are essential parts of the contract negotiations and highly complex. Thus, although they have a major impact on issues such as contract validity, remedies and enforcement, these issues can only be briefly discussed in this chapter.

4.4.1 *Legally Recognized Capacity*

A contract will only be enforceable if it is fairly entered into. There is a basic principle recognized in most countries that contract law should not be a tool that enables one person or entity to take unfair advantage of another. This fairness is sometimes described as a "level playing field."

Contractually, a level playing field exists when all parties have an equal right to negotiate for the best deal, and that no intervening factor (*e.g.* lack of statutory capacity; limited actual capacity/understanding; and/or fraud or nondisclosure) is creating an unfair advantage. The concept of legally recognized capacity is designed to ensure that no party is at a grossly unfair disadvantage. By analogy, it ensures that a greedy uncle cannot obtain the fortune belonging to his five year old nephew by getting the child's signature on a contract. For this reason, if a contract is formally agreed and executed, but one party is later found to lack legal capacity, be included within a protected class, or be deemed a third-party beneficiary to the contract, the contract may either be unenforceable, or it may be interpreted in a way that the parties do not expect.

In the context of ABS, this principle means that a large and sophisticated multinational conglomerate of companies that seeks access to genetic resources cannot take advantage of the lack of experience of a rural farmer or indigenous community that is negotiating as provider. The law of most countries include a range of provisions that can protect these less commercially sophisticated providers. Many of these are addressed in other parts of this book;[124] however, it is also important to determine whether any relevant country's contract law places limits on who may contract. Such limits are generally referred to as principles of "legal capacity," but will be referred to in this book as "legally recognized capacity."[125]

Like legal personality, the question of legally recognized capacity is viewed as the first prerequisite of a valid contract with any individual. And as with legal personality, if a contracting party lacks legally recognized capacity, the contract's enforceability will be doubtful at best. The issues are alike in another way as well: One cannot avoid them by simply adopting a clause stating that all parties have legal capacity. If legally-recognized-capacity issues are not addressed by pre-contract investigation, these issues can invalidate the contract even if it includes such a statement.[126]

---

124 In particular, ¶ 8.3.3, discusses the concepts of unconscionable contracts, and the problems with model and standard contracts that might be considered to be "contracts of adhesion."

125 This chapter will use the term "legally recognized capacity" to avoid confusion of the legal term with the very different concepts discussed in CBD and NP policy forums under the heading of "capacity." In a large number of resolutions, the CBD and many other multilateral environmental agreements use the term capacity as a generic term referring to each country's or individual's actual ability to undertake a task or action under discussion. Thus in that context, "capacity" includes expert training, the availability of necessary equipment, the ability to pay critical costs, access to information and other factors. As discussed above, "legally recognized capacity" does not address any of these concepts.

126 For a brief discussion of the essential nature of legal capacity issues as they arise in ABS contracts, see ¶¶ 2.3–2.4 of Young, 2009.

Many of the factors affecting legally recognized capacity are not very relevant to ABS contracts. For example, the law in most countries states a minimum age below which a person may not enter into a contract directly.[127] Often, the age varies according to the type of contract under consideration (*e.g.*, a marriage contract, property transfer, *etc.*)[128] Rather clearly, it is rare that an ABS contract will be negotiated directly with a child. Other common factors affecting legally recognized capacity to contract include mental impairment and incarceration. Here also it is unlikely that an ABS contract will be negotiated with a person suffering from a mental disorder or a person who is in prison.

There are however, two areas in which an ABS contract may need to address legally recognized capacity: contracts involving bankrupt persons and contracts with indigenous communities. As noted above, bankruptcy is far too complicated and diverse among countries to be addressed in detail in this book. Parties are strongly advised to do whatever is necessary to assure themselves that they are protected if any other party is bankrupt or near bankruptcy.

The issue of legally recognized capacity of indigenous persons and communities is also relevant in the ABS context. In some countries, the law protects people whose lifestyles are based on social separation (including indigenous peoples and those living in isolated rural communities) by declaring that they lack legally recognized capacity.[129] This type of provision will essentially state that such a person cannot enter into a contract directly, but must have independent help and advice. It can apply even if the specific individual or community in question is demonstrably able to protect his/its own interests. Where a category of persons is defined as lacking legally recognized capacity, the contract can be invalidated regardless of the specific characteristics of the individual or

---

127 The underage person may still enter into a contract, through a responsible adult, acting in the child's behalf.

128 While many developed countries set the minimum legal age as high as 18 or 21, other countries set the minimum age 7 years of age. In some countries, the legal age to enter into a marriage may be as low as 13 years, even if a 13-year-old would not be considered to have legally recognized capacity to enter into other contracts.

129 See, 5 *Williston on Contracts* § 9:1 (4th ed.) (*emphasis added.*) Cases on this issue have been decided in the United States, very recently. See UNITED STATES *Penobscot Indian Nation* v. *Key Bank of Maine*; see also *U.S. v. Ahtanum Irr. Dist.*, and *Davis v. Jones*. Given that these cases and laws were specifically directed to indigenous tribes within the US, it is not clear whether or how it might be applied in an action to enforce a contract involving indigenous peoples from outside the US.

group involved, unless the negotiation process complies with legally required protections to ensure that the person's/group's interests are protected.[130]

In the ABS context, this issue can be hidden or camouflaged. The question of negotiation with indigenous communities and private individuals is frequently addressed in national ABS measures and may be a point of controversy. Some countries have adopted ABS laws that specifically allow private individuals and/or indigenous communities to be considered the "providers" of particular genetic resources, indicating that these providers and should negotiate ABS contracts directly (with or without a later approval, confirmation or other decision by the government). In many other countries, the law may be unclear about which person has the rights to grant access and/or share benefits. These laws too are often interpreted by users as authorizing individuals to enter into ABS agreements directly.

Once they have worked out this issue in the ABS law, many parties may overlook the need to comply with other national laws that consider indigenous and traditional communities as "protected groups." As far as the authors know, however, no ABS law specifically addresses the overlap and potential conflict between ABS provisions relating to negotiation with providers and the country's laws or policies regarding the legally recognized capacity of such individuals to enter into contracts.

TIP

There does not appear to be any written clause that can resolve a problem with any of the above issues, because, the law will not recognize a provision in a contract that violates these laws. For example, one who lacks legally recognized capacity to enter into a contract cannot be bound by any clause in that contract.[131] This means that anytime there is any doubt about capacity of any party in a negotiation, negotiations should cease until it is *clearly proven* that all parties have legally recognized capacity to enter into contracts. In resolving doubts regarding the capacity of any participant in the negotiations of an ABS contract, clear evidence of

130 Where the special protection requirements are not met, the contract may be invalidated at the request of the protected person, or enforced only if the protected person seeks enforcement.

131 If the parties all agree on a contract clause that says "all parties agree that all parties have legally recognized capacity to enter into this contract," that agreement will be invalidated, when the contract is invalidated.

capacity should be provided and examined. It is advisable to maintain detailed records or copies of all such evidence, in case the issue comes up again at a later date.

4.4.2 *The Rights of Non-parties and "Third-party Beneficiaries"*

Any consideration of the question of whether the ABS Contract involves the "right parties" must also consider the possibility that other persons, who are not named as parties, will have some rights under the contract. In legal terminology, such persons are referred to as "third-party beneficiaries."[132] All parties to an ABS contract should make an effort to investigate this issue for a simple reason. If some person or group is later found to be a third-party beneficiary under a contract, they will have a right to try to enforce their interest in the contract, but will not be bound by the contract. The third-party beneficiary's enforcement of his rights could cause the contract to produce legal results very different from what the parties intended.

Third-party beneficiaries are not specifically bound to the contract obligations (because they have not signed the contract.) In many countries, however, the law may give them the power to assert their rights under the contract.[133] It is very complex, legally, to determine which persons are "third-party beneficiaries" entitled to bring action under the contract, and which are not.[134] Some of these legal issues are detailed in ¶ 6.6, *infra*. It is clear, however, that if a person or group is eventually found to be a third-party beneficiary, the obligations and rights of the parties that have entered into the contract can be impacted. Thus, whenever any person or group appears to be benefitted by a proposed contract, the parties negotiating that contract should make an effort to determine whether he/they will have the rights of a third-party beneficiary.

132 There are hundreds of potential examples of third-parties (persons who are not parties to the contract) that are benefited by the contract, for example, The agreement to build a new factory, for example, may benefit all of those who live in the neighbourhood of the factory (because they may find jobs there) and all local businesses (whose receipts may increase as the number of people coming to the area increases.).

133 In a contract to build a factory, for example, local residents and businesses (who would gain jobs, businesses and other benefits if the contract is fulfilled) might be given the authority to seek enforcement of the building contract, in the event of a breach that would prevent the factory from being built. In other contracts which require one party to build special infrastructure, in exchange for a permit or other desired right, third party beneficiaries might have the right to try to enforce the infrastructure requirement.

134 It is clear, for example, that where the user or user government negotiates the ABS agreement with the provider government, the provider government is often acting on behalf

If so, or if there is doubt, the parties should consider whether it is advisable and feasible to include the possible third-party beneficiaries as parties to the contract, thereby clarifying and concretizing their rights.

If it is not possible or desirable to bring the third-party beneficiaries into the contract, the parties can attempt to draft their agreement with the object of specifying the limits of those rights. Here also, one cannot simply alleviate the problem with a clause stating that there are no third-party beneficiaries to the contract. A court will reconsider this question, particularly if the contract involves the resources owned, regulated or managed by the government or a community on behalf of its people.

This conclusion is particularly important in ABS contracts, since many countries, communities and commentators believe that the mandatory objectives of any ABS contract are (or should be) sharing benefits with the provider country or community, promoting conservation and sustainable use of biological diversity and/or promoting social welfare. This perception of the objectives of ABS may prompt environmentalists, indigenous communities and others to try to affect or enforce the ABS contract claiming to be "third-party beneficiaries."

4.5 Legal Authority to Act on Behalf of a Party

Strongly connected to the issue of legal personality is the need to address the responsibility, right and authority of the contract parties, and the question of who may represent an entity in contract negotiations and execution. Even after establishing that all parties have legal personality and capacity, one must also ask whether the particular individuals signing the contract have the authority to bind the entities for which they are acting. There are many legal sources to

---

of some or all of its citizens or communities, and that the benefit-sharing will flow to them, directly or indirectly. These potential recipients of benefit-sharing may be legally considered to be third-party beneficiaries, and may have, for example, the right to bring an action to compel performance of the contract, and potentially even the right to seek interpretation of the actual benefit-sharing provisions (possibly even to seek to compel that the user make direct payment to themselves, rather than paying the funds to the provider agency, who will distribute them as the law determines.) Similarly, in cases involving indigenous knowledge, locally derived varieties/subspecies and farmers' rights, the specific authority of an individual holder of the knowledge or variety/subspecies may be legally tied to the community welfare. For example, where a community's traditional medicinal knowledge is traditionally passed down from one designated shaman or other healer to his/her successor, sometimes within a single family line, the critical question is whether and to what extent that knowledge "belongs" to the individual healer or family, or constitutes a traditional knowledge resource of the entire community.

the answers to these legal questions, including documents establishing the relationship between individuals and the company, the documents constituting the establishment of the company itself and the laws on the country under which it has been established.

In addition, party selection analysis is used to determine which persons are "necessary" and must be included in the contract. This analysis is not only applicable to users; it also arises in determining whether the providers named in an ABS contract have the actual legal right and ability to grant access. For example, in the short history of ABS, there have been many situations in which a contract is signed by a provider of genetic resources or ATK, but it is later claimed that this provider does not have the legal authority to provide those assets.[135] Often this problem arose from one of the following types of basic misunderstanding:

- The parties have sometimes incorrectly assumed that, where there is no clear ABS law in the country, this means that there is no restriction on any person providing GR or ATK to any user;[136] or
- Where national ABS law exists, it is often ambiguous. Although the parties may interpret it in a way that gives the erstwhile provider the right to enter into an ABS contract, others (in government or elsewhere) may have a different interpretation – one that casts doubt on the legal validity of the contract and the rights of the user.

Clearly, the question of whether the person negotiating on behalf of a party is authorized to make the commitments contained in the contract is critical to its validity. This issue applies to both providers and users.

---

135 In 1993, for example the US National Cancer Institute entered into a Letter of Intent (essentially a kind of ABS contract) with regard to a plant found in Cameroon, which was thought to have potential as a "promising HIV agent." The specific person signing the agreement on the provider side was the Dean of the Center for Health Services of the University of Yaounde. Later, the Government of Cameroon cancelled the Letter of Intent, stating that the University did not have authority to enter into such a contract. See discussion in Laird, *et al.* 1999, at 345, 352.

136 This view has been expressed by a range of national CBD delegates representing developed countries. As noted in ¶ 11.5.1 *infra*, however, even where there is no law specifically mentioning ABS, GR and/or ATK, each country has national law governing transactions, and determining who owns or has the right to dispose of all types of property, *etc.* It violates the basic principle of national sovereignty to assume that, where Country X does not have direct law on a specific point, a foreign user and/or his country's laws should determine what legal rights exist with regard to property and activities within Country X.

4.5.1 *"Authorized Representatives"*

The question of authorized representation is a very important one, closely tied to the issue of legal personality, because most companies and other corporate entities are represented by one or more individuals (officers, shareholders, employees, advisors, *etc.*) in the negotiations. The parties often rely on these persons to provide information about the company, and especially to agree to specific provisions and compromises in a manner that binds the company. The following sections consider how a corporate or governmental entity[137] authorizes someone to represent it.

(a) Who Represents a Corporate Entity?

In general, even where a corporate entity has legal personality, it can only be bound where the contract that is signed by the entity's "authorized representative" – someone with legal authority to bind that entity. The question of whether one is the authorized representative may often be affected by the law of the country in which it was formed, and of the countries in which it operates.

These issues vary greatly from country to country. Many developed countries have had long experience with the sharp practices of the unscrupulous and/or the sloppy legal protective measures taken by some companies that produce unexpected results. The lack of clear standards of authorization has a serious impact on whether companies are willing or able to enter into contracts – it can disrupt the commercial environment. As a result, developed countries have very detailed and specific rules relating to corporate entities, to ensure that no person who does not have authority to do so may bind a corporation by contract.[138] In addition, the manner the company is organized will add to answering the question whether the persons' signatures can bind the company. Thus, for example, in Norway, the law is designed to ensure that the funding documents of any company contain information regarding who can sign on its behalf.

---

137 Similar issues are tied to the question of legally capacity, because when there is a doubt about the legally recognized capacity of a particular person or group to enter into a contract, it is commonly recommended that the other parties should find (and sometimes pay for) an appropriately qualified and knowledgeable advisor to advise and possibly represent the person or group in negotiations. See ¶ 4.6, *infra*

138 In the United States, for example, all types of corporate entities must formally identify an "agent for service of process" in their government registration documents. In some states other designated individuals must also be named. See, generally, Cornell University, Legal Information Institute, links to state law at https://www.law.cornell.edu/wex/table_corporations. These laws do not limit the company's right/ability to authorize other representatives, without changing their corporate documents. A very complex web of laws and

The "authorized representative" issue often leads to misunderstandings that can effectively annul a contract. Consider, for example an ABS contract between the provider country or community and a researcher, where that contract frequently mentions the name of a specific company or institution under whose auspices the researcher's work is being conducted. Although all parties believe that other body is involved in the contract, in many cases either (i) the researcher signs the contract only in his own name and not on behalf of the entity or (ii) the researcher signs on behalf of the corporate entity without providing any evidence that he/she has the right to take actions that are binding on that corporate entity. Later, when the corporate entity disavows the contract and/or refuses to make payments as provided in the contract, a professional review of the contract discloses that the corporate entity is not bound by the contract, and that the researcher does not have sufficient assets to cover the payments required.[139]

As noted above, these concerns are not one-sided. While these questions often focus on the legal authority of an individual to bind a user company or institution, the question regarding who may execute a contract on behalf of an indigenous group or local community is equally challenging, and, if not properly addressed, may also result in a contract that is not legally binding.

(b) The Obligations of an "Agent" Representing a Party

Another important concept is that of "agency." This term refers to any situation in which a person or group claims that they are acting with authority on behalf of some other person or entity. The role of agency law in international contracts is one of only a few key contractual issues on which international commercial instruments may be of help, as discussed in ¶ 10.4.2, *infra*. In general, both international and national principles impose very stringent civil and criminal liability in cases of agency.[140]

---

judicial decisions governs the cases in which an individual who did not have a company's permission to do so, enters into a contract binding that company. In most countries, however, there is no requirement that the company formally register all persons who may ever be designated to act on their behalf. For this reason, as discussed below, most contracts with companies include guarantees that the person signing is acting on behalf of the corporation, and these are (or should be) backed up by investigation.

139 As noted above, a similar situation occurred under the Teff Agreement, when the user company claimed that the contract did not bind its subsidiaries and directors, but the user company had gone bankrupt and could no longer be required to make compensation.

140 If the person is claiming to act on behalf of a company and the other parties rely on this claim as one of the reasons they entered into the contract, and if they have taken actions under the contract such as allowing the person to remove samples, then the agent may be guilty of misrepresentation or fraud. In addition, the law will normally either rewrite

These principles may not be very consoling, however, where a provider thought he was dealing with a financially sound company and discovers after it is too late that the people he was dealing with were not authorized representatives. In such cases, the company will usually be protected from liability, and the false agent may not have enough assets to redress the harm suffered by the provider.

(c) Other Representation Issues: Negotiating with Government Entities

As noted in ¶ 3.2.2, the legal personality of government entities and other institutions is somewhat unpredictable. In addition to the general questions listed above, applicable to all corporate entities, a governmental entity that seeks to enter into a contract is often bound by additional laws and restrictions. Those restrictions may include limits on which persons may represent the government entity in negotiations. They may also limit the powers of such representative.[141]

Thus, additional investigation, beyond that necessary in all questions of authorized representation, may be needed when a representative purports to bind a governmental entity. In addition to confirming that some person in government has authorized the representative, it may be necessary to determine if that authorizing action was legally permitted.

4.5.2 *Contractual Provisions on Authorized Representatives*

Up to now, although many ABS contracts involve a variety of different types of entities, the basic questions of authorization of the persons signing the contract have not been addressed in most ABS contracts. In order to be certain that a contract with a company, community, institution or agency is actually binding, it may be necessary to undertake in-depth research and analysis. As noted earlier, the person signing may actually believe that he/she has authority to bind the company/institution/agency/community and be unaware that this

---

the contract, naming the false agent as a formal party, or impose obligations to complete the contract under some other legal theory. (See, *e.g.*, Corbin on Contracts, "Contracting Under Color of Authority"). Beyond this, if the person's failure to obtain clear representative authority means that the entity is not a party to a valuable contract, the person who failed to establish it properly may be liable to the other members within the legal entity.

141 See ¶ 4.2.2(c), *supra*. In the US, for example, various state and federal laws and constitutional provisions place major procedural restrictions on the representatives of governmental entities that are assigned to enter into contracts binding their agency or institution, and on the extent to which federal agencies can be held liable under contracts.

belief is incorrect. It is clearly not sufficient to rely on that person's individual assurances. That reliance is risky for the purported representative, as well as the other parties. If the contract does not bind the corporate entity, it may be wholly binding on the representative, who may also be liable under other theories, such as misrepresentation. Compelling this person to perform the entity's obligations, however, or to pay damages will often be useless, if he lacks the necessary legal power or financial ability.

TIP

No contract provision will bind an entity, if that contract is signed by a purported representative who is not properly authorized. In an ABS contract with a corporate entity (company, organization, institution, agency or community), independent verification of representative authority is necessary. The most effective approach is to contact that entity's management directly (using a means of communication that is not controlled by the purported representative) and/or contact the relevant governmental institution that determines its status. At a minimum, the home office of the entity or the responsible government institution should provide a formal letter of written assurance stating that the particular person is authorized to execute binding instruments on the corporate entity's behalf. It will normally be a good idea to have an expert review that letter and to annex it to the contract, backed by a warrantee (see Chapter 9.)

4.6 Including and Properly Binding All Necessary Parties

A contract is only binding on the persons and entities that agree to be its parties. This means that when the contract is formally executed, it must include all parties who will be expected to perform obligations under it – that is, all "necessary participants." This presupposes as we have seen that the parties have legal capacity, that the entity is represented by its representative and that parties that that might be made responsible for the implementation of the contract are bound by it. But another main question must also be addressed, as explored in this section: whether the contracts binds the "necessary parties" – *i.e.*, the parties able to actually take the actions agreed to in the contract. Given that ABS contracts are frequently "international contracts," involving at least two countries, the question of whether the contract includes all of the parties necessary to perform its obligations may become critical.

This issue is a continuation or next step after the challenges set out above – whether any entity involved in the contract has legal personality, whether all persons acting in the negotiations are authorized to act, and most basically, whether the parties have legally recognized capacity to enter into the contract.

The next determination must clearly be this: which parties to the contract are "necessary" and how are the parties bound to achieve the contractual objectives? The main necessary-participants question is whether the parties are actually able to take the agreed actions and/or actually bound to ensure that they are taken. This analysis embodies two issues:

- Does the contract include all of the persons who would have to be bound in order to achieve the desired result? and
- Does the contract contain a loophole that would unintentionally allow any person to get some part of the contractual benefit without paying for it?

4.6.1 *Who Can Take Actions under ABS Contracts?*

The question of whether the proposed parties to the contract can take the required actions is complex. It can best be answered by considering a buy/sell contract for a car, in which X agrees to sell a specific car to Y for a specific price, to be paid in cash. The problem in this contract arises because at the time of execution, X does not own that car and Y does not have that amount of money. There are a variety of possible solutions. The simplest way would be to add one or two new parties to the contract; W (the car's owner) and/or Z (Y's rich parent.) Unfortunately, this simple solution is impossible in most commercial situations. Instead, the contract goes forward on the assumptions that X's commitment includes a promise to acquire the car before the transfer date; while Y's includes a commitment to obtain the necessary cash by that date. Although a court would normally find that the contract is based on these assumptions, it is best to write them out in the contract, and also to specify what consequences each party will suffer if either party fails to meet these requirements.[142] Such a provision proves the parties a basis on which to solve any problems that might arise, and complete the contract without going to court.

142 Failure to address these issues in the contract, as well as by investigation, can result in financial disaster. For example, a common fraud scenario, sometimes referred to as "selling the Brooklyn Bridge" involves a swindler who tries to sell property that he does not own, claiming that he has the right to sell it. If he convinces someone to buy it, he then takes their money, gives them a false deed, and leaves them with no remedy for their loss.

In ABS contracts, necessary-participants issues are relatively clear with regard to providers. Either those negotiating as providers have clearly established authority to grant access to genetic resources, or they are expected to obtain it in time for the transfer.[143] With regard to the users, however, these issues may be less clear. As the Teff Agreement demonstrates (¶ 4.1), it is entirely possible for a user to use a "shell" corporation (a corporation that has been cleaned out of all assets) as a shield, protecting the actual users of genetic resources in a manner that cannot be challenged without an expensive and unpredictable lawsuit. Unless there has been appropriate pre-contract investigation coupled with proper efforts to join other parties and/or take other measures to ensure that all user-side parties are properly bound (see ¶ 4.5.2), there is a risk that the providers will be left in a situation in which they have no remedy for non-compliance.

Normally, if a person or entity commits to pay money, but does not intend to pay, that person or entity is probably guilty of the crime or tort of fraud or deceit. This means that the defrauded party may have the option of pursuing a tort law remedy, even if there is no contract. Unfortunately, it will normally require a lawsuit to obtain such a remedy. Even then, the challenge comes in finding objective proof of the fraudulent intent. By contrast, in many ABS contract situations, a user company may enter into a contract to purchase goods, rights or other *res* from a provider with the intent to use the purchased *res* in a product or include it in another transaction. The user intends to pay the provider from the profits of this later activity, if any. This is not a fraudulent intent. Rather, it is a contractual way of placing some or all of the financial risk of the second sale on the original provider. The contract should make this clear, and all parties should understand it.

Thus, one important step in the parties' negotiation plan is to determine who will be bound by the contract, and what assumptions the contract is making regarding how they will take the actions required of them. The plan must examine, item-by-item, which party bears each expected responsibility; who controls physical/financial aspects of each activity. If any factor is outside of the parties' control, the parties must clarify how it will be achieved, and who bears the risk that the uncontrolled factor will not behave as expected.

143 The contract may assign this responsibility to the providers, or it may allocate some duty to assist in it to the users.

TIP

As further discussed in Chapter 4, many necessary-participant analyses cannot be undertaken until the provider's country has clarified key questions such as "who owns GR/ATK?," "Who has a right to enter into an ABS contract for particular GR/ATK?." This is yet another reason that it will be advisable for parties to eliminate all ABS terminology or references and include more detail about the precise actions each party will undertake. Even after the provider country has adopted appropriate legislation, this course may be advisable, given the uncertainty of providers' rights under most developed countries' ABS legislation.

At all events, parties should take care to obtain official confirmation that all parties to the ABS contract have obtained, or are obligated to obtain, the legal ability to take all of the actions to which they are committing.

One example of the importance of clarity on this issue is found by examining the financial result of the Teff Agreement. According to reports, HPFI (the user in that contract) incorrectly estimated the value and profits it could earn, and based its benefit-sharing commitment on that bad estimate.[144] Owing to bad financial planning and other internal problems, HPFI subsequently became bankrupt, and under the Teff Agreement no other person or entity was responsible for the user's obligations. In essence, HPFI had transferred some of its financial risk to Ethiopia, and when HPFI went bankrupt, Ethiopia's contractual expectations of payment and other benefit-sharing were lost.

When entering into a contract with any company or individual, it is potentially irresponsible not to confirm that the company or individual will have the right and ability to take all relevant actions that will be required under the contract. For example, in an ABS contract, if the user is expected to engage in R&D, develop and market a product, and share benefits from that product, the contract has an entirely different meaning if the user does not have an R&D capacity. In essence, it changes the contract, if rather than engaging in R&D, product development and marketing, the user's role will be to find those willing to conduct R&D, develop the product and market it. Although there are

144 Andersen and Winge, 2012, Executive Summary.

numerous kinds of contracts to address these activities, it is clear that, as the contract was initially envisioned, the necessary parties are not included.

As shown in the Teff Agreement example (¶ 4.1, *supra,*) ignoring the step of ensuring that all "necessary participants" are bound, can have serious consequences. Perhaps if the providers had understood the precarious state of the user entity – a start-up with two main individuals having all beneficial ownership – they might have insisted that the two individual directors should be personally bound, or required them to provide third party guarantees (see ¶ 9.4, *infra*). If they had realized that all assets, including the Teff patent, could be transferred out of the user entity without the requirement of notice to the user entity's creditors, they might have required that the patent (and perhaps other assets) be held as security for the user's performance under the Teff Agreement. All of these precautions begin with the legal requirements relating to identification of the parties and the basic rule of this Chapter – make sure that all parties are properly bound with regard to all of necessary actions.

Even where a party's only obligation will be to pay money, it is potentially irresponsible not to confirm the party's financial status, as part of the analysis of whether all of the necessary parties have been included in the contract. This evaluation will tie into later contractual negotiations over whether and to what extent it is necessary to guard against situations in which a bankruptcy by that person or entity will leave one unprotected or impose significant financial harm. The only exception is where the party who expects payment agrees that such payment will be conditional on the other party's financial success – *i.e.*, accepts the risk of non-payment.[145]

TIP

A number of conventional legal mechanisms may be applied in these cases, including

- adding other parties to the contract who will share in the payment obligation,
- requiring third-party guarantees;
- creating and funding an escrow or other security account;
- imposing a mortgage or trust arrangement giving the payee rights in valuable property, pending full payment; and

145 In this case, however, the provider becomes, in essence, an "investor" in the user's business, in the sense that his right to benefits (a valuable asset) is inaccessible to him until/unless the company makes a profit. Benefit-sharing obligations arise out of "utilization

– negotiation of a coordinating relationship between the user-country and provider-country, to enable more effective ABS implementation.

Any of these or other contractual or legal solutions may require the assistance of a commercial lawyer with experience in international law.

4.6.2 *Avoiding Loopholes*

As further discussed in Chapter 5, *infra*, the specific wording of obligations in a contract can create loopholes that enable parties and non-parties to obtain and use desired resources and rights without complying with the contract.[146] These challenges, however, are closely intertwined with the basic challenge of identifying the "right parties" for the contract, and/or investigating the persons with whom you are negotiating. Although most participants in ABS contracts are negotiating honestly, there have been situations in which a user has (apparently intentionally) used a shell corporation or other legal mechanism as a means to avoid its ongoing benefit-sharing responsibility.

Loopholes of this type create a "free rider" situation, not binding all present and future participants involved in the utilization of genetic resources or ATK under and ABS contract. Some person or entity not a party to the contract could gain access to genetic resources or ATK without being bound by a benefit-sharing obligation.

These determinations are significantly impacted by the type of entities involved in the contract, whether they have recognized legal personality, and whether their actions and commitments fall within the scope of that legal personality. If all potential users and user-side parties cannot be formally made party to the contract, it will be essential to address their future actions and the

of genetic resources," rather than out of "earning a profit," which is a very material difference, as demonstrated by the Teff Agreement. (See ¶ 4.1, *supra*.) Under conventional contractual law, there are many practical means of protecting the investor in such situations, and often the law imposes specific protective requirements, that will apply, regardless of the title or wording of the contract, wherever the transaction is effectively an investment transaction, which need to be investigated and applied in ABS transactions. This practice is further discussed in the context of third-party rights, at ¶ 5.5, *infra*.

146 This is one reason underlying the recommendation that, when negotiating a contract where one does not already have a long-established relationship of commercial trust, it is usually advisable to obtain professional assistance. Even with trusted trade partners, it may be best to have a commercial lawyer experienced in international contracts review the ABS agreement.

benefit-sharing obligations in other ways, such as through re-drafting the basic obligations (Chapter 5); finding mechanisms to control post-contract transfers (Chapter 7); applying legally valid enforcement provisions (Chapters 7 and 8); and requiring guarantees, warranties, bonds and other security (Chapter 9.) All of these negotiating and drafting activities must be guided and focused on key information and analysis regarding the nature of the parties, their legally recognized ability to be bound by a contract, the authority of the persons negotiating on their behalf, and their actual ability to take the actions required under the contract.

As noted above, if any of the "right parties" issues presents a problem, simple solutions are not usually enough to solve those problems. Adding more entities to the contract, for example, may only make the compliance issue even more complex and less predictable. Instead, it is important to link the party-selection issue analysis discussed in this chapter with the various legal drafting issues discussed above.

CHAPTER 5

"Be Specific and Concrete": The Subject Matter (Res), Functional Clauses and Objective of the Contract

The negotiation of an ABS contract has, broadly speaking, two goals. The first is to decide what the contract will do and how. The second is to write it all down, clearly and concretely.

The first goal is achieved through discussions and negotiations. Once the key operations and prerequisites are clearly established with regard to the contractual relationship, the remaining challenge focuses on documenting that relationship. In an ABS contract, which addresses a new type of *res* and/or contractual function, it is necessary for the parties to negotiate a shared understanding of exactly what their rights and obligations will be and how they will operate. While ABS remains uncertain or uncommon, contracts will have to be rather detailed and specific. If they are not, any disagreement or controversy among the parties cannot be resolved by the terms of the contract. This situation will increase the chances that the contract will be breached. If the parties take the issue to court, it is possible that the court will determine that the contract is invalid or unenforceable. Over time, however, as ABS parties develop and share contractual experiences and best practices, those practices may eventually be recognized as "standards" for the ABS contracts. This can enable future contracts to be shorter and negotiations to be streamlined. With time, such shared experiences might also enable countries to develop background laws on ABS contracts that make it easier to enforce them. The current ABS situation, however, is not conducive to the enforcement of contracts.

The achievement of the second goal (concrete, specific drafting) is the work of the negotiators and contract draftsmen. It is detailed work, and as the old saying goes, "the devil is in the details." The drafters' challenge is to ensure, to the greatest extent possible, that all relevant questions that may arise in future can be resolved in the language of the contract. In order for any contract to be implemented without disagreement (and to resolve disagreements in a way that allows/requires implementation) all parties must have a clear and concrete understanding of precisely what the contract covers and requires.

The objective and operative provisions of the ABS contract provide an excellent example of the basic rule described in this chapter – "Be Specific and Concrete." Accordingly, this chapter will focus on how contractual precision

 | DOI 10.1163/9789004356573_006

and ambiguity issues should be dealt with in the operational provisions of an ABS contract. Specifically, it will look at the clauses that (i) describe the *res*, (ii) set out the overall objective of the contract, and (iii) clearly detail the obligations and rights of each party. These are not, of course, the only clauses requiring concreteness and specificity – the principles of contractual specificity apply equally to all clauses. This chapter underscores the relationship between the need for precise terminology and the absolute importance of NOT relying on the ambiguous terminology of the NP and other international ABS policy instruments.

Up to now, ABS contracts have been notoriously imprecise, often relying on general terminology (such as "genetic resources" and "benefit sharing") that is too ambiguous to be subject to established contract law.[147] This chapter shows how essential it is for ABS contracts to move away from reliance on or use of generic terms and descriptions, towards specificity and precision.[148] It begins (¶ 5.1) with a more detailed discussion of the importance of concrete drafting and the potential harm that may be caused if the contract is ambiguous. Following that, in ¶¶ 5.2 through 5.4, it addresses the key operational elements of the identification and stipulation of the *res* and basic operative descriptions of the parties' obligations. In ¶ 5.5, it will consider the triggers or other factors that link them, discussing the particular challenges that arise in documenting the objective and the *res* in an ABS-related contract. The overarching role of objective clauses in contracts is discussed in ¶ 5.6, with particular attention to their special importance in ABS contracts. The chapter will close with a brief look at one of the greatest challenges facing ABS contracts – change of use or intent with regard to the *res* (¶ 5.7).

With time, shared experiences might also enable countries to develop background laws on ABS contracts that make it easier to enforce them. In the current ABS situation, however (as discussed above, and in Chapters 1 through 4), there is a complete lack of agreed definitions and few, if any, countries have enacted or adopted any legislation to clarify the basic concept and how it fits into their national regulatory and commercial legal frameworks. This situation is not conducive to the negotiation, creation, implementation and enforcement of ABS contracts.

---

147 The basic challenge of ABS ambiguities are discussed in more detail in Chapters 1, 2 and 11, and generally throughout this book.

148 For a discussion and comparism of the manner to define the res in ABS laws, ABS contracts and in patents, see Tvedt 2013.

5.1 Contractual Precision – Ambiguity Kills Contracts

As a point of departure, it is important to consider the consequences of contractual ambiguity and the reasons underlying this book's second rule: "BE SPECIFIC AND CONCRETE." The reasons behind this rule all derive from the relationship between ABS and contract law. As discussed in Chapter 2, the NP and the CBD were designed with the expectation that they should be implemented through private contracts. Thus, by definition, ABS is based on contract law.[149] In turn, contract law is based on clarity, precision and mutual understanding. Its underlying purpose is to create a predictable basis for implementation and enforcement. This predictability helps to minimize the need for the courts or arbitrators. The main road to contractual predictability and certainty is a precise contract that clearly and concretely states what the contract requires of all parties and what they expect to receive.

One of the challenges for all contracts, and particularly for ABS contracts arises out of the fact that contracts must (as explained above) be fixed and concrete, while their implementation happens in a "real world" in which assets, conditions and parties all experience unexpected changes. In ABS contracts, for example, all parties expect that the genetic material being collected and researched will lead to new knowledge and possibilities; however, nobody knows what those possibilities will be. Parties are sometimes less aware of other types of dynamic change that may occur in the future. The parties to the contract may experience financial or other major changes, for example; or the geographic, biological, climatic physical or political situations in the countries involved may change. Other researchers may achieve new discoveries that influence the users' research agenda in some way. It is literally impossible to predict these changes; yet the fixed contract must be the primary tool for addressing them. This need to create a tool that will help in the future beyond the conclusion of the contract is the most important challenge facing those who negotiate and draft the contract – not only to address known areas of agreement and concern, but to provide a basis for addressing new issues that might arise in future – and all without being considered legally "vague" or "ambiguous", and therefore "unenforceable."

As explained in more detail below and in Chapters 6, 7, 8 and 9, an ambiguous contract is difficult or impossible to implement and legally it cannot be enforced. Consider, for example an employment contract where the terms and requirements are ambiguous. The employee would never know what to

149 Rosendal *et al.*, 2014.

do, and the employer would never know what to expect. They could not settle any disagreement between themselves by reference to the contract, because each side would interpret the ambiguity differently. If their disagreement went before a judge, that judge would have no basis on which to know what the parties expected. Although he might be able to rule under other principles of law or tort, the judge could not use their contract as a basis for his ruling. In most countries, the contract would be considered invalid, and the judge would not even be allowed to issue a ruling.

In ABS contracts, this situation is even worse. Unlike employment law, there is no other supporting body of law relative to ABS. This means that if the ABS contract does not contain a precise statement of what the parties are expected to do and when, there is little possibility that they can later come to a compromise, when a disagreement or conflict arises. There is virtually no possibility that a court could find any other basis to rule on their case. If the drafters are not able to provide clarity in the text when concluding the contract, one cannot expect a judge to create such clarity later. While any type of contract must clearly state the parties' objective, subject matter and functional provisions, this need is double in in ABS contracts, in which there is no general agreement on the meanings, objects, and activities that will be addressed in every ABS contract. The lack of such clarity and concreteness will often be fatal to the entire relationship among the parties.

5.2 The Operative Provisions / What Does the Contract Do?

The subject matter of the contract (sometimes referred to as the *res* of the contract[150]) and the specific obligations/actions required of the parties are often the most intensely negotiated aspect of ABS contracts, but frequently these provisions are not drafted very clearly. These clauses, along with the contract's stated objective and the clauses that specify the duties and rights of the parties, together comprise the "core" of the contract. When one describes what the contract does or requires, he normally describes these critical elements. In ABS, these core clauses need to specify (i) the resources accessed (genetic resources or ATK), (ii) the user's rights and expectations, (iii) the provider's rights and expectations, (iv) the user's obligations, (v) the provider's obligations and (vi) the overall contract objective. It is critical that each of these

150 In ABS contracts, the *res* generally refers to the genetic resources and/or ATK that is the primary focus of the contract.

items be unambiguously detailed and specific. The text of the contract must convey exactly what is included and what the parties have agreed to do, in a level of detail that includes, for example, the deadline or due date for each action, as discussed below. To date, the manner in which these elements have been planned and described in ABS contracts has not considered or applied the essential principles of contract law.

In drafting a contract, the parties have full control over how the contract will describe its objectives and all of its operative elements. In a contractual relationship, this flexibility enables them to state their objective and all of their obligations and expectations clearly, precisely, understandably and in detail. It is important for them to do so. It must be possible for all parties to objectively determine whether contract requirements are being met. In some contracts this mandate might necessitate more than just an affirmative statement of rights and duties – the parties may also need to specifically designate activities that are prohibited.[151] Even these must be formulated in a manner which is externally verifiable.

Moreover, as detailed in Chapter 3 the operative clauses of the contract must be linked in a practical way, closely tied to actual "on the ground" activities and events. No matter how beautifully written, a contract will not function unless the drafters have carefully linked every obligation and right to a clear method by which each party is able to know what actions are taken (or not taken), which triggering events have occurred, and which conditions have been satisfied.

It is also important to ensure that performances, triggers and requirements are "externally verifiable" – that is, requirements that one party can confirm by relying only on sources that are not within or influenced by the other party. A contract that relies on the user's report, for example, as the basis for determining whether one of the user's obligations has been triggered may not function well. If other parties do not have some other way of verifying the triggering action or event, then they may not be aware of a need to make inquiry or take other actions to call for, encourage or force the user's compliance. Even

151 As a task for the contract drafter, a clause that prohibits certain activities is very difficult. Exclusion is a legally problematic concept, as discussed in Chapters 1, 2 and 4. Rather than prohibiting an activity, it is often more desirable to specifically discuss that activity, and state additional notifications, rights and obligations that will arise in the event that a party undertakes it. In any event, the contract drafters should emphasize inclusion/definition as the primary mode of concretizing the parties' agreement, using exclusions only as an added description, for clarity.

a formal enforcement action might be impossible, unless the various obligations, triggers and other critical events are not only clearly stated in the contract, but also externally verifiable. No party's rights should be dependent on the other party's honesty in sharing internal information that cannot be confirmed any other way.

These issues are also important, in the rare case in which formal legal action (litigation or arbitration) is necessary to resolve a dispute. It must be possible for the judge or arbitrator, who may not have legal access to the user's records or the biological knowledge on which to assess them, to determine whether the parties' obligations under the contract have been triggered and complied with. For the negotiation and drafting of a contract, it is critical to be aware of the legal rights of the owners and operators of a private enterprise or entity. These owners need to be free from external interference or search of their premises, in the absence of a court order. In ABS contract practice, independent verification of the users' contractual compliance and reports is a critical and difficult necessity for which there are few dependable mechanisms.

As discussed in more detail in Chapters 7, 8 and 9, it may also be important to specifically state the consequences of any party's failure to take actions required, or to comply with agreed limitations on action. A clear knowledge of the consequences of non-compliance with a contractual requirement or limitation is often as important as clarity about the requirements/limitations themselves. Although contractual law specifies many kinds of consequences, it generally depends on the contract, in order to determine whether or how they apply. In order for the parties to have access to legal remedies (to impose consequences) for a breach of the contract, the contract must first have been very clear about what it requires. No remedy is available if the contract does not give enough detail to make it clear whether there has been a breach.

Moreover, as discussed in Chapter 9, there are certain contract mechanisms that enable the aggrieved party to seek private redress, without formal legal action. These mechanisms, too, are only available where it is concretely and precisely clear that a breach occurred.

5.3 What is Transferred? – The Need for Precision about the *Res*

When considering the core clauses of ABS contracts, many commentators break them down into two main contractual relationships: the provider side, which authorizes the utilisation of "genetic resources" and/or ATK; and the user side, which utilizes those resources, sharing the benefits arising from that utilization. Virtually every ABS contract will be more complex than this, because many other activities, events and factors must be addressed. Although the ABS contract may have many parties, there are two positions (provider and user) that have a role in virtually all aspects of the ABS contract, including responsibilities well beyond the grant of access, the utilization of resources and benefit-sharing. For this reason, the authors have separated the resource-oriented provisions (the *res*), discussed in the following sections, from the intangible obligations and expectations of the parties, discussed in ¶ 5.4. The value and effectiveness of any ABS contract can be directly linked to the precision and concreteness of its descriptions of the *res*.

5.3.1 *What is Offered?*

From the CBD and the NP, the only thing that is known about the provider side of an ABS contract is found in general statements indicating that the *provider* is expected to grant the user *access* to *genetic resources* and/or *traditional knowledge associated with genetic resources* for purposes of their *utilization*. Unfortunately, as discussed in Chapter 2, there is no general substantive agreement as to the meaning of any of the italicized terms. The CBD and NP provide ambiguous definitions, or none at all. In this way, the negotiators kept the entire concept of ABS so ambiguous that all of the negotiating countries would agree to adopt it.[152] Although a useful strategy for getting the final international instrument adopted, this approach was decidedly unhelpful for those hoping that the negotiations would provide the precision needed to enable functional ABS contracts.

The ambiguities in the CBD and NP are particularly problematic when the parties to an ABS contract attempt to concretely identify the subject matter that the provider is offering.[153] If the parties rely on the CBD and NP for this, it is not even clear whether "genetic resources" should refer to physical samples

152 Tvedt has expressed worries that the manner in which the subject matter is defined in ABS being too unspecific compared to for examples how the subject matter is defined in patent law. Tvedt, 2013.

153 In ABS the two most well recognized types of assets or subject matters transferred are "genetic resources" and "traditional knowledge associated with genetic resources" (ATK). Although both of these are specifically addressed in the CBD and NP, neither of those instruments provides any guidance or legal basis for concretely determining what is transferred when one simply agrees to transfer "genetic resources" or "ATK."

or some informational component. Nor is it clear when or how genetic resources or ATK are transferred.[154]

At the time that they enter into an ABS contract, the parties need to agree specifically on what the providers are offering, and the exact form in which the users will collect or receive it. In order for the contract to function, this information must be clear and exact. It is entirely too ambiguous to simply say that "provider X grants user Y access to genetic resource Z in exchange for 'benefit-sharing.'" Depending on how X and Y interpret ambiguous terms like "access" and "genetic resource," one of them could assume, for example, that the contract allows large-scale collection of an unlimited volume of samples of Z, to be removed and used in any manner the user wishes, and compensated by an up-front payment. Conversely, the other party might assume that the contract allowed only limited sample collection, to be done by the provider, allowing the user only to identify usable extracts and genetic sequences and thereafter to use that information only for particular types of research and development, in exchange for a profit-share and access to research results. Both of these views reflect descriptions of the meaning of ABS, as expressed by key participants after the adoption of the NP.[155]

The challenge in describing/defining the genetic resource/ATK covered by the ABS contract is to ensure that it is functional as a term in a contract. Often, at the time the resource is accessed (collected), the precise list of samples accessed may be clear to both user and provider. Even in that case, however, the contractual challenge lies in the need to make it clear to all parties exactly what right or asset the recipient is receiving under the contract?[156]

---

154 When a genetic material is regulated in the contract, is the digital sequence data from that material also transferred to the user for open use? If the benefit-sharing obligation does not clarify these kinds of questions, then it will not provide sufficient clarity. A contract must use more specific terms than those that are italicized in text, above, in order to be enforceable.

155 See footnote 153. In Tvedt, 2013, the author discusses four main potential ways of understanding the term "genetic material": (1) that it means the same as biological resources; (2) that it refers to micro-physical material; (3) that it is are informational in nature, and (4) that it has both micro-physical and informational components. See also Vogel, *et al.*, 2011 (genetic resources as purely informational resources) and Kamau, *et al.*, 2011. The interpretation of the term "genetic resources" has varied among international organisations working in the field, also among UN organisations. See Schei and Tvedt, 2010. These usages are inconsistent and reduce the certainty of the system.

156 Schei and Tvedt, 2010; and Tvedt and Schei, 2014.

5.3.2 *How to "Be Concrete" about the* Res

It is absolutely critical for the parties to an ABS contract to agree on what the provider will be providing. In this connection, there are a number of questions that need to be answered, including the following:

- *For contracts involving genetic resources*: taxonomically, how does the contract identify the genetic resources included? (This may be specific or general, depending on what the parties agree. For example, it may be limited to a particular subspecies or variety, or it may include generally collecting samples within an entire genus or higher taxonomic level.)
- *For ATK*: how do the parties describe the information to be accessed? (Here also, the description may be very specific or very general.)
- Geographically, what are the limits of access granted? (This may often be specified in terms of GPS coordinates.)
- When and by whom will specimens or data be collected?
- Is there a limit on the number of specimens that may be obtained?
- If the user is collecting specimens directly, must his collecting activities be monitored? If so, how and by whom?
- What other parameters limit or extend the specifications? (For example, does the contract focus on bioprospecting for a certain kind of compound?)
- Are there time, location or activity limits relative to the user's activities? (These questions are more fully addressed in ¶ 5.4.)
- Is the provider granting access to these resources on an exclusive basis? If so what is the coverage, nature and time-limit of that exclusivity? (This issue is further addressed in ¶ 5.4.2.)
- *Commencement*: Many ABS contracts appear to begin to operate at the time that samples are transferred from the provider to the user. Others begin sooner, clearly covering all bioprospecting preparation and collection activities.

It is clearly in the best interests of all parties for all of these matters to be precisely and exactly stated and agreed in writing. In particular, it is important for the parties to agree on the precise nature of the resources granted – that is, whether the user receives unbounded rights to use the sample, or only a right to the information embedded in the genes of the samples transferred.[157]

Where the user is allowed to collect samples in specific areas or in specific categories of biological material, the element of monitoring also may become

157 Vogel, *et al.*, 2011.

important. The most effective way of minimizing the need for long-term vigilance is to find users who are willing to pay an appropriate price in exchange of a long-term custodial right to collect and remove a broad range of samples in exchange for a significant "up-front" payment. Once the provider has received all the payment due under the contract, its need for monitoring may be limited to ensuring that the user does not collect anything it is not entitled to, that he complies with collection procedures, and that he reports properly regarding any matters on which reports are needed. These matters are more fully discussed in ¶ 5.4., regarding the user's obligations.

All of these provisions may be later amended, if bioprospectors observe a potentially desirable specimen outside the scope of their contract, if researchers need additional wild-collected samples, or for many other reasons. In any of these cases, a user may return to the provider seeking an amendment of the contract. Or the contract can establish a mechanism for adding them into the contract without the time and effort of a formal, written amendment negotiation.

Where the ABS contract is intended to continue for a long time, it needs to include procedures for further collecting activities. (See ¶ 3.6.3, *supra*.) Here one can stipulate either that the material will be included under the same terms as the original contract, or that specific (different) terms and conditions will apply, or that new collection or new samples may only happen pursuant to a formal amendment at that time. Also in a long term contractual relationship there is a need for milestones at which the parties review the collaboration and assess and ad on the relationship.

The Teff Agreement between Ethiopia and the Dutch company HPFI, discussed in Chapter 4,[158] provides an example of one approach to some of these specificity issues. Samples of several teff plant varieties were transferred to the Netherlands. The contract annex identified the varieties accessed by their official names as registered in Ethiopia. For examples, one variety was designated as "DZ-Cr-255." These Ethiopian official names are listed correspondingly with the varieties' names in the company's records (*e.g.*, "S&C10"). This approach made it easier deal with the material. In theory, it could also enable more effective tracing and tracking of its movement to other users and uses. On the other hand, this level of specificity might sometimes provide support to claims that other varieties were used that were not subject to the contract. The determination of how to describe and identify the *res* in a contract is thus integrated with a detailed analysis of how the description of the *res* affects or is affected by other contract terms.

158 The Teff case is described in ¶ 4.1, and referred to in later sections of Chapter 4 as well.

5.4 Obligation/Action Clauses: The Duties and Expectations of the Parties

The user's side of the subject matter of the ABS contract is embodied in a number of less tangible clauses, including not only benefit-sharing, but complying with the access requirements. In addition, in some cases the providers may make commitments, such as exclusivity. These obligations, too, are a key element of the contract and must be specified concretely, even though they are, in many ways, intangible.

The rule of specificity is also essential with regard to the obligations, actions and rights of the parties to the contract. As noted in Chapter 4, *supra*, these clauses must be closely interlinked with both the description of the *res* and the determination of which persons and entities must be parties to the contract. As each of these clauses is mapped, negotiated, drafted and revised (see Chapter 3), it is essential to reconsider all of them, to ensure that they can function in a concrete and specific way, and that their fulfillment will achieve the desired or expected results and objectives.

5.4.1 *The Benefit-sharing Obligation*

Of all of the ABS contract's elements, its provisions for benefit-sharing are generally the most ambiguous. In one demonstration project, project staff was tasked to bring a user and provider community together and facilitate the negotiation of an ABS contract. Although a user was found who agreed to participate (*i.e.*, to have its negotiations observed, scrutinized and reported) and a community was contacted which could provide the type of resources the user sought, the project was ultimately unable to achieve a final contract. The user indicated that its main problem was that the provider community had not come to its own conclusion about what the resources were worth, but was unwilling to commit to a specific agreement (preferring to keep its options open, fearing to settle for an amount less than the maximum the user might ultimately be willing to pay).

In most commercial contracts, it is most important to demonstrate concreteness and precision in every clause that relates to money or value. In general, courts or arbitrators cannot or will not enforce a commercial contracts financial terms, unless they are "sufficiently specific."[159] In some contracts, this requirement is easily met. For example, a contract for the purchase of a

159 These issues are among the few areas in which CISG and UNIDROIT principles offer Guidance. See, *e.g.*, UNIDROIT principles 2010, Chapter 6; and CISG, Articles 55 through 59. Neither of these standard approaches is particularly helpful in the ABS context.

specific item or group of items may require only the specification of a particular sum to be paid (also specifying the currency in which the payment must be made). If, at the time of the contract, the parties are not able to specify how many items will be purchased, the contract may state a particular price per item or per ounce.

Where there are other factors that impact the amount or value, however, the financial clauses of the contract may become very complex indeed. It is necessary to pin down the price or value computation mechanism so precisely that both parties, and perhaps another person (judge or arbitrator), would reach the same result independently.

ABS parties, especially providers, frequently want to express the benefit-sharing obligation in terms of a percentage share of the user's profits from utilization of the genetic resource or ATK. In some cases, they add other types of benefit-sharing (sharing samples and/or research results, *etc.*) Although no court has yet been called on to interpret or enforce such a payment, we can learn major lessons about them from other kinds of commercial contracts.

(a) Calculation

There are many types of commercial contracts that calculate the payment owed on the basis of a particular share of the paying party's profits in a specified venture. In order to be "sufficiently detailed," these provisions are sometimes highly complex. An excellent way to describe the level of concreteness required and why it is needed is to use a common example: payment provisions in commercial leases of retail space. These payments are often based on a complex calculation. The monthly rental under such leases are sometimes calculated as a base amount plus a specified percentage of the month's receipts. Even though commercial lease payment clauses are somewhat standardized, they still must be very lengthy and detailed. Among other things, the lease must specify whether the percentage applies to gross receipts[160] or net receipts.[161] If net receipts, it must specify which expenses may be set off against gross receipts for purpose of this determination. It must also specify the manner in which the calculation is verified – *i.e.,* the landlord's rights to

160 This term is usually defined in the instrument. Where it is not, in the US, "gross receipts" is interpreted to mean all money paid in during the specified period.

161 Similarly, in the US, "net receipts," where not formally defined is usually interpreted to mean gross receipts minus authorized costs. For these purposes, authorized costs is a matter of agreement, so that a company's net receipts, as calculated for the lease may be different from its net receipts when calculated for another purpose.

check the tenant's books and take other measures to confirm that the tenant is reporting receipts correctly.

In ABS contracts, the challenge is still more complex, although some ABS negotiators view the calculation of the benefit-share as a relatively simple process. Unfortunately, it is far from simple and raises many different kinds of practical and legal challenges. The contractual draftsman must understand and clearly describe the specific factors that form the basis of the computation. Since accounting terminology and usage differs from country to country, it is necessary to describe the benefit-sharing computation in detail.[162] A statement that "the benefit share will be X% of net income from the sale of products developed utilizing the genetic resources of species X," for example, may have widely different meanings to various parties to the contract. It is not possible to rely on "common usage by accountants," because there are no accepted standards in this area. Even when everyone can agree on a specific meanings of "net income" and "sale of products" (problem clauses in most international contracts), ABS adds another problematic question – how will the provider know or confirm that a product has been developed utilizing the genetic resources accessed under the contract?[163]

There have been many attempts to find wording that will make percentage-based benefit-share clear, simple and enforceable. To date, no satisfactory approach has been offered. The following are two examples from contracts negotiated by others (not the authors), including an indication of their functionality/enforcement challenges:

- The Teff Agreement[164] based its benefit-sharing obligation on a highly ambiguous and contradictory term – the user's "gross net income" for a specified three-year period. If payment had ever been made under this agreement, this term alone would have raised serious controversy and possibly invalidated the entire contract.

162 Drafting a contract by using or referring to accounting terminology from one country, without carefully defining it, can have the same type of negative impacts as using the term "genetic resources," without definition.

163 See generally, ¶ 5.3, *supra*. The contract needs to provide clarity also on this question. For some types of uses of genetic resources, there is a close connection between the genetic material and a product in a market (for example where a virus is used to develop a new vaccine with RNA coded into the vaccine). For other uses, there is larger distance between the accessed material and the product that eventually makes its way to the market. Often multiple accessions of genetic material have been used to develop one product. Tvedt, *et al.*, 2016.

164 Described in ¶ 4.1.

- Another draft contract used the formulation "net sales according to the company's accountance [*sic*] standards." This clause is rendered virtually useless by two factors. First, the contract failed to define "net sales" or to specify "sales of what?" Second, although the contract refers to the company's accounting standards, it does not specify what those standards are, nor does it attach them to the contract. For these reasons, this clause is probably too ambiguous to be enforced. Even if it were upheld, however, it is one-sided, in that the company could theoretically alter its accounting standards at any time, and thereby undermine the calculation.

(b) "Fair and Equitable"

Another source of ambiguity in the benefit-sharing clause arises where parties use the CBD language "fair and equitable benefit sharing" in their contract, assuming that it provides a sufficient standard on which to determine the eventual benefit share. In general, the authors are not aware of any court that would enforce a benefit-sharing obligation that merely requires a "fair and equitable share." Very rarely, in conventional contracts, courts have been willing to determine what is fair and equitable, even if the contract omits the payment clause entirely. This only happens, however, where the court can identify established valuation principles, and use them to determine a fair and equitable value.

That means that a court could probably not make such a ruling with regard to an ABS contract, because there is little or no public information about other contracts that could be used to enable the court to fairly estimate an equitable payment. Eventually, this might become possible, but not until the world has a great deal more experience with ABS contracts. Until then, a contract using the term "fair and equitable share" will probably be declared invalid due to lack of specificity.

(c) Benefit-sharing Clauses

The foregoing paragraphs have focused on the concept of specifying a percentage of profits arising from utilization of genetic resources/ATK, as the "benefit-share" to be paid. The authors have described this approach primarily because this discussion has arisen every time they have advised any type of ABS contract negotiation. It must be noted; however, that benefit-sharing of this type has so far not produced significant results. Early on, it was stated that the lack of reported payments of percentage-based benefit-sharing was simply due to the long lead time necessary for a user to go from resource collection to marketable product. At present, however, nearly 25 years have passed since the completion of the earliest benefit-sharing contracts.[165] The claims about the "long lead time" are wearing thin.

The alternate theory is that, as noted in ¶¶ 1.1.2 and 2.2, a contract's functionality is based on a combination of motivation and legal obligation. Once a user has obtained the genetic resources and/or ATK and has no further need to return to the provider country, his motivation declines, and benefit-sharing obligations begin to slip down the priority list. Given that the provider has little or no means of knowing whether the genetic resource or ATK has resulted in a useful compound or product, the user may simply decide to "forget" to share benefits. In terms of legal obligation, an additional factor may further deter compliance, where the contract is not properly drafted. For example, if an ABS contract relies on the NP's vague and ambiguous definition of "derivative," the user might formally cease his R&D when it has created a preliminary product for which there is no market, and then sell that preliminary product to a subsidiary or related company for its "market value" of $0.00. At that point, the original user's percentage benefit sharing obligation is $0.00, and the related company, which has no contractual relationship with the provider, may undertake further R&D. (In addition to demonstrating that the percentage approach is unlikely to produce actual benefit sharing, this example shows that proper contractual drafting makes a major difference in whether the ABS contract will function.)

There are, however, many other types of benefit-sharing mechanisms. Costa Rica, for example, has obtained critical equipment (used gene sequencers, *etc.*) and up-front payments from users who obtain samples of Costa Rican biodiversity. Based on informal interviews with biological and taxonomic researchers around the world, it appears that many academic and research institutions have provided seminars, training, and even scholarships as means of sharing their research results and other benefits of their work. Several providers have focused on requiring the bioprospectors to share one or more of each type of sample collected with appropriate institutions within the provider country. In some ABS contract the provider country or community asked only to be credited in any published research resulting from the researcher's access to genetic resources or ATK.

Similarly, some countries have adopted legislation requiring the user to enter into partnership with provider-country companies or residents. In some cases they are also required to set up analytical, research and/or production facilities within the provider country and staffed at least in part by local residents. These requirements cannot prevent the foreign users from informally

165 Reid *et al.*, 1993.

taking or sending the samples and knowledge obtained out of the country or conducting R&D away from the provider country's observation. Still, the capitalization of a local partnership, the establishment and construction of local technical facilities and/or the training of facility staff are important potential benefits to the provider country.

5.4.2 *Scope of Obligations, Actions and Rights*

The ABS contract's main operative provisions can specify a variety of types of obligations, actions and rights. These include obligations to transfer assets, to pay money or to put up security to help guarantee ones performance. Contracts may also specify particular services and future actions to be performed by the parties. Once again, no matter which type of operative clause is used, it can be legally functional only if it is sufficiently specific and concrete that an external observer can determine what is required.

In ABS contracts, the challenge of properly stating the nature, scope and extent of particular rights and responsibilities is acute. It is essential to specify the exact activities that each party agrees to undertake. Two points are relevant here. First, each contract is different, so the authors do not think it will be possible or useful to attempt to provide examples of the drafting of possible clauses.[166] Second, the clearest and most precise operative clauses are those that describe each required action in specific detail, including the date, location, time and other requirements. Similarly, promises to refrain from certain actions need to be clearly explained.[167] At the time an ABS contract is being negotiated, the parties should make a sincere effort to be as detailed and complete as possible. Where a particular type of activity is expected/possible, but details are not available, the contract should describe the precise purpose for which such activity will be undertaken, specifying as many parameters as are currently known and detailing the manner in which actual parameters will be calculated or otherwise finalized.

The importance of precision in these clauses should not be underestimated. No matter how specifically an ABS contract defines/describes the *res* and parties, it will be legally unenforceable if its obligation clause says only that "the provider grants access to the *res*; the user will utilize the *res* and the user will share benefits from that utilization." Such a contract would be legally

166 A number of examples culled from 75 contracts which were identified by their parties as "ABS contracts" can be found in Young and Bhatti, 2009.

167 As discussed in ¶ 5.3 and in greater detail in Chapters 6, 7, 8 and 9, it is often more difficult legally to enforce a contractual prohibition on certain actions, than to restate it as an activity that triggers additional obligations and/or consequences.

unenforceable due to uncertainty. If such a contract were executed, each party might have a different understanding of terms like "grant access" "utilize" and "share benefits." Those differences would almost guarantee that, even if the parties try, in good faith, to fulfil their contract, it will not be completed in a way that is satisfactory to all. The more specifically and exactly a contract spells out the activities that the parties are allowed or required to undertake, the more enforceable it will be.

The tools described in Chapter 3 can play a very important role in the negotiation of these clauses. The creation of the optimum-contract map requires each party to develop a concrete idea of what he believes the contract should require. The map itself is also useful in that it can help a party know how changes to any of the core provisions (res, obligations and objective) can impact the others or other parts of the contract strategy. The party analysis can provide important insight into the types of activities the other party will want or need to undertake.

Several other points have proven useful in specifying the obligations of parties in an ABS contract, including the following:

- The use of GPS coordinates in defining the range of the sampling;
- Requiring that the bioprospectors' collection notes (and/or duplicate prepared samples) be left with the appropriate national authority;
- Requiring that such notes be later updated with additional taxonomic information as it becomes available; and
- Identifying specific bioprospecting or germplasm collection protocols that must be followed.

5.4.3 *Limiting the Scope of Obligations, Actions and Rights*

An important aspect of the development of concrete core provisions, is the concrete specification of limits on those provisions. This section will consider two approaches to limiting the scope of the rights and obligations under an ABS contract. The first involves streamlining the operative provisions, to accord with the users' specific statements about their intended activities. The second involves the use of explicit clauses that specify directly state that certain activities, or categories of activities that are not permitted.

(a) Focused User Situations

In some situations, the ABS contract may not need to address the full range of ABS-related activities. As noted in ¶¶ 3.4.2 and 3.4.3, it may be appropriate to create a narrower contract for users with highly focused intentions.

Consider, for example, a specialized company working in a narrow field of products seeking the right to collect and utilize samples of a specific group of species, for use in its specific field. Many of the broader clauses in a more general ABS contract are not relevant for this user. The parties might wish to eliminate many elements from the ABS contract, so that it directly focuses only on elements of his research and development processes.

One such example could be a pharmaceutical company which works with development of vaccines and requires access to a particular novel strain of deadly viruses. By focusing on the branch in which the company operates and the type of genetic material accessed, the other parties may get a strong indication of the manner in which that the company is going to use the virus samples. A precise and exact obligation clause might then be appropriate to link the access and genetic resources, allowing specific targeting of the contract toward this particular product development.

The focused contract, however, is often a source of loopholes.[168] For this reason, it may be appropriate to also include explicit exceptions (next section) to ensure that the user is prevented from using the opportunity to enable inappropriate access.

(b) Explicit Exceptions and Prohibitions

Another type of limiting provision either specifies that particular rights are excluded from the contract or imposes commitments on particular parties to refrain from taking certain actions. There are many reasons that such exceptions to be included. Here, too, however, these provisions are effective only if they are specific, and they must be carefully drafted to avoid creating inappropriate loopholes. Often, as discussed above, it is more effective to avoid the use of prohibitions, where possible, substituting positive obligations, that will arise in the event a party takes the action of concern.

There are many reasons that a contract must be specific not only about what is required or permitted, but also about the scope and limits of those requirements and permissions. One example of an exception clause, in a simple contract might say "If X will pay $10 per year, Landowner Y will allow X and his companions to enter Y's apple orchard without separate permission. While in the orchard, X and his friends may picnic, climb trees, pick apples,

168 For example, many commentators have suggested that the highly focused SMTA under the ITPGRFA (which limits the users rights to utilizing the genetic resources for of food and agricultural purposes) may have created an unsupervised loophole that enables users to obtain samples and then use or transfer them for pharmaceutical and other purposes.

and eat apples." Under a literal reading of this contract, X may bring an unlimited number of "friends" into Landowner's orchard, and harvest all of the apples in the entire orchard if he chooses, in exchange for $10/year. Although the contract is unambiguous and thus potentially enforceable, this is probably not what Landowner intended. The drafting of the contract in this case is clearly insufficient. A few well place phrases beginning with the words "not more than" would have made the above contract reflect the Landowner's intent better, without impacting the contract's legal functionality.

In addition to stating the scope of the party's obligations in an affirmative way, the parties may often want to clarify the external boundary of that scope by directly stipulating what is not allowed. The contract could include both types of provisions. This is particularly relevant in an ABS contract. A specific genetic material can be used in a number of ways. The contract might allow only one or a few specific uses. Exceptions and prohibitions in the paragraph describing the permitted uses can tailor the contract to what it is meant to allow. As noted, however, the provider must then assume the challenge of surveillance and vigilance, since he will need some way to monitor what the user is doing.

(c) Exclusivity in ABS Contracts

Although most examples of explicit exception clauses (above) focus on user activities, one important type – the exclusivity clause – is usually directed at the provider. Exclusivity is often a strongly emphasized aspect of the negotiations, particularly desirable to certain users who hope their research and products can be protected with intellectual property rights. These parties call for a clause by which the provider agrees not to give access to the same *res* to another user. An exclusivity clause needs to be very specific, especially regarding precisely what is exclusive, and how the exclusivity provision will operate when other parties seek access to the same or different resources from the same provider. In addition, exclusivity is generally not eternal, so the clause is usually bounded by a specified time period.

From the perspective of the user, securing the exclusivity of his right to the material can be of critical importance – one of his priorities in the negotiations. If so, then from the perspective of the provider, exclusivity can be a bargaining chip. The provider may propose adjustments to other elements of the concept. He may, for example, propose a limit on the time-period of the exclusivity. Doing so could be of great value to the provider. It could create an important incentive for the user to invest and get results from the genetic material. Another possibility is to focus the exclusivity in terms of the proposed use, leaving the provider be free to contract with other users who propose other uses. A third area of possible negotiation would be to tie in oversight elements – to build milestones regarding the user's progress into the clause, as an ongoing prerequisite of exclusivity.

(d) Ending of the Contractual Relationship

As has been noted by many commentators, particularly in the ITPGRFA's SMTA revision process,[169] there are many commercial reasons why users will avoid ABS contracts under which genetic resources and/or ATK are only transferred if the user agrees to tie them to a virtually unending benefit-sharing obligation. Less frequently remarked, however, is the fact that providers may be generally unwilling to grant broad rights of access, utilization and exclusivity to users under a contract that ties benefit-sharing to their own activities, but does not include any commitment regarding how soon they will undertake those activities. In recognition of the relationship between both of these, it may be useful or advisable to negotiate a clause relating to the manner in which the contract will end.

Such a clause should specify any or all of the following

(i) whether there is a specific point at which the contract will expire because it has been fulfilled, and if so what that point is;
(ii) what happens when the contract expires (which obligations, if any, continue to function[170]);
(iii) what each party must do in order to keep the contract in force, how a party may terminate the contract if the other party is not living up to these requirements; and
(iv) what happens in the event of such a termination of the contract (return of the resources, rights of the parties against one another, *etc*).[171]

5.4.4 *Monitoring*

Where the user is allowed to collect samples in specific areas or in specific categories of biological material, the element of monitoring also may become

169 Discussed in "Options for Introducing a Termination Clause"; FAO Document IT/OWG-EFMLS-3/15/Inf.7 at http://www.planttreaty.org/sites/default/files/OWG%20EFMLS%20 3-15-Inf7%20Termination%20Clause.pdf.

170 For example, confidentiality obligations and warranties frequently continue even after the contract has been fully executed.

171 In early ABS contracts, one of the authors has seen contracts that stated that they would terminate after a certain number of years, without any additional information about, for

important. Monitoring is very difficult to implement and enforce. It is also sometimes expensive.

The most effective way to minimize the need for long-term vigilance is to find users willing to pay an appropriate price "up-front," in exchange of a long-term custodial right to collect and remove a broad range of samples. Once the provider has received all the payment due under the contract, its duty of monitoring is limited to ensuring three aspects: (i) that the user does not collect anything it is not entitled to, (ii) that he complies with collection procedures and (iii) that he reports properly regarding any matters on which reports are needed.

5.4.5 *Operational Provisions Relating to Patents and Other IPRs*

The combination of patent law and contract law can sometimes pose significant challenges. When drafting an ABS contract the use or filing of intellectual property rights, particularly patents, is frequently a major point addressed within the negotiations. This attention is quite justified. If an ABS contract does not pay attention to patent law issues, that omission can have a very negative impact on the parties' rights and expectations. At the same time, excessive focus on patent concepts has often led negotiators to overlook issues, options and possibilities that are ultimately much more critical to the real situations that arise.

In the past, providers have viewed patents as an option that harms their own rights and interests. This has led to a common concept, claiming that ABS contracts should generally prohibit the users from ever applying for patents. There are a number of reasons, however, why such a clause might not be advisable.

(a) Ineffectiveness Due to Differences in the Legal Regimes

Patent law is distinct from contract law. In many instances, it is possible that a clause that operates well under contract law would have little or no impact on the grant of a patent. For example, a contractual prohibition on patenting material covered by the contract have no legal effect on applicable patent laws or conventions.[172] A patent or other intellectual property right is "a creation

---

example, the disposition of laboratory samples held by the user on that final date. As discussed in more detail in Chapters 6, 7, and 8, a contract that is silent on what happens at termination, presents serious challenges for its parties.

172 *European Patent Convention*, 5 October 1973, as amended on 17 December 1991, 21 December 1978, 13 December 1994, 20 October 1995, 5 December 1996, 10 December 1998 and 27 October 2005 and 29 November 2000.

of law." This means that its issuance and existence is based on the logic and criteria set out in the patent system of the particular legal entity/jurisdiction that grants the patent. In most cases, the patent applicant need not provide any documentation that he has obtained legal access to the genetic or biological material or ATK used in the invention. Even where the patent law calls for such documentation, it is not considered a "patent criteria." Thus, even if it is shown that the applicant erroneously stated that no access was required or made some other misstatement, the patent will not be invalidated. A contract provision prohibiting a user from applying for a patent would have a similar result – even if proven, that prohibition will not affect any patent granted and will have no consequences within the patent system. This suggests that the most likely result from a contractual prohibition of patenting could be that it will motivate the user to find legal justifications for claiming that the *res* of the ABS contract is not relevant to the patent.

A better strategy than for dealing with the relationship between the contract and patent law is for the contract to regulate matters relevant for the contractual relationship, leaving other patent issues to be addressed at the appropriate time and in the appropriate way. It is very seldom that the genetic material is patented in the form received. Thus, it is difficult to identify when or whether a certain patented invention is based on the material that was accessed under this ABS contract. The contract might aim at building in mechanisms through which the user provides evidence that a forthcoming patented invention arose out of the utilization of specific genetic material acquired under the contract. Rather than attempting to prohibit the user from securing an exclusive right to an invention, the contract should establish clear rights for the provider to share in the benefits of the patent. The application and grant of a patent is externally verifiable, and is thus well-suited as a trigger point for a benefit-sharing obligation.

For this reason, and given that patent law and its relationship to ABS is a topic that would fill another book this size, the authors have opted that this book will not include any attempt to deal with the law of creating enforceable, functional patent instruments and related contracts. Clearly, the contract parties should obtain advice about patent issues, both prior to the negotiation of the ABS contract and in the event that the ABS contract leads to the patenting of ABS-derived innovations

(b) Ineffectiveness Due to Contractual Drafting Issues

The wording of the patent itself may defeat an ABS contract's patent prohibition. A patent grants an exclusive right to an invention described by the applicant in the patent claims. The manner in which the patent applicant writes the patent claims is not restricted with regard to the genetic material/ATK issue. The applicant's description may be specifically designed to ensure that there is no claim that the patent covers a "genetic resource." He may also carefully word it to ensure that he can claim that there is no overlap between his patent and the *res* of the contract.

Before considering the contract, looking only at the two bodies of law, it was already clear that the provider cannot challenge a patent based on the legal argument that its applicant was not allowed to patent a genetic resource. Looking to the contractual prohibition, the result is the same. The prohibition in an ABS contract cannot prevent a patent office from granting the patent, because it is not a party to the contract. The provider's only avenue of remedy is direct action against the user under the contract. Even here, however, the user's application will not necessarily be a breach of the contractual prohibition, because in most cases, the user does not patent a genetic resource/ATK. Instead, the application is written in a way that targets something more specific. Again if the contract uses the undefined terms in the CBD and NP, that would increase the chance that the provider would not be able to secure a share of the benefits arising from the patent.

The foregoing analysis is based on the type of patent prohibition stated in the Teff Agreement. This clause exemplifies the lesson that a patent prohibition clause is not an appropriate way to promote the benefit-sharing goal of an ABS contract. The failure of the Teff Agreement's patent prohibition is easiest to interpret by comparing the wording of the Agreement on this point with the wording of the patent claim that was filed:

Teff agreement	Teff patent
5.1 The Company shall neither claim nor obtain intellectual property rights over the **genetic resources** of Teff or over any component of the genetic resources.	**Claims 1. A flour of a grain** belonging to the genus Eragrostis, preferably Eragrostis tef, **characterized in** that the falling number of the grain at the moment of grinding is at least 250, preferably at least 300, more preferably at least 340, most preferably at least 380.

Comparing the two, it is obvious that the subject matter of the contractual prohibition is "teff genetic resources" or "components of the genetic resources." The subject matter of the patent claim, however, is not a genetic resource, but a flour with a specific characteristic concerning the "falling number."[173] This means that the *res* of the Teff Agreement does not overlap with the subject matter of the Teff patent. The insight and innovation that formed the basis for the Teff patent claims does not appear to overlap with the term "genetic resources of Teff or over any component of the genetic resources" as is the term in the contract. Additionally, the ABS claim would depend on the providers' ability to make a very difficult proof: that there was a clear link between the genetic resources accessed under the Teff Agreement and the patented invention. Proving this linkage to the satisfaction of a court might require both clear evidence and the ability to "teach" the court about the science of the development of genetic resources. These discrepancies formed the bases of the user's statements that its patent application did not breach the contract.[174]

(c) Probable Outcomes and Motivation Issues

As the foregoing sections show, it would be very difficult (perhaps impossible) to convince a court that applying for a patent in the manner described above infringes or breaches the contract. In order to uphold the position of the provider in the Teff Agreement described above, the court would have to come to critical decisions about the practical application of the term "genetic resources," the linkage between the resources accessed and the subject matter of the patent, and various other practical and legal questions. The general ambiguity surrounding the meaning of the term "genetic resources," coupled with most courts' unwillingness to second-guess scientific decisions by government agencies would often prevent any court from making such a decision. These observations make it clear that a no-patent clause may have little or no legal effect in courts or patent agencies. Moreover, if the parties focus too much of their negotiating efforts on the patent issue, their contract may fail to address other potential challenges or loopholes over which they would otherwise have a greater level of control.

Thus, at this point, it is appropriate to recall a second key motivational impact that a no-patent approach might have on the objectives of the ABS

173 The falling number is not linked to the particular genes but stems from the manner in which processors are able to after-ripen the harvested seeds.

174 No court decided this, however it was a part of the provider's analysis, which eventually concluded that no litigation should be filed.

contract. In addition to potentially encouraging users to create and take advantage of legal loopholes, a patent prohibition may also discourage users from, relying on the patent mechanism, from utilizing any genetic resource or ATK in a commercially valuable way or even from entering into ABS contracts, at all. Before deciding to prohibit the other party from patenting an innovation that either utilizes genetic resources/ATK or was developed through their utilization, a provider should recognize that patenting is only one of the mechanisms by which users generate benefits from research and development. If it is sufficiently restrictive to actually deter a user from patenting his innovation, a patent prohibition in an ABS contract could also be a means of eliminating that user's ability to produce benefits to share.

In most ABS contracts, the most commercially sensible approach would probably be to design the contract around the users' possible need to patent their innovations. The contract should recognize this need, while it also clarifies the providers' rights and expectations with regard to its genetic resources and ATK in the event that such a patent is filed. Rather that attempting to prevent patent filings, the provider might be better served by recognizing patents as an important commercial benefit arising from the utilization of genetic resources, and negotiating to claim an interest in it. As noted by many negotiators during the NP's development, a patent is one of the few externally verifiable legal facts regarding what the user is doing, as such, many believe that the patent system could or should be a primary a mechanism for triggering benefit sharing.

(d) Approach to Ownership to Information and Knowledge and Patent Clauses

In some academic or commercial ABS contracts, the contractual activities using genetic material are undertaken with the goal of understanding the DNA and genes of the organism. These contracts would therefore need to regulate rights to data, genetic information (for example, digital sequence data and knowledge generated on the basis of the genetic material). Questions relating to the patenting of an invention based on the material are important aspects of regulating benefit sharing.

To date, however, ABS contracts have usually delayed the question of how to deal with patents and commercialization, declaring it to be the subject of a new negotiation, when such issue has arisen. As detailed in ¶ 3.6, *supra,* this is not a fruitful strategy and the parties to a contract at the point of access need to find a balance between negotiating "ghost" issues that are not yet in existence and creating a situation in which later behavior will "trigger" a negotiation at a time when the user has no motivation or willingness to return to the negotiating table.

5.4.6 *Middlemen, Interim Users, Collectors and Transferees*

Many of those who bioprospect or collect samples under ABS contracts do not plan to use the material themselves, but intend to transfer it to third parties. Such parties might be unable (or unwilling) to commit to a contract that identifies one or more specific permitted and/or excluded uses. In such a situation, the collector normally expects to transfer the material from its own entity to other companies (giving rise to the challenges described in Chapter 6.) This possibility, along with the prevalence of middlemen, interim users, collectors and transferees in ABS discussions and in practice, should stand as a clear indication of the importance of independent research into the activities and history of the parties with whom you are negotiating, and the importance of addressing transfer and other unexpected post-access events in every ABS contract.

5.5 Triggering Contractual Rights and Duties

Contractually, a party's obligation, no matter how beautifully stated, means little if the contract is not clear about what factors or conditions determine when the obligation is owed. Those factors or conditions are sometimes called "triggers" or "triggering mechanisms." In ABS contract negotiations, the parties have sometimes overlooked the discussion of triggers, because they are relying on their perception that, the CBD and the NP have firmly established, as a "general principles of international law," that the fair and equitable benefit-sharing obligation is automatically triggered by the "utilization of genetic resources."

Regardless of whether/how the global regime negotiations have addressed this issue,[175] the concept is not yet sufficiently well established for contractual parties to consider it "accepted" where the contract does not include any direct contractual clause on the point. In order for a contractual trigger to be functional, it too, must be concrete. Specifically, it must unambiguously state exactly what action, condition or factors triggers the obligation and exactly what action is mandated or allowed at the time.

175 The authors have discussed this issue in the context of the international ABS regime and the need for national legislation implementing these obligations. See, Tvedt and Young, 2007. As these "regime" discussions make it clear, there is no general agreement on any part of this "assumption." As such, it cannot be relied on as an unwritten part of any ABS contract.

In contract drafting, the primary objective is to ensure that every such trigger is an external verifiable action, and that the contract clearly and precisely states exactly which obligations are triggered by each triggering event or condition and how those obligations are satisfied. If a contract states that a particular type and amount of benefit must be shared as soon as the user has engaged in the "utilization of genetic resources," then there may be no basis for claim, in the event that no benefit is ever shared. To make a claim, the provider would not only have to prove exactly what the user had done with the genetic resource, but would also have to prove that that activity constituted the "utilization of genetic resources," as that term is used in the CBD and NP. The first proof is only nearly impossible, while the latter is completely impossible, since the CBD and NP's use and definitions of those terms are not precise enough to apply to a particular action. No matter how clearly the benefit-sharing obligation is specified, it will not be enforceable, if the trigger cannot be proven.

The following sections discuss the various types of triggers that can be included in an ABS contract, and the various challenges that arise with regard to their drafting and application.

5.5.1 *Trigger Challenges*

The trigger issue challenges the parties to clarify the precise actions that link one party's obligation to another party's right/expectation. To build this link, the contractual wording must again be clear and unambiguous, particularly because the trigger is a highly controversial moment in the life of a contract obligation. When one party believes the other party's obligation is triggered, it is important that the other party should think so as well. Any other situation may lead to breach, controversy, litigation and possibly contractual failure.

There are very few examples of clear (or unclear) ABS triggers. One that is readily available is found in the ITPGRFA's SMTA, which provides that its benefit-sharing provisions are triggered when the recipient "**commercializes** a **Product** that is a **Plant Genetic Resource for Food and Agriculture** and that incorporates **Material** as referred to in Article 3 of **this Agreement**, and where such **Product** is not **available without restriction** to others for further research and breeding."[176] The benefit obligation here is for the user[177] to transfer a fixed 1.1 per cent of the net sales of the product into the ITPGRFA's multilateral fund. The drafting and functionality of this trigger have been strongly

---

176 *Standard Material Transfer Agreement*, ITPGRFA Governing Body, 16 June 2006, Resolution 1/2006 Annex 2, Art. 6.7. (*emphasis in original*) This clause is considered in more detail in Tvedt, 2015.

177 Termed the "Recipient" in the SMTA.

criticized. Thus, even though it stands as one of the few ABS contracts that have attempted to tie all benefit-sharing to the actual receipt of commercial benefits, it is also an example of how poorly constructed triggers can defeat the functionality of a contract. As such, it demonstrates the most important practical challenges in establishing triggering mechanisms: external verifiability.

In particular, over time it has become clear that the ITPGRFA SMTA's trigger-provision is not very accurately phrased. Some have suggested, for example, that inclusion of the phrase "where such Product is not available without restrictions" implies that all plant breeders' rights fall outside the scope of the trigger point. If that were true, it would effectively exclude the breeding of new plant varieties (a primary raison d'être for the Multilateral System) from the benefit-sharing obligation. Another challenge arises from the fact that the UPOV conventions allow unfettered "further research and breeding" on a new plant variety. As a result, the above-quoted SMTA trigger would appear to focus on patenting. This raises the multiple problems of using patent triggers. Most importantly, the SMTA states that the trigger applies only where the "Product ... is a Plant Genetic Resource." As noted in ¶ 5.4.5, above, patent claims are rarely if ever formulated in a way that would describe their subject matter as a plant genetic resource. They more usually describe it very narrowly, as a product or process. All of these factors, illustrate the complex challenges involved in describing a benefit-sharing trigger based on commercial marketing and/or sales.

Over all, the greatest trigger challenge is simply that the triggering event will be known only to (and within the sole control of) the user. Hence, a major and mostly unsolved challenge in many types of triggers is the need for provider vigilance – independent surveillance that will enable the provider to know when an obligation of the user is triggered.

Not only will the provider need to know when the trigger occurs, but he will also need to be able to document it with clear evidence, showing not only that the triggering event or condition has been met, but also any other factors that impact the user's obligation. In the SMTA trigger described above, for example, the triggering event is not only the commercialization, but the earning of "net sales," without which it would be impossible to calculate the amount owed.

5.5.2 *Designing Functional Trigger Points*

To date, there has been much discussion of the nature of the link between the user's receipt of benefits from his utilization of genetic resources and/or ATK and the user's duty to share benefits with the provider. No matter how those issues are resolved, however, the actual triggers of the user's benefit-sharing obligation are the actions, events and conditions that are specified in the ABS contract. Apart from the contract, there is no requirement anywhere that specifies when benefit-sharing obligations must be fulfilled nor even how or when the provider's benefit-share should be calculated.

This means that benefit-sharing obligations may be estimated, concretized and triggered at the very beginning of the contract, if the parties agree. At this point, of course, the benefit itself will be very speculative because the parties cannot have any certainty that the user's research will actually produce any benefit worth sharing. As always, where a party seeks a secure up-front payment, rather than waiting to find out if the *res* will prove to be extremely valuable, the party receiving the up-front payment will be expected to accept a much smaller payment. There are two reasons for this. First, of course, a secure small payment is often considered to be comparable in value to a speculative large payment. Second, a payment now is generally thought of as more valuable than a payment later.

As noted in Chapter 2, and also in ¶¶ 3.6 and 5.5.1, the primary problem with ABS functionality arises where benefit-sharing is delayed until a point at which the user is no longer motivated to comply with the contract. That is, if the benefit-sharing is deferred until the user has already obtained and utilized the genetic resources – until he has actually received benefits from that utilization – then the provider's rights must be strong and enforceable to overcome the user's strong motivation to "forget" his benefit-sharing obligation. By that time, the provider can only have a strong, enforceable right if he can prove that the triggering event has occurred. As noted above, however, by this time most providers cannot even know for certain what the user is doing, much less prove it. As a result, most providers may well desire to restructure the ABS contract so that all user obligations occur in the early stages, when the user may be present or represented in the provider country, and may also have an interest in preserving a good working relationship with the provider and the provider country.

There is no contractual reason that the benefit-trigger cannot be an event or condition that occurs in the beginning phases of the contract. In virtually all contracts, the parties come to an agreement based on a compromise between their respective objectives and valuations, to be paid at a time or upon a condition that may occur long before the purpose of the contract has been fulfilled or even triggered. As discussed in greater detail in ¶ 9.5, there are many structural options for triggering benefit-sharing, once one discards the idea that benefit-sharing should only happen after the user has obtained a benefit.

The availability of such different structures also gives rise to a range of options regarding triggers that may be much easier to verify.

As examples, some possible options for benefit-sharing triggers include the following, any of which is externally verifiable:

- The execution (formal signing) of the ABS contract (an event that, by definition, is known to all parties) or other key ABS documents;
- The collection or transfer of specimens; or
- The removal of specimens from the country.

It may also be appropriate to specify a certain number of days before any of these events. In that case, the event cannot happen until that number of days has passed after the benefit-sharing has been completed. Recalling that benefit-sharing may include obligations beyond the payments of money, it is clear that more than one trigger may happen under a single ABS contract. The choice of trigger may sometimes be tied to the nature of the benefit-sharing. For example, a duty to provide duplicate samples might be triggered by the collection of specimens and a duty to share taxonomic information by their removal from the country. It is equally appropriate in some cases simply to assign a specific date as the trigger. As discussed in Chapters 8 and 9, a user's failure to make any triggered benefit-sharing requirement may sometimes be considered a breach of the entire contract, giving rise to judicial or non-judicial remedies.

5.5.3 *Products and Processes in the Market*

It seems clear that the presence in the market of products or processes arising from the utilization of the *res* have a two-sided influence on the trigger question. On one hand, it will obviously be very difficult for a provider to canvass the genetic underpinnings of every product on the market to determine whether a particular genetic resource is found within it or was used in its production.[178] It remains for legislation to be developed that would help create some kind of link between ABS compliance and the appearance of new products and processes on the market. On the other hand, however, if such canvassing were possible (*i.e,* if a multi-country effort was feasible and the necessary scientific process was viable and cost effective), the public nature of the market would serve as an excellent venue for independent confirmation.

In some situations, public filing requirements can operate as externally verifiable triggers. For example, in the Teff Agreement, benefit sharing was to be triggered by elements of the annual accounting processes of the user company. This could have been useful, if the parties had been certain of three

178 See Tvedt *et al.*, 2016.

things: First, they needed to confirm that the user country's national reporting requirements would, in fact, disclose all factors relevant to determining whether the triggering condition had occurred. Second, they needed to determine whether and how the provider would be able to access all relevant filings in the user country (in some countries, such matters are publicly available to all, but in many countries they are tightly restricted.) Third, the provider would have to actually do what was necessary to access that information on a regular basis – both to confirm that the proper filings were made, and to evaluate them to verify user's statements or silence regarding whether benefit-sharing had been triggered. Often, even when public access is available, it is difficult and costly both to obtain access and to undertake the relevant research. Where all three of these factors are substantiated, however, public governmental filings can be a useful, but potentially expensive, trigger point.

5.6 "Objective" or "Purpose" Clauses

Two basic principles of the negotiation of any contract are first that there must always be at least two parties, and second that it is unlikely that the parties to the negotiation have matching interests and objectives. A party to a contractual negotiation should never assume that the other parties' objectives are the same as his own, or that their view of the contract's requirements will be the same. This is the key reason that all contractual provisions must be precise and specific. For this reason, most contracts begin with one or more clauses that state the parties' agreed objectives and the reasons they are entering into the contract as a potential aid in interpretation of the remaining provisions.

No matter how carefully crafted they are, the main operative clauses of the contract (the clauses describing the *res* and stating the parties rights and obligations, as discussed in ¶¶ 5.3–5.5, above) often require interpretation. Whether due to disagreement or to unexpected occurrence, they need to determine what the contract actually requires in practice. Interpretation might be needed to figure out how a particular change in circumstances or conditions might impact each party's obligations. It might also be sought to determine whether a particular action (not specifically mentioned in the text of the contract) will satisfy or breach a party's obligation. In seeking clarification the parties, judge or arbitrator may need to look at the "contract as a whole" to answer the question in a way that does not defeat the contract's overall objective or purpose. For this reason, many contracts include formal clauses explaining the parties' overall agreed intent in entering into the contract.

These "objective" or "purpose" clauses are thus designed to provide a clear record of the parties' "agreed intent," which often describes a combination or compromise of their original individual negotiating objectives. Such clauses can be a useful tool in helping the parties to resolve their differences without legal action. They cannot, however, be used as a basis for adding obligations, limitations or rights, however, only for interpreting the operational clauses already in the contract.

In light of their interpretative role, objective/purposes clauses can be very important. They are not just nice statements of the parties cooperative attitude and shared goodwill. Parties should carefully examine all parts of any proposed objective clause, to confirm that it is a reasonable statement of their negotiated agreement as to the purpose and ultimate goals of the contract. Failure to do so can have a devastating impact, in the event that a court or other external person or agency makes any interpretation of one of the contract's operative clauses.

5.6.1 *The Role of a Purpose/Objective Clause*

There is no requirement that a contract must have a clause stating its objective or purpose, but as noted above, most contracts do so, either as one or more clauses within the main text, or as preambular material (usually called "recitals" or "whereas clauses.") They do not purport to list all objectives of all parties, but only to memorialize these that are shared or "agreed."[179] As such, they can be used to resolve ambiguities, as noted above, but not to impose obligations.

The role of the objective clause should not be misunderstood. The parties are clarifying a shared understanding of their agreed goals and the purpose of the contract. They should not expect this clause to include all of their negotiating priorities, but they must ensure that the clause is carefully and precisely drafted to conform to their mutual understanding of what the overall contract is intended to do. They should also recall that no matter how excellently written it is, the objective clause cannot replace contractual precision

179 It is important to make a clear distinction between the "objective clauses" of a contract and the objectives of the parties to the contract. The parties respective priorities, expectations and desires vary greatly. A party can have many objectives underlying his participation in the contract negotiations. Some of these objectives cannot be disclosed during the negotiations, whether because they are strategic in nature (disclosing the value of the contract to one party might give the other party unfair leverage) or because, as is sometimes claimed, they are nefarious. Only the objectives that have been shared with and agreed by all parties are part of the objective clause of the contract.

and exactness in the core contractual provisions, nor can it remedy the lack of such concreteness.

In the operative (res and obligation) clauses, the goal of contractual precision is predominant. The purpose clauses clarify these matters in a different way. They are intended to address a basic reality of all contracts – that during the time that the contract remains in force, circumstances and conditions will often change in ways that the contractual negotiations and text not consider or address. The need to ensure that the contract will still function in such a case pits two critical concepts against one another: the need for contractual specificity and the need to ensure that the contract allows for dynamic developments. The "objective/purpose clauses" are designed to help the contract address this serendipity by providing an outcome-based view. This is why, as noted above, courts and parties can often rely on them as bases for interpreting the more specific res, obligation/rights, trigger and enforcement clauses (described in ¶¶ 5.3–5.5, *supra* and Chapters 8 and 9, *infra*), when determining how the contract should be interpreted in response to unexpected change.

5.6.2 *Balancing Precision with Dynamic Development*

Given their role in re-thinking how the contract will address unforeseen changes, objective clauses are, on some ways, the "loose cannons" of the contract. They may be used as a means of "dynamic development" of the contract, but by definition, that development can only happen in the event that something unforeseen happens. As such, it is unreasonable to council proactivity in this context. Instead, what the authors do council is twofold.

First the parties should aim to minimize uncertainty, by attempting to ensure that their operative provisions take into account as many possibilities as they can foresee. If the functional clauses can be reasonably interpreted to include a particular situation or condition, then there will be no need for the court to turn to the objective/purpose clause in order to address it. In general, if the core provisions are clearly and concretely stated, the best result for the parties is their implementation/enforcement. A legal, arbitral or compromise decision that is based on the purpose/objective clause adds a level of uncertainty to the contract, and may alter the delicate balance represented by the parties' agreement. To the maximum extent possible, the parties should strive never to need to apply the purpose/objective clause.

Second, however, they should carefully consider the purpose/objective clause by asking the question – if the contract achieves everything stated in the objective clause, will that mean that our reasonable objectives and agreement are fulfilled? This question encompasses the value of the purpose/objective clause – it may save a contract that might otherwise be legally terminated or invalidated by unforeseen changes. Objective clauses inject a level of controlled flexibility in the operation and interpretation of the contract. Such a clause is best, where it indicates the balance between the parties and their shared view of the overall desired outcome.

5.7 Change of Use or Intent

A number of particularly thorny problems have arisen in ABS, for which no clear solution has yet been found. One of the most difficult challenges for ABS contract negotiators relates to the possibility of a post-access change of use or intent with regard to the genetic resource or ATK. This issue has posed a significant challenge in nearly every ABS negotiation that either of the authors have advised.

Briefly, the concept of "change of use" recognizes that ABS does not govern all transactions in any material containing DNA. There are a great many non-ABS reasons why a party might want to acquire samples that contain genetic resources, or to obtain information about ATK. These include purchasing a part of a plant or animal to eat, wear, carve, weave or mount on the wall, or learning about ATK as part of anthropological or cross-cultural studies. These "other purposes" are entirely legal and often may not have any ABS-related implications. The challenge arises when the acquirer changes his mind about the genetic resources or ATK that are part of what he has acquired, and begins the processes of "utilizing" them for purposes of commercial or technical development.

As ABS is designed, that change converts the purchaser into an ABS "user" (or perhaps a middleman.) At that point, the user may be obliged under national ABS law or primary principles of national sovereignty to obtain PIC and establish MAT with the provider country. Depending on national law, he may also be required to enter into an ABS contract with one or more specific individuals, entities, agencies or communities. There are broadly two categories of change of intent situations (often overlapping): (i) the decision to use legally acquired biological material in a manner that constitutes "utilization of genetic resources"; and (ii) the decision to transfer material that may already be subject to an ABS contract to a third party. The following sections provide some suggestions for addressing these two concerns.

5.7.1 *Change of Intent by the Person/Entity that Acquired the Material*

Where a person has obtained biological material legally, but then later decides to undertake activities that constitute "utilization of genetic resources," the ABS requirements should apply, so a huge loophole in the ABS regime is not created. If that user is already operating under a contract or permit, then there may be a value to including contractual provisions to prevent or regulate such changes of use or intent. Unfortunately, in many cases, the user's original access to the material did not require any contract or permit. In those situations, there is no contractual method of addressing the change of intent.

(a) Genetic Material Acquired for Non-ABS Purposes

A user who has legally acquired biological material for some non-ABS purpose is probably not bound by any particular contract or permit with regard to his future use of that material. He may have collected it himself, purchased it in a street market, or acquired it in some other legal way. Thus, his decision to undertake actions that constitute "utilization of its genetic resources" presents a very complex challenge. He cannot be accused of violating his contract or permit, since he has none.

Given that this type of "change of use" is not a contractual issue, the person who engages in this change of use can only be directly accused of violation of the provider country's national law if he does not immediately comply with ABS requirements when he decides to change his use. At present, no legislative remedy is normally available where the material has already been taken out of the provider country by the time the change of use occurs. Even in the few user countries that have attempted to address this need legislatively, the law allows that user country to take a legal action against the user, but does not require or allow it to return the genetic material or any payment or other remedy to the provider country.

There is little need to consider this issue in ABS contracts. By definition, PIC, MAT and ABS contracts are only obtained by persons who intend to utilize genetic resources or ATK in accordance with the NP or domestic ABS laws. Thus, unless an ABS contract requirement is imposed on every person who purchases or otherwise acquires any biological sample (an option that would have a major negative impact on virtually all commerce), the provider will not normally have any contractual remedy available for this type of change of use.

For this reason, the most important change-of-use challenge is to create an incentive for the user to enter into such an agreement.

TIPS

1. "Change of use" from a legal use to an action that constitutes "utilization of genetic resources" or ATK cannot be regulated by ABS contracts or other ABS documents. It must be addressed through international cooperation among governments – recognition of all countries' obligation to ensure that ABS functions.

2. In the meantime, it could be legally useful for provider countries to adopt legislation requiring every person removing any biological material from the country to sign a statement agreeing that the material will not be used for any purpose defined as "utilization of genetic resources or ATK" under the provider country's national ABS law, without first obtaining PIC, MAT and whatever permit, contract or other document or approval is required. The signing of such a statement may not prevent the person from "misusing"[180] the genetic resources or ATK he takes out of the country. It may, however, improve the provider's chances in the event that it seeks to enforce its ABS rights in another country – contractual violations and false legal statements are more easily enforced in foreign courts and arbitrations than national laws of the provider country.

(b) Change from a "Special," "Non-commercial" or Exempt ABS Use to a Commercial or Other Non-exempt Use

There is, however, one situation involving a change of use by a user under an ABS contract that can and should be addressed by the ABS contract. That situation arises where the provider country has adopted a streamlined process or special category or other exception with regard to certain academic and/or non-commercial uses. The application of ABS to these activities was intensively discussed in the NP negotiations. The result of those negotiations is that, at present, the NP allows, but does not require, countries to make a distinction in their national ABS legislation between "commercial" and "non-commercial" utilization of genetic resources or ATK.[181] Clearly, as noted above, the ABS contract is not governed by, and should never attempt to incorporate, the vague concepts and terminology of the NP and/or national ABS legislation. Even so, the distinction between non-commercial/exempt/special uses and commercial uses may have an impact on ABS contracts.

For example, if a provider country's national law does not apply to noncommercial users who collect samples, then the collection of samples by such

180 The special uses of the terms "misappropriation" and "misuse" of GR and ATK, that were frequently used during the NP negotiations are discussed in Young, T. 2006. As noted therein, it is not advisable to assume that these special uses are universal, even in the context of ABS.

181 The NP recommends that countries consider streamlining their ABS process by minimizing the requirements that apply to users who are seeking access for purposes of "non-commercial research." To this end, Art. 8(a) provides, "In the development and implementation of its access and benefit-sharing legislation or regulatory requirements, each Party shall: (a) Create conditions to promote and encourage research

users would essentially be identical to the acquisition of biological material for a non-ABS purpose, as described in ¶ 5.7.1.a, above.

In some national legislation, however, the non-commercial and/or exempt user is still subject to regulation. That is, if they must comply with streamlined requirements and/or obtain a special permit or contract. These latter situations require special provisions in the applicable permit or contract. The provider might then have an obligation to provide access, but also some right to oversee or control the collection of samples by these entities. Where the law requires some special or streamlined PIC, MAT or contract, it is essential to determine if the purported exempt or non-commercial user continues to qualify for the exemption.

To date, only a few countries have adopted this type of distinction. Of these, the most well publicized is Australia's law governing use of genetic resources of some Commonwealth areas. That law allows any user to obtain a "non-commercial research permit," if it signs a statement that it is undertaking only non-commercial research. To date, according to national online data, out of several hundred ABS permits issued, only three were issued for commercial purposes, and all three of these were issued to the same governmentally funded research institution. Australian law does not appear to impose monitoring or oversight requirements on non-commercial research activities, and does not state any penalty for undertaking commercial research under a non-commercial permit. Although it requires that the user must obtain an ABS contract with the provider in the event that it obtains a commercial permit, it does not discuss the relationship between the user and provider in the event of non-commercial activities. Given that the law only addresses certain central government lands. It is not clear whether or to what extent this approach is replicated in state/territory law and/or applicable to indigenous communities or private providers.[182]

which contributes to the conservation and sustainable use of biological diversity, particularly in developing countries, including through simplified measures on access for non-commercial research purposes, taking into account the need to address a change of intent for such research." After intense discussion of the need for streamlining the ABS processes for non-commercial research any gains made by negotiators of that clause were subsequently eclipsed when those negotiators did not stay involved in the process. Eventually, as shown above, Art 8(a) is phrased so ambiguously that it does not require streamlined processes, and does not interlink with other NP provisions that appear to completely obviate it. See, *e.g.*, Young, T. 2011.

182 The Australian Commonwealth provisions are also discussed in ¶ 3.6.2, *supra*. They are, in effect a "two-step ABS contract system" of a type that the authors believe should be avoided in new ABS contracts, where the parties seek to create a functional ABS contract.

For the ABS contract being negotiated in a special "non-commercial or exempt" user situation, a contractual change-of-use clause appears essential. In drafting such a clause, the parties must be aware of the basic theme of this Chapter: the need to be specific and concrete in drafting. Thus, the special use provisions should attempt to focus only on concrete, observable actions and conditions. For example, the contract must be very specific in stating which particular research activities that are included within the exemption – *e.g.*, which actions that are considered "non-commercial,"[183] and which will be deemed "commercial activities."

It may also be necessary for the contract to address the more difficult question of oversight. Unless the user has some other specific motivation to comply with the "no-change-of-use-without-permission" provision, it will be difficult for the provider to have any confidence that the user will satisfy these obligations. It would appear that there are only two primary ways for a provider to increase the likelihood of compliance and/or enhance enforceability of such a provision:

- First, appropriate amendments to the draft contract may create some motivational interest for the non-commercial user – in essence giving that user a long-term reason to support and foster the provider's interest.
- Second, depending on the nature of the resources transferred and of the proposed uses, the contract could also state that the non-commercial user will be personally liable for a specified sum. This could apply in the event that the genetic resources or ATK comes to be used in the development of any commercial application or any action apart from those specifically permitted. The contract should include an obligation on the non-commercial user to ensure that the full commercial-use ABS process be undertaken by any person or entity with whom the genetic resources/ATK is shared. This second option may be rather draconian in some situations (*i.e.*, where there is already commercial research ongoing, *etc.*) and may be inappropriate or require significant modification to avoid being considered "unconscionable" (see ¶ 7.3.3).[184] A non-commercial contract should stipulate clear consequences for the non-commercial user if embarking on commercial uses.

183 It will also need to consider the possibility that the non-commercial user may wish to publish his results, or to discuss his work with some other person(s) from a facility that is not bound by the ABS contract. In order to avoid the possibility that the non-commercial user will transfer valuable information or specimens in a way that causes them to leave the provider's oversight, such activities should be allowed only after obtaining specific permission from the provider/provider country (see ¶ 5.7.2, *infra*, and Chapter 6.).

184 See also ¶ 4.4.

5.7.2 *Third-Party Transfers that Represent a Change of Use or Intent*

The concept of post-access transfer of genetic resources and/or ATK is generally discussed in Chapter 6, *infra.* The following sections briefly consider the situations in which such transfers represent not only a transfer, but also a change of use/intent. Two primary situations relevant to this issue are transfers by academic/non-commercial users and transfers by collections.

(a) Transfer by a Non-commercial or Academic User

Academic research is not only the most common type of non-commercial use, but also the most common example of post access transfers into commercial use. This section discusses five common situations in which an academic researcher or institution that is a party to the contract transfers samples or research results:

- The research institution transfers materials/publishes research subject to its pre-existing rules and regulations;
- The transfer occurs as part of an ongoing collaboration with a commercial actor;
- The institution enters into a new collaboration with a commercial partner;
- Researchers in the institution use their findings as basis for a start-up company;
- Researchers publish research results including genetic information (gene sequence or biochemical formula) or ATK.[185]

These situations give rise to a need for a transfer clause, as described in ¶¶ 6.3 and 6.4, *infra*, but also need to be considered with regard to the change of intent reflected by the transfer. The common factor of all five situations is their foreseeability. This means that they can be justifiably raised as issues that must be addressed in the negotiation of an ABS contract for academic or non-commercial research. To maximize concreteness, precision and control in the ABS contract, therefore, these issues must be carefully considered in the drafting of the core (*res* and obligation) clauses of the contract as well.

In the modern world, academic and other research activities face increasing funding difficulties. Given that the standard objective of most academic and other non-commercial research institutions is to find ways to use their research results to help fund their futures, their practices have had to evolve

185 Even if the researcher does not seek direct financial benefits, he will normally find it essential to publish his results (seeking professional or academic benefits), thereby enabling other institutions to utilize his discoveries (indirect transfer.).

in many ways. In particular, when a researcher finds or stumbles on a valuable genetic or biochemical characteristic, he will often contact a commercial R&D institution or company, as a way of converting that discovery into financial support for himself or his institution. This practice is so common that it has become institutionalized in many countries.[186] In the current financial climate, academic institutions seldom have solely non-commercial goals for their research activities. Increasingly, students and other non-commercial researchers are confronted with demands that they sign documents regulating the terms and conditions for ownership and property rights in the case of commercialization.

Academic institutions sometimes have funding agreements with commercial actors, through which the latter sponsor research as part of a social program with no strings attached. More often, however, a sponsorship is linked to an expectation from the company to get something back in respect of a research result or a lead towards a product. The commercial partner will typically have an interest in having access to the results from the apparently non-commercial academic research. The academic institution may choose not to publicize such ongoing collaborations with commercial actors, and may choose not to provide this information in the negotiation of an ABS arrangement. These public-private partnerships in research are blurring the sharp line between non-commercial and commercial research and development.[187] Where an academic institution began its relationship as a pure non-commercial actor, its motivation might change for a variety of reasons.

---

186 Many academic institutions have rules and regulations for commercialization of their research findings. One example is the US "Bayh-Dole Act," which mandates that universities patent and commercialize academic research conducted with federal funding. Under the Bayh-Dole Act, universities retain ownership of inventions made under federally funded research, but are expected to file patents and to ensure commercialization upon licensing. Following the enactment of Bayh-Dole, the number of patents obtained by US universities went from approximately 250/year in 1980 to nearly 3100/year in 2009. The trend is so widespread that it is now common practice for universities to have their own patent departments. The research council of Norway, for example, now requires from each applicant for project funding an estimate of the number of patents the project expects, to be reported as well in the final report of the project.

187 For a number of commercially successful start-up companies, the basic commercial idea on which they were founded stems from non-commercial, academic research, sometimes by the same persons who have founded the start-up company. A researcher who starts out with pure academic motivation for his or her research can change his or her strategy when research discloses a valuable lead towards a product or a process.

The prevalence of these practices in the ABS context may have a major impact on the likelihood that provider countries will be willing to grant exemptions for non-commercial and academic users at all. They also represent critical issues that must be recognized in the drafting and negotiation of ABS contracts for academic and other non-commercial research. For this reason, when entering into an ABS contract with an academic institution the provider should investigate whether any such agreement exists that could apply to the *res* or obligations of the ABS contract. (Or one could include a guarantee from the user on this point.) This investigation could have a major impact on the resulting ABS contract. For example, it might appear necessary for the contract to bind not only the researcher, but also the academic institution supporting him, and even possibly the commercial organization that is supporting that institution, in order to have "named the right parties" as described in Chapter 4, *supra*. The core contractual provisions must also be reconsidered (see ¶¶ 5.3–5.5). Recalling that researchers often have little ability to make up front payments or to guarantee later benefit-sharing obligations, it may be necessary to find other ways to restructure the ABS agreement. One such restructuring tool would be to limit the *res* to ensure that it only addresses specified activities. Another tool would be to include monitoring requirements. A third tool might involve revising the benefit-sharing commitment entirely, so that it does not unduly impair academic/commercial research, but also does not allow these researchers to deprive providers of benefit-sharing from commercial activities. Finally, of course, these challenges could lead to a greater contractual attention to strengthening controls and oversight regarding transfers (Chapter 6).

(b) Transfer from a Collection

The discussions relating to academic and non-commercial users have often been stretched to include genetic resources held in collections (herbaria, botanical gardens, zoos, spermbanks *etc*). The primary difference between collections and the institutions described under heading (a), above, is the justified perception that for many collections, the institution's *raison d'être* revolves around providing samples and access to other persons and entities.[188] Even a

188 For example, the CGIAR collections are almost entirely focused on this objective. According to a database that has since been removed from the internet, most of the material in these collections was obtained from persons who were undertaking research in foreign countries, but provided samples to the collection. There is no indication that such researchers even informed the provider country or community, much less obtained its permission or approval, before placing their samples in the collection.

collection that is primarily focused on conserving biodiversity and/or enabling non-commercial research may find it difficult to distinguish between commercial and non-commercial users. Such institutions, too, are facing a decline in traditional sources of funding and recognize the need to obtain some funds by enabling access for outside users, and even preparing and providing samples for them. Thus, according to the EU Commission (in a report issued during the development of its regulation on ABS), a high percentage of the material used in European biotechnology companies has been found in a collections rather than directly collected by the user in a provider country.

Clearly, one cannot assume that a collection has no commercial intentions and objectives when accessing genetic resources. This, however, is generally an issue of greater relevance to national legislation, rather than to contract. If a collection is entering into a contract, then the rules and provisions described in this book will apply, and the manner in which the collection transfers samples, and the entities to which those transfers are made can be addressed through the negotiations, as discussed below.

Given the expectation that any collection will provide third parties with access to all of its specimens, the contractual solutions for ABS agreements with collections are significantly different than a provider might consider in the situations described under (a), above. Although every collection's situation and desires are potentially different, there are already examples of generic models for ABS contracts with collections.[189] The authors are not comfortable recommending any of these as fully functional models for ABS contracts. It may be useful, however, to consider a few of the many challenges arising with respect to these documents, to demonstrate the transfer/change of use issues that need to be considered in the course of any ABS negotiation with a collection.

For purposes of this section's discussion of change of intent, a key challenge in any contract based on specialized use or exemption is the need to limit the scope of the access granted. Many users support the approach of either specifically listing the permitted uses or specifically explaining which uses are not permitted. Thus, for example, The Swiss Academy of sciences has prepared a model that states the users rights in primarily terms of the kinds of uses that are not allowed:

189 Two examples are the ITPGRFA's SMTA (briefly discussed in ¶ 11.3, *infra*, and mentioned in many other contexts throughout this book) and the Swiss Academy of Sciences document entitled "Agreement on Access and Benefit Sharing for Non-Commercial Research: Sector specific approach containing Model Clauses" (available online at http://www.naturalsciences.ch/organisations/biodiversity/abs/publications/36817-sample-abs-agreement-for-non-commercial-research-2010.) The SMTA is not an appropriate example

> The User shall not use the Genetic Resource nor derivatives generated in the research for any commercial purposes, nor shall the User commercialize any Product derived from the Genetic Resource, unless with the written consent of the Provider.
>
> The User is obliged to take all reasonable precautions to prevent the Genetic Resource coming into the possession of any Unauthorized Person.
>
> The User is obliged to inform the Provider about any unforeseen research results that are of potential commercial interest, prior to any disclosure of this information to the public.[190]

By contrast, the SMTA defines the "Recipient's" (user's) activities initially in terms of what is included, followed by a listing of some types of uses that are not included:

> The **Recipient** undertakes that the **Material** shall be used or conserved only for the purposes of research, breeding and training for food and agriculture. Such purposes shall not include chemical, pharmaceutical and/ or other non-food/feed industrial uses.[191]

Both of these provisions are basically rendered unenforceable by many factors. Initially, in both cases the terms used are ambiguous, and either undefined or rely on the vague and ambiguous language of the NP. Secondly, of course, both clauses specify obligations that cannot be externally verified. The only party who can know whether the user/recipient is in compliance is the user/ recipient. In addition, the application of the most basic rules of contractual interpretation would make it clear that these terms are internally inconsistent, and inconsistent with the stated objective of their respective contracts.[192] For purposes of addressing the change of use/intent issue, it is vital to ensure that the recipient/user's activities are limited, but also to ensure that those limits

---

for this chapter, because it is essentially a contract between a middleman that has no contract with the provider and a Third-party user. The Swiss Academy document provides a classic example of a contract that appears to assume that the NP is binding on parties to ABS contracts, using NP terms and definitions. Both of these instruments contain major flaws that may render them unenforceable and possibly even void as contracts, even in the courts of the countries in which they were developed. They patently do not conform to the rules described in this book.

190 Swiss Academy, *ibid.,* at p. 21.

191 ITPGRFA SMTA, Art. 6.1.

192 For example, by stating that "research, breeding and training" are allowed when these actions are taken for food and agriculture, the ITPGR SMTA creates many open questions,

prevent him from later transfers that give his transferee more rights/abilities than the original user/recipient had. The creation of a concrete, specific and externally verifiable description of the uses allowed and/or those that are not allowed is an important first step in this process.

The second drafting challenge in regard to transfers that involve changes of intent is, obviously, the need to address transfers. While this issue is primarily addressed in Chapter 6, it is useful to reiterate here that, where change of intent is a possibility, any restriction on transfer must also integrate with the limitation of the *res* and of the rights and duties granted to the user. It is critical to determine in the initial contract with the collection how the subsequent transferee will be bound to the ABS contract, and what penalties or other consequences will apply, in the event that a transfer is undertaken that violates these requirements.

As a final comment on collections, it is worth noting that both provider and collection could theoretically benefit if they viewed their relationship as a mutually supportive partnership. To the extent that collections view themselves as acting in concert with users and potentially adversaries of providers, the tensions that are limiting access to genetic resources will continue. Not only is this a negative consequence for collections, but it cuts providers off from a potentially valuable ally in the identification of and negotiation with commercial and other users.

---

including the following: Would breeding for biofuel be allowed? Are the stated areas of permission and prohibition the only ones, or does the principle of *ejusdem generis* apply? When one starts to list specific allowed or prohibited activities, it is important to be clear about whether the list is exemplar or definitive. It is also very difficult to get a court to rule on a prohibition of any specific use.

CHAPTER 6

"Manage and Address Major Risks": The Third-party Transfer Challenge

This chapter deals with a question that is potential an issue in virtually all ABS contract situations: "third-party transfer". This means the possibility that, after the contract is drafted and executed, a party to the contract might transfer key resources, rights and obligations to a person or entity that is not previously bound by the contract and unrelated to the current parties. In the ABS context, this possibility presents challenges that have sometimes been thought to be virtually un-solvable. This chapter addresses these issues and considers some possible contract-based approaches that solve them, at least in part.

Only a few ABS contracts have not experienced some kind of post access transfer of genetic resources or ATK. In those contracts, the original "user" accessed the genetic material or ATK and directly used it in the development and production of a final product that was eventually commercialized. Such situations are rare. In most ABS contracts the user that originally obtains access will transfer of genetic resources or ATK to some other person or entity at some point in the development/production process. Thus, the third-party challenge is an issue of concern in virtually all ABS negotiations.

In negotiating and drafting an ABS contract, it is always necessary to address in some way the possibility that a party may attempt to sell or otherwise transfer the genetic resources, ATK and/or rights or duties under the ABS contract. This possibility may have multiple impacts on the contract's provisions. In addition to a specific clause regarding such transfer, negotiators and draftsmen should also carefully consider to address impact of such transfer possibility on other clauses of the contract. The greatest potential impact will normally be on the identification and binding of the parties (discussed in Chapter 4); the clauses that define the res, clarify contract objectives and set the obligations and rights of the parties (discussed in Chapter 5); the clauses that discuss the possibility of amending the contract (¶ 6.5); and those that allocate the duty to comply with national legislative requirements (including the question of whether a new or amended PIC and/or MAT may be required). The following sections address these transfer and amendment issues and the particular concerns they create in the context of ABS contracts.

In addressing third-party transfers, the ABS contract's negotiators must integrate many of the topics discussed in the previous chapter on the *res* of the contract, as well as the primary concepts discussed in that Chapter. It begins,

 | DOI 10.1163/9789004356573_007

in ¶ 6.1 with an overview of the third-party transfer challenge. In ¶ 6.2, the authors seek to provide an insight into the consequences that may result if the ABS contract does not satisfactorily address the transfer issue. Section 6.3 then discusses how the parties should find an answer to the key question – Should this contract even attempt to include a third-party transfer clause? Thereafter, ¶ 6.4 discusses some of the key elements to address if the parties decide to adopt such a clause; ¶ 6.5 offers some direct assistance with drafting such clauses and advice on how to apply them; and ¶ 6.6 addresses special types of transfer (bankruptcy, corporate restructuring, *etc.*)

6.1 The Transfer of Genetic Resources, ATK or Preliminary Research Results to Third Parties

As discussed in detail in Chapter 4, it is essential to include all of the "necessary parties" as parties to an ABS contract, because the contract will bind only parties that are specifically included. Normally,[193] if the parties expect someone who is not a party to take action, pay money, hold/utilize the genetic resource or pay the benefit share, then they can only hope that the non-party will act voluntarily – he will not be legally obligated to do so. In other commercial contexts, it is common for the contract to specifically state what will happen to the contract and/or which party bears the risk, in the even that such an un-bound party fails to do as expected.[194]

The impact of un-bound persons on ABS contracts constitutes an important limitation affecting those contracts in many ways. ABS research and development activities often involve the transfer of research materials (specific

193 In some cases, it might be possible to bring a lawsuit against the person and compel him to comply, but such lawsuits are rare, expensive and unpredictable. This book focuses on creating precise, predictable legal obligations that all parties will recognize as binding and enforceable.

194 For example, the government is sometimes not a party to an ABS contract (*e.g.*, where the law gives "provider" status directly to individual landowners, local residents and/or indigenous communities, authorizing them to negotiate ABS contracts for themselves, without oversight.) In those situations, national legislation might require specific compliance with other national actions (PIC, MAT, and/or permit/certificate issuance) as a prerequisite to any activities covered by national ABS law. Although the government is not a party to the ABS contract, that contract is built on the assumption that the required government actions will be taken. The negotiators/drafters should address the possibility that the needed government approvals will be delayed or denied, explaining what will happen to the contract in detail.

genetic resources, ATK and other information.) Employees of user entities may have a long history of sharing specimens, samples, interim research and other information through informal transfers between researchers. When a company obtains genetic resources or ATK under an ABS contract, its employees and other researchers might assume that they can share those resources in this way, without concern for the company's contractual responsibilities. ABS contracts are thus intensely affected by the general practices among researchers and commercial entities working in biotechnology-related industries.

Unfortunately, persons who receive such informally transferred resources are usually not parties to the ABS contract. Many companies have a standard practice of allowing and not overseeing informal transfers by their employees and researchers. This means that neither the company that obtained the genetic resources/ATK under an ABS contract nor the company whose researcher receives those resources will engage in any monitoring of its researchers or such transfers. As a result, the resources can often find their way into the hands of a "third party" – a person or company who is not bound by that ABS contract. The ABS challenge arises where that third party feels that he is permitted to use the transferred material or information in a way that the transferor could not – to take actions without complying with the ABS contract.

As noted above, this situation is so common in ABS that it is rare to find any ABS transaction in which some type of third-party transfer has not occurred after the initial collection/access. Around the world, it is generally recognized that such transfers present a problem that was not solved by the NP, but still requires a solution. Therefore, the solution must be contractual. Each ABS contract must actively find solutions for regulating the transfer in a manner that adequately binds the new user.

In ABS contracts, there are few ways to controls third-party transfers effectively. This fact has led to criticism from many providers, stating that a solution is urgently needed. In some other strata, however, ABS is roundly criticized for the opposite reasons. In the realm of botanical and zoological collections, herbaria and genebanks (including CGIAR collections), for example, two very different primary complaints are levelled against ABS. First, they argue that ABS "may prevent" post collection transfers, block or reduce access and transfer of genetic resources for research and development purposes.[195] Some of these commentators have claimed that the facilitation of these activities is the *raison d'être* of their collections and the instruments establishing them.[196]

195 Schloen, *et al.*, 2011.

196 The ITPGRFA, for example, created its "Multilateral System of Access and Benefit-sharing" (MLS) for the express purpose of creating an "efficient, effective, and transparent [means],

Although the authors recognize that many collections are founded for very different reasons, even those collections generally focus on providing access to third parties in some way.[197]

The contractual challenge in addressing post-access third-party transfers in ABS contracts is to find ways to control and oversee transfers that are reasonable and externally verifiable, and do not negatively affect the benefit-sharing and other rights and obligations in the contract. The external verification aspect is especially difficult, because the transferee may not be known or disclosed to the provider. The provider might not even have any way to know whether a transfer has occurred at all. Transfers of the contract's genetic resources or ATK may have a profound impact on an ABS contract, affecting the intentions of the parties, the ability of the contract to achieve its objectives and its intended results. Such a transfer can have a significant practical impact on the ability of the provider to obtain performance, including benefit-sharing, under the contract.

Despite the fact that the third-party situation is both common and challenging in all ABS contracts, neither the NP nor the CBD have addressed this topic in any manner that is useful to the parties to an ABS contract.[198] Even international sources do not provide any clear solutions to this challenging situation.[199] The issue takes on greater importance and difficulty in ABS, both because it affects the ultimate achievement of the contract's objective (fair and

both to facilitate access to plant genetic resources for food and agriculture, and to share, in a fair and equitable way, the benefits arising from the utilization of these resources, on a complementary and mutually reinforcing basis." ITPGRFA, Art.10.2. The CGIAR collections are also established by of international instruments, although party oversight of the collections is less intense.

197 See ¶ 5.7.2(b), *supra*.

198 The nearest either instrument comes to the point is where the CBD calls on user-side States to take measures "with the aim of sharing in a fair and equitable way" (CBD Art 15.7) rather than specifically requiring measures to require users to meet their obligations ABS arrangements. Similarly, rather than requiring that user countries enforce ABS contracts, the NP's benefit-sharing clause specifically states that "benefits arising from the utilization of genetic resources as well as subsequent applications and commercialization shall be shared in a fair and equitable way with the Party providing such resources that is the country of origin of such resources or a Party that has acquired the genetic resources in accordance with the Convention" (NP, Art 5.1). Presumably, these mandates include an obligation to prevent the user from evading ABS through the use of third-party transfers, but even so, neither instrument provides any guidance on how to do this.

199 The law on transfer of contractual rights and on the enforceability of contractual restrictions on transfer of any asset is well established in most countries, with regard to domestic contracts and transfers between persons/entities within a single country. Although

equitable utilization and benefit-sharing) and because one party (the provider) has little or no way to determine if any transfer has occurred.

In other contracts, there are many types of clauses and approaches to address the transfer of contractual obligations to third parties who are not bound by the initial contract. Those "standard" transfer clauses and approaches are often complex. In general, they rely on factors that externalize the evidence of transfer. Such factors are not applicable within the ABS system. None of these approaches provides a functional solution for ABS situations. For example, the transfer clause may often require the transferor and transferee to notify the other contract parties, in order for the transfer to be effective. In an ABS transfer, there is little actual inducement for the user and transferee to do this. The provider has little or no way to monitor such transfers, and even if he found out about the transfer he might not be financially or practically able to take action. The only incentive for users and transferees to give the notice would be their desire to comply with the contract provision. In legal terms, we would say that this kind of provision relies on "self-reporting" by the user and transferee. Contract professionals generally agree that it is important to avoid creating or relying on self-reporting situations. The generally recommended alternative is to set up the contract in a way that carefully addresses transfers, while giving all parties an independent means of confirming compliance and/or an independent ongoing motivation or incentive to comply.

6.2 Laws and Consequences Regarding Transfers of Resources and Rights

A transfer of the *res* to a third party may often prevent any future operation of the contract, unless the contract addresses the possibility of transfer. If the third-party transferee is not subsequently bound by the contract then the other parties may not rely on him to fulfil the transferor's obligations. If the transferor also believes that the transfer effectively terminates his obligations, then nobody will fulfil those obligations. Under an ABS contract, the transfer by a user to a transferee could mean that the provider may not be able to obtain performance of any user obligations that are not yet fulfilled.

ABS contractual transfer issues are still not easy to address where these laws apply, the general commercial laws have been designed to give parties a degree of certainty regarding the transfer issue, and the manner in which it arises in conventional contracts.

6.2.1 *Contract Law on Transfers*

Unfortunately, most countries' national legal systems are designed to promote and support reasonable commerce, and therefore to encourage more transactions. As a result national law is often designed in a way that prevents any party from limiting other parties' right to sell or otherwise transfer any valuable property or right they possess. The countries' goal is to preserve the right of any person to freely sell his own property and rights. In addition, countries have a strong desire to ensure that the parties do not need to constantly turn to the courts for solutions. These laws are usually expressed as a series of presumptions about what is reasonable in commercial life. In essence, one may freely sell or transfer anything he owns, unless there is a specific legal reason why he cannot. As with any general presumption, most countries' law and policy include specific exceptions to this presumption, as well as specific laws that prohibit or regulate transfers of certain types of assets.

To promote free transferability, most national courts and commercial practices impose practical and legal rules that limit the extent to which any party can be prevented from selling or otherwise transferring any asset, right or obligation it possesses. These rules add legal challenges to drafting contractual clauses relating to third-party transfer; however, as noted above, the most significant transfer challenges for ABS are practical. The following is an extreme simplification/generalization of the law regarding transfers of contractual rights and duties.[200] It is offered in the hope that it will provide sufficient guidance to the negotiators and drafters in the initial stages of negotiating an ABS contract.

Normally, the law interprets contractual transfers with two assumptions: First, when a party transfers his right to receive payment of money or other specific value, the transferee automatically replaces the transferor in the contract. When a party transfers his contractual obligation, however, that transfer is only a contract between transferor and transferee. The transferor will continue to be obligated under the original contract, unless all parties to that original contract agree to substitute the transferee for the transferor.[201] Thus a transfer of obligations may sometimes lead to automatic substitution of the transferor, but not always.

If the contract is silent on transfer questions, these rules apply and transfers may be considered to substitute the transferee as a party to the contract "by operation of law," even if no specific change has been made by the parties.[202]

200 This paragraph simplifies the basic contract law principles (which become very complex in regard to litigation) into a "basic rule of thumb" for writing contracts that hope to avoid any need for future complex litigation.

201 See Furmston, 2001.

202 *Ibid*, at 580.

In such cases, a court may note the behavior of the other parties to the original contract to prove that they have accepted the transferee.[203]

Where the contract includes specific transfer clauses and procedures, however, those provisions will govern the transfer unless they are ambiguous or illegal. A transfer notification or amendment will usually not be legally effective unless it is in writing.

Although the above summary reflects the practices of many countries, it may not be universal. National law and practice on these questions may vary and should be investigated with regard to the primary national jurisdictions involved in the initial contract.[204]

6.2.2 *Application to ABS Contracts*

In conventional contracts, the easiest approach to the transferability issue is to carefully design the contract, limiting its *res* to something that cannot be transferred. In ABS, this would call on the contract draftsmen to ensure that the contract grants the user only a limited interest in the genetic resource or ATK – an interest that is intended to be personal or non-transferable. As explained in ¶¶ 6.3 and 6.4, such a provision will not eliminate the possibility of transfer, but it will make it clear that transfer is subject to the approval of the parties. Even if it specifies that the *res* and/or the contractual rights or obligations are non-transferable, an ABS contract will still need a transfer clause to address the impacts of permitted and unpermitted transfers. Such a clause will not be automatically effective, however, unless the parties can find ways to address the many practical challenges discussed below.

To date, the authors have not yet seen any ABS contracts in which providers attempted to assign or transfer their right to receive payment. Our only experience with transfers have involved the user's rights to undertake research and/or development. In ABS contracts, the user's rights and duties are inextricably linked to the genetic resources and ATK and to the results of research and/or development activities. This means that most ABS transfers, even if only samples or information is transferred, are actually transfers of the user's rights and duties as well.

In most ABS situations, a user may be considered to be trying to transfer his rights and duties any time he transfers all or any part of the genetic resources or ATK. Unless the contract states otherwise, however, he cannot be

203 *Ibid.*

204 At a minimum these would include all countries with jurisdiction over any user or provider, the country whose law is designated as the contract's "governing law" if different, and any country with jurisdiction over probable transferees, if known.

legally released from those obligations, unless the other parties agree to amend and re-form the contract to substitute the transferee for the user. Such amendments are sometimes called "novations."

6.3 Assessing the Parties' Options Regarding Third-party Transfer

In dealing with transfer in an ABS contract, the negotiators/drafters have the same three basic options as any parties to a conventional contract: the contract can be silent; it can call for or mandate termination[205] (with specific liquidated damages[206]) in the event of a transfer; or, it can include one or more other clauses directly addressing/regulating transfer. As with any such situation, the parties must balance the risks and benefits of these options. For each option, there are four key points to consider:

(i) The obligations of the original user (and whether they would apply to him even after transfer, or would be legally considered to pass to the transferee);
(ii) The availability and practicality of enforcement in the case of a non-permitted transfer;
(iii) The extent to which a provider would find out about a transfer from a source other than the original user; and
(iv) The extent to which the contract can provide an incentive or motivation to for the initial user and any third-party transferee to comply with a third-party transfer clause.

The following sections provide an overview of the risks and benefits and all of these factors, as applied to each of the three options. Given that most transfers are by users, this overview is stated from the provider's perspective.

6.3.1 *The Silence Option*

The first option – that the contract should remain silent on the topic of transfer – is the most uncertain, legally speaking, of the three basic options. If a court were faced with the question of whether a transfer is permitted under a contract that is silent on the topic, it would probably allow the transfer, and might also release the transferring party from all remaining obligations (depending on other clauses in the contract.)

205 Discussed in more detail in ¶¶ 6.3 and 6.5.1.

206 See ¶ 8.3.4, *infra*.

Applying the four factors listed above to the silence option yields different results in different situations. First and most important, the provider must determine whether the initial user's obligations are stated in such a way that the user would remain liable even if the resource is transferred. If so, then silence may be a workable solution.

Second, however, the enforcement question (discussed in more detail in Chapter 7) analyzes whether the user's obligations require costly legal action to enforce them in the event of a breach? If so, this fact may counterbalance the first point's advantage, unless the initial user maintains significant operations or assets in the provider's country.

The third factor – the provider's ability to know when/if a transfer has occurred – is discussed in more detail below. If the provider cannot expect to find out whether a transfer has taken place, what is the value of a transfer clause? This may indicate a need for a different approach to the overall issue.

Finally, regarding motivation, a party will comply with his obligations under a contract, if sufficiently motivated to do so. If the contract does not provide such a motivation, then he might balance costs and benefits, in order to determine whether to comply. Motivation is a practical matter – a dynamic and possibly unstated element of the contract. Does the user have a strong practical incentive or motivation that causes him to believe that compliance with the contract will be easier, less problematic and more beneficial than avoidance of the contract would be? If so, then he will be prevented from engaging in such a transfer by self-interest – the best mechanism – and there may be less need for a transfer clause.

6.3.2 *Termination-on-Transfer*

In many ABS negotiations, the providers start out with the idea that they can solve the transfer problem with a clause that terminates the contract upon transfer (discussed in more detail in ¶ 5.5.1 and Chapter 7). Termination of the contract, however, would terminate the obligations of the original user. Hence a termination-on-transfer clause can only be positive if other changes are also made.[207] Thus, this option is not as simple as some may think.

For example, the first evaluation factor (the contents of the obligation clause) will determine whether and how the provider could enforce other requirements, such as a liquidation of damages clause, in the case of a transfer.

207 For example, in some cases, a termination clause could be effective if the contract imposes a strict "liquidated damages" clause that would be triggered on termination, and then, only if the satisfaction of that clause is a prerequisite to (or survives) termination (see ¶ 8.3.4, *infra.*)

As above, if the provider does not have a reliable way to find out about a transfer from a source other than the original user, the existence of a termination clause, even if supported by liquidated damages may mean nothing in the event of a willful attempt to transfer the resources without notice to the provider.

As for the second factor (availability/ease of enforcement), a key question is whether the users has operations or substantial assets within the provider's country. If not, even a clear right of enforcement will not produce a benefit.

If there is a way for the contract can provide an incentive or motivation to comply with a third-party transfer clause, then the termination and liquidation clauses must be closely integrated with the elements that provide that incentive/motivation. In ¶¶ 6.5, 6.6 and 8.3, *infra*, this book includes additional advice that may be useful in the drafting and implementation of termination-on-transfer clauses.

6.3.3 *The Use of a "Transfer Clause"*

The third option is the insertion of a clause that regulates transfer without terminating the contract. For most contracts, the best approach to the transfer issue is a clause that allows transfers, but only if the transferring party meets certain requirements and with certain specific obligations on him. The parties would be well advised, however, to apply this section's four-element analysis before adopting this approach. Such an analysis will not only help determine whether how the contract should address transfer, but also what types of activities the transfer clause should include.

Regarding the first key point of analysis, the transfer clause must make clear to the user exactly how a permitted transfer will affect the rights and obligations of the original user and all other parties to the ABS contract. It must not only state whether and/or how the initial user is released from his obligations after transfer, but must clearly explain the legal basis of his future obligation and/or liability. These issues are discussed in detail in ¶ 6.5, *infra*.

The second analytical point (availability and practicality of enforcement) is also affected by the drafting of the transfer clause. If the initial user is to have continuing obligations, those obligations must also be tied to some mechanism for asserting and enforcing that liability. Under this heading, it is also relevant to consider what rights, if any, the provider might have against the transferee, in the event of a transfer in violation of the transfer clause. Although mentioned in ¶¶ 6.4 and 6.5, *infra*, these issues are more specifically discussed in Chapters 7 and 9, *infra*.

Unfortunately, even the best-drafted transfer clause does not eliminate the provider's most difficult necessity – the need to maintain vigilance so that he can find out about a transfer from a source other than the original user (analysis point iii.) The individual circumstances of the particular transaction may indicate a greater or lesser level of concern with regard to this issue.

Finally (analysis point iv), as noted above, the primary force that instigates contractual compliance by any user entity is its own evaluation of the costs/benefits of compliance *vs* the costs/benefits of non-compliance. Any transfer-regulating clause must be drafted keeping this issue in mind, and in coordination with the other clauses that work together to concretely motivate all parties to comply with the ABS contract. Although they are critical to the drafting process, these factors are individual to each situation, and form a special element of the overall contract process. As such they are addressed in Chapters 7, 8 and 9, *infra*.

6.4 Key Legal Elements of a Transfer Clause

As noted in ¶¶ 6.1 and 6.2, *supra*, most countries' systems of commercial/contract law are intended to promote and encourage transactions. As such, they usually prefer to support each person/entity's right to transfer assets, rights and/or duties that he has legally obtained under a contract. An entire commercial area has grown up around the practice of obtaining contracts or permits relating to certain types of commercial activity, and then selling them to others who will go forward and develop those opportunities into fully functional commercial activities or entities.[208] This means that, in legal forums, there is a basic preference in favor of allowing transfers, whenever the issue is in doubt. In common practice, however, there are many exceptions to this basic preference. Many types of transfer restrictions are commonly included in conventional contracts and enforced by the courts. These examples may be particularly useful in drafting ABS contracts.

In general, acceptable transfer restrictions often are based on the premise that the parties do not oppose the entire concept of transfer, but want to retain certain rights. Among the rights retained are the following: the right to control and/or approve which person or entity the right or asset is transferred to; the

208 A common example involves a person or entity that obtains real property (by purchase or lease, or by obtaining an option to purchase) and then invests the money, time and effort needed to get development permits and other contractual preparations, after which he sells the entire package (property, permits, *etc.*), which is the considered a "business opportunity" to a third party who will build the facility and put it into operation.

right to ensure that the transferee is properly bound by the contract; and (in some cases) the right to ensure that the transferor is not released from liability.

In ABS contracts, however, there is a second level of possible restrictions as well. The national law of the provider country may include specific limits or standards regarding the transfer of required ABS permits or other instruments (in ABS, the PIC, MAT, ABS contract, or IRCC.) These laws may limit who may hold the user's interests as well as possibly imposing additional requirements at the time of transfer.[209]

The decision to include a transfer limitation clause is not automatic, however, and even where the parties decide to include such a clause, its effectiveness is not assured. The drafting process presents several critical challenges, not only of legality and functionality, but also of expectations. If a provider's rights under a contract are dependent on the other parties' compliance with a third-party transfer clause, it is important for the provider to remain aware of that dependence. He should not expect performance to happen smoothly based on the existence of a third-party transfer clause. In all contracts, where a party who relaxes his vigilance and oversight because he thinks the contract protects him, he vastly increases the chance that he might lose opportunities to assert his rights, identify breaches, or take other action at a time when something can still be done. By the time he awakens, he may have no option left to protect himself against these losses.

There are generally three legally recognized justifications underlying a contractual party's ability to limit the transfer of the other party's contractual rights: (i) that the transferee (also known as the "successor" to the transferring party) is at least equally capable of performing the transferred duties as the transferring party would be; (ii) that the transferee is equally worthy of receiving the rights granted; and/or (iii) that the non-transferring party is not in a worse position after the transfer, including with regard to guarantees and remedies. Although the parties to a particular transaction may have other

---

209 A clause in the contract or permit process will often formal describe the prerequisites for transfer and whether the transferring party will continue to be bound by the contract and/or responsible for performance of the contract after the transfer is complete. This is a critical underlying issue that must be considered in all transfer situations. The release of the transferor from contractual or permit obligations would change the balance in the original contract. Where one of the parties to the original contract was required to provide guarantees, or otherwise take actions to ensure that the other party will be properly compensated under the contract/permit, the non-transferring party may have a keen interest in ensuring that those protections remain valid and in-place.

concerns, these three items are the basic legal elements that most courts use to determine if a limit on transfer is permitted. Thus, in drafting the contract, it is best to present all transfer restrictions in these terms.

These basic points justify the provider's *right* to limit post-contract transfers, but they do not give any mechanism or other indication of *how* to do it. That practical question gives rise to a number of key points for the parties to consider, including the following:

(a) The inadvisability, in most cases, of a clause which terminates the contract on transfer (see ¶ 6.3.2, *supra*);
(b) The transferee's relationship with the original ABS contract;
(c) The manner in which the contract addresses/describes the transfer of genetic resources or ATK;
(d) The manner in which the contract addresses/describes the transfer of genetic resources or ATK; and
(e) The common practice among researchers of "casual sharing" of samples and interim data.

There are not, as yet, any agreed or "standard" solutions to the transfer issue in the ABS context. Although some particular language is offered in ¶ 6.5, *infra*, the text of final transfer clauses will vary greatly from transaction to transaction.

In contract practice, there are very few "self-executing" provisions (clauses that operate automatically without action or assertion by one or more parties). ABS contracts, perhaps more than others, require constant awareness, monitoring and communication. Inserting a transfer clause does not solve the transfer problem; it merely gives the provider guidance on one aspect of his awareness and monitoring with regard to transfer issues. The following sections offer brief discussions of particular issues of concern that arise when trying to develop and/or implement a clause that regulates post-execution transfer in an ABS contract.

6.4.1 *Does/Should Transfer Terminate the Contract?*

As noted in ¶ 6.3.2, *supra*, some negotiators have sometimes viewed "termination on transfer" as an easy solution to the transfer problem. Rarely, however, does this type of clause provide the simple result these parties anticipate. The ABS contract creates and defines the legally enforceable relationship between the provider and the user. Thus, a clause that automatically terminates the contract eliminates that relationship, depriving the provider of contractual remedies. His only remaining option is legally uncertain – attempting to enforce the provider-country's national ABS laws against the user.[210] This is the primary reason that the authors have recommended that ABS contract parties should avoid automatic termination-on-transfer clauses. As noted above, in many situations, transfer of genetic resources or ATK may be a precursor to the realization of benefits from its utilization. Hence, the provider may not be best served by a clause that totally prohibits transfer. It may be better to allow transfers, subject to specific requirements.

In a few negotiations, the provider may feel that no transfer of the genetic resource/ATK and/or of the user's rights and duties should ever be allowed. In those situations, a flat prohibition of transfer or a "termination-on-transfer" clause is legally risky, in light of the fact, noted above, that most legal systems have a preference for transferability.[211] Instead of an out-and-out prohibition in these cases, a modified approach to the termination clause can be effective and useful. The transfer elements of this type of clause are basically the same as those discussed in ¶ 6.5. It is important to consider all aspects of the each termination situation – what actions give rise to termination; what rights and duties if any "survive" after termination; and respect for the fact that termination is a clause that may be asserted in many cases by any party to the contract.

6.4.2 *Approving the Transferee as a Party to the Original ABS Contract*

The basic legal question with regard to any transfer of a party's rights or duties under a contract is always the same: Does the transfer change the original contract between the original parties, or is it only a separate agreement between the transferor and transferee, leaving intact the transferor's duties under the original contract? The following discussion focuses on one aspect of that question – how to justify the decision of the non-transferring party to accept or reject the substitution of transferee into the original contract.

In many transfer situations, the transferee will be unknown to the provider. This is often tied to the user's hope to free himself from all remaining rights and obligations under the contract by transferring them away. In general contract law,

210 As discussed in Chapter 2, the ABS concept is so vague and ambiguous that it is essentially impossible to predict how, or whether, a court or arbitrator will take action under it.

211 The particular contents and use of termination clauses are discussed in more detail in Chapter 8. As noted, although essential, a termination clause is legally difficult, particularly in a contract that may be transferred to, or interpreted by, someone in another country. A provider's aggressive approach to the termination clause may bounce back against him, especially if the user should claim that the provider is not fulfilling some part of its obligations, and seek to terminate the contract.

this situation is clearly addressed. The contract may give the provider a right to evaluate the transferee, in order to determine whether he would be able to meet the original user's obligations to an appropriate standard. In general, this need to "pre-qualify" the transferee should involve the same level of investigation and documentation that is recommended in Chapter 4, with regard to the original parties.

The second element justifying a provider's concern with regard to a proposed transfer is expressed in terms of the transferee's "worthiness" – *i.e.*, whether he deserves to become a transferee. As a practical matter, however, it is more appropriate to consider this element as an evaluation of the contract with attention to whether any part of it was a special benefit to the transferor. If, for example, the original contract was negotiated with a person or company that had a long-standing relationship with the provider, it might include provisions that the provider would not be willing to give to a stranger. Similarly, in conventional contracts, the law sometimes recognizes that the *res* has a special importance to one party. For example, a man gives his great-grandfather's watch to his nephew, on the condition that the nephew may never sell this family heirloom (must either give it back or pass it along to the next heir.) This is a contract that controls transfer. The law often allows this type of special circumstance as a justification for restricting transfer. A similar justification may easily apply to the ATK of a traditional community, or even to genetic resources from lands or over which the community and/or country has special responsibilities.[212]

As discussed in more detail in ¶ 6.5, it is challenging to draft a provision regarding the right to investigate and approve a potential transferee – even more challenging than the task of pre-contract investigation of the original parties. Such a clause must enable these activities in an unknown and potentially unpredictable future situation. This issue is closely interlinked with the issue discussed in ¶ 6.4.3(b) regarding the transfer of duties – whether the transferee will become a party to the original ABS contract.

In many transfer situations, however, these legal capacity, personality and authority issues have not been addressed, or not addressed with the same diligence as in the original negotiation. This could result in the same problems as those described in earlier parts of Chapter 4. Therefore, one element in the transfer is that all the same questions regarding the parties to the contracts need to be dealt with.

212 In some countries, for example, national law forbids a foreign buyer from taking certain types of icons and cultural items (old or new) out of the country without a license. These laws are completely legal, and not even considered a restraint of trade.

In this connection, it is necessary eventually to come to a conclusion regarding the post-transfer situation. Specifically, once the transfer is completed, will the transfer simply be an agreement between the first user and the new user, leaving the original contract parties intact? Or will the transferee become substituted for the transferor, and thus a direct party to the transfer contract? It is also possible to merge the two, so that the transferee is added to the contract, but the transferor is not released. The transfer clause can choose one of these, or it may adopt them all as options, leaving the particular choice to be made at the time of the transfer. No matter what choice is made, the transfer clause should be as concrete and complete as possible, enabling the parties to establish a clear structure of rights and obligations following the transfer. At all events, the transfer clause must stipulate a precise and exact procedure to address any transfer, and particular consequences where transfers occur without following that procedure.

6.4.3 *Types of Transfers*

As noted in ¶ 6.2, transfers are relatively common in genetic resource research situations. (As noted, such transfers occur casually, presenting special concerns.) For the transfer clause to regulate or prevent transfer, it must be carefully and precisely drafted. In particular, it must clearly specify both the types of activity that constitute a transfer, and the manner in which a transfer is regulated. In this connection, it is possible (and sometimes essential) to deal with transfers of the genetic resource/ATK as a separate issue from transfers of the user's rights and obligations. The contract may also apply different requirements to different types of transfer. The next two sections discuss, first, transfers of the genetic resources and/or ATK and then transfers of the user's rights and/or obligations.

In both contexts, the negotiation and drafting of the transfer clause requires the same care in drafting as applies to the primary clauses of the contract. The clauses describing the resources, rights and duties covered by the contract and the clause describing the *res*, obligations and triggers (see ¶¶ 5.3–5.5, *supra*) are clearly relevant to and affected by the transfer clause. The added challenge of the transfer of clause, however, arises from difficulty faced by a provider, even if he tries to discover a post-access transfer. In some cases, such a transfer may be unknown to the user as well, because the actual transfer was an independent, informal action of the user's employees.

(a) Transfer of the Genetic Resource and/or ATK

Once genetic resources and/or ATK have been transferred to the user or middleman, the provider may lose all practical ability to monitor or track them.

Even where national ABS law requires the user to establish an operation in the provider country, and only utilize the genetic resource or ATK there, actual awareness of compliance by the provider is drastically limited. If the provider is non-governmental, its ability to monitor in such a situation would depend on a combination of contractual provisions allowing such monitoring and the provider's ability to enforce those rights, if necessary. This latter ability may depend on its ability to mobilize local law enforcement in support of monitoring where necessary. Even where the provider is governmental, such monitoring can only be effective when based on trust, on the users' motivation to comply, or on intensive full-time surveillance. In general, none of these options is particularly strong at present.

Another challenge in this connection relates to the character of the resources transferred. When a user or researcher transfers genetic resources or ATK, the actual material or information transferred may be very different from the material that user originally received. For example, the transfer may involve extracted or reproduced genetic material, research results, or data. By contrast, the primary clause in the ABS contract that describes the genetic resource or ATK covered by the contract may focus on the originally accessed material or knowledge. Clearly, any transfer clause may need to include a separate description of the kinds of material or data whose transfer is controlled under the clause.

This means that this aspect of the transfer restriction must meet two needs – one (relatively) simple and one difficult. The simple one involves determining who bears the risk of actions taken outside the knowledge of either party, where those actions function as a transfer under the contract. As noted elsewhere in this book,[213] such allocations of risk are common in conventional contracts, and present few added challenges in the ABS context.

The more difficult challenge, however, is the obvious one – how to ensure that the provider (and user) know whether a transfer has occurred. Although there are examples of relatively extreme solutions that might function, in the negotiation/ drafting stage, such solutions are often nearly impossible since the parties may not be able to agree on such aggressive measures.

(b) Transfer of the User's Contractual Rights and/or Duties

The drafting of a clause regulating the transfer of contractual rights and obligations involves issues that are quite different from the transfer of the *res*. Here also, in drafting transfer clauses, it may be necessary and/or appropriate

213 See Chapters 8 and 9.

to differentiate among various types of rights and duties that may or may not be transferred.

Three primary questions must be addressed in the negotiation and drafting of this aspect of the transfer clause: (i) whether and to what extent the transferee must or may become a party to the original contract; (ii) whether and to what extent the original party who is transferring his interest shall or may be released from future involvement in or obligations under the contract; and (iii) whether and to what extent the original contract must or may be amended in connection with the transfer.

6.4.4 *Casual Sharing/Transfer Issues*

As noted above, the common practice of casual sharing of genetic resources, research and ATK presents a particularly difficult challenge in ABS situations. Even the user company's officials may not be aware of the fact that its employees at the hands-on level (*e.g.*, R&D technicians) have a practice of "casually transferring" such resources. Such an employee may assuming that the materials used in the laboratory are the property of his employer, which he has always been allowed to share with colleagues from other companies. Thus, as he had done in pre-ABS days, he may inadvertently share material or information covered by the ABS contract's transfer restriction. The employer might not be aware of this type of casual sharing. In these very common situations, a contract clause stating that "no transfer of the genetic resources may occur without approval from the provider" might have no direct impact. The employees who do the sharing may not be aware of the restriction and their employer may not be aware of the sharing.

This type of casual sharing is also involved where professional researchers and other employees are allowed or encouraged to publish unusual findings in professional journals. Given that ATK, biochemical formulas and genetic data can often be transferred in text, in a manner sufficient to enable others to reproduce them, such publication could also constitute a transfer of genetic resources or ATK. In many cases, professional employees are given wide latitude to publish in professional journals, so long as the publication does not expose the employers' "trade secrets" (a term that may not encompass genetic resources and/or ATK). Similar situations arise where a researcher or institution has obtained a streamlined permission to access genetic resources or ATK for "research purposes" or "non-commercial" purposes. For most researchers, publication is the *sine qua non* of their work. Such publication is usually in a professional journal with a relatively high subscription cost. This means that only other professionals in companies and institutions in the same field will read it, essentially receiving a transfer of the genetic resource and/or

ATK without having any contact with either the researcher or the provider/provider-country.[214]

These unintentional transfers are an additional complication with regard to transfer of the *res* under an ABS contract. If such a user or collector is seeking to evade ABS responsibilities, it is currently difficult (perhaps impossible) to detect a transfer of those genetic resources or ATK or to backtrack the resulting products, research results or other benefits, to determine where the genetic resources or ATK were accessed.[215] As noted in ¶ 6.5, *infra*, there appear to be two primary mechanisms for dealing with the "casual transfer" situation. One would be for the contract to require all individual researchers or others within a user entity to sign an instrument agreeing to accept individual responsibility for any such transfer. The second would be to specifically allocate the financial risk of such transfer to one or more of the parties, regardless of how the transfer occurred. Neither of these, however, solves the basic vigilance problem (that the parties have little chance of knowing whether a transfer has occurred.)

6.5 Advice on Drafting Provisions Addressing Third-party Transfer

The lesson of Chapter 5 regarding the importance of precise drafting is clearly important to all aspects of the contract. When negotiating and drafting clauses directed at preventing or addressing future risks, however, other rules may be equally important. A "concrete" clause addressing a future risk may be so precise and specific that it excludes whatever risk actually arises. For example, if one makes a list of all possible types of actions that can be considered a "transfer," the parties, courts or arbitrators may later find that the list does not include a specific action taken by the user, so that the transfer clause will not apply to that action. In any contractual provision that is designed to address unknown future situations, while concreteness is important, flexibility in the sense of comprehensiveness is also important.

214 Case examples of this phenomenon in ABS situations are described in detail in Mgbeoji, 2005.

215 Given that the users of genetic resources or ATK are often working in countries that have not adopted user-side ABS legislative, administrative or other measures, there may be an additional problem. Under the user country's law, it may not be a violation or an actionable offense to transfer genetic resources or ATK that are subject to a restricted ABS permit. This may make it difficult or impossible to obtain enforcement and thus provide little or no incentive to those users to participate in mediation or in compromise discussions.

Thus, it might be more useful to describe the characteristics or results that indicate a transfer, rather than naming certain types of transactions. Such characteristics might simply include, for example, "any situation in which genetic material or samples thereof are held by persons not party to this contract, unless the other parties have agreed in accordance with XXX of this contract." Obviously, other result descriptions should also be included, as the foregoing example does not include information transfers, right/obligation transfers and situations that release a party from his/its responsibilities under the contract.

Beyond this, most providers expect ABS contracts to operate without continued oversight by the provider, in part because, in ABS contract situations, the genetic resources or ATK from the provider country are often taken out of the provider country to another country (where the user operates) for most R&D and other utilization activities. The distance and cost of oversight add to the likelihood that the provider will be unable to monitor the user closely enough to detect transfers to third parties. Thus, the contract must be clear, but not too restrictive in describing which activities are (or are not) transfers, how the user will document compliance with transfer restrictions, how that documentation will be verified and what external factors will be indicate that a violation has occurred. As detailed in Chapter 8, the contract will also need to specify at some point what will happen in the event of a violation of these provisions.

In describing its operation, a transfer clause must begins by identifying various triggers that give rise to an immediate obligation to comply with the transfer procedures. Next, there are several key elements that must be considered in the negotiation/drafting of a transfer clause, including the need to clearly determine which actions constitute a transfer covered by the clause; the contents of a prohibition clause (if that option is chosen); the approval/disapproval procedure; and the question of whether and how a transfer amends or re-forms the contract. Given that there are, at present, no "standard practices" that have been proven to function effectively in ABS contracts, these clauses should be individually negotiated by the parties, and cannot, as yet, be addressed by models. The following sections attempt to offer "tips" and "examples" that separately address particular aspects of drafting a transfer clause.

6.5.1 *Which Actions Constitute a "Transfer"?*

As a practical task, determining what constitutes a "transfer" under an ABS contract is similar to, but even more difficult than the challenge of describing the materials, data and rights covered by the contract, as discussed in ¶ 5.3. As noted in ¶ 6.4.3, in most bio-survey and genetic-resource collection processes, it is common to obtain multiple samples of each subspecies, population or variety. It is relatively easy to physically transfer some of these samples to third parties and relatively difficult for any other person to detect such a transfer. Beyond that, however, every sample is potentially divisible, with each part containing the sample's DNA. Many samples are replicable, whether by agricultural multiplication or test-tube or other chemical/biological processes. Most important, in modern laboratories it is possible not only to fully map the sample's DNA and biochemistry, but to build a reproduction of it based solely on such a map, without any physical material. The transfer issue becomes even more challenging, when applied to ATK, which is information only and can be transferred in writing or even in conversation.

In many instances, transfer of either the genetic code or biochemical formula of a genetic resource or of the elements of ATK may have a wide circulation where the researcher or company publishes research results or other discoveries. It is not possible to track the individual recipients of such information. It may, however, be reasonable to assume based on the high-costs of subscriptions and/or online access to professional journals, that they are primarily commercial researchers, corporate R&D departments, developed-country governmental units, and developed-country institutions/universities. In light of their limited budgets, few developing countries and non-profit organizations place a priority on such subscriptions.

Clearly, if the ABS contract's goal is to regulate transfers, it may not be sufficient to say that the transfer clause applies to "transfer of a genetic resource." Such a clause might not be concrete enough to trigger the operation of a transfer clause. Often, it is not the same material that was accessed which is being transferred and it might be transferred in a modified format. It is not advisable to rely solely on a transfer clause to regulate transfer activities, unless one can be certain that both the transferor and/or transferee will continue to have significant motivation or incentive to comply throughout the life of the contract. Such motivation will be generated in part by other clauses of the contract and in part by factors outside of the contract entirely.[216]

There are two primary legal requirements of a transfer definition: First, it must be sufficiently specific and clear that a reader will have no doubt about what is included. Second, however, it must be sufficiently broad to include all relevant ways in which a transfer might occur. To date, the authors have

216 One potential factor that may affect the user's ability to transfer and incentive to comply with the contract may be the outcome of ongoing international action implementing the NP. The overall process being undertaken at the international level is briefly described in Chapter 11. It may create new incentive/motivations for users to be able to prove that they have entered and are in compliance with ABS contracts. See, Morgera, *et al.*, 2014.

not encountered a form of words to describe the transfer of genetic resources and ATK for purposes of a contract clause that meets these two objectives, although examples of unsuccessful attempts abound. The following example is offered to assist negotiators in developing their own clause – it is a starting point, not a model:

> EXAMPLE: DEFINITION OF "TRANSFER OF GENETIC RESOURCE ATK"
>
> For purposes of this paragraph, the term "transfer of the genetic resource or ATK" shall mean and include any action that results in a third party to this contract receiving all or any part of the biological samples/ATK covered by this contract, as defined in clause XXX; as well as any fraction, extract or reproduction of that material and/or any research results which enable such third person to construct or use the genetic or traditional information embodied in the biological samples/ATK covered by this contract.

In addition, the parties should consider inclusion of a definition of "transfer/assignment of rights and duties under this contract." Such clauses are not uncommon, and the parties should identify appropriate language, based on the nature of the parties and the countries whose law is relevant to the contract.

The text of the transfer clause has a significant impact on (and is significantly affected by) another important legal issue – the "burden of proof." Clearly, a provider who believes that a transfer has occurred in violation of the transfer clause cannot simply obtain a judgment on the basis of that belief. In such cases, the result may depend on which party has the burden of proof. If the provider has the burden of proof, he must prove that an illegal transfer has occurred. If not, he need only allege the facts giving rise to his belief, shifting the burden to the user to rebut that belief. Clearly, if a clause is ambiguous, that ambiguity benefits the party that does not have the burden of proof.

6.5.2 *Exclusivity*

Many other issues that impact the determination of which actions should constitute a transfer of genetic resources or ATK under the contract. In some contracts, for example, there is some element of "exclusiveness" – that is, the provider seeks some assurance that no other user will have access to the genetic resources of a particular species. Such a provision would clearly need to be negotiated in conjunction with the transfer clause. In an exclusivity-based contract, any indication that the resource (where specific origin is determinable) is being utilized by third party would clearly indicate that one of the following had occurred: user has transferred the genetic resource in violation of the transfer clause; the provider has violated the exclusivity clause; or the third party has violated the ABS rights of user and provider. A contract including both transfer and exclusivity clauses will have to address this possibility.

> TIP
> EXCLUSIVITY
>
> Unfortunately, the range of options and issues relevant to exclusivity clauses is so great that the authors cannot in conscience provide appropriate examples, without unduly extending the length of this book. As a substitute, we offer the following advice:
>
> - Be very concrete and detailed about exactly what is exclusive. Use of phrases like "user shall receive the exclusive right to XXX" should be very carefully examined. Make sure that all parties agree about what actions or promises are implied, and what actions or promises are not permitted by this phrase;
> - Specify the term of exclusivity;
> - Specify any factors that might lead to cancellation of exclusivity (for example, if exclusivity is granted only in exchange for active R&D efforts, leading to a product or patent within a specific time);
> - If the exclusivity can be cancelled, as described above, specify any procedures or notification that applies.

6.5.3 *Transfer of Contract Rights or Obligations*

Within the question of transfer, it is also important to consider the "contractual assignment of a party's rights and obligations under a contract," as discussed in ¶ 5.5.4, *supra*. This issue essentially focuses on whether the transferor should be released from the initial contract, and whether the transferee should become a party to it. As noted, there may be many reasons that a party to a contract may seek to transfer his rights/obligations to another party, and many possible reasons that other parties may insist on at least notice of and possibly a right of approval over such a transfer. An important factor in this situation is the linkage between the transferred rights/obligations and the genetic resources or ATK that is also transferred. In many countries, if the parties to a contract transfer an asset that is associated with certain contractual rights or duties, the law may presume that the rights/duties are also transferred ("assigned"). This presumption may operate to release the transferring party from further duties under the contract. Where such a presumption exists, however, it can be rebutted by a provision in the contract that specifically explains the relationship between the transfer of the asset and the assignment of the transferor's rights and/or obligations under the contract (see the following example[217]).

> EXAMPLE: EFFECT OF TRANSFER ON THE TRANSFERRING PARTY'S OBLIGATIONS UNDER THIS CONTRACT
>
> The Parties agree that even where done in full compliance with this [transfer clause], the transfer of resources and/or rights as described above shall not operate to release the transferor from any obligation under this contract, unless and to the extent that the transfer of those obligations is also specifically included in the notification provided under clause XXX of this contract and specifically approved by the non-transferring part[ies]. The parties agree that, unless and to the extent that the notification and approval state otherwise, the transferee receiving any approved transfer of resources and/or rights must thereafter be jointly and severally responsible[218] for all obligations of the transferor under this contract.

One must also ask, to what extent the initial provider should be brought onboard as the party to the transfer contract?

There is a psychological component of this decision, as well as a legal one. If he does not become a party to the initial contract, the transferee will typically feel less obliged by the initial contract and its objectives. For this reason, it may be a very good idea to formally include the transferee as a party to the original contract through a formal amendment process. This will enable all parties to

217 The authors have been unable to find any reliable comprehensive source of information on how this point is addressed across the range of national contract law and practice in various countries and legal traditions.

218 The term "joint and several responsibility" means that each parties subject to that responsibility must ensure that the responsibility is fulfilled. If three parties are jointly and severally responsible and two of them become bankrupt, then the third must bear the entire responsibility.

openly determine how this change will affect their own plans and motivations. In addition, of course, where the transferee is not in a direct contractual relationship with the provider, he will not have any direct right against him. His right will be against the transferor, who will then have to take action against the transferee to recover any damages or penalties paid to the provider. Where the provider is not confident that the transferor will be solvent and available in the future, he may wish to "eliminate the middleman," to ensure that he has a direct right against the transferee (both judicially and non-judicially.)

In drafting the transfer provisions of an ABS contract, one should not be blind to the possibility that the transfer issues that will arise may be different from the ones you are expecting. Thus, the range of options available should not prevent the parties from eventually deciding to directly substitute the transferee for the transferor in the initial contract, renegotiation/amendment of the entire agreement, and many other options.

6.5.4 *Casual Transfer*

A transfer clause must also address the significant possibility that any transfer will involve the actions of individual researchers or employees – occurring casually or outside of the knowledge of the directors and managers of any company, institution or entity that is a party to the contract. As discussed above, in most ABS situations, there is concern that it may be difficult for any other party (or even other employees of the same party) to become aware of or get information about such individual transfers. This uncertainty can easily carry over into a dispute among the parties following such transfer, with one party claiming that it cannot be held responsible for the independent acts of these individuals. Although a court might hold any entity responsible for contract violations caused by independent action of its employees, that result is uncertain and variable. Accordingly, it is preferable for the parties to address the question directly.

One option to close that loophole would be a clause stating that the user company or institution must require all employees using or having access to the genetic resource to sign a specific agreement not to share any part of the resource (subject to the same drafting issues described above) in any way without the advance written consent of the provider. This employee agreement could be drafted in a manner that makes it legally enforceable by the provider. In that case, the associated termination clause could be written in a way that holds the user specially liable for breach of the ABS contract,[219] if any employee or other individual gains access to the genetic resource without having signed such employee agreement. This option may be considered too extreme by some users,

219 Special liability clauses are discussed in Chapters 8 and 9, *infra*.

and although closing the potential loophole, does not alleviate the provider's need for vigilance. Moreover, if an individual employee violates the employee agreement, the provider's only remedy might be an action against that individual, whose assets might not be sufficient to compensate the loss caused to the provider as a result of the transfer.

6.5.5 *Drafting a Transfer Prohibition*

A transfer prohibition is a necessary starting point in any contract, except one that is intentionally silent on transfer. This is because, even where the parties agree that the ABS contract should not prohibit transfer, it is important for them to do so in a manner that will not provide a court with an easy justification for invalidating the contract.[220] Although its goal is only to regulate transfer, the contract must begin with a prohibition on transfer, applicable to any transfer that does not comply with the other provisions of the transfer clause. Where the parties intend to allow transfer subject to restrictions, the clause will usually begin with the words "Except where undertaken in compliance with [the clauses that set out the process for regulating transfer]…" Where they intend to unequivocally prohibit transfer, the prohibition language is the same, but that introductory phrase will not be used.

In drafting any transfer prohibition, it is always more defensible if the provision is not absolute. The contract should provide some mechanism or process by which a party may at least seek consent for a transfer. Hence, it is usually advisable to include the possibility that the non-transferring party may give consent to a transfer:

> EXAMPLE: TRANSFER RESTRICTION
>
> [Except in accordance with this agreement,] the [users] shall not transfer any component of [the genetic resources described in paragraph XX of this contract] or his rights and/or obligations under this contract without first obtaining explicit written consent from [provider or designated person within the provider community].

220 As noted in ¶ 6.2, supra, commercial law in most countries begins from a presumption that a party may transfer any property or rights that he owns/holds at the time of transfer. Even where a contract places limits on transfer, it is more effective to phrase those limits as "transfer is not allowed unless…" rather than "a party who transfers his interest must…."

To be effective, a transfer prohibition should be integrated with all other aspects of the contract (*i.e.*, provisions that define transfer or discuss amendment, penalty/enforcement clauses, and any other clause addressing an activity that might give rise to a possible application of the transfer process.) It will be important to include or integrate the transfer clause in the contract's clauses on amendment and termination, as discussed in ¶ 6.5.8 and Chapter 8, *infra*.

6.5.6 *Trigger and Notification*

As with any duty under a contract, the specific action or conditions that trigger that duty are critical to its legal effectiveness. In any clause which regulates transfer of genetic resources, ATK, contractual rights or contractual duties, the trigger for active compliance should be earlier than the transfer itself.[221] In some contracts, the trigger could be the party's decision to transfer; however, this trigger is known only to the transferring party. Hence, it is common to trigger the transferor's duty on an externally provable event – either a specified number of days after negotiations of the transfer began or a specified number of days before the date set for transfer. The following is a relatively standard approach to such a notification requirement, as used in conventional types of contracts.

EXAMPLE: PRIOR NOTIFICATION ON TRANSFER

In the event that any party to this agreement shall wish to transfer, as described in section XXX, any of the resources described in section XXX[222] or any part of his rights or obligations as described in section XXX[223] to any other party or to any third person, the transferring party shall provide advance notification of that proposed transfer, in accordance with section XXX [notification procedures clause[224]] not later than the earlier of the following:

- XX days after the transferring party has begun negotiations or discussions with a proposed transferee; or

221 If the contract does not state a different trigger, the obligation to notify the non-transferring party may be deemed to be triggered by the transfer, itself.

222 Description of the resources transferred is discussed in ¶ 5.3, *supra*.

223 Discussed in ¶ 5.4, *supra*.

224 A notification clause is a type of clause that is properly considered "boilerplate" as it is relatively similar in most contracts and generally not negotiated. It states the addresses

– XX days prior to the date [tentatively] set for the proposed transfer.

If any transfer occurs without such notification, or before the tentative date as set out above, that transfer shall be deemed a breach of this contract and dealt with according to section XXX [enforcement clauses[225]], in addition, such a transfer shall be deemed a "fraudulent transfer,"[226] under the laws of [country which would have jurisdiction over such a claim[227]] and may be prosecuted as such to the full extent of applicable law.

Clearly, this sub-clause may need to be adjusted to reflect the parties agreements regarding other elements of the transfer requirement, as mentioned below. For example, the parties may decide to limit only certain types of transfers, or to address transfers with some type of response other than a declaration of breach and/or action for fraud. It is also clear that the extent to which this language provides a "safe harbour" depends on two critical factors. The first of these is the contract itself, specifically the quality of the drafting of the descriptions of the *res* (¶ 5.3, *supra*), operative provisions (¶ 5.4, *supra*), actions constituting transfer (¶ 6.5.1, *supra*), and consequences of breach of the contract (Chapter 8, *infra*.) Second, and equally essential, however, is the non-transferring parties' vigilance and ability to know when/whether a transfer has occurred.

6.5.7 *Procedure for Approval/Rejection of the Transfer*

Where a transfer may be allowed if it fulfils certain contractual requirements, the parties should specifically agree on how the transfer requirements will function. This agreement turns on a choice among two primary options: In the first option, the non-transferring party will have a right of approval/disapproval of the transfer proposal. The second approach will not restrict the parties' rights to transfer, but will instead impose certain specific requirements following any transfer. The specific elements of these processes are discussed at ¶ 6.5.8, *infra.*

---

at which contract notifications shall be received, and the manner in which they may be given (i.e., whether only a mailed or hand-delivered written notification is allowed, or whether e-mail and/or telephonic or oral communication will also satisfy a notification requirement), as well as the manner in which the parties can document that they have duly given a notification and that it has been received by the other parties.

225 Discussed in Chapter 8 *infra*.

226 See Chapter 8, *infra*.

227 See Chapter 10, *infra*.

> TIP
> RIGHT OF APPROVAL/DISAPPROVAL
>
> In drafting transfer clauses, the first priority will be to address the rights of the non-transferring parties (usually the provider.) Specifically, a transfer clause that includes a right of approval/disapproval should include the following procedural elements:
>
> - Whether the non-transferring parties have a right to investigate the transferee and approve/reject the proposed transfer;[228]
> - If the non-transferring parties have a right of approval, how much time they have after the triggering event or receipt of notification[229] in which to make this decision;
> - Where any party consists of multiple individuals (*i.e.*, an agency, government, institution, community, family, *etc.*) which persons (usually stated by position, rather than by name) shall have the right/ability to make and/or convey the approval/disapproval decision;
> - Whether failure to respond should indicate consent to the transfer, and whether in this event an additional notification should be required;
> - What rights the transferring party and the proposed transferee have in the event that the proposed transfer is not approved;[230] and
> - Whether and when the transferring party will reimburse the reasonable costs incurred by the non-transferring party in investigating transferee and how those costs shall be estimated and or documented.

As noted above, when any transfer notification is received, it is strongly recommended that the non-transferring party investigate the transferee in detail. Without full exercise of the parties' rights and options under it, a transfer clause protects no one.

6.5.8 *Integrating Transfer with Clause on Amendment or Re-formation*

A critical question in any transfer of the contractual *res*, rights and/or obligations is how that transfer affects the status of both the transferor and transferee

228 As discussed in ¶ 6.4, in drafting this element must bear a close relationship to the issue of whether the original user is released from his contract obligations after the transfer.

229 Discussed in ¶ 6.5.6.

230 The answer to this point is also addressed in the transfer clause's provisions regarding amendment/reformation of the contract. See ¶ 6.5. 8.

with regard to the contract. In other words: Does/Should the transfer substitute the transferee for the transferor, releasing the latter from all future connection with the contract? As described above, there may be many reasons why one or more parties would answer this question very differently from the others. If the contract does not address it, this point may well engender a conflict among the parties, preventing the contract from functioning, and potentially requiring legal action.

There are a variety of contractual options with regard to this issue, including the following:

- Automatic commencement of the amendment process to specifically replace the transferring party with the approved transferee (transferor only released when/if transferee is formally bound);
- Decision as to whether to amend the contract and replace the transferring party with the transferee is separate from approval of transfer. Pending such formal amendment, transferor and transferee are both (jointly and severally) responsible for transferor's obligations under the ABS contract; or
- Transferor is responsible for all performance under the ABS contract, including performances taken on by transferor.

The advantages and disadvantages of these and other options may vary from one ABS contract to another. For example, if the ABS contract included special provisions in light of the special status of one of the parties, or a pre-existing relationship between or among them, then it may be preferable to prevent that party from making any transfer. Even where a transfer prohibition is not desirable or feasible, however, the parties may not feel comfortable about any clause that allows the special-status party or the party who built the contract on the basis of a pre-existing relationship to leave the contract.

By contrast, if the transferee is investigated and found to be as solid and financially sound and dependable as the original party, the non-transferring party might prefer to take all possible steps to ensure that the transferee is bound by the ABS contract, including by formally amending the contract to include the transferee as a party and signatory. This may be particularly true if the parties or the relevant law of the countries involved will hold that the obligations under the contract are legally tied to the genetic resources/ATK.

Some legal advisors will state that it is legally insecure to rely on a clause that requires the transferor to bind the transferee. Others, however, will note that, if the provider becomes aware of the transfer, it will be relatively easy for him to demonstrate a breach of such a clause. It would be relatively simple to prove (1) that the transferor did not meet its obligations to properly bind the transferee, and (2) that the provider did not receive the contractually required share of benefits.[231] These two proofs may be a sufficient basis for a judgment against the transferor. Some advisors also claim that amending the contract to include the transferee has a psychological impact, causing the transferee to feel less separate from the ABS relationship, and potentially to enter into negotiations to make sure that the ABS contract includes a more appropriate reflection of his needs.

The question of whether to release the transferor from all or part of his obligations is more difficult, as detailed in ¶ 6.5.3. The basic challenge here arises from two facts. First, as noted above, genetic resources and ATK are almost infinitely shareable because they can often be reduced to writing (formulae, genetic code, research notes). Even where physical samples are required, relatively small collected materials can be split into increasingly small samples and may often be multiplied in the lab or in the field. The extent of sharing of written maps of gene sequences (as well as transcriptions of ATK) is essentially infinite. Second, however, the ABS contract is often focused on the physical samples and/or their collection but includes many legal rights to utilize those resources.

After a user has transferred the genetic resources, he may have retained some part of the sample and he may have the results of pre-transfer research and development on the received material or information. The transfer does not necessarily transfer or terminate his practical ability to continue such R&D. If the user is released from the contract (replaced by the transferee), however, he may take the position that he is no longer bound with regard to the ABS contract, even as to the ongoing R&D, commenced on the basis of pre-transfer information and research results.

In some negotiations, the parties may claim that it would be better to wait, rather than address transfer issues in the initial negotiations. They suggest that the parties only need to deal with a transfer if a transfer is proposed, rather than try to plan for something that may never occur. By the time a transfer occurs, however, the parties to the contract may find themselves in changed situations, unable to agree on any of the issues described above. The transfer clause is useful because it is agreed in advance. At the time of the transfer, the particular motivations of the transferring party may not include the best interests of the non-transferring parties. Transfer-related decision-making is not left solely in the hands of the transferring party, and does not wait until

231 This second factor will depend on the wording contents of the basic operational provision of the contracts – in particular, on how the user's benefit-sharing obligation is stated.

a problem or conflict arises. Although an amendment/re-formation clause is often long and detailed, it can be very useful in avoiding conflict.

EXAMPLE: AMENDMENT/RE-FORMATION OF THE CONTRACT ON TRANSFER

Automatic or Decision-based Amendment:

In the event that a transfer, as described in subparagraph XX, of any party's assets, rights and/or duties under this ABS contract has been [approved, properly notified, *etc.*] in accordance with [trigger/notice and/or approval sub-clauses], the parties shall confer with the transferee to [decide whether to] formally amend this ABS Contract to include transferee as a formal signatory and party to this ABS Contract, fully responsible for all obligations transferred in accordance with this [transfer clause]. Any amendment pursuant to this clause [shall/shall not] reopen the negotiation of any other clause of this contract. No such amendment shall have any legal effect on the respective duties of any of the parties and/or transferee, until it has been finally agreed and fully executed by all parties to this contract and by the transferee. Nothing in this sub-clause shall be interpreted as releasing the transferor from any obligation or liability under this contract, except as and if expressly agreed in writing, in accordance with [clause on release of the transferor].

[Note: If the contract required the original user to obtain "employee agreements" as discussed in ¶ 6.5.4, *supra,* it may be advisable to specifically discuss how that requirement and any other requirement specifically limited to the party that is transferring his interest should apply to the transferee.]

Post-transfer Rights and Obligations of the Transferor:

Nothing in this transfer clause or elsewhere in this ABS Contract shall operate to reduce or eliminate any party's direct obligation to perform any responsibilities assigned to it under this ABS Contract[, except if the parties have fully complied with this sub-paragraph XX, with the express objective of relieving specified parties from specified obligations in connection with a transfer of all or any part of the genetic resources/ATK transferred under this contract, as defined in clause XX, or any rights granted to that party pursuant to clause XX.] In the event of such a transfer, the transferring party may apply to the other parties to this ABS Contract, seeking amendment of this contract with regard to any of the following [the following items are offered as an exemplar list,[232] parties to select which options will be included in the contract]:

- To reduce or eliminate any direct liability of transferor for amounts owing or liquidated damages arising solely from the actions of the transferee, if and to the extent that the transferee has been approved as a party to the contract and the contract has been amended to reflect that status, and fully executed by the transferee and all parties;
- To establish a priority of actions, in seeking to resolve any allegations of breach of this agreement by the transferee, where the transferor may have a derivative liability, whether as a result of the transfer or arising out of some relationship between them;
- To specify the transferor's direct obligations with regard to any part of the genetic resource/ATK retained in any form (including data and research results) by the transferor and/or any future research, development or other commercial or non-commercial use thereof;
- To specify the transferor's direct obligations with regard to any research results of other information developed prior to the transfer and/or any future research, development or other commercial or non-commercial use of that information or future-developed information based on the genetic resources or ATK;
- To revise any financial assurances of the transferor, so that the transferee is substituted as the assurer, to the extent of transferee's share in the assets and/or actions to which such assurances are addressed; and/or
- To replace an appropriate share of any committed security provided by the transferor with security provided by the transferee, to the extent that such security is of the same or higher value, both in terms of the actual value of the security and in terms of the commitments given by the security provider and the transferee's apparent ability to meet those commitments.

232 The example provides only some possible options. Many of these may not apply in some contracts.

> Amendments applied for under this transfer clause shall be considered by the parties in accordance with the procedures and requirements of clause XX [the clause addressing amendment to the ABS Contract more generally], and shall not affect the relationship among the parties to this ABS Contract in any way unless and until fully agreed and executed by all parties. Nothing in this transfer sub-clause shall prevent the non-transferring party from proposing other amendments to this contract at the time of transfer, pursuant to clause XX [the clause addressing amendment to the ABS Contract more generally].
>
> In the absence of any amendment of the contract, the transferor shall remain fully responsible for compliance with all obligations, rights and limitations imposed by this ABS Contract, regardless of any transfer.

The second part of this clause ("Post-transfer Rights and Obligations of the Transferor") is still necessary, even if the parties agree that a transfer in compliance with this contract should reduce or completely relieve all of the transferor's future obligation or liability under the ABS contract. In that case, however, the list of permitted amendments will differ markedly. All of the main issues addressed in the above exemplar list of amendments (*i.e.,* relationship between the transferor and transferee, transferor's liability for actions of the transferee; and transferor's post-transfer responsibilities with regard to utilization of any retained genetic material and/or pre-transfer research results) should also be considered in determining whether how and when to amend the contract following transfer.

6.5.9 *Where Transfer Cannot be Independently Monitored*

An ABS pessimist reviewing this section might snort and say that all of this effort is meaningless because normally the provider cannot independently discover whether a transfer of genetic resources has occurred. Moreover, monitoring relies on the user's active cooperation – even though his compliance is potentially costly in time, personnel, legal services, and money. Worse, he is aware that he may not have to endure any negative consequences, even if his non-compliance is discovered.

While these factors certainly affect the value of the entire contract, they are no more relevant to transfer clauses than to the rest of the ABS contract. Accordingly, it is only appropriate to mention that, as discussed in Chapters 8 and 9, the drafting and negotiation of contracts can be designed to make compliance with transfer provisions more attractive to the user. A well crafted transfer clause, coupled with such a general incentive might extend the desirability of compliance to the transferee as well.

6.6 Special Third-party Transfer Risks

Contractually speaking, there are three main categories of transfer/assignment: voluntary transfers, "involuntary transfers" and "incidental transfers." A contract's transfer provisions address only the first of these. This section considers the other two, addressing transfers and assignments that occur as a result of events and actions that may be outside of the control of the transferring party. Specifically, this section briefly considers bankruptcies (one of the most common types of involuntary transfers[233]); and the effect of corporate merger/acquisitions – a type of transaction that can "incidentally" transfer rights under ABS contracts. Although each of these areas is extremely complex and detailed, most of those complexities are not relevant to the objective of this book. Accordingly, these two sections focus only on specific aspects that are different where these issues arise in connection with ABS contracts.

6.6.1 *Bankruptcy*

Although most people use the term "bankruptcy," not everyone is aware of its legal meaning. In fact, a "bankruptcy" is a formal legal declaration that a person or company (the "bankrupt") is unable to pay its debts and/or satisfy its other obligations. Following that declaration, all assets and funds belonging to the bankrupt are managed by a court-appointed trustee, who oversees the sale of the bankrupt's assets, marshals all of the sale proceeds and other funds (the "bankruptcy estate"), compiles a list of all of the bankrupt's creditors and the specific debts owed to each, and apportions the contents of the bankruptcy estate among the bankrupt's creditors, according to a framework of very specific laws. This is called the "bankruptcy settlement."[234] In a bankruptcy settlement, the trustee will distribute the bankrupt's remaining assets among the creditors, after first satisfying certain "priority debts." After these distributions are completed, the bankruptcy is "discharged" and no creditor may seek to enforce any existing debts or liabilities against the bankrupt. Obviously, most debtors would like it if their debt was considered a priority debt. This can be difficult (see also Chapter 9, *infra*).[235]

233 Other types of involuntary transfer include the death or dissolution of a party.

234 In some countries, another type of bankruptcy may also be available, in which the court "reorganizes" the bankrupt's obligations, setting a new schedule for payment of his creditors over time.

235 The rights of the holder of a secured debt are complex, and must usually be addressed in a special provision or separate agreement.

Many bankruptcies are entirely involuntary – where the bankrupt's creditors bring a legal action to declare him bankrupt – but it is also possible for the bankrupt to choose this path himself. Often, the bankrupt uses bankruptcy as a way of evading its responsibilities to creditors. Although bankruptcy laws normally include rules designed to avoid this abuse, some companies have colluded to transfer all of their assets to other companies or individuals, before declaring bankruptcy.[236] This is essentially a fraud on the other creditors of the bankrupt. In order to challenge such an abuse, a creditor must bring an objection before the court or trustee supervising the bankruptcy within the legally specified time.

Regardless of who initiates the procedure, however, if bankruptcy arises regarding one of the parties to a contract, that contract's operation may become uncertain. Bankruptcy causes a serious interruption in all commercial transactions involving the bankrupt.[237] The proceedings may involve a lengthy examination of the assets of the bankrupt and possibly also their transfer or sale.

Predictably, bankruptcy law varies widely from country to country, and the procedures and requirements of those laws are all very intricate and complex. Fortunately, there is no need for in-depth discussion of bankruptcy law and process, in this book. We will consider how bankruptcy issues are addressed in contracts.

The bankruptcy of a party may affect an ABS contract in three primary ways: First, the user's bankruptcy may terminate his present or future obligation to pay money or transfer value, possibly including his benefit-sharing obligation. Second, even if a user's obligation is not terminated by bankruptcy, it may be seriously delayed or much more complicated. Finally, if the user is holding any samples or data (genetic resources, ATK, research results) at the time of the bankruptcy, those assets may become part of the bankruptcy. In dealing with them, the bankruptcy trustee may not be obliged to comply with the contractual transfer restrictions.

All of these impacts are particularly problematic in ABS contracts. In addition, there may be less common impacts of bankruptcy in ABS contracts.[238]

---

236 There is some indication that this is what happened in the Teff Agreement. See Andersen, and Winge, 2012.

237 Similar problems arise with other types of involuntary transfers, including the death of a party (transfer to the heirs), the dissolution of a corporate party (transfer to shareholders) or transfer by governmental fiat (as where an asset is nationalized or taken for a priority government purpose.)

238 ABS contracts are frequently signed in the provider country, and sometimes includes a provision stating that the provider country's law is the "governing law" of the contract. See Chapter 8, *infra,* which explains why the "governing law" clause is often misinterpreted

Perhaps the worst aspect of bankruptcy, however is that it brings an entirely separate body of law into the ABS contract. If a bankruptcy is filed, the various vague and ambiguous aspects of ABS will have to be decided in the context of an entirely separate body of regulation by courts that know nothing about ABS.[239] Hence, if possible it would be preferable to find a way to keep ABS samples, rights and assets out of bankruptcy estates and other involuntary transfers.

6.6.2 *Addressing Future Bankruptcy in ABS Contracts*

As noted above, bankruptcy law is very specific and may have a major impact on the contract. Accordingly, the parties' goal in drafting a bankruptcy clause in a contract is to find ways to avoid the three basic problems mentioned above (loss of expected benefit-sharing, destruction of samples, interruption of implementation, and involuntary asset transfer) in a manner that will be found legally acceptable by the bankruptcy court and/or trustee. In order to do this, the contract draftsmen must separately address all three potential impacts. Although most contracts include a "bankruptcy clause," such a clause will function properly only if all other parts of the contract are written in a way that coordinates with it.

To begin with, any contractual provision relating to bankruptcy, must normally begin with a definition of the meaning of the term "bankruptcy," as used in the contract. There is no accepted definition; however if your contractual definition is too narrow it may create a loophole in the contract.

EXAMPLE: DEFINING THE ACTIONS INCLUDED WITHIN THE CLAUSE ADDRESSING BANKRUPTCY?

"Bankruptcy": with respect to any Person, shall mean that such Person shall have become insolvent or generally failed to pay, or admitted in writing his or its inability to pay, debts as they become due; or shall have applied for, consented to, or acquiesced in the appointment of, a trustee, receiver or other custodian for such Person or any property of such Person, or such Person makes a general assignment for the benefit of creditors; or, in the absence of such application, consent or acquiescence, a

and does not give the legal protection that providers often expect. A bankruptcy of the user may be filed in a different country. This creates special potential problems and concerns that need to be addressed in the contract, as well.

239 It may be difficult to integrate bankruptcy law with the interlinkage between the *res* in an ABS contract, the rights of utilization and the benefit-sharing obligation. Whenever a transfer of assets or rights occurs by operation of law, there is a possibility that the

> trustee, receiver or other custodian is appointed for such Person or for a substantial part of the property of such Person and is not discharged with sixty days; or any bankruptcy, reorganization, debt arrangement, or other case or proceeding under any bankruptcy or insolvency law, or any dissolution or liquidation proceeding is commenced in respect of such Person and if such case or proceeding is not commenced by such Person, it is consented to or acquiesced in by such Person or remains for sixty days un-dismissed; or such Person takes any action to authorize, or in furtherance of, any of the foregoing.

The above example is taken from a domestic contract in the US. It represents an effort to include all situations in which a person is or may become bankrupt, described in a way that will include all possible types of transfers that may be made with the intent of using bankruptcy to escape from a contractual responsibility.

As noted above there are three main contractual impacts of bankruptcy. In an ABS contract, the first of these is the effect of bankruptcy on the provider's benefit-sharing expectation. With regard to this type challenge, the most apparent contractual solution is not found in any bankruptcy clause. Rather, the description of the provider's interests should specifically take the possibility of future bankruptcy into account. As further discussed in Chapter 9 (which covers guarantees and financial responsibility issues,) one potentially effective means of doing this is for each user's financial obligations under the ABS contract to be formally "secured" making it a "priority debt" in any bankruptcy.

The second impact is collection. Here the options are virtually non-existent. In general, if the provider can file as a creditor in bankruptcy, his potential for recovery is limited. One possible approach to addressing this challenge is to draft a clause which declares that it is a breach of the contract for any party to enter into a bankruptcy. Unfortunately, this type of clause, sometimes called an *ipso facto* clause, is not effective in many countries. If you decide to try such a clause, it will be necessary to ensure that the ABS contract has an appropriately drafted "liquidated damages" clause (a clause which states a specific amount that a breaching party must pay, in the event of certain types of breach), as discussed in Chapter 7. The idea behind the use of an *ipso facto* clause would be for the entire liquidated damage amount to be considered to be a debt of

---

transferee will assume that they hold the asset or right, free of former contractual restrictions. While such an assumption can be challenged, the cost of such a challenge can be high and the results uncertain.

the bankruptcy estate. If this works in the country in which the bankruptcy is filed, and if the user's obligation is secured in a way that qualifies as a "priority debt," this might even allow the liquidated damage amount to be paid directly out of the proceeds of sale of the security.

Finally, with regard to the physical transfer or sale of specimens, the authors' experience indicates that there are few options, and they must be approached with care. In essence, the simplest of these involves modifying the description of the user's rights in the genetic resources or ATK, so that, if the user files bankruptcy or is declared to be bankrupt, those assets are not considered to "belong" to the user. This approach can be problematic because bankruptcy law normally does not allow the bankrupt to transfer assets before the bankruptcy as a ploy to keep them outside of the bankruptcy.[240] Such a ploy may be considered a criminal act or, at minimum, give rise to a civil penalty. Accordingly, this type of bankruptcy protection must be addressed very carefully, in reliance on specific legal advice.

6.6.3 *Mergers and Corporate Restructuring*

Following an acquisition of all or part of a corporate entity by a new entity, the sale of a significant part of the entity's assets, the merger of the two entities, or even the restructure of a corporate entity, similar legal questions may arise. If a user under an ABS contract engages in one of these activities, the provider must ask whether the merger or restructuring operates as a "transfer" of the genetic resource or ATK and/or of the user's rights and obligations under that contract. Any of these transactions may change the nature of the entity or limit its ability to make payments or take other action under the contract. In these ways, it is essentially a type of transfer, even if the resulting entity has the same name and still holds the genetic resources and contractual obligations. In many other ways, these transactions are very different from standard transfers. Most important, the definition of what constitutes a transfer in each case is very different.

There are many reasons why most contracts discuss the possibility of future mergers and acquisitions. Most important, the relationship among companies, their shareholders, their management, and their parent, subsidiary and other entities is often rather convoluted. As discussed in Chapter 4, it is important for all parties to be aware of these relationships, to ensure that all necessary entities have been bound by the contract. It is also important to maintain awareness of these relationships after the contract is in force.

240 Such a transfer would be considered an attempt to defraud other creditors who have a right to a share of the bankruptcy estate.

6.6.4 *ABS Contractual Clauses on Mergers and Acquisitions*

An entity's commitment to the pre-existing contract may change, even if it keeps the same name and staff following a merger, acquisition, division or restructure. To guard against changes that negatively impact the parties, most contracts include a provision that specifically states that any time a party participates in a merger, acquisition and other corporate restructuring, it must consider that event to be a transfer, triggering the contract's transfer provisions.

The most important part of a clause on mergers is the definition element – describing which actions are considered to be "mergers, acquisitions, divisions and other corporate restructuring." These four types of changes are distinct and would require distinct solutions. Once this definition is written, then the remaining question is "what happens if a party is involved in a merger, acquisition, division or other corporate restructuring?" There are, of course, a range of options. One is to consider any such event to be a "transfer," triggering the application of the transfer clause as mentioned above. When this option applies, if the entity can show that its merger, acquisition, division of other corporate restructuring did not impact its performance under the contract, then the other party or parties can easily agree that the contract should go on unchanged. Another approach would tie the issue to the percent change in ownership or capital structure of the entity, as compared with the time it entered into the contract.

CHAPTER 7

"Know the Possibilities and Limitations of Contract Law": Contract Validity, Equity and Enforceability

To be enforceable, ABS contracts must focus on basic contract law, rather than repeating unenforceable language from international ABS conventions and protocols, national legislation and other documents. The ABS contract must be recognized as "valid," "equitable" and enforceable under national contract law. Although relevant contractual law varies from country to country, the basic standards that determine validity, equity and enforceability are generally similar enough that they can be summarized in this chapter.

These issues are legally critical, but they are also important from a practical perspective. Specifically, commercial entities are far less likely to comply with an instrument that is legally invalid or unenforceable, even if called a "contract." As noted in Chapter 2, an ABS contract that is not legally enforceable is little more than a statement of goodwill – it can only have legal effect if all parties implement it "voluntarily." By contrast, even where the other party is unlikely to bring a lawsuit, a party is more likely to implement and complete an enforceable contract. This chapter will not attempt to teach a course in contract law. Instead it will focus on providing practical guidance on how to make your ABS contract a valid and enforceable contract. Its sections very briefly outline the breadth of these issues:

- the concept of a "valid contract" from the negotiators' perspective (¶ 7.1);
- the basic principles underlying that concept (¶ 7.2);
- the particular elements that determine validity of a contract (¶ 7.3);
- the consequence of finding that a contract is invalid (¶ 7.4);
- the options that may still be available if a contract is determined to be unenforceable (¶ 7.5);
- particular elements that might be relevant under the applicable national law and special aspects of addressing ABS contracts and ATK (¶ 7.6); and
- the potential role of "industry standards" in streamlining ABS contracts (¶ 7.7).

7.1 Valid or Void – What Makes Your Document a Contract?

Many types of instruments (even some that are titled "Contract") are not legally considered to be "contracts," and as such cannot be enforced using contract

 | DOI 10.1163/9789004356573_008

law. The primary difference between such an instrument and a legal contract is the legal test of "validity."

A valid contract is the only type of contract that can be legally binding on its parties. This determination affects all legal aspects of the contract. Most important, validity is a legal requirement that cannot be "worked around" – that is, the parties cannot simply write a clause stating that they agree that the instrument is a valid contract. Such a statement will have no meaning if the contract does not meet the relevant criteria for validity. If the contract is legally invalid, then the only way to make its terms enforceable is to draft a new valid contract.

Throughout this chapter, the reader should keep in mind that, as briefly examined in Chapters 2 and 10, there is no simple answer to the question of which national law will apply to determine whether a contract is valid. Every time the question is asked, the answer may change. Unfortunately, that answer is very important, every time the question is asked. If two separate arbitrations or lawsuits are filed in different countries concerning the same issue under the same contract, it is likely that they would come to different results. If the same issue comes up later in a suit filed by or against a transferee in a third country, that court may come to yet another answer.

Although contractual law is not the parties' only legal option, it is usually the most concrete. Even where a contract fails the legal test of validity, an aggrieved party may seek legal redress in some other way (*i.e.,* in cases alleging fraud, misrepresentation, violation of consumer protection laws, usury, misappropriation of property or information, *etc.*) Unfortunately, these solutions are less predictable than contractual enforcement, as the variation among countries' law on these topics is much greater. Moreover, the aggrieved party can only obtain redress through these theories if he brings a court case. As a result, these theories are not particularly helpful to most providers[241] and should not be relied on in drafting the contract.

7.2 Basic Concepts and Principles of Contractual Functionality

As summarized in Chapter 2, a contract is a self-standing legal document that is intended to fully regulate the relationship between its parties. If the parties disagree about basic issues in the contract, they can apply commercial or contract law to resolve that conflict. This does not mean that they must litigate,

241 The desire to maximize enforceability, without the need to actually go to court or file an arbitration is discussed in Chapters 8 and 9, *infra.*

rather that they have the law as a basis or guidance, on which to develop negotiated solutions. Contrary to the claims of many, an emphasis on ensuring that ABS contracts are legally clear, concrete, valid and enforceable is not a way of promoting litigation, but rather a way of avoiding it.

Where the contract is not clearly valid and enforceable, the law cannot provide a basis for enabling compromise. In the event of a disagreement or breach, the contract's parties might face a bitter choice. Their only options would be either to take a chance by bringing an action under other types of law[242] (a case that will not be likely to succeed, and will be costly to file and prosecute) or to simply give up their rights and expectations.[243]

There are four key adjectives, which determine the legal status of any contract (in the following order): "**valid**" (a valid contract is one that a court would recognize as a legal instrument); "**binding**" (a binding contract imposes legally recognized obligations on the parties); "**implementable**" (an implementable contract can be performed according to its terms without the need to resort to courts or arbitration); and "**enforceable**" (an enforceable contract is one that a court or other authority could enforce, either by mandating compliance or by ordering a money judgment or penalty for non-compliance).

The challenge in negotiating and drafting ABS contracts is to find a way to apply these legal principles so that the law will recognize them as binding "duties" of the respective parties. This challenge is enhanced by the fact that ABS transactions involve parties from multiple countries, whose legal systems, including their law of contract differ markedly. Beyond this, as discussed in detail in Chapter 6, ABS transactions face a very difficult challenge arising from the possibility that the user might transfer the genetic resource/ATK and related obligations to third parties. In determining whether a contract is valid, binding or enforceable, therefore, the drafters must not only comply with the contract law of the provider country but also take into account the possibility that it will need to be enforced or evaluated in other countries.

---

242 As noted above, tort principles, such as fraud, misrepresentation and unjust enrichment, as well as a range of trade and intellectual property laws are among the possible legal bases for such an action. These matters are also discussed in ¶¶ 7.3.4 and 7.4.

243 An example of this situation is the "Teff Agreement," described in ¶ 4.1. After reviewing their ABS contract to determine whether they could bring suit against a user in breech or contract, the Ethiopian government and their attorneys concluded that their contract did not have all of the elements necessary to enable them to obtain legal recognition and enforcement. They described their contract as "a Gentlemen's Agreement," which relies on the good faith of the parties in lieu of legal enforceability. Anderson and Winge, 2012.

The following discussions examine the primary concepts that determine whether a contract is valid, implementable and enforceable. Section 7.2.1 looks at the primary issue of validity; ¶ 7.2.2 looks at the binding contracts; ¶ 7.2.3 considers implementability and ¶ 7.2.4 looks at enforceability, dividing that issue into discussions of legal certainty and functionality.

7.2.1 *Contractual "Validity"*

The first question that must be asked in any interpretation of contractual obligations is whether the contract is valid. If a contract is invalid, questions of whether it is binding, implementable and enforceable can never arise. Contractual validity forms the basis for all of these points. Although it is possible that a valid contract will not be binding, implementable or enforceable, that situation is rare.

In general, every country's courts have identified specific elements that must be met in order for a contract to be valid. As detailed in ¶ 7.3, although each country's elements differ, they are similar enough that they can be discussed under three general categories: mutuality/intention, concreteness, and equity. These elements determine a contract's validity *as of the day on which it was executed.* After that date, the actions of the parties may violate the contract or cause it to be cancelled or annulled,[244] but those actions will not change the fact that a valid contract was created, nor will it alter the commitments made by the parties.[245]

> "**valid contract**": an instrument or contract that complies with all the relevant legal requirements that would allow a particular court to recognize the contract as a legal instrument under that country's legal system.

In negotiating an ABS contract, therefore, it is essential from the outset to focus on ensuring that the instrument will be valid under both the law of the country in which the contract is being negotiated and any other country whose law might apply. Section 7.3, below provides some guidance regarding how a contract draftsman might ensure that his product includes the primary elements of contractual validity.

244 *E.g.,* fraud, misrepresentation, extortion, unconscionable pressure, *etc.* As discussed in this chapter, if any of these actions happens in the negotiation of the contract, then the contract will not be valid at all.

245 After a valid contract exists, the commitments in it may be changed by all parties agreeing to amend the contract or to replace it with a revised contract. If those activities are legally proper, then they result in a valid contract.

7.2.2 *"Binding" Contracts*

A contract is "binding" when it creates legal obligations from which the two parties cannot escape without consequences. That is, a binding contract is one that creates an obligation that a court can enforce. A contract that is valid is usually also binding, unless the obligations that are created are either legally forbidden (a contract to violate the law) or impossible to either understand or perform.

> "**binding contract**": a valid contract under which all contractual parties are legally bound to perform. Where a contract is binding on a party and that party breaches the contract or refuses to perform his obligations, the other party may take legal action.

In an ABS contract, the obligations created are generally understood as follows: the provider agrees to allow access to and certain uses of genetic material or ATK, and the user agrees to share a portion of the benefits arising from its utilization of those genetic resources or ATK. Unless the contract attempts to circumvent national ABS legislation or sovereign rights, these obligations will not violate the law. There is some concern however, that their precise meaning might be difficult for a court to understand, and that it might be difficult for a court to order specific performance or remedies, in the case of a breach. As this book shows, it is possible through careful drafting to create an ABS contract with terms that are clearly legally binding (see Chapters 5, 8 and 9.)

7.2.3 *"Implementable" Contracts*

In most contracts, the parties' objective is implementation – that is, they intend to take all actions necessary to ensure that all parties (including themselves) fulfill their obligations under the contract. For this reason, the question of a contract's implementability is of primary importance. In essence, a well-written contract describes a clear "pathway of implementation." As noted in Chapter 5, such a pathway is created by describing in precise detail the specific commitments of all parties (the specific actions or behavior required), the timing or triggers of such commitments, and the consequences or options when those commitments are not fulfilled.

As a practical matter, a contract that is not valid, binding or enforceable might still be implemented, as a "gentleman's agreement."[246] In this situation,

246 See ¶ 4.1, where we discuss this concept of a contract that is not binding, but on which the parties trust to each other's "goodwill" to encourage the fulfilment of the contract. By using this term, the authors (one of whom is female) do not mean to suggest that only the male of the species is capable of goodwill in fulfilling a contract that has validity problems.

however, the user may often feel that it is not obligated to comply, and that belief may become its justification for not implementing the contract.

A contract is implementable where each party's obligations are clear and not impossible. Once a contract is found to be valid and binding, its implementability is usually assured. There are however, potential implementability challenges relating to the factual situations surrounding implementation. For example, if a country changes its ABS law after the ABS contract is formally agreed, then the question will arise as to whether the parties may still take the required actions. Thus, the legal questions relevant to the implementability of an ABS contract focus on asking whether the terms of that contract is legally certain, and whether it is functional in the current situation at the time the question is asked. Both of these issues are discussed in detail in connection with enforceability, below.

> "**contract implementation**": the actions of the parties to fulfill the terms of the contract.

7.2.4 *"Enforceable" Contracts*

Formal contract enforcement (bringing a case in court or binding arbitration) is a final option for the parties. It is done only when no resolution is possible through informal means. This option is only available where the contract is "**enforceable**" – that is, where its terms are written in a way that a court or other authority could issue a decision to enforce them, either by mandating compliance or by ordering payment of a monetary remedy or penalty.

> "**enforceable contract**": a binding contract on which a court or arbitrator is legally able compel a violating breaching party either to perform its obligation or to pay remedies or penalties for that breach.

In emphasizing the importance of an enforceable contract, the authors are not suggesting that the parties intend to rely on the courts to satisfy their disputes. As noted above in ¶¶ 1.1, 7.1 and throughout this book, even in very litigious countries (*e.g.*, the US, Europe, and South East Asia) the fact that a contract is binding and enforceable means that its parties will be less likely to violate their contractual obligations, even where they know that the other party is unlikely to take legal action. In general, each company's duty to its shareholders is to balance the costs and benefits of implementing the contract,

247 When commercial entities, companies and individuals enter into contracts, they are doing so within the boundaries of operating budgets, concerns about the economy, and

against the risks of non-compliance.[247] Those risks are seen as much greater, where the contract is enforceable, and virtually non-existent where it is not. It is possible, through careful drafting, to ensure that the terms of a contract are clearly enforceable; thereby increasing the likelihood that parties to that contract will implement it without being forced to do so.

In the case where a company has established a corporate social responsibility (CSR) program, social/charitable reasons could justify giving benefits from a certain line of production to specific objectives in the country where it operates. This is not certain, however; in some cases, the purpose of the creation of the CSR program may be to gain good publicity, rather than to enable social/charitable corporate actions. In general, contract negotiations are premised on the assumptions that both parties will pursue their own interests and priorities, and that they will comply with the law, where it applies.

Although a contract that is valid and binding is usually also enforceable, legal actions for breach or interpretation of contracts normally include a separate consideration of enforceability. In this analysis, they look at concepts that have been applied in ABS under the headings "legal certainty" and "functionality." In addition, there is, unfortunately, another aspect of enforceability – actual ability to perform or pay. As a practical matter, the ability of commercial entities, companies and even many individuals to perform their obligations under contracts, is limited by other factors, such as operating budgets, concerns about the economy, and the demands of shareholders or creditors. The following sections consider the legal certainty/functionality issues, and then turn to the issue of the parties' respective ability to meet their obligations.

(a) "Legal Certainty"

In the CBD and NP negotiations, it was frequently stated, almost as a matter of faith, that ABS would be implemented through contracts. Often, negotiators specifically declared that this decision resolved the complex legal challenges of

---

demands of shareholders or creditors. In most countries, private companies are *legally required* to make all due efforts to maximize profits for shareholders, or to limit themselves to those actions that promote the company's stated objectives. Relatively few companies have the stated objective of giving profits away. Companies do not want to be sued, but this concern disappears if the contract is unenforceable.

It should also be remembered that this is a *practical* balancing. If a company knew it could get comparable samples from a country that does not impose ABS user measures, that company will normally not consider samples obtained from the provider country as one of the benefits of its ABS contract. This fact indicates the importance of ensuring that the ABS contracts provide users with other significant benefits and motivations to comply with the contract.

248 See, e.g., Glowka, 1998, at 2.1.3; and Laird, 1993.

ABS.[248] Their belief was that all ABS implementation issues could be addressed under national contractual and commercial law. On the basis of this view, many (non-lawyer) ABS experts gave advice based on the assumption that contracts are a simple matter. Often, they addressed the entire issue of ABS contracts with only a few words or paragraphs.[249] As a result of this early approach, authors gave virtually no attention to the contractual legal issues of ABS during the first 20 years of ABS, despite the fact that comparative contract law (discussing the differences in contract principles and practices in various countries) is globally one of the most intensively studied legal issues.[250]

> "**legal certainty**": the ability for any person to know with certainty what both parties rights and obligations under the law are, and when those rights attach

Eventually, many of the critical unanswered questions regarding ABS contracts arose in the NP negotiations under the heading of "**legal certainty**" – concern expressed by users about how they could ensure that their contractual rights and obligations were "certain" and not revocable. Over time, it came to be recognized that legal certainty concerns apply to both parties. On one hand, the potential user wants to be certain that the provider in the negotiations actually has the legal right to grant access to the GR and/or ATK. The user also needs certainty in the contract about the exact requirements he must meet, and who is responsible for other legal requirements, (satisfaction of all elements of the country's PIC, MAT, permit and certificate requirements, *etc.* under national ABS frameworks). Conversely, potential providers have their own needs for certainty – they need to be able to prove that they have the legal right to grant access or the right to utilize regarding the particular genetic resources or ATK, and they also need some certainty that the potential user will be able to meet its obligations. Other providers raised the general question of "functionality" – the concern that the ABS system is designed to fail. In particular, they noticed

249 See, *e.g.*, Gollin, 2002. In this document, purporting to clarify the drafting of ABS contract, the author's entire coverage of the contract law was as follows: "The essential elements of any contract throughout the world include (i) competent parties able to be bound by the agreement through their representatives; (ii) meeting of the minds regarding the subject of the agreement – the understanding of what will be done or not done; (iii) mutual assent – a voluntary commitment to perform under the agreement; (iv) consideration – an exchange of valuable tangible things, money, promises or rights; (v) enforceability – the promises of the parties must comply with legal requirements." [no citation]. Not only does this summary assume that contract law is identical the world over, but two of its five listed elements are not, in fact, elements of contract validity in a large number of countries. See also Laird, 1999.

250 Reinmann and Zimmermann, 2006, at p. 900.

a number of issues that cannot be addressed in a functional way unless both provider countries and user countries (and possibly the bodies implementing the global ABS regime[251]) develop comprehensive measures that ensure that ABS obligations are enforced against users even outside the provider country, and that the various monitoring/oversight mechanisms actually function as tools to protect the rights of providers.

With regard to enforceability, legal certainty and functionality are the central issues of ABS. Even where contract law applies, the courts may not usually decide a contracts lawsuit, if the contract is ambiguous or not sufficiently certain regarding the main obligations and other key elements. In the end primary questions affecting functionality and legal certainty were not addressed by the adoption of the NP. Most developed countries have strongly indicated that they do not intend to address ABS functionality challenges in their national law, regulations or other measures.[252] As a result, the task of ensuring that ABS functions is left entirely to provider country legislation and other measures on one hand, and the ABS contracts themselves on the other (see Chapter 5.) Given that provider country measures are nearly impossible to enforce outside the provider country, this means that ABS can function only through legally certain contracts, and only if they are valid, binding, implementable and enforceable in all countries in which they might be tested.

(b) Ability to Perform

Another aspect of enforceability relates to whether the parties are actually able to perform their obligations. The issues underlying this discussion are of two primary types – obstacles that existed before the contract was executed and those that arose later. In general, if an obstacle that prevents a party from fulfilling its obligation existed during the negotiations, then contractually speaking that obstacle is a risk assumed by one or more of the parties. To determine which party assumed the risk, a court or arbitrator will look to the structure of the contract. For example, if a seller agrees to sell a certain asset, but does not own the asset at the time of the negotiations, then that seller is essentially also committing to acquire the asset on or before the date on which it must be transferred.

By contrast, if the obstacle arises after the contract is executed, other factors determine its impact. In the foregoing example, if the asset is destroyed after the contract is signed, but before the date of transfer, then the question of what happens to the contract depends on whether the destruction was caused by the seller, whether it was predictable, and other factors.

---

251 Listed in ¶ 11.3, *infra*.

252 Bavikatte and Meienberg, 2014.

As discussed in more detail in Chapter 4, in some cases, a party might be unable to perform because it is not the right party. For example, a subsidiary company or an individual may promise to take actions that only the parent corporation could do. If the parent company has not agreed to the action, then the contract will fail due to inability to perform. In some cases, this could mean that the contract is invalid. The injured party will not be able to utilize contract law in order to obtain performance or a remedy. Depending on other factors, however, it may give rise to a claim that the subsidiary or individual assumed the duty of obtaining the parent corporation's agreement. In some cases, it might even serve as a basis for an action against that subsidiary or individual alleging fraud, misrepresentation or some other legal claim.

Often in these situations, however, the contract will still be valid, but it will be effectively unenforceable. The original parties are still subject to enforcement action, but when the court or arbitrator issues an order, that order cannot be enforced. This happens when the breaching party is insolvent, so in addition to being unable to perform its obligations, it is unable to pay the ordered remedy or penalty. This is the worst kind of unenforceability, because it happens after the parties have invested time and money in bringing an enforcement action.

7.3 Drafting Issues of Validity for ABS Contracts

As noted above, all of the basic concepts of contractual functionality turn on the determination of the contract's validity. Depending on which country's law applies (see Chapter 10, *infra*), the validity of a contract may involve anywhere between two and six elements, which vary greatly from country to country.[253] To maximize the enforceability of a contract that could be interpreted by parties, arbitrators, judges and others in many countries, it is advisable to take a conservative approach – to try to ensure that the contract meets as many as possible of these validity factors.

Across all of the varying approaches to contractual validity, it is possible to identify three general categories that encompass all of the elements of validity that are known to the authors,[254] which we have called "mutuality and

253 The most common elements are generally stated as intent, offer, acceptance, consideration, capacity and congruity with public policy, but different terminology or translations may apply.

254 The authors give no assurance that this is a complete summary of all elements of validity from all 200+ states currently in existence, however they have, between them worked with

intention," "concreteness" and "equity and public policy." Not all countries require all three types of elements. It is advisable in drafting an ABS contract, to attempt to satisfy each of them as much as possible. The following summaries provide some general understanding of each category and indicate the range of national approaches that apply.

7.3.1 *Mutuality and/or Intention*

The most common examples of "mutuality and intention" are often referred to by one of two standard phrases "offer and acceptance" or "offer, acceptance and consideration."[255] The use of these phrases provides a view of contracts that is somewhat antiquated, in terms of actual practice, in which there are many drafts and revisions, resulting eventually in an agreement. Despite their outdated approach however, offer/acceptance and offer/acceptance/consideration approaches are still the official view in some countries' national contract law.[256]

The more modern view recognizes that, no matter how the contract is created, and no matter how many different parties are involved, the primary requirement is that all parties share a mutual intent, as of the time that the contract enters into force. The six most commonly recognized elements of mutual intent are as follows: intent, offer, acceptance, consideration, capacity and congruence with public policy. To understand mutuality/intention elements, it is useful to start from the offer/acceptance models, and then examine the

---

the contract law of over 20 countries, and have researched several others for this book. This summary is based on that experience.

255 The old-fashioned offer/acceptance and offer/acceptance/consideration models are most often found in countries that do not have a full commercial code, but rather base national contractual law on a single "Contract Act," which is often quite old. The adoption of a more detailed "Commercial Code," which is the accepted approach in most developed countries, enables a less simplistic and vastly more realistic and useful approach to modern contract practices. Even countries such as the UK that have historically relied on precedent-based "common law" to govern contracts now have enacted bodies of formal legislation governing and limiting not only contract validity, but also contract equity.

256 In many countries, commercial codes are included in a larger code entitled the "civil code," however this book will not use this term, as it causes confusion among readers who assume that it refers only to countries whose legal systems are based on the "code Napoleon" or "Roman" models. Even countries that have evolved to a broader view of mutuality include offer and acceptance concepts within their contractual codes, recognizing the need to continue to accommodate old-fashioned approaches, to the extent that they can be justified through the application of mutuality concepts.

manner in which most countries' contractual law (and virtually all modern commercial practice) have evolved beyond them. The following general summary is limited to the basic point regarding why and how to reflect mutuality in an ABS contract.

(a) Mutuality

The "offer and acceptance" model is based on the idea that a contract involves two parties – the "offeror" and the "offeree." The offeror makes an offer, which becomes a contract when the offeree accepts the offer.

This approach was the basis of the earliest contract cases. A large body of law developed over the question of when one could conclude that a particular statement or action constituted an offer or an acceptance. The challenge was relatively simple: Contracts can be created by actions, verbal statements and written statements, even where the parties do not clearly state that they are offering or accepting a contract. Often, for example, an exchange of letters might discuss what the parties want or plan to do, without any particular statement that an offer has been made or accepted. In many cases, such an exchange of letters or oral statements was found to be a binding contract, even without a formally signed contract instrument. Further challenges related to post-contract changes in the contract (transfers, amendments, termination, *etc.*), and again validity was based on the view that one party proposes the change and another accepts it.

Although appropriate in the 11th century (and earlier), the offer/acceptance model has become increasingly difficult to apply, because in modern times the actual practice of contract negotiation and drafting is quite different. Today's contracts often involve multiple parties, bound by a web of interconnecting obligations and rights. Contract processes have evolved to include complex negotiations, in which the parties essentially produce a jointly written instrument that memorializes the agreement among all parties.[257] As a consequence, modern contract practice and most commercial codes do not bother with the detailed questions of "offer," "acceptance" or consideration, but focus instead on a more useful issue: "mutuality."

257 Typically, after general discussions leading to the agreement to go ahead and negotiate a contract on the basis of a generally agreed concept, one party or a jointly hired legal advisor writes a draft which is circulated to all for comments. Comments, whether general or specific, are made in the form of "markups," letters, verbal discussions and even the submission of entirely new drafts. Eventually, if all parties can accept a "final" version, the contract is executed. If not, the negotiations end with no contract. It is difficult to break this process down into an "offer" and an "acceptance."

The mutuality construct focuses on the question of whether and at what point the parties all agreed that the contract was complete, agreed on its objectives and contents, and also agreed that they would be bound by it. Particularly in a complex relationship in which no universally agreed "standards" are recognized (see ¶ 6.7.3, *infra*), the most effective mechanism for concretely establishing mutuality is a signed written contract.

One challenge is to ensure that all aspects of the agreement are reflected in the contract. If the parties had orally agreed to additional terms that were not included in the written contract, then their contract could become ambiguous. The oral statements may either be found to be meaningless or controlling. If the former, than the person who relied on the oral statements may lose benefits he had been expecting. If the latter, the written contract may be drastically changed. These rules are often complex, but the most effective way to avoid any problem is first to ensure that *every* assurance made in the negotiations is included in the written contract and then to include a clause (called an "integration" clause) that specifically states that no oral agreement can alter the written terms:[258]

(b) Intention

Another focus of the offer/acceptance model is the question of intention. In the offer-acceptance era, the question was this: Was the offer intended as an "offer"

EXAMPLE: INTEGRATION CLAUSE

This Agreement [together with the documents or annexes listed on Exhibit A] constitutes the entire understanding and agreement of the parties hereto with respect to the subject matter hereof and supersedes all prior and contemporaneous agreements or understandings, inducements or conditions, express or implied, written or oral, between the parties with respect hereto. In particular, the express terms as defined herein control and supersede any other usage, including in the international ABS regime, national ABS legislation, or the [pharmaceutical, research and development, agricultural, *etc.* include all that are relevant] industry[ies].

258 Similar, but separate, issues are addressed in the "amendments" clause, discussed in ¶ 6.5.8, *supra*.

or just an "idea for future discussion"? If the latter, then it would not become a contract upon acceptance. In fact, that "acceptance" may be seen as simply a new offer. Often, this issue was resolved by looking at "consideration" -- did either party do or give something valuable to lock the contract into place?

Today, the underlying question is "what do the parties intend?" A common example of the role of intention in contracts is an uncle who promises that he will bequeath his father's watch to his nephew, if the nephew promises to keep it as an heirloom and pass it on to a family member, in due time. The nephew accepts the offer and makes the promise his uncle has asked for. To some, this may sound like an offer and acceptance. At the time of their promises, however, neither party has *done* anything that would indicate a contractual intention. If the uncle leaves the watch to someone else, the nephew cannot claim any right based on the earlier exchange of promises. Again, the key question goes beyond asking whether there was an offer and acceptance, to ask whether there is *evidence* of a shared intention to be bound by a contract.

Unfortunately, intention is a thought process. It is not currently possible to determine with any precision what the parties were thinking at a given time. As a result, in contract law, the only evidences of intention are (in order of usefulness) (i) the contents of the contract itself; (ii) the parties' actions; and (iii) the parties' statements about what they intended.

Normally, the validity of the contract is an issue that arises after the contract is signed. At that point, the parties, court or arbitrator will first look to the contract itself. This is why the contents of the contract should be carefully drafted. Any remaining doubts are resolved by considering proof of the actions and statements of the parties – whether they acted and spoke as if they believed they were bound by a contract.

In practice, many interpretations can be placed on any action. For this reason, some countries have specified particular components of intention. One primary example is the concept of "consideration" (money or something of value.) The intention element may be proven by the fact that one party formally transferred (or made a binding/irrevocable commitment to transfer) some consideration to the other party. Even countries that do not specifically identify "consideration" as a required element of validity will normally consider that a contract exists where some transfer of value has occurred.

The mere fact that a document contains a promise to act in future may not constitute evidence of intention. To increase certainty that the parties intend to enter into a contract, it is useful to include a phrase or clause regarding consideration:

In addition to the above "consideration language," it is also useful to draft the contract so that it will not commence until some specific transfer of value

EXAMPLE: "ACKNOWLEDGEMENT OF CONSIDERATION" LANGUAGE

In consideration of the receipt of [here identify the value transferred, e.g., samples, ATK and monetary and non-monetary transfers] pursuant to paragraph XXX herein, all promises and covenants herein contained, and other good and valuable consideration, the receipt and sufficiency of which are hereby acknowledged, the parties agree as follows:

[Note: This language frequently appears between the "recitals" (sometimes called "whereas clauses") and the first of the functional clauses of the contract.]

has occurred, such as the collection of the first sample, an up-front payment of money, and/or a transfer of equipment or other value.

7.3.2 *Concreteness*

In most legal systems, validity and "enforceability" are closely linked – a contract will be invalid if it is not concrete enough to be specifically enforced.[259] This underscores our basic advice on drafting contracts, as contained in Chapter 5. It also demonstrates how important it is to carry that advice over to *all* contractual provisions. If a contract is concretely specific about the *res* and the obligations of the parties, but vague or ambiguous regarding other key legal elements, the contract may still prove unenforceable. At this point, it may be useful to explain how lack of concreteness and contract validity are impacted by future events, and the manner in which contracts can "concretely" address uncertain and changing conditions.

One aspect of concreteness involves ensuring that the contract is clear about how it will operate. If the contract fails to explain/address some essential question, or is ambiguous about it, there is a possibility that the contract will be declared to be invalid due to incompleteness or ambiguity. It is often difficult to predict which issues a court will find to be "essential" for this purpose,

259 In the offer/acceptance model, an offer is not an offer unless it is specific enough that, upon acceptance, the parties, arbitrator and/or court will know exactly what each party is required to do. Mutuality and intention models also recognize that a contract cannot reflect mutual agreement and intention if it is not concrete enough that the parties are clearly agreeing to the same things – that their intentions are mutual.

or how much uncertainty will be permitted, especially in an international contract.[260]

Another aspect of the concreteness elements relates to industry standards, as discussed in ¶ 7.7, *infra*. Standards can become important because the arbitrator or court may find that a contract containing gaps is still enforceable and thus valid, where it is possible to fill those gaps by applying "industry standards." As noted below, however, it is not currently advisable or even possible for ABS contracts to rely on this, because at present no generally recognized ABS contractual standards exist. The ABS concept is relatively new, there have only been a few dozen ABS contracts negotiated worldwide (compared with hundreds of thousands every year for most other industries with "standards.") In addition, most of the ABS contracts that do exist or have existed have not been made available due to confidentiality clauses. Only time and the amalgamation of generally shared practices and examples can change this situation.

TIP

Although it is clearly important to ensure that the ABS operational elements of the contract are very concretely expressed, do not let the difficulty of this task prevent the careful inclusion of concrete provisions addressing more conventional issues, including the specific elements of payment, the manner in which transfers are made, the procedures that must be followed in the event of breach of contract, *etc.*

7.3.3 *Equity and Public Policy Elements*

Many countries refuse to recognize any contract that does not meet the country's equity standards or that violates the country's "public policy." These issues are generally unique to each country. The following discussions provide a bit of understanding of some of the most common equity and public policy issues that may impact a contract's validity; however, the uncertainties in this area make it difficult to propose contractual solutions or protections.

The following sections provide a brief summary of some of the most common equity and public policy issues that might arise in ABS contracts.

260 These issues are discussed in more detail in Chapter 10, *infra*.

> TIP
>
> Unless or until the Parties to the Nagoya Protocol can agree on standards that every country specifically commits to uphold,[261] the only advice that can be given is to make efforts to ensure that the ABS contract is equitable and reflects positively on general political and social policy issues, and seek advice from contractual experts regarding contractual validity and public policy in every country whose law is or may become potentially relevant to the contract (*i.e.*, the countries of the user, provider, arbitrator, governing law, and likely transferees.)

(a) Inequality of Parties; Protected Classes

As noted in Chapter 4, contractual/commercial law frequently includes special protections for categories of parties that are legally considered to be vulnerable – less sophisticated or powerful. These laws are intended to protect those vulnerable parties from more powerful or sophisticated persons or entities that might (intentionally or unintentionally) take advantage of their weak position, inexperience and lack of commercial knowledge.

In some cases, a contract with a member of a protected class may be found to be invalid, or even, in some countries, rewritten to ensure that it operates equitably. Most of these factors are discussed in Chapter 4. This section is only intended to remind the reader that, if there is any doubt about whether a party is a member of a legally protected class, those doubts should be addressed as a matter of urgency, because they can cause the invalidation of the entire contract. In addition, as noted in Chapter 4, it is not sufficient to simply address them by writing a paragraph in which the parties all agree that their legal status allows them to enter into a valid contract. Such a paragraph will not prevent a court from invalidating the contract.

Applying this issue to ABS contracts, it is important to note that many countries' law specially protects people who are not properly prepared for modern transactional negotiations, such as people whose lifestyles are based on social separation (*e.g.*, indigenous peoples and those living in isolated rural communities).[262] Thus, indigenous persons and communities, particularly those

261 Young and Tvedt, 2009.

262 Unfortunately, many of these laws equate the protection of indigenous people with protection of those who are mentally or educationally impaired (and sometimes of persons

whose entire lives have been in separate from the main part of the country's commercial system, may be a protected class.[263] This means that the general law may require special protections for them in the course of the negotiations. Where those requirements are not met, the contract may be invalidated at the request of the protected person, or enforced only if the protected person seeks enforcement.

As described in Chapter 4, the most important means of addressing this issue is through pre-negotiation investigation. In general, the ability of all parties to enter into and perform the contract should normally be addressed and/or proven *before* anyone signs the contract, in time to confirm the parties' claims and resolve any legal problems.

In some limited cases, special laws are designed to protect private individuals any time they are involved in a contract with more sophisticated commercial companies.[264] In many commercial transactions, the parties may not be aware that these clauses are relevant, due to the fact that they are frequently called by generic names such as "consumer protection" statutes. It may come as a shock to a company that is dealing with a private individual in a contract that is not *per se* a consumer transaction, to find that such laws apply. The outcome may have unexpected negative impacts on the company's actual rights and obligations. In ABS, this kind of situation could arise where, for example, the user is committing to transfer some benefit other than money (*e.g.*, equipment, services, scholarships, *etc.*) to the provider in a situation in which the court or relevant agency assumes that the individual might normally simply receive money.[265]

---

disabled by insanity or intoxication.) The basic contractual law tome in the United States, *Williston on Contracts*, notes the following as the primary classes of persons that have been declared in various states to lack the capacity to contract: "infants [*e.g.*, underage children], insane persons, intoxicated persons, married women, convicts, spendthrifts, aged persons, corporations, *and Native Americans*." *Williston on Contracts* § 9:1 (4th ed.) (*emphasis added.*) A detailed discussion of this issue is found in Furmston, 1993, at pp. 399–444; and see Shelton, 2014.

263 See, *e.g.*, UNITED STATES *Penobscot Indian Nation* v. *Key Bank of Maine*; *U.S. v. Ahtanum Irr. Dist.*; and *Davis v. Jones*.

264 Many countries' commercial codes include specific legislation addressing specialized aspects of fair commercial practices, sometimes called "consumer protection" statutes.

265 The authors have not seen this happen in ABS contracts, as yet, but one of them has been involved in two natural-resource-related contractual situations where these issues have arisen to disrupt the contract.

TIP
REGARDING PROTECTED CLASSES

It is essential to work with a commercial lawyer in the provider country or whichever country the ABS contract is being negotiated in. That advisor should provide an "opinion letter" (a letter in which the lawyer essentially guarantees that he is properly describing the state of the relevant national law and practice. Such a letter is normally carefully written, because if the lawyer is not careful and accurate, he could be liable for any harm that his inaccuracy caused to the party he addressed the letter to) explaining the applicability or inapplicability of national consumer protection laws to the transaction.

(b) Inequity of Contract Terms – Unconscionable Contracts and Contracts of Adhesion

There are other potential legal challenges that may arise with regard to national standards of equity. As further discussed in Chapter 8, there is a possibility in many countries that a court or arbitrator will unilaterally rewrite an inequitable contract, to make it fairer to the parties involved. In this chapter, however, we will consider only the possibility that a court will invalidate an inequitable contract – *i.e.*, that it will declare the contract to be void or voidable,[266] due to the inequity. The most common contract equity issues arise where a contract is alleged to be a "contract of adhesion" or an "unconscionable contract." If it is found to be so, the contract may be declared invalid.

Unconscionable contracts, including contracts of adhesion, may generally be defined as contracts in which a legally stronger party controls the contracting process, so that the text of the contract may be unfair to the weaker party,

266 A contract that is potentially invalid because of inequity to one of the parties may be declared "voidable" rather than completely void. The party that was potentially the victim of its inequity has the option to go forward with the contract, if he wishes. If he does not wish to go forward with the contract, he can "void" it. The other party has no such option. It must go forward with the contract if the victim wishes, or consider it void if the victim chooses that option. See UNITED STATES *Forrest Associates v. Passamaquoddy Tribe*; *Narragansett Indian Tribe v.* RIBO, Inc.; *Taylor v. Grant*; and Cohen, *Handbook of Federal Indian Law*, 1982. This result may depend on the nature of the protected party. The law will often hold this person responsible to comply with part of the contract, in order to assure fairness. See, *e.g.*, UNITED STATES *Taylor v. Grant*. The person who lacks capacity may, for example, have to pay a reasonable amount for goods or services, but will not be held to a higher, unreasonable, contractual price.

who has no ability to change it. In a contract of adhesion, the stronger party provides a "required form"[267] and insists that the weaker party must sign with no amendment possible. Non-form-based contracts may also be invalidated as "unconscionable," where the stronger party uses its superior bargaining position to insist on terms that are found to be unfair or excessive.[268]

The common factor in these kinds of impermissible contracts is that the weaker or less sophisticated party may be told or led to believe that he has no choice. Sometimes he is told that the terms in the document he is asked to sign are fixed or standard within the industry so that no alteration is possible or advisable.[269] Often, the weaker party may welcome this information, as a reason that he need not try to understand the contract. But if he fails to read and understand it, he may find himself bound to an inequitable contract and terms he would not have agreed to had he been given a choice.

To avoid these abuses, conventional contract law in many countries imposes strict controls on the use of form contracts. If a form is used that is found to be a contract of adhesion, then the court may declare it invalid, and release the weaker party, but only if the weaker party wants to be released. Under these principles, not all form contracts are illegal, because it is clear that form contracts can often be very helpful to less sophisticated parties. Contract law seeks to *enable* the use of forms by imposing legal standards. A contract can avoid being considered as a contract of adhesion, if it meets the following standards:

- The contract is generally fair and balanced;
- The contract takes the needs and interests of both parties into account; and
- The contract is only used in the particular situation for which it is designed, and the weaker party is given a "fair understanding of his options."

On the surface, these standards may seem very subjective, but are actually fairly concrete. Over the centuries, court cases have provided many examples,

267 Wherever one party gives the other a printed form contract or says that the contract he offers is "standard," and states or implies that no changes to the contract will be allowed – *i.e.*, that the other party must either sign the contract as-is or walk away entirely, that contract is possibly a "contract of adhesion" (sometimes described as a "take-it-or-leave-it contract.")

268 Some contracts may be considered unconscionable where a commercially stronger party uses this strength to obtain an unfair advantage (a ridiculously low price, for example) over the weaker party.

269 Many countries have adopted consumer protection laws and other statutes to protect parties in other unequal negotiation situations. See, *e.g.*, UNITED STATES 8 *Williston on Contracts* §§ 18.1–18.20 "Unconscionable Agreements."

both of form contracts that have been deemed acceptable and those that have been declared to be contracts of adhesion.[270] The form contracts used by reputable organizations are normally carefully drafted to ensure that they meet these standards and that all of their contracts and negotiations with weaker or less sophisticated parties are implemented in a manner that avoids these controversies.

In the context of ABS, there are two situations in which an ABS party may be legally recognized to be weaker in terms of commercial matters (poorer, less knowledgeable about contracts, *etc.*):

- In a few countries, the law states that private individuals and/or indigenous communities and may be direct "providers" of genetic resources and should negotiate ABS contracts directly (with or without a later approval, confirmation or other decision by the government); or
- In others, the law may be unclear about which person has the right to grant access and get benefit-sharing with regard to a particular species. Often in these countries, users assume that this means that any individual, entity or community may enter into an ABS agreement without governmental oversight or provisions.[271]

Both types of laws can sometimes place significant strain on the provider, and may create an unintentional coercive situation.

As a key means of avoiding such unfairness, some of countries have specifically adopted ABS form contracts, most of which are still new enough that they have not yet been tested or proven in practice. In addition, a number of

---

270 Generally discussed in UNITED STATES 1 *Williston on Contracts* §§ 1:20 ("Void bargains and voidable contracts") and 1:21 ("Unenforceable contracts").

271 In some countries the law simply says that any owner of a particular plant or animal owns (or may grant access to) its genetic material. Every person who owns an example of a particular plant/animal species is aware that there are potentially dozens of other persons in the same situation. If any of them is able to successfully complete an ABS contract negotiation, they will be in a type of competition. The first company to obtain a patent could effectively remove all incentive for other companies to continue to work on the same genetic resource. All other providers might lose their expectation of benefits. (As noted in the case of the Teff Agreement, such arrangements can eventually even claim to exclude the original provider from such uses. See Andersen and Winge, 2012, at Chapter 6.) This creates a "race to contract," potentially pushing many providers to act improvidently. Fortunately, to date only a very small minority of countries have left the ownership of genetic resources and ATK solely in the hands of the individuals who own specimens.

companies (as well as the ITPGRFA[272] and the WHO Pandemic Influenza Preparedness (PIP) framework[273]) impose "unchangeable"/"non-negotiable" form contracts.[274] As noted above, these instruments are not necessarily contracts of adhesion; the determination of their validity may be based on the analysis of many factors. In this connection, ITPGRFA Parties have asserted that the ITPGRFA-SMTA[275] is narrowly focused, given that it is not available to just anyone and may be used only by developers of agricultural plant varieties and only for agricultural variety development.[276]

The WHO Pandemic Influenza Preparedness (PIP) Framework originally included two SMTAs, one of which was also non-negotiable. That agreement – WHO-SMTA1 –, although an even better example of a non-adhesion ABS form

272 Discussed in more detail in ¶ 11.5.3.d, *infra*. Unlike most other ABS-related form contracts, the SMTA has been frequently used. It has been the subject of significant recent analysis regarding its function (See FAO Report of the Expert Panel, 2016, "Options for Introducing a Termination Clause") and is currently the subject of ongoing review by technical experts considering possible revisions. By and large, these discussions have not focused on whether or to what extent it is a contract of adhesion; however, this issue was addressed in memoranda produced by FAO during the negotiations of the ITPGRFA and of the SMTA. Those memoranda are no longer accessible online.

273 Pandemic Influenza Preparedness Framework for the sharing of influenza viruses and access to vaccines and other benefits ("PIP Framework").

274 In Young, 2009, table 3–1.1 (p. 80) lists a large number of contracts that were then in the World Intellectual Property Organization (WIPO) database of documents that had been submitted to and designated as "ABS contracts" by the party submitting them. Most of these documents are printed forms, offered by their drafters to be used in the field without amendment.

275 Moore and Tymowski, 2005. The SMTA negotiations are alleged by some as assurance that the SMTA cannot be considered coercive. The SMTA was negotiated in a very public process by a broad base of negotiators, and is being reviewed, again by a balanced team of experts from around the world, with the primary objective of ensuring that the SMTA would ultimately be fair to all users, collectors (middlemen) and providers of genetic material. ITPGRFA § 12.3(a).

276 There have been many criticisms of this SMTA, based on the fact that this limitation is not monitored, so that users are the only persons who know whether they are complying with this restriction or not. During the negotiations, many participants made it clear that they were agreeing to the proposed terms only because they were appropriate in that limited situation. Commentators have also noted that the specific situation to which the SMTA is addressed is the situation in which there is a pre-existing international body of collections of specific plant genetic resources (*e.g.*, the CGIAR centres) developed for that specified narrow purpose. This situation is not duplicated with regard to any other type of GR. During the negotiations, many participants made it clear that they were agreeing to the proposed terms only because they were appropriate in that limited situation. This

contract, appears to have been deleted from the agency's options, in the year between submission and final proofreading of this manuscript. The following discussion is retained, because it is instructive regarding the crafting of mandatory documents: WHO SMTA1 made up for its non-negotiability by including provisions that address most of potential criticisms. Specifically, it was narrowly focused, both in terms of the *res* (setting a clear limitation of the precise genetic resources covered, making it clear that all other genetic resources, even if transferred at the same time, would be subject to other rules[277]) and of the parties who may participate;[278] inclusion of a specimen in a contract-related transfer may happen only with approval from the provider country;[279] it clearly stated benefit-sharing provisions;[280] and clearly specified tiered pricing of the vaccines thus created;[281] it included specific statements about the benefits of compliance by the user as well as the provider;[282] and specific provisions protecting the interest of providers.[283] Perhaps most relevant to its ABS

indicates that the SMTA is probably not an appropriate model for other kinds of genetic resource utilization situations and ABS contracts.

277 PIP Framework, § 4.1.

278 WHO-SMTA1 applied only to parties that have specifically agreed to the PIP. For labs that have not agreed, WHO-SMTA2 is much less prescriptive, with most headings followed by the words "to be agreed." WHO-SMTA2 also includes detailed benefit-sharing requirements for manufacturers of vaccines and/or antivirals (with comparable provisions for other manufacturers of products relevant to pandemic influenza preparedness and response). Among other provisions it requires the manufacturer to reserve a specific percentage of the vaccine for distribution by WHO "at affordable prices," to donate a specified amount for use by WHO, and to license it in developing countries on fair and reasonable terms or enable royalty-free use.

279 PIP Framework, § 5.1.2.

280 Regarding the "general benefit" from the use of its genetic resources it required that "Genetic sequence data, and analyses arising from that data, … should be shared in a rapid, timely and systematic manner with the originating laboratory and among WHO GISRS laboratories" (PIP, § 5.2.1) and further benefits developing countries through its recognition and addressing of their needs in its benefit sharing system (PIP, § 6.7.)

281 PIP Framework, § 6.12.

282 Specifically, it called on Member States to "urge influenza vaccine, diagnostic and pharmaceutical manufacturers to make specific efforts to transfer these technologies to other countries, particularly developing countries, as appropriate" and specifically asks that such transfer "empower developing countries to study and manufacture influenza vaccines, diagnostics and pharmaceuticals." PIP Framework, § 6.13.

283 It placed obligations on the collection to protect the interests of providers by requiring that "The Director-General, … put in place in a timely manner a transparent traceability mechanism that uses an electronic system in order to track in real time the movement of

compatibility, fully half of the costs of the WHO-PIP programme that provides benefits is funded by specified financial contributions from the pharmaceutical companies that will use the viruses.[284]

> TIP
>
> To avoid the pitfalls and uncertainties connected to unconscionable contracts and contracts of adhesion, contract parties should take a number of generally recognized steps to ensure that their contract is not coercive, where the contract involves a commercial and institutional user and a rural or traditional provider. One of the most effective ways would be for the commercially sophisticated user to provide separate legal and technical advisors who can help the provider understand and protect its rights.[285] Another possible approach is for the provider and user countries to adopt open and fair processes to specifically identify particular forms and models that their legal processes will be clearly accept as "fair and reasonable."

(c) Disclosure and Free Will – Preventing and Combatting Fraud, Coercion, Misrepresentation and Non-disclosure

Disclosure issues arise under both equity and mutuality. Equity predominates, because a contract founded on a lack of full disclosure is not fair, also where a party enters into a contract on the basis of a misunderstanding caused (intentionally or unintentionally) by another party, there is no "mutuality of

PIP biological materials into, within, and out of the WHO GISRS" (PIP, § 5.3.) In addition, WHO accepts some responsibility for actions to redress breaches of the WHO-SMTAS (PIP Framework, § 7, and WHO-SMTA1, Article 7.) WHO-SMTA1 also included a provision that forbids user and provider from patenting any of the transferred materials (WHO-SMTA1, Article 6. This clause was relatively non-specific and may not have been sufficient to avoid the challenges faced by providers in other ABS situations, such as the Teff Agreement challenges, discussed in § 5.4.5). It also mandated binding arbitration.

284 PIP Framework, § 6.14. In 2010, the companies were to provide US$28.3 million. (PIP Framework, page 18, footnote 1.)

285 The Biotrade initiative provides detailed guidance about this issue. *BioTrade Verification Framework for Native Natural Ingredients*, § 3.1.1, Union for Ethical BioTrade, International Standard 1, Proposed Draft 3 – Clean 2007-06-20 (http://www.biotrade.org/ResourcesPublications/BT_Verification_framework_NI_June07_en.pdf), last accessed on 15 January 2015. Possibly over-optimistically it defines the following indicator of fairness in ABS transactions: "There are no disputes related to the use of biodiversity and traditional knowledge of substantial magnitude involving a significant number of interests."

intent" and the contract can be invalidated under that heading as well. It is well beyond the scope of this book to detail the law on these types of civil and criminal misbehavior. Instead, we will be satisfied with briefly discussing the difference between "retaining confidential information" and impermissibly misleading or failing to disclose.

The obligations of disclosure are not limited to contracts with "protected classes" or unsophisticated parties. These principles apply to all parties in all contracts. Thus, they fall equally on users and providers. These concepts focus on the harms that arise when one party intentionally or unintentionally deceives the other or fails to disclose critical information. In most countries contractual/commercial law includes a number of provisions or practices designed to protect all parties from this kind of harm. These include legal concepts such as fraud, misrepresentation, deceit, non-disclosure, coercion, duress, corrupt practices, *etc.* The laws and practices addressing these concepts protect both sides of the transaction.

These issues arise at the intersection of two potentially conflicting principles: the right of confidentiality and the right to full and accurate disclosure. On one hand, the negotiation of a contract involves multiple parties, each of whom has its own reasons for participating. Each such party has come to its own internal determination of the value of the contract to its own objectives and activities. As discussed in ¶ 3.2.1, each well prepared party has also determined which potential rights it must receive and/or protect and which obligations it is willing to commit to. They also have come to decisions regarding how much flexibility they will have with regard to all of these facts. The contract negotiation involves all the parties convincing one another to agree to particular provisions or accept particular compromises. The fairness of that process depends on each party being able to maintain the confidentiality of its private determinations of value, willingness to commit and flexibility.

On the other hand, in most modern transactions, some relevant fact may be known only to one party. For example, in a contract involving a corporation, the corporation's directors and officers may be the only persons who know all key factors regarding its current financial condition. They have a strong motivation to keep this information confidential. If the corporation is nearly bankrupt, the other party may not wish to go forward with the contract. The fact that the other party cannot find out independently is a key factor. Obviously, there is a delicate balance between confidentiality and the full and accurate disclosure. National legal principles and laws on this issue may vary. As set out in ¶ 3.2.1, *supra*, there are several practical rules of thumb that should guide negotiators.

(d) Contracts "Against Public Policy"

Many countries view a contract that violates "public policy" as invalid, because it is not appropriate to use the legal processes of a country in a way that subverts that country's policy. This principle normally does not refer to particular policy documents, instruments or statements adopted by the government, but rather focuses on basic social, moral and economic values – the "social contract" that ties the national society together.

To a large extent, these basic values are similar in all countries, and include many issues that can be linked in some way to ABS contracts and their implementation.[286] Each State has a sovereign right to invalidate contracts or refuse to enforce foreign laws or judgments, on the ground that they are "contrary to [that State's] public policy."[287]

Each country has its own views on what is specifically included within the ambit of public policy for these purposes. In some countries, it has been reported that any contract or law which prevents a landowner from doing whatever he wants on his own land, would violate public policy. In other countries, certain religious values are considered to be public policies which can be used as the basis for declaring a contract to be null and void.

As we have noted, there is no general agreement on the meaning, interpretation and implementation of the concepts of ABS and its components under the CBD and NP. As a result, it is not clear whether any ABS contract might be declared invalid as "against public policy" in a country that holds a different view from the provider country, regarding the interpretation of certain ABS concepts.

7.4 Effect of Contract Invalidation

What happens if a contract is found to be invalid, impermissibly inequitable, illegal, unconscionable or a contract of adhesion? The short answer is as

286 Critical "public policy" values include the impartiality and neutrality of the legal system; the sanctity of life; the protection of family/community values and rights (especially gender issues); the doctrine that ignorance or evasion of the law does not excuse violation (except in the case of some of the special classes of people discussed in ¶ 7.3.3(a), *supra*); legal certainty; acknowledgement of the legal system as the primary method or resolving disputes that cannot be amicably settled; political equality; governmental transparency; societal flexibility; and economic growth.

287 Two simple examples of contracts that have been invalidated on the basis of public policy are contracts for euthanasia and contracts to commit a crime.

> TIP
> CONTRACTS AND PUBLIC POLICY
>
> At present, there is no agreement among countries (not even those that are Parties to the NP) on the nature of ABS, or on basic principles or models of ABS contract that they will all recognize as valid and enforceable. As a result, each country's public policy principles must be considered in the negotiation of any ABS contract. In particular, the parties should investigate the public policy decisions relating to contracts, especially contracts for various types of property, in all countries that they know or expect may be relevant to the contract (the countries of the user, provider, arbitrator, and likely transferees). Where an innovative clause is developed, special attention should be given to analysing it in terms of public policy.

follows: The results may vary. In some cases, the unfair contract may be declared to be invalid and it may be either immediately voided or formally terminated. In these situations, the best legal solution may be to "unwind" the contract, with each party's performances returned to him or compensated. Often, however, termination or voiding the contract produces an inequitable result. For example, if an ABS contract is declared void or terminated after samples have been transferred, it is not possible to be certain that the user will not continue to use the genetic information or ATK obtained, even if the user returns the samples. The provider whose contract was terminated will have no contractual basis for monitoring or taking other action against the user. For this reason, as more fully examined in Chapter 8, many contracts include a term that specifically calls for the contract to continue to exist following breach. In addition, some countries' courts are authorized to "reform" contracts that are invalid, in order to allow them to continue as binding contracts.

7.5 Valid but Unenforceable – What Can be Done with "Soft" Obligations?

As noted above, the lack of sufficient specificity regarding contract obligations may render the contract completely invalid. In other situations the contract may be ruled valid; however, it is possible that it will still be unenforceable. Specifically, in countries where concreteness is not included among the tests of validity; a contract may be both valid and too unspecific to enforce. Even in countries which include concreteness as an element of validity, a contract that is not specific on all major points may still be deemed valid. When the time comes to enforce these contracts, the legal system may conclude that they are not specific enough for a court to enforce. In that case, there are several possible options. The first possibility is that the parties will go forward with the contract anyway, as a "gentlemen's agreement"[288] – that is, an expression of the intentions of parties, to be respected and implemented as a mark of mutual respect and goodwill.

Where legal action is needed, however (*i.e.*, where there is a disagreement or conflict among the parties that cannot be resolved informally), the aggrieved party may choose to take the case to court or arbitration anyway – *i.e.*, to ask the court to fill the gaps that make the contract unenforceable. In most countries, this will only happen where the court or arbitrator determines that there are existing standards which the parties were relying on, when they agreed to an incomplete contract. In a few countries, however, there is a standard of practice where contracts are incomplete or inequitable by which the court will essentially rewrite the contract, so that it is enforceable and equitable. As noted in ¶ 6.6, *supra*, if there are "well established industry standards" applicable to the contract, it may also be possible to use them to "fix" an unenforceable contract. At present, there are, as yet, few if any agreed "ABS standards."

Another option might be for the aggrieved party to seek a different kind of remedy (under tort law or some other legal theory). These options are all discussed in Chapters 8 and 9.

7.6 Contract Classification Issues

The laws governing contracts vary greatly according to the subject matter and other elements of the contract. Thus for example, in most countries the laws governing contracts involving real/immovable property are very different from those governing contracts for movable, tangible property, and both of these are quite different from contracts relating to intangible property. Although all of these types of transactions are also governed by basic contract principles, the law includes special additional rules for each one. There are also such separate rules governing, *inter alia,* personal service contracts, insurance contracts, loan contracts, investment contracts and intellectual property contracts, to name but a few.

288 See footnote 243, *supra.*

In many countries (especially those with "civil law" systems), the law adds another categorization system – dividing public and private law, and further dividing private law into "civil" and "commercial" categories. All of these groupings involve different legal requirements. Contracts, particularly those that are tied to national patrimony or permit requirements, may be categorized as either public or private. If private, their content and parties will normally be determinative of whether they are civil or commercial.

In all countries, then, it is critical to determine how the national legal system views genetic resources and/or ATK and how it categorizes ABS contracts. This decision may vary from country to country; even countries that apply the same type of legal system may come to different decisions about it. In some cases, parties have attempted to change the classification of their contract by rewriting the basic descriptions of the *res* or the parties obligations. These efforts are dangerous however. In most countries, the determination of classification is based on the analysis of the underlying substance of the contract. Thus, for example, it is possible to change classifications by changing the entire contract from a transfer of rights to access and utilize genetic resources to an agreement on the rights to apply for particular patents. In order to actually change classification, however, that change must completely alter the rights of the parties. If the rewrite is intended to keep the contract substantially the same, while changing the wording to avoid a particular classification, it will nearly always fail to achieve this objective.

As another example, some countries may determine that the immovable wildlife (trees, plants and fungi) found on a landowner's property are governed by the law of immovable/real property,[289] so that the landowner has the rights of a "provider" with regard to those assets. In many countries, however, the landowners' rights with regard to trees on their property are not absolute – those countries may place limits on, for example, felling some or all trees or harvesting certain parts of those trees. In those countries, even if the law stated

289 In many countries with strong agricultural histories, crops or timber or wildlife on land are considered to be real or immovable property, where the contract is negotiated before they are harvested and removed from the site. However there is no uniformity on this point. Some analysis of ABS contractual rights appears to assume that in all countries all genetic resource and ATK will be governed by national laws governing real/immovable property. See, *e.g.*, CBD Secretariat, 2007. This assumption is incorrect from a legal perspective. It would be useful to re-conduct that research to determine whether national law actually addresses the nature of genetic resources, and if not, at least to confirm how its law views or categorizes the ownership of natural resources (plants and animals).

that the landowner has the rights of a provider as to plants on its land, there may be uncertainties regarding whether the legal limits on felling or harvesting operate to limit those rights. The situation with regard to movable wildlife (animals, insects, microorganisms) may be even less clear. With regard to ATK, it may be still more obscure.

Globally, there is no uniform agreed categorization of genetic resources or ATK. As noted in Chapters 1 and 2, and throughout this book, the instruments in the international ABS regime are far too vague to provide any reliable uniformity. As a result, under international legal principles, this determination is left to each country's discretion, in the course of their respective implementation of the CBD, NP and other instruments. It is quite likely that, when they address this issue, various countries will come to varying conclusions regarding which categor(ies) of property law should govern genetic resources and ATK, and which bod(ies) of contract law should apply to the various types of ABS contracts.

7.7 Industry Standards

In every country, the sheer number of oral and written contracts has not only led to the creation of detailed law (so that most contract parties need not resort to the courts or arbitrators), it has also eventually resulted in a high level similarity among some types of contracts. When a particular contract term or practice is successful, it may be imitated in other contracts within its sector. Eventually, the courts in that country may recognize nationally accepted "**standard commercial/industrial practices**" (*see box*) in that particular industry or type of contract. Once the country's courts have recognized a standard practice in an industry, then that practice will govern contracts within that industry, unless the particular contract clearly adopts a different practice.

> "**Standard commercial/industrial practices**": Practices of a particular industry or commercial segment in a country that are so common within that group that the courts of that country have come to recognize them as universal, and to apply them to contracts in that industry or segment, unless the contract specifies otherwise.

In addition, where the particular industry is frequently addressed in international contracts, the collected body of nationally accepted standards may gradually merge into internationally accepted standards, through a combination of contractual practice (many international contracts incorporating the standard) and formal interpretation by courts and arbitrators.[290]

Once legal standards have come to be recognized for a particular type of contract, the contracts of that type can incorporate them by reference, and thereby become much shorter. Many of the challenges of legal validity and enforceability will become less problematic. Within an industry that has evolved enough to recognize such standards, so long as a contract has been drafted carefully and well, it can be written relatively simply. The parties need only address a particular standard area where they want to deviate from the standard terms or practices.

At present, however, ABS is a very new concept. Few commercial and contractual ABS practices have evolved or been publicized. Indeed, where particular contracts have been touted as pioneer efforts in the development of ABS practice, they have often met with failure.[291] As a result, there are virtually no accepted standards of ABS commercial and contractual practice. This is yet another reason that the authors feel that it is not advisable to rely on the CBD, the NP, or even national ABS legislation and principles as a legal basis for an ABS contract. Such principles will produce an instrument that is too ambiguous to be legally recognized or considered enforceable in most countries' legal systems. When the courts consider the contract, they will not have accepted standards to rely on. Most courts will likely conclude that the contract is either invalid or unenforceable. Courts that decide to revise it, with the goal of making it enforceable and equitable, will not be acting on the basis of predictable

290 When a particular industry or commercial segment's contractual practices have received "standard practice" recognition in many countries, efforts are made to ensure that they are interpreted similarly by all countries. Unfortunately, the processes for legal recognition of a standard practice vary from country to country, and are often unpredictable. For this reason, international non-profit standards organizations, such as the International Standards Organization (ISO), ASTM International (an engineering standards body that developed from the American Society for Testing and Materials) and similar bodies seek to create uniform non biased standards that can be applied in various industries, and are often legally recognized as international standards. Given that ABS contracts involve technical and scientific, as well as legal, issues, these organizations' ongoing work might provide some idea of how international ABS standards could eventually be formalized.

291 See, *e.g.*, the Teff Agreement in Ethiopia (see Andersen and Winge, 2012), discussed in more detail in ¶¶ 4.1 and 5.4.5, *supra*. An older example, the Hoodia contractd involving the San people in Southern Africa, met with a similar fate. Highly touted in 2002 as major ABS achievements, one of the original commercial users went bankrupt, shortly thereafter. The contract went forward as a domestic agreement with a government agency, and is seen today as a cautionary example (see "Overview of the San Hoodia ABS Experience").

standards, but applying their own perceptions, possibly leading to a result that does not satisfy the parties' needs.

In the future, it seems probable that the challenges of ABS will almost certainly be met by changes and developments in many aspects of ABS contractual practices. Based on the examples in other relatively new types of contracts that have developed over the past century (radio and television broadcasting/air rights; the software industry; database development; the exchange of microorganisms; *etc.*), new types of contracts mechanisms, escrow systems, guarantee programs and transferrable permits are among the options that might come to be internationally accepted using recognized standards that most national legal systems recognize as valid.[292] In the early years, however, ABS contracts will need to be relatively long as the parties and their lawyers struggle to find provisions that protect all parties and clarify their rights and expectations. Over time, however, these initial solutions will certainly be refined and standardized by laws, court decisions and common practice, resulting in a practice in which contracts can be relatively short, because the parties are able to rely on the experiences of past contracts, which will come to be seen as "ABS industry standards."

---

292 Without such efforts, the commercial world (and the courts/arbitrators) often do not have sufficient familiarity with ABS to provide consistency and legal certainty in the interpretation and enforcement of ABS contracts. It is essential to help develop the field of ABS contract law to a level of certainty, so that the parties can predict how any court might come down on primary questions of contract validity and enforceability.

CHAPTER 8

"Expect the Best; Plan for the Worst": Contract Provisions that Improve Enforceability and Address Contract Amendment

It may seem strange that we provide a detailed chapter on legal enforcement provisions, given the number of times we have stated that the most effective and functional contracts do not rely on legal enforcement as their primary tool for settling disputes. In this connection, however, it is important to recollect the true purpose of "enforceability" – as a motivation for each party to implement the contract. In modern business practice, if a contract is not legally enforceable, then the commercial world will view it as a "gentleman's agreement" at most. In essence a business entity will feel that it *may* implement such a contract, but not feel that it is legally bound to do so.[293] Often it will assume that the other parties must also have known from the outset that the contract was unenforceable. So it will assume that there will be "no hard feelings" when it chooses not to implement it. Thus, the concept of legal enforceability bears a close relationship both to full implementation and to the goodwill of the parties.

This chapter considers how an ABS contract can and/or should address the issues of enforcement and compliance. It attempts to provide a basic level of practical understanding of the following major points: (i) the reasons that legal enforcement contract provisions are necessary and relevant (¶ 8.1); (ii) the types of enforcement (¶ 8.2); (iii) how ABS contract provisions should address enforcement challenges, including the role of contract amendment clauses (¶ 8.3); (iv) the most effective means of preventing legal procedural problems from arising (¶ 8.4); (v) arbitration and mediation clauses (¶ 8.5); and (vi) the

293 An example of this object lesson is found in the Teff Agreement (also described in ¶ 4.2.2, *supra*, and later on in this section.) As its various financial and operational problems developed, the user company (HLPI) evaluated its contractual obligations to the providers (Ethiopia) on a purely commercial / legal basis. In essence, the value of its new patent, the need for money and the relatively low likelihood that Ethiopia could or would take enforcement action combined with the existence of a low-level legal justification for its decision to motivate HPFI to effectively renounce the Teff Agreement.

possibility that some other person or entity will take up the case, either on their own behalf or on behalf of one of the parties to the contract (¶ 8.6).

8.1 Why Not Wait until Enforcement Is Needed? Addressing Enforceability in the Text

At the time of negotiations, the parties to any contract do not want or expect ever to find themselves in a position that requires them to undertake legal enforcement processes. It is essential to the functionality of the contract however, to ensure that they could do so if necessary. As noted above, commercial entities and businessmen are much more likely to negotiate or compromise on contract disputes, if the instrument they are implementing is a "binding contract," even where there is little chance that the other party would ever bring a case for formal enforcement.

The lack of clear international precedents on ABS enforcement is often cited as a reason for doubting that ABS contracts could ever be enforced. There is, however, a legal reason to care about enforceability. Specifically, there are two primary ABS situations in which formal enforcement is not only possible but recommended: First, where the user has assets and/or operations in the provider country; and/or second where the provider is able to litigate (even outside the provider country) or an NGO or civil society group is willing to do so on behalf of the provider.[294] In both of these situations, parties negotiating ABS contracts can seriously affect the possibility of formal enforcement. This illustrates just one reason that every ABS contract should consider and address the full range of contractual enforcement issues.

As discussed in more detail in Chapters 4 through 7, the enforceability of a contract is initially determined by two key legal questions – whether it is legally "valid" and whether it is concrete enough that a court could implement it.[295] Even if it satisfies these requirements, however, many other issues affect enforceability, as further explained in the later sections of this chapter.

294 In many comparable situations involving the environment or social welfare, such groups may sometimes take on the task and costs of litigation, whether as an aid to plaintiffs who cannot afford to act in their own interest, or in an effort to create a body of decisions supporting the law or principle of the case. It is possible that such cases may at some point be brought to support the mandates and objectives of ABS.

295 As discussed in ¶ 5.3, a contract that is not specific enough will not be considered by courts that operate on the principles of legal certainty and the rule of law, because it would be unfair to the parties to have some third-party (judge or arbitrator) deciding what the contract covers, after the negotiations have been completed. As further explained in Chapter 12, where generally accepted "industry standards" have developed, those standards may

All of this leads to the question heading this section: Why deal with enforcement issues in the negotiations – why not wait until we know if there is a problem? The answer is simple: Although it is not always possible to predict and solve enforcement problems and obstacles in advance, it is almost certainly not possible to resolve them once a dispute has arisen. The primary reason that it is important to address issues like breach, dispute, termination or amendment during the negotiations is this: When a dispute arises, the parties are rarely in a conciliatory mood; thus, if the contract is not already clear regarding what will happen in case of a disagreement, it is unlikely that the parties will be in the right frame of mind to negotiate them.

In most countries, contractual or commercial laws include "default" principles – laws and standards that can be applied by a court or arbitrator to address disputes if the contract that is not clear on enforcement. It is generally not recommended that parties rely solely on these unstated enforcement principles, however, especially in two situations: (i) when using a new type of contract, because it is not clear in advance whether or how a court or arbitrator will apply those principles; and/or (ii) where there is a possibility that the contract will operate or be interpreted in another country or legal system. Both of these situations apply to ABS. For these reasons, it is very unwise for an ABS contract to rely on "general enforcement principles." The court/arbitrator may simply decide that ABS contracts are different and declare the contract unenforceable. In the alternative, it may apply its own views of what the contract should provide, resulting in a contract that neither party would ever have agreed to. In the event of a dispute or implementation problem, the parties, knowing this, may be unwilling to compromise.[296]

The foregoing is best illustrated by the "Teff Agreement" (discussed in ¶ 4.1), which was negotiated in detail between Ethiopia and HLPI, a Dutch company. When the contract was eventually breached creating an *impasse* that could not be resolved, its default and enforcement provisions were found to be unhelpful. Many of the explanations for the contract's failure also explain why the parties were unable to effectively work out the enforcement problems at the time of the breach. The provider's view of the primary reasons that the Teff Agreement failed included, *inter alia*, "the fact that the Dutch company had originally overestimated the market potential for teff and was overly optimistic about

be applied, as if they are part of the contract – shoring up the contract's legal certainty. At this writing such standards have not developed for ABS contracts.

296 Some users may prefer that the contract's enforcement provisions be ambiguous or absent, converting the ABS contract into a "gentlemen's agreement" that they feel they can ignore.

potential profits," as well as "the company's inability to fulfil the benefit-sharing obligations in the contract" and "the loss/deterioration of HPFI's commitment to the Teff Agreement."[297] In essence, the contract was no longer interesting to the user since the teff material was in their hand, and at that point the user had little or no incentive to negotiate any compromise or to clarify the providers' enforcement rights. From the user side, HLPI reportedly complained of "coordination problems on the Ethiopian side," "limited flow of information" and "export restrictions affecting later movement of teff from Ethiopia to HLPI." Both sides alleged that there were "communication problems," and "a lack of professionalism." Plainly, the parties were no longer operating in a negotiating environment in which it would be easy to clarify ambiguous or unaddressed enforcement issues.[298] When contract was signed, however, they might have been willing to do so.[299]

8.2 Types of Legal Remedies Available and How the Contract Can Affect Them

A "legal remedy" is defined as "one of the types of judgment that a court can issue." The formal enforcement of a contract always depends on the legal powers of the court or arbitrator.[300] This is best described by a quote attributed to a great British jurist of the 1770s: "For every legal right, there is a remedy; *where there is no remedy, there is no right*."[301] Although a contract may include any provision it wishes, if a provision does not give rise to a "legal remedy," it may have little meaning or effectiveness.

Arbitrators often have greater latitude in the kinds of awards they may order; however, they too must issue their awards on the basis of the commercial system. Given that this system is built around legal issues, arbitration awards most often follow the rules governing legal remedies.

297 Andersen and Winge, 2012, at pp. 110–113.

298 Ultimately, for a variety of reasons, the providers were unable and/or unwilling to bring an action for the contract's enforcement or seeking damages for its breach. *Ibid.*

299 Many of the particular problems that brought about this result, including apparent bad faith of the users (as evidenced by, inter alia, their use of bankruptcy as a means of blocking future claims against transferees of the res), could not have been resolved by a contractual provision. Even so, if the contract had been enforceable, and if there had been less ambiguity regarding whether it had been breached, it is entirely possible that the users would have felt a greater obligation to negotiate with Ethiopia following the breach.

300 Courts are "creations of statute" and as such are limited in their powers. They are normally unable to act outside of the scope of their empowering legislation.

301 Attributed to Blackstone (1765). (*emphasis added.*)

The following sections briefly describe the three main categories of contractual remedies, and the particular challenges each poses for the drafter of an ABS contract: declaratory remedies, such as interpretation (¶ 8.2.1); compensatory remedies, *i.e.*, "damages" (¶ 8.2.2); and coercive remedies, which are sometimes called "equitable remedies" (¶ 8.2.3). Although these categorizations are not found in all legal systems, most of the remedies discussed below are available in one form or another in nearly every legal system.

8.2.1 *Declaratory Remedies and the Rules of Interpretation*

In some enforcement situations, the only remedy that the parties need is contractual interpretation – a court's or arbitrator's decision on how the contract should be applied to a particular situation. Even in most other controversies and decision-making processes, interpretation of the contract is an essential first step. Every judge, arbitrator or party engages in "contractual interpretation" whenever he considers the obligations of the parties to a contract, or determines whether the contract has been breached. The following sections provide overviews of contractual interpretation, and of the role of interpretation as a remedy.

(a) Rules of Contractual Interpretation

"Contractual interpretation" may be defined as "determining what a particular contract provision means, when applied to specific facts, conditions or actions." This definition, however, is sometimes misunderstood. Parties, especially non-lawyers, may not be aware that "contractual interpretation" is strictly controlled. Courts, arbitrators and parties look to "rules of interpretation" (refined over many decades and centuries) to guide them regarding how a particular provision should be interpreted. Such rules are found in national law, recognized industry standards, and sometimes the rulings of previous cases. This means that there are usually clear right (and wrong) answers to most interpretation questions. No matter how strongly you assert your opinion, your assertion might well be wrong, if it is not in accordance with the legal rules of interpretation.

As a point of departure, in any detailed lesson in contract interpretation, must normally begin by attempting to identify a single generally accepted meaning for each term used (*i.e.*, their "dictionary" meaning) or where relevant its meaning in particular professional contexts. This is the basic rule of interpretation, but does not easily get results, where the parties offer multiple views regarding the "generally accepted meaning" of particular words. From that point, if there is any uncertainty as to how the term applies to particu lar actions, conditions, parties or items, it is necessary to apply the formally accepted "rules of interpretation."

As we have noted elsewhere, few, if any, ABS concepts have been unambiguously defined, and most operative provisions under ABS contracts discuss actions, abstentions and conditions that have not normally been included in other types of contracts. Hence, it will probably be necessary for the court to apply rules of interpretation. It would not be useful, however, to provide a short list of the rules of interpretation. Such a parroting of the shorthand versions of rules could often leads to misunderstanding.

One example of this type of misunderstanding is the frequently mentioned rule that "a contract provision is interpreted against the party who drafted it." This rule is designed to prevent one party from taking advantage of another party's lack of legal knowledge or commercial experience by writing an obscure clause and later insisting that it has a particular meaning that benefits his interests. The rule is often misunderstood, however, by lawyers and others who consider it as a warning. They assume that it means that they should avoid taking on the primary responsibility for drafting the contract, for fear that the contract will be "interpreted against you." In reality, this rule is very complex and the best advice is often the opposite.

First, this rule applies *only* where the contract is ambiguous or vague. If the disputed clause of the contract is clear and complete, then the rule does not apply. Other rules may be applied to the interpretation of that clause, but the question of which party drafted the clause will not have any effect on how that clause is interpreted or applied.

Second, the determination of which party is "the drafter" is far from clear. As noted in Chapter 6.3.1, in modern contractual practice, contracts usually have more than two parties, and the process of drafting a contract virtually never consists of a direct and clear offer followed by a simple and clear acceptance.[302] The parties may discuss the contract in detail, and often multiple "drafts" of the contract pass back and forth among them, with each party suggesting amendments on each draft that he reviews. Eventually, a

302 The problem for contract drafting, is that a few countries still have laws that assume that contracts are entered into by the old offer/acceptance method. In ¶ 6.3.1, *supra*, this book discusses this in more detail. The main modern situation in which the simple "offer, followed by acceptance" still applies is in the marketing and purchase of products in a store-type situation (in person or on-line.) The product is displayed, with its price stated. The buyer's payment of that price constitutes an implied acceptance, even if no words are spoken. The other terms of the contract are determined under the relevant country's laws on such contracts (default provisions) and/or "industry standards" (See ¶ 12.2, *infra*), if any.

final text is agreed on. Regardless of who prepared the original draft,[303] the court or arbitrator applying the "interpretation-against-the-drafter" rule must determine who specifically inserted the words that gave rise to the argument. It will do this by examining the history of the negotiations in detail. Hence, although the rule cannot be discarded (owing to the need to protect the parties, as noted), its modern application is unpredictable.

The overarching moral of this example is once again that it is best to strive for a non-ambiguous, non-vague contract. This goal is often achieved by taking on primary drafting duties, or engaging appropriate advisors to do so.

> TIP
> DRAFTING PROCESS
>
> On the chance that the interpretation-against-the-drafter rule should ever arise, the parties should each maintain the file of all of the negotiations (copies of all drafts and markups, letters, notes of meetings, *etc.*) in case it becomes necessary to prove which party was the source of a particular ambiguity.

(b) Informational and Declaratory Remedies: Interpretation as Enforcement

In many instances, interpretation is the only remedy sought or needed. The parties just want an unbiased finding on the meaning of a particular clause. In some countries, nearly all such cases are welcomed; in others, however, the law is specific that no "advisory opinions" may be sought.[304] In the latter countries, no party may seek a speculative interpretation before there is an "actual controversy" (*i.e.*, one party has taken an action which another party views as a breach or default under the contract.) Only at that point, may either party bring an action asking the court to interpret the contract, and a "declaratory judgment" as to whether the action was a breach/default or not. This divergence among legal systems may become important in some contracts.

---

303 In many contracts, where the parties have reached a general understanding on some or all of the main terms of the contract (*e.g.*, *res*, price, terms, *etc.*), they join together to hire an attorney or other advisor to prepare the first draft.

304 These countries hold that the parties should not be allowed fair to use the courts as a form of loss protection – that is, they may not use the courts as a tool for deciding whether to violate the contract.

One common type of informational remedy arises when one or both parties ask a court or arbitrator to determine how much is owed under a contract which includes complex computation clauses for determining how much is to be paid in a given situation. This remedy is often tied to an "accounting" – by which the party who has access to information on the assets, costs and receipts relevant to determining the payment amount is compelled to provide that information. In general, a courts may only provide this type of decision where the contract is sufficiently specific on key issues relevant to this calculation.[305]

8.2.2 *Damages and Other Direct Compensation*

Some legal systems have two categories of compensation: remedies that involve the payment of a specified amount of money ("damages" or "compensatory remedies") and those that address some specified unfairness in the contract or in the actions of one or more of its parties (sometimes referred to as "equitable remedies.") For the parties to ABS contracts, this distinction may be important, even if it is not found in the "governing law" of the contract,[306] given the possibility that enforcement might be sought in the courts and officials of some other country.[307]

(a) Compensation for Loss, Harm or Damage

Historically, the development of enforcement processes under any legal system began from a focus on compensation for loss, harm or damage – that is, a court orders a defendant to pay the plaintiff a specified amount to "compensate" the plaintiff for the loss, harm or damage suffered.[308] Although compensation is not always the best remedy for a particular breach, it is usually the first choice of courts and arbitrators, wherever they can come to a concrete ruling regarding the amount to be paid.

---

305 As discussed in Chapter 5, payment provisions must be as concrete as possible regarding the extent to which the payer is bound (*i.e.*, whether his "satisfaction" figures into the deal), the manner in which the payment amount is calculated, the date on which payment is to be made, the currency involved, responsibility for shipment of any material that is transferred, *etc.*

306 See Chapter 10, *infra*.

307 For example, a country in which that party is conducting R&D or into which the original *res* has been transferred. See Chapter 6, *supra*.

308 For these purposes, "loss" normally means a financial cost or loss of an expected financial gain, "damage" refers to any action's or event's negative impact on property of any sort; and "harm" refers to injury to persons.

As further discussed in ¶ 8.5, *infra*, the challenge for those drafting an ABS contract is to make sure that the contract enables an appropriate and final money judgment. It must be clear how the court would rule, should the case be put before them. From the enforcement perspective, it is essential that the value and costs arising in the event of any breach of the agreement be stated as concretely as possible. The parties are less likely to breach the agreement and much more likely to cooperate and create a compromise, if the probable compensation amount is clear.[309]

(b) Liquidated Damages

The actual damage to one party if another party breaches the contract may be much greater than simply the amount of money due. In conventional contracts, the most common example is late payment, which can affect the recipient's ability to pay his own contracts on time.

In ABS contracts, the determination of "actual damage" is even more difficult. For example, where a party has obtained genetic resource samples and ATK, but failed to perform some of contractual obligations, the other party may have lost far more than the payment owed. It may have lost its ability to control future utilization of the genetic resources or ATK that have been taken. That loss may be much greater in value than the court is aware. It can be very difficult to prove these economic losses, however, and even more challenging to prove that they were caused by the action breaching the contract.

The best time for addressing this issue is during the negotiations. As further discussed in ¶ 8.3.4 and Chapter 9 *infra*, it may be possible to agree in advance that a particular payment, transfer and/or other specific remedy shall be due to compensate the non-breaching party in the event that the contract is breached. This type of contract provision – a "liquidated damages clause" – may sometimes allow the parties an easy way to resolve conflicts without going to court.

(c) Punitive Remedies

In cases in which the breaching party has acted in "bad faith" – unfairly and intentionally seeking to avoid his contractual responsibilities – another type of compensatory remedy may apply: The court may order that party to pay "punitive damages" or other amounts designed to punish the offending party. In some cases, this may provide a significant "bonus" to the plaintiff, to whom the penalty is paid. This is because the amount of a punitive remedy is determined

309 For example, see footnote 302, *supra*, regarding the need for concreteness in many aspects of payment.

on the basis of whether the amount would deter the defendant (and others like him) from engaging in the same bad-faith actions in the future. Where the defendant is a large corporate enterprise, only a fairly substantial sum would effectively serve as such a penalty or deterrent. Rules concerning punitive remedies vary greatly between countries.

In contractual drafting, especially in the context of ABS, it may be effective to use the possibility of punitive damages as an incentive, by emphasizing that certain kinds of procedural breaches, such as failure to inform the other parties of a transfer of the *res*, would be considered evidence of "bad faith" of the party who took such action.[310] Given that punitive damages are not contractual, and may only be awarded by a court, the provider should not build negotiation, implementation or litigation plans solely on the basis of possible punitive damages.

(d) Costs and Fees

Although in some countries the losing party in litigation must pay the other party's court costs and attorneys fees, this is not a universal rule. In many countries and legal systems, the general rule is essentially the opposite: each party must be responsible for his own litigation costs (the costs of filing the action and the fees paid to one or more attorneys), unless the court or arbitrator specially orders that the loser pay them This type of award is partly compensation and partly punitive. When awarded to the plaintiff, this indicates that the court feels that the defendant should not have forced the plaintiff to litigate. If the plaintiff loses and the court feels that his legal action without merit, then the plaintiff may be ordered to pay the defendant's costs and/or fees.

In some countries, an award of the "costs" of litigation is limited to the court costs and filing fees. A separate award would be necessary to compel the losing party to pay the winning party's attorney fees. In those countries, the payment of attorney fees is essentially another punitive remedy. For the parties to an ABS contract, however, both court costs and attorney fees are among the financial obstacles that might prevent the non-breaching party from taking legal action. To ensure that attorney fees and other costs are awarded, it is common to include a clause that specifically requires the losing party to pay both lawyer fees and other costs arising out of a dispute under that contract:

---

310 See example in ¶ 8.3.2, *infra*. The warrantee and breach clauses in this chapter and Chapter 9 are generally set up to address the most significant types of bad faith – failure to disclose or misrepresentation of relevant facts.

> EXAMPLE: COURT COSTS AND ATTORNEY FEES
>
> In the event of any action to enforce rights under this Agreement, the prevailing party[311] shall be entitled to reimbursement of its costs and expenses, including reasonable attorneys fees, in connection with such action.

8.2.3 *Coercive ("Equitable") Remedies*

Over the centuries, it has been recognized that the payment of money may not provide an adequate remedy in some cases. A range of other kinds of remedies have developed, where the court may order a party to take or stop taking certain actions. In common law countries, these remedies are generally grouped together under the heading "equitable" remedies, because their purposes is to address situations in which the standard remedies could produce unfair ("inequitable") results. In ABS, the special nature of genetic resources and ATK, and of the actions authorized by the ABS contract may increase the importance of this type of remedies.

Equitable remedies are limited some jurisdictions. There, the plaintiff may only seek the remedies described in this section, if he can prove that the payment of money would not be "make him whole" (adequately address his injury/damage.)[312]

(a) Specific Performance, Injunctions and Other Mandates

One type of equitable remedy is "specific performance" This is a remedy which orders the defendant to take (or stop taking) a specific action (*e.g.* to comply with the contract.)[313] There are numerous forms of this remedy, in addition to "specific performance":

---

311 The clause may grant attorneys' fees only to particular parties (*i.e.*, instead of "the prevailing party" it might name one or more of the specific parties to the agreement). If such a limited right was obtained inequitably, however, a court may refuse to enforce it. See, *e.g.*, *Henderson v. Henderson Investment Properties*,; and Idaho Annotated Code § 53–613

312 In the US, for example, equitable remedies are sometimes not available as where compensatory remedies are adequate. For example, under the Uniform Commercial Code specific performance in a sales contract can only be sought where the items sought are "unique." UCC § 2–716. "Buyer's Right to Specific Performance or Replevin."

313 Some countries will not allow "specific performance" lawsuits, where the plaintiff seeks only an order to pay the money owed, because such payment is thought of as "damages," and therefore subject to rules on compensation. To add complication, there is one situation in which payment of money is considered an "equitable remedy" – restitution,

- Restitution (return of illegally obtained property);
- Rescission/cancellation (cancelling the contract and "unwinding" everything that has been done under it to date);
- *"Quantum meruit"* (in which a court may order that, despite the terms of the contract, that one party *deserves* more or less compensation);
- Writ of Mandate (a court ordering the defendant to do some particular thing, such as to perform or deliver what he promised under the contract);
- Writ of Prohibition (a court ordering the defendant to cease some particular activity that the court feels is a breach of the contract or of the relevant law).

It can be difficult, procedurally, to convince a court to issue one of these remedies, especially in an ABS situation. Where for example, a provider seeks an order prohibiting future utilization of a specific genetic resources or particular ATK, the court may be unwilling to issue the order because of the difficulty in monitoring/proving compliance. The surveillance challenge – the task of ensuring that the user actually ends all utilization of the specified material – is well beyond most normal types of specific performance. This will be even more difficult with regard to ATK. In essence it would constitute an order not to remember what the user has learned. These issues parallel the challenges described in ¶¶ 5.7 and 6.3–6.5, with regard to the return of genetic resources or ATK upon contract termination or after a judgment that they have been illegally obtained.

(b) Contract Reformation

In some countries, the powers of the courts with regard to contracts are more extensive, so that the court may essentially rewrite a contract, if it determines that the contract is not fair as written.[314] This may occur even if the contract is legally valid and has met all other legal requirements.

In Norwegian contract law, for example, there is a continuum between "interpretation" and "reformation" of the contract. Section 36 of the Norwegian Contract Act provides, "A contract may be fully or partially set aside or modified insofar as it would seem unreasonable or be contrary to good business practices to make it current." This gives each court broad discretion when considering whether the contract or part thereof is unreasonable. On this point, the Act states that the court shall take "into account not only the content of

in which a court decides to "unwind" the contract, forcing each party to return what it has received. This option is called "rescission (or 'cancellation') and restitution."

314 Contract Act of Norway § 36.

the agreement, the parties' position and conditions at the time of signing the agreement, but also to later occurred conditions and circumstances." Thus, the court is instructed to take a broad perspective, considering all the elements when deciding whether to reform the contract or not.

The existence of this law and others like it increases the uncertainty of ABS contracts. Parties cannot know whether some part of the contract (*res*, rights, obligations) may eventually be transferred to a Norwegian user and/or prosecuted under this law. However, the threshold for a court to rewrite a contract is high and it does not happen very frequently. In addition, since ABS contracts have not been widely seen or litigated, it is not remotely possible to predict or even imagine all the possible ways in which a court may re-form an ABS contract, should it choose to do so. Currently, in Norway, it is an open question whether and how the court would apply this principle to an ABS contract.

8.3 Enforcement-related Provisions in ABS Contracts

Even if the ABS contract is valid, there are three main obstacles that may impair enforcement:

(1) Judges and arbitrators may find it difficult to determine whether the contract has been breached and whether a remedy is possible, because ABS concept is so new that they have not considered it before;
(2) The cost/complexity of enforcement may be prohibitive for providers with limited assets.[315]
(3) Once an award is obtained, it is often difficult or impossible to enforce it a foreign country.

The importance of the first obstacle must be emphasized. It is not possible for ABS contracts to predict or address everything that might happen in the future. A few examples include the bankruptcy of one or more parties, the informal

315 Modern commercial law favours persons and companies with large operating budgets, because it is only they that can afford to bring suit to protect their interests. In the context of intellectual property rights, for example, it is only they that can afford to monitor broadly enough to know when their rights are infringed. Of late, the work of non-profit organizations and citizens' groups have focused on empowering smaller and less well financed persons and entities to take action, particularly now that significant aspects of social welfare are being put into the hands of modern commercial law through mechanisms like ABS.

transfer of the *res* to a third party, or a drought or flooding in the sampling area affecting the target species. Any of these and hundreds more may prevent the contract from being completed.

Wherever such a factor intervenes, however, the parties turn first to the contract to find out what to do. If the contract does not satisfy, then the solution must be either compromises between the parties or recourse to the courts and/or arbitration. Clearly, the best solution is for the parties to agree on these issues as concretely as possible while they are still driven by the motivating force that brought them to the negotiating table. The second best solution is for the parties to find compromises. As discussed above, they are more likely to be motivated to do so, where it is clear that a court would find the contract binding and enforceable. The last-choice solution would be to actually seek enforcement in court. In all three situations, the most effective and positive results arise where the text of the contract provides support in advance. The following sections look at the key aspects of the contract relating to enforcement:

- Clarifying which actions and failures to act constitute breach or default under the contract (¶ 8.3.1);
- Setting up a reasonable procedure for situations in which one party defaults (breaches or fails to act) under the contract (¶ 8.3.2);
- Addressing possible areas of exclusion (¶ 8.3.3);
- Defining the value of the contract and each of its elements, in order to specify "liquidated damages," for purposes of remedies (¶ 8.3.4); and
- Addressing the enforcement aspects of particular challenges (*e.g.*, transfer, bankruptcy and other amendment of the contract) (¶ 8.3.5).

8.3.1 *What Constitutes a Breach of an ABS Contract?*

For many contracts, the question of whether a party has breached his contractual obligations may seem clear-cut. If the contract says that he must and he does not, then he has breached the contract. The issue is more difficult than it seems, however, with many factors adding complexity. It involves asking first whether any of the obligations in the contract have been breached, and second whether the contract specifies the response required with regard to that particular type of breach. In drafting an ABS contract, one must be clear about both of these points.

At the outset, the draftsman must be clear about precisely what types of misconduct that would be considered as breach of contract, how such breaches can be detected, and what consequences apply to each type of breach.

(a) "Minor Breach"

The distinction between a minor breach and a more important breach is sometimes easy to make. For example, most written contracts say that each party must mail written notice of certain events to all other parties, specifying the addresses of each party's "contact person." Does the fact that notification occurred orally, or was sent via e-mail, constitute a breach of the contract? It may be only a minor matter in most cases; however, if, because the error, the notification was never received, greater questions are raised: Is the failure of notification a minor error? Which party bears the risk that notification is not received? What is the appropriate remedy? Is this potentially worth terminating the contract?

Without some indicator of the value and/or importance of such a requirement, it may be considered only a "deviation" rather than an actual breach of the contract. In general contract practice, a court or arbitrator may dismiss such a claim, find only nominal damage,[316] or simply order the other party to provide proper notification in future.

Where the breach occurred in an ABS contract, however, the typical responses may be very different. There are many situations in which a user's failure to notify the provider (for example, about a transfer of the genetic resources, ATK or their derivatives) might have a very significant impact on valuable rights of the provider. A user that fails to properly comply with a notification provision may effectively eliminate important rights and expectations of the provider.

(b) Conditions

A related concept is that of a "condition" in a contract In essence a condition is a fact or situation on which all or part of the contract depends. For example, a purchase contract for apples may be written conditionally: "If Farmer A produces Granny Smith apples that naturally contain more than X% of natural sugars, the Marketer B will be obligated to purchase Farmer A's entire harvest at the specified price." The test results of the apple harvest are a condition of the contract. If the crop does not achieve the specified level of sugars, then there is no obligation to purchase. For each such condition, the contract must specifically answer a critical question: Which party bears the risk of the failure of a condition?

316 In some courts, a "minor breach" may only be compensated with damages – no specific performance or other coercive remedy will be granted. Then, a court or arbitrator, on finding that the plaintiff was right, but that the breach was minor will award only a token amount in damages to the plaintiff.

In ABS contracts, many obligations may be subject to conditions. For example, in an early ABS contract, the user's obligation to share benefits was conditional on whether research and development regarding a particular specimen resulted in a product or other value for the user.[317] Unfortunately, this condition was only known to the user, who took the specimens to his own facility for research. The contract did not impose any obligation on the user to expedite or even to undertake research.

The contract's terms are the easiest and best means of clarifying which provisions are obligations and which are merely conditions and who bears the risk of a condition's failure.[318] Where the contract is not clear, however, the parties would once again have to rely on a court's interpretation.

(c) Delay as a Breach of Contract

In some cases, courts or arbitrators have refused to consider delays to be breach of the contract. For the party expecting payment, however, any unplanned delay is potentially problematic. Here also, it is useful to make timely payment a contractual requirement, and to make it clear that delay in payment constitutes a material breach. In contracts, this can often be handled simply, by including a "timeliness" clause in the contract (*see* ¶ 8.4.1, *infra*.)

(d) Drafting Suggestions

In all of these contexts, and many others, the parties to ABS contracts should not simply wait to see if there is a breach. The parties to an ABS contract should ensure that the enforceable text of the contract clarifies the importance of key provisions, and guides the court on how to value them.

As a first step in this process, the contract may include a clause specifying which particular violations must be considered as "material breaches" of the contract, and which other actions shall be considered as "actionable breaches." In this context, a "material breach" is one that can be a justification for termination of the contract by the injured party, if he so desires, in addition to action for remedies; an "actionable breach" is one that gives only a basis for legal action without the option of termination of the contract. This list will operate in tandem with the "default" and "liquidated damages" clauses, as discussed in ¶¶ 8.3.2 and 8.3.4.

317 Described in Reid, *et al.*, 1993.

318 A particular clause may often be both. This is called a "dependent promise," which means that if it is breached then all of the other promises that depend on it are terminated because the failure of a dependent promise is also the failure of a condition for those other actions.

EXAMPLE: BREACH OF CONTRACT CLAUSE

1. For purposes of this contract,
   - failure to comply with any or all of the following clauses shall constitute "Material Breach" of this contract:
     - [Here list selected clauses. Each item should be as specific as possible, for example: "Paragraph [XX] [the notification clause], to the extent that any breach or mis-performance under that clause shall result in a failure to notify the designated contact person or a delay of more than [XX] days in that person's receipt of such notification."]
   - failure to comply with all or any of the following clauses shall constitute an "Actionable Breach" of the contract, giving rise to an action for damages and/or specific performance under this contract, but not termination hereof unless and to the extent that paragraph [XX] of this contract applies.
     - [Here also, the list should be as specific as possible.]
2. Nothing in this paragraph shall prevent any party from bringing any legal action or arbitration to address any wilful, reckless or negligent act of any party or its affiliate.

8.3.2 *Basic Default Clauses*

One way to address default in a contract is to include clauses that specify a reasonable process by which the parties will deal with any violations. Default clauses are usually focused on making sure all parties are aware of any controversy or conflict that is brewing. They emphasize each party's duty to inform the others if it believes a default has happened or may happen, and to organize a procedure for the parties to work out a compromise, while the contract continues to operate as normally as possible. The goal of such a clause is to maximize the parties' ability to keep the contract functioning in the event of a breach or disagreement concerning any party's performance:

EXAMPLE: OPTIONS UPON BREACH OF CONTRACT

1. If either party commits a Material Breach (as defined in paragraph [XX]) under this Contract, the other party (if not itself in Material Breach) may choose among the following options:

(a) It may terminate this contract, subject to all of the provisions of paragraphs [XX and XX], by giving the breaching party at least [XX] days' prior notice.
(b) It may notify the breaching party of the breach, calling for a specified cure of the breach within a specified period (not less than [XX] days from the date of such notification).

2 Whichever of the options set out in clause 1 is chosen, the following shall apply:
(a) If the breaching party cures the default within the specified notification/cure period, this contract shall continue as set forth herein.
(b) If the breaching party responds within the specified period, but does not cure the default in a timely manner, the non-breaching party may choose among the following options:
   (i) It may terminate the contract in compliance with this paragraph and paragraphs [XX and XX]; or
   (ii) it may agree in writing to continue the contract for a specified period of not less than [XX] days during which the parties shall seek to develop an appropriate compromise, thereby amending the contract, in accordance with paragraph [XX] of this contract. If no compromise is reached within the continuation period, the breaching party may terminate the contract in accordance with clause 1(a) of this paragraph.

3 If either party commits an Actionable Breach of this contract, as defined in paragraph [XX], the other party may notify the breaching party of the breach, calling for a specified cure of or remedy for the breach within a specified period (not less than [XX] days from the date of such notification). In the event that the breach is not cured or remedied within the cure period, the non-breaching party may bring an action seeking damages or any other non-termination remedy. This contract shall not terminate as a result of such action, and all obligations of both parties shall continue unless the contract is terminated for other reasons.

4 The failure of the breaching party to respond to notification duly made under clauses 1, 2 or 3 of this paragraph shall constitute an indication of bad faith[319] on the part of the breaching party. If the

319 See discussion in ¶ 7.2.2(c), *supra*.

breaching party responds by explaining that it has reasonably concluded that it is not in breach and giving reasons for that conclusion, that response shall not be considered evidence of bad faith. If the parties fail to reach agreement under clause 2(b)(ii), that failure alone, shall not be considered evidence of bad faith.

8.3.3 *Exclusion Clauses*

Connected to the default clause, the "exclusion clause" is normally designed to clarify situations in which the parties agree that certain events or occurrences will not give rise to a material or actionable breach of contract. These clauses are also sometimes called "non-responsibility" clauses, because they frequently begin with the phrase "[Party X] shall not be responsible if…." They are frequently used to make it clear that a party that is offering goods or services for particular use (*e.g.*, sports equipment) is not responsible if the other party gets injured while using the *res* (that is, the company selling the football or the lessor of the pitch is not responsible if some of the players are injured in the course of the game).[320]

Exclusion clauses essentially shift responsibility among the parties. In the sporting example above, for instance, even though the lessor of the football pitch is not responsible for injuries to the players, he remains responsible to provide a safe and appropriate facility, but the clause has shifted the responsibility for matters such as safety gear and medical staff to the team. There are many types of legal limitations on the use of exclusion clauses, primarily focused on ensuring that all parties were aware of such clauses before entering into the contract, and that the exclusion does not violate or promote/excuse violation of relevant law.[321]

In ABS contracts, there are many areas of potential exclusion for both sides. If the contract includes collection and bioprospecting, one or both parties may have concerns about incurring liabilities for situations outside their control. For example, a user may wish to exclude responsibility for ecosystem damage caused in connection with collection, where such user has fully complied with all regulations imposed by the ABS contract, ABS permit, PIC, MAT and

320 Another type of exclusion involves the acts of third parties. For example, the owner of a public carpark or other leased premises will seek exclusion from liability for the acts of others who cause damage in or thieve from the area.

321 See the Australian case of *Thornton v Shoe Lane Parking Ltd.*, which found that although there was a binding contract, the exclusion clause could not apply.

other relevant laws. A provider might wish to ensure that he will not be held responsible, if the target species cannot be found easily, the search needs to be extended onto other areas, or the samples collected are unsatisfactory.

Because they are so individual, it is not possible to provide a useful general model or example of an exclusion clause. Instead, we note that courts or arbitrators reviewing exclusion clauses generally read them very narrowly, and resolve any doubts in favor of any member(s) of legally protected classes of parties.[322] It must also be reiterated that the exclusion must not violate, promote violation of, or excuse violation of relevant law.

TIP

EXCLUSION CLAUSES

The law governing exclusion clauses is often complex, even if the clause looks deceptively simple. At the risk of "sounding like typical lawyers" we must advise that the parties obtain legal advice on any exclusion clause.

8.3.4 *Liquidated Damages Clauses*

From the negotiator's/draftsman's perspective, the concept of a "liquidated damages" clause is potentially one of the most important in this chapter. If used properly, a liquidated damages clause can help the parties get past one of the most difficult enforcement challenges that an ABS contract must face – uncertainties regarding the valuation of the *res* and of the parties' expectations.[323] It does this by specifying a particular sum as "liquidated damages" – *i.e.,* the amount that must be paid in the event of a certain type of breach. This means that, if there is a breach of contract, the plaintiff does not have to prove the value and amount of damage suffered, nor address most causation issues. All that he must prove is that there was a breach. Once that is proven, the court will award the liquidated damage amount. The most valuable aspect of a liquidated damages clause, however, is its impact on the parties before any

322 As discussed in ¶ 4.4.1, the law recognizes special concerns, when considering the contractual rights of certain groups, including indigenous communities that are generally living apart.

323 In courts and arbitration, the problem of proving the amount of damage suffered is often a very time-consuming, expensive and unpredictable part of the process. Liquidated damages clauses take much of this duty away from the court or arbitrator by specifying the award in the contract.

enforcement action is filed. Although a court can enforce a liquidated damages clause of a contract, the primary purpose of such a clause is to create a remedy that can be used without recourse to the courts (as discussed in Chapter 9).

In its simplest form, a liquidated damages clause might say "If Party A breaches his obligation under paragraph XX, then Party B shall have the option to recover $XXX." Where this appears in a contract that is signed by both A and B, the court can reasonably order Party A to make the specified payment – the parties' intent is clear. So clear, in fact that the parties may not bother with the court. A will just go ahead and make the payment.

Unfortunately, such clauses are rarely simple. The parties have many concerns that must be addressed, to ensure that the clause is fair. In addition, courts and arbitrators will not enforce a liquidation clause if the amount is set too high.[324] In drafting a liquidated damages clause, the parties should include an explanation of the reasons they feel that the clause sets out a reasonable estimate of the value of the omitted performance and the financial remedy of other harm or damage. Such justification should focus on the difficulty of quantifying actual damages and the parties' agreement that the named sum or formula will provide a reasonable approximation of the damages that may be anticipated.

In order to minimize legal challenge to the application of liquidated damages, the clause should be as clear as possible about which particular breaches it covers and how it is triggered. To the greatest extent possible, the trigger should be entirely objective – an observable fact, rather than a supposition or assumption. It should not involve value judgments or refer to the satisfaction of either party. If liquidated damages are imposed for late payment, the clause should also specify whether it is triggered by any delay or only by delay caused by the breaching party.

In conventional contracts, the main use of liquidated damages clauses is in contracts for the sale if goods. Courts and arbitrators are most comfortable when applying a liquidated damages clause to the failure to deliver specific goods or to make payment for them in a timely fashion, and similar situations. In ABS contracts, however, very different obligations are important: failure to give notification of transfer; failure to share benefits where one party

---

324 Thus, liquidated damage clauses must be very carefully calculated, to represent a reasonable amount, considering all aspects of damage that are addressed (for example, loss of reputation, loss of future use of formerly exclusive rights, *etc.*), in addition to the failure to pay or other direct loss of expected benefit. These clauses should be phrased as mandatory, rather than giving the non-breaching party the option whether to use them. In most cases "optional" liquidated damages clauses are unenforceable. See, *e.g.*, *Avery v. Hughes*.

believes that a benefit-share is owed; misappropriation or misuse of genetic resources/ATK; or actions/inactions that enable some other person to misappropriate or misuse these resources. It is possible to draft liquidated damages provisions to address these kinds of breaches, but it is not at all clear how a court would interpret them. Even so, especially in an ABS contract, a liquidated damages clause may still be very important. It can give a court or arbitrator a useful standard on which to base an award, but only if the clause provides proper specificity and legal justification, and if the trigger is clear and agreed.

As a result, this book advises all ABS parties to consider the inclusion of a liquidated damages clause in their ABS contracts. After including it, however, they should not rely on such a clause to eliminate the other challenges discussed in this book.

EXAMPLE: LIQUIDATED DAMAGES[325]

Notwithstanding any other provision of this contract,

1. If [Breaching Party] breaches its obligation to give notice prior to the transfer of all or any part of the *res* of this contract as set forth in paragraph [XX] or by virtue of any other actions/inactions enable some other person to misappropriate or misuse these resources,
   a. [Damaged Party[326]] shall recover the sum of $[XX], as liquidated damages.
   b. The liquidated damages amount in clause 1(a) is intended to cover the damage to [Damaged Party]'s interest in the res, due to lack of privity of contract with persons who hold and are able to engage in research and development with regard to it, as well as the loss of future right and ability to enter into contracts with others, who might in future seek to use the *res*, without contacting or compensating [Damaged Party].

325 The format of the clause follows the generally used format for many liquidated damages clauses that are recognized to be effective and functional in immovable property transactions, natural resource prospecting permits and "sale of goods" contracts. None of the provisions in this example have been tested in the courts or other ABS actions.

326 *Ibid.*

2. If [Breaching Party] should breach its obligation to make timely payment, including payment of a "benefit share," that shall become due pursuant to paragraphs [XX and XX],
    a. [Damaged Party] shall recover, in addition to the full amount of the payment owed, the sum of $[X] per day for each day of delay, as liquidated damages.
    b. The liquidated damages amount in clause 2(a) is intended to cover the potential financial challenge to [Damaged Party] and the persons, communities and institutions that are expecting to receive some share of such payment, both in terms of the need to obtain other funding to the cover goods and services to be financed by said payment, and to address the reputational and other losses suffered by [Damaged Party], arising from its failure to timely distribute such proceeds among individuals and communities.
3. In the event that [Breaching Party] should breach its obligation to comply with relevant [national] law as described in paragraph [XX],
    a. [Damaged Party] shall recover the sum of $[XX] per day, for each day in which the violation of law continues uncured, as liquidated damages.
    b. The liquidated damages amount described in clause 3(a) is intended to cover penalties, reputational losses to the ABS program in the country, and other losses or costs incurred by [Damaged Party].
4. In the event that [Breaching Party] should breach its obligation to limit its activities involving the *res* to specific activities described in paragraph [XX],
    a. [Damaged Party] shall recover the sum of $[XX] as liquidated damages.
    b. The liquidated damages amount in clause 4(a) is intended to cover the damage to [Damaged Party]'s interest in the *res*, by virtue of [Breaching Party]'s exercise of rights not included in this contract without compensating [Damaged Party], as well as the loss of future right and ability to enter into contracts with others, who might in future seek to use the *res* in this way.
5 The parties agree that, for clauses 1–4, quantifying losses arising from the stated events or violations is inherently difficult – any of the

foregoing violations may impact the party entitled to liquidated damages, by affecting that party's legal rights and ability to assert those rights in future, or in some instances necessitating that that party provide substitute payments, rather than legally agreed distributions to individuals and communities.

6 The agreed sums set out in this paragraph are not intended as a penalty, but rather represent a reasonable measure of the damages that may result from the violation.

7 Nothing in the foregoing liquidated damages provisions shall operate to limit or prevent other action by the aggrieved party, or the recovery of additional damages, in the event that the breach causes or contributes to environmental damage or direct harm to individuals, or in the event that the party obligated to pay liquidated damages has violated paragraph [XX – intellectual property rights] of this contract.

8.3.5 *Amendment*

As discussed in ¶¶ 5.7 and 6.6, *supra*, the parties' rights and expectations under an ABS contract may be seriously impacted by transfers, bankruptcies, business alterations, and other activities. In order for the contract to stay relevant in each of these situations, it is essential to tie all such changes to a primary obligation to amend the contract to reflect the change. In discussing the identification of parties (Chapter 4), enumeration of contract duties (Chapter 5) and transfer, bankruptcy and major business alterations (Chapter 6), this book has included examples of a variety of contract provisions, that refer to and must coordinate with the amendment process under the contract. The following is an example of an amendment clause.

EXAMPLE: AMENDMENT OR ALTERATION CLAUSE

1. Notwithstanding any other provision of this contract, this contract may not be amended, nor any obligation, right, or interest therein waived or altered in any way, unless such change is in writing, signed by all parties to this contract.
2. In the event that any party shall seek to amend or alter this contract, including to [transfer or] waive any right, obligation or interest herein, that party shall provide written notification to all parties,

in accordance with paragraph [XX], and such notice shall include a complete written statement regarding the nature of the amendment sought or the full text of the amended contract with the amendment clearly delineated.

3. If the notification provided under clause 2 of this paragraph includes the full text of the amended contract with the amendment clearly delineated, and if all parties are in agreement with the amendment as therein proposed, the parties may execute the amendment in counterparts, at it shall go into effect upon receipt by all parties of a notification, in accordance with paragraph [XX], that all parties have so executed.
4. If the notification provided under clause 2 of this paragraph does not include the full text of the amended contract with the amendment clearly delineated, the notification shall include the proposed date, place and time of a meeting to discuss and negotiate regarding the proposed amendment. Each party shall respond within [XX] days of receipt of such notification as to whether the proposed meeting is acceptable.
5. If any party does not agree to an amendment as proposed, the part[ies] that do not agree shall so notify all parties in accordance with paragraph [XX]. Within [XX] days of receipt of such notification, the proposing party shall notify all parties of the proposed date, place and time of a meeting to discuss and negotiate regarding the proposed amendment, following the process set out in clause 4. If no such meeting is proposed within the specified period, the proposed amendment shall be dropped and this contract shall continue in force.
6. From the date of any meeting set under clause 4 or 5 of this paragraph, the parties shall have not less than [XX] days to come to a final decision regarding the proposed amendment. They may extend this deadline by mutual agreement. If no agreement is reached within the agreed period, the proposed amendment shall be dropped and this contract shall continue in force.
7. The fact that an amendment is under discussion as set forth in this paragraph shall not alter any of the obligations, rights or interests of any party during the pendency of such negotiations. Unless a particular clause of the contract is specifically identified in the proposed amendment, the fact that an amendment is proposed shall not reopen the negotiation of that clause.

8. No amendment shall have any legal effect on the respective duties of any of the parties, until it has been finally agreed and fully executed by all persons or entities that are at the time parties to this contract.
9. In the event that any action is taken that requires amendment of this contract, such action shall not be binding on, or have any impact on, any party to this contract unless and until the amendment has been finally agreed and fully executed by all parties.
10. Nothing in the paragraph shall prevent any party from taking action to enforce this contract, or from seeking remedies or compensation for damages hereunder.

8.4 Practical and Procedural Elements Relating to Enforcement of ABS Contracts

There are many other legal issues that might have a significant impact on enforcement actions, although they do not directly affect enforceability. Addressing these issues in the contract may improve the parties' situation, should an enforcement action be needed. The following sections discuss a few of the issues that might come up in an enforcement action, where such an action may be made easier by including appropriate language in the ABS contract.

8.4.1 *Timeliness*

Although most contracts carefully specify the dates on which particular obligations must be met, and even include penalties for delay in meeting such obligations, many courts are slightly resistant to imposing penalties or finding a breach where the payment is "only late."[327] To avoid losing a case for this reason, most contracts include a "timeliness" clause:

EXAMPLE: TIMELINESS

Time is of the essence in the performance of all obligations of any party under this contract.

327 It can be difficult to prove that a party has gone from being late to making it clear that he does not intend to pay.

8.4.2 *Filing, Standing and Other Issues*

Where the parties are certain which country enforcement actions will be brought,[328] the contract can pre-address a number of procedural challenges that might interfere with an enforcement action. Such issues could include "standing to sue" in the designated country's courts, choice of forum issues, statute of limitations[329] and other matters. A model or advice should be sought from a contracts expert in that designated country.

8.4.3 *Burden of Proof*

The issue of burden of proof is at once both simple and complex. In essence, the party with the burden of proof is the party that must bring evidence on the issue in question. In most cases, where a party brings an action seeking damages or other "affirmative remedies"[330] for violation of a particular contractual obligation, that party (the "plaintiff") has the initial burden of proof, to demonstrate that his claim is justified and timely. He must, initially, prove (i) that the obligation existed, (ii) that it binds the defendant, and (iii) that all events had occurred giving rise to the duty to perform.[331] If he cannot bring sufficient evidence on these points, then his claim will be dropped and he will have no relief. The other party need not bring evidence, unless the party with the burden of proof has provided sufficient evidence, at which point any other party may bring evidence to contradict or throw doubt on the original evidence.

The first two of these points may sound quite simple, on the assumption that the contract provides evidence of the obligation. In fact, however, they are key points that must be clarified carefully in the course of drafting (*see* Chapters 4 and 5, *supra*). Thus, for example, contract document shows the text of the contract, but the plaintiffs burden is to prove the wording of the contract imposes an obligation on that defendant. As we have seen, most ABS terminology

---

328 As discussed in ¶ 10.1, *infra*, this is a very difficult and challenging question.

329 The particular time period from the date of the default, in which an action may be brought. This varies. For example, in US jurisdictions, the time in which a contract action must be brought varies, with some states saying that such action must be filed within 3 years from the date that the plaintiff discovered the breach, and others setting that limit as high as 6 years.

330 Where the plaintiff is asking for declaratory relief or interpretation, the burden of proof may be different, in many countries.

331 In legal parlance, this is called the "*prima facie* case" for breach of contract. Each type of claim has a different *prima facie* case. In ABS, this means that different prima facie cases may apply to other parts of the litigation – where for example, the plaintiff also includes claims for bad faith, fraud or misrepresentation, misappropriation, violation of national law, permit violation, other torts or even conspiracy.

(even terms that are defined in the CBD and/or NP) is legally uncertain. The burden is not met if the contract discusses the defendant's "utilization of genetic resources" and/or "derivatives," without concretely indicating which actions are covered, what the defendant must do, and what triggers those obligations.

Similarly, although the contract document provides evidence that certain individuals signed the contract, the burden of proof that the contract binds the parties is met only where the plaintiff can provide substantial evidence that individuals who signed on behalf of the defendant were authorized to bind him to the contract.[332]

The third stage of the plaintiff's burden (proof that defendant has not met his obligation) is dependent on careful drafting. If an obligation is too vague, the court may not agree that it has been triggered. Even the would-be plaintiff may not be certain of this. Consider for example, a user's obligation to make specified payments within a specific time after any new product has been developed from the *res* through R&D. How can the provider know what is happening in the user's facilities? Even if the provider obtains objective information from a third party, who will determine whether the user's activities constitute "utilization of genetic resources or derivatives"? Instead of using these ambiguous terms, the contract needs to state *objectively verifiable* obligations. For example, the provider could easily document in a legally useful way the number of samples taken and the date of their collection. It would be simple contractually to trigger one or more of the user's obligations on the expiration of a specific time number of days after that date, giving the user a procedure to extend the deadline if he provides additional information on what is being done.

Often, burden of proof issues are not stated directly in the contract. They are inferred from the way a clause is phrased. This makes identifying the party who bears the burden of proof an imprecise legal determination. For this reason, it is normally best to allocate the burden definitively, as to each relevant issue. The parties' strategies with regard to allocating the burden of proof must therefore be interrelated with the challenge of precision in drafting the contract. The clearer the contract language is, the less difficult it will be to prove a breach of the obligation.

Normally, after the plaintiff has met his initial burden, the burden shifts to the defendant to disprove what the plaintiff has said – to prove, for example,

---

332 As noted in ¶ 4.5, *supra*, where a provider has obtained clear statements in writing on this point from the user, that is probably sufficient. The user would then have to prove that the statement either does not address the point, or that it is a lie. If the latter, then a case for fraud is probably proven.

that there is a reason to declare the contract invalid, that the obligations in the contract have been altered in some way, or that there is an exclusion or other reason not to enforce the obligation.

As the contract nears completion, another important step may be necessary. The parties should carefully re-evaluate every clause to determine if a violation of that clause could give rise to an enforcement action or could be a factor in proving the case. If so, the party should ask himself whether it could be proven objectively. If not, it is advisable to find a better way and more objective way of stating the point. In addition, many contracts include a contract clause that directly addresses the burden of proof. In essence, such a clause creates a presumption. The burden of proof shifts to the party that wishes to rebut that presumption:

> EXAMPLE: BURDEN OF PROOF
>
> For purposes of any action to enforce this contract, if a question arises as to whether [identify particular issue of concern that is not objectively provable by or entirely within the knowledge of both parties], the court or arbitrator shall presume that [presumption about that issue], unless disproven by good and substantial evidence.

8.4.4 *Calculating Amounts Owed*

In general, the enforcement of a claim for payment depends on the plaintiff's ability to concretely prove all relevant facts about the payment. The Convention on the International Sale of Goods (CISG)[333] provides some useful examples on the contents of an enforceable payment clause.

Very few commercial contracts state payment clauses simply (*i.e.*, "Party A shall pay Party B $XXX.") In the vast majority of contracts, the total amount to be paid is based on other factors that must be clarified in the contract. For example, the date of payment must be stated, as well as any added fee for late payment. The contract should also state who bears the responsibility for transport of goods or samples (as well as shipping and insurance costs), and the costs assessed by any bank or other institution involved in the money transfer.

333 As noted in ¶ 10.3, *infra*, the CISG is not particularly useful as a legal basis for ABS contracts. One issue on which it provides useful examples however is the payment of money in an international contract situation.

Where the contract is international, it is also necessary to state the currency in which the payment will be made, and how and when the value of that payment will be calculated. Parties often negotiate prices in dollars or Euros when the exchange rate between that currency and their country's currency is particularly favorable. By the time that payment is due, the exchange rate may have shifted, and the party owing the payment may delay in hopes that it will shift further.

Many contracts apply additional factors to the determination of payment. In agricultural contracts, for example, the amount to be paid will depend on how many barrels of produce are provided, and may also change based on agricultural grading standards (*i.e.*, the price will be stated per barrel, with different prices for Grade A, Grade B, *etc.*)

In some contracts (including some ABS contracts) the payment is sometimes described as a percentage of the amount the payer earns on a particular asset or activity.[334] These provisions can be very difficult to enforce unless they are very detailed.[335] In addition, of course, the calculation depends on information that is entirely in the control of the payer. His records must be obtained and their veracity confirmed, in order to prove how much is owed. This is a time-consuming and expensive undertaking. Liquidated damages clauses (see ¶ 8.3.4, *supra*) may help, but it may be difficult to justify them, where the question is how much is owed under the contract or how to calculate it.

For the drafters of ABS contracts, the above discussion underscores an important lesson. Even though they may feel that their payment clauses are clear and concrete, there are many factors that add uncertainty and may prevent enforcement. Those negotiating on behalf of providers are faced with a very practical question: Are you willing to give up the (uncertain) possibility of a "great bonus" (if the genetic resource or ATK produces a new product of enormous value, and if the user pays the specified share) in exchange for the certainty of a more concrete and enforceable payment? As an example of this type of trade-off, consider an ABS contract in which the user seeks to collect plant samples in a specific area and to use them in pharmaceutical research and possibly develop new pharmaceuticals out of that research. The negotiator has many options regarding payment including the following two:

334 For example, in leases of retail stores, the monthly rent often includes a specified percentage of the tenant's intake or profit during the previous month.

335 This challenge is also discussed in ¶ 5.4.1(a). The contract must specify what earnings are included, whether/how expenses should be deducted, *etc.*

(1) to require the user to pay a specific share of the benefits arising from any products or interim products of his R&D activities; or (2) to require a lower (earlier or up-front) payment of a specified amount, calculated on the basis of concrete objective facts – number of specimens taken, particular known qualities of the species involved, *etc.*

Although the first type of provision may have the chance of a higher return, that chance depends on not only whether the resource has a pharmaceutical value, but especially whether the user will comply. Enforcement may be impossible. In all probability, the information necessary to prove a triggering event will be held tightly by the user. In the first type of payment provision, there are many factors that a court or arbitrator may well find either unproven or too vague to serve as a basis for an award. For example, how will the provider prove that a particular product is based on genetic resources obtained under his contract? This issue involves, *inter alia*, proving a connection to a specific species, proving that the user's activities were "utilization" of genetic resources, rather than some other activity, and proving that the particular specimens used were obtained from provider. It is very difficult for the contract to resolve these challenges. Due to uncertainties, the user may conclude that payment is optional.

The second kind of provision can be relatively certain if the provision is well drafted. If it is clear that the triggering events (taking samples and the passage of time or other specified trigger) have occurred, the other questions that pose obstacles to enforcing the first option's provision would not apply. A user might be more likely to view this second type of payment clause as non-optional, because it will know that a court or arbitrator will order payment, and the negative publicity connected with such an order would be unwelcome.

8.4.5 *Waiver and Estoppel*

The concepts of "waiver" and "estoppel" arise where one party has indicated, by words or conduct that he will not object to a particular breach or violation of the contract. For example, Party A fails to provide required notification to Party B in writing but gives notice orally to a member of B's on-site staff. If B does not object immediately, A may claim that B has "waived" any right to take action with regard to this faulty notification. A may also claim that B is "estopped" (legally prevented) from requiring written notification under that clause in future.

Most ABS contracts are implemented by persons with limited commercial and contractual experience. As a result, there is a considerable danger of actions giving rise to claims of waiver and/or estoppel. Every ABS negotiator should at least consider including a no-waiver clause:

EXAMPLE: WAIVER/ESTOPPEL CLAUSE

The failure of any party to take any permitted action under this contract or otherwise with respect to any breach that may occur shall not constitute a waiver of the non-breaching party's right to take action for redress of such breach, or to insist on performance of that provision in future, in the absence of a signed written statement or an amendment to the agreement waiving these rights. No party's failure to take action on any breach be held to excuse future breaches of the same type.

8.4.6 *Anticipatory Breach and Repudiation*

Once a contract is completed and all parties have signed it, there is a possibility that one or more parties may later decide not to implement it. In some cases, rather than simply fail to perform, that party will tell the other parties that he wants out, and state that he will no longer perform his duties under that contract. There may be many reasons for this, ranging from "hardship" (the party can no longer afford the contract) to the fact that the repudiating party can get a better deal elsewhere.

In some countries, this statement is considered an "anticipatory breach" of the entire contract.[336] If the repudiation is not clearly stated, however, and if the contract does not discuss this, the non-breaching parties may lose many of their enforcement rights.[337] In ABS, anticipatory breach may be particularly problematic where the repudiating party has already obtained samples of genetic resources and ATK. In addition, the rumor of such repudiation may cause further damage to the providers' expectations and rights. Although it is not certain that all courts will recognize it, a contract clause that addresses repudiation/renunciation of the contract may be of help in this type of situation:

336 See, *e.g.*, UK cases: *Federal Commerce & Navigation Cov Molena Alpha Inc* (the "Nanfri") and *Hong Kong Fir Shipping v Kawasaki Kishen Kaisha*. Others do not take this approach. See *e.g.*, Allen & Overy, 2009.

337 If a user repudiates the contract, the provider may be forced to wait until some obligation is past due, and may be limited to bringing an action solely on that obligation.

EXAMPLE: REPUDIATION OR RENUNCIATION

In the event that, after this contract is completed and signed, any party (the "renouncing party") to this contract shall state that he no longer intends to perform his obligations under this contract, no matter who the statement is made to or how such statement shall come to the attention of another party, any other party shall have the option to consider that statement to be a Material Breach of all of the renouncing party's obligations, which shall be due in full as of the date that the other party received or got notice of the statement, and the other part[ies] may on that basis bring action for damages, restitution, or other remedies.

8.4.7 *Survival*

As explained in detail in ¶¶ 5.4.3 and 6.3.2, the termination of a contract as a result of the breach of the contract by one or more parties may have very serious negative consequences for all parties, since many other obligations and statements of both parties can only be enforced if the contract is in force. Even where the contract terminates "according to its terms" (*i.e.*, the contract ends because all parties have performed all remaining obligations that could come due) there may be elements of the contract (statements or representations made by one or more parties, warrantees and guarantees, governing law provisions, arbitration clauses, *etc.*) that may still be relevant if facts are later discovered indicating that some dispute or unresolved obligation still exists. These possibilities are particularly important in the ABS context, because new developments continue to improve the parties' technological ability to confirm the utilization of particular genetic resources or ATK and/or to pin the particular resources to a specific location. A contractual "survival" clause is generally understood, and may provide added assurance on this point:

EXAMPLE: SURVIVAL CLAUSE

Any provision of this agreement which imposes an obligation after termination, including [here list clauses such as confidentiality or exclusivity or other provisions that include a termination date that might be later than the termination of the contract] or any representation of facts or intentions by one or more parties, warrantee or guarantee by one or more parties, or any provision which specifies the rights or duties of the parties in the event of breach of any obligation hereunder, including its clause relating to arbitration, shall remain in effect [indefinitely/ for XX months/days/years][338] after the termination or expiration of this contract.

8.5 Arbitration and Mediation Clauses

In most contract negotiations, there are both pros and cons to the question of whether disputes should be subject to commercial arbitration and/or mediation. Many factors affect this determination, and the assumption that arbitration processes are faster, cheaper and easier than litigation is often untrue. Most arbitrators can provide examples of arbitration clauses or arbitration agreements that have been effective in their country or jurisdiction. In using these, it is important to keep two things in mind.

First, it is much easier to agree on all of the relevant aspects at the time that the contract is being negotiated, than at the time that a dispute has arisen. If requiring or allowing arbitration, it is normally preferable to state all relevant requirements in the contract.

Second, arbitration clauses are effective only if they contain all of the information that the law requires, leaving little room for negotiation over whether the arbitration is mandatory or voluntary, and/or what rules and procedures apply. Among the issues that should always be addressed are the following: whether the arbitration and/or mediation will be mandatory or not (and if not what the parties must do if they wish to submit to arbitration); which arbitration rules apply and whether a particular arbitral body will oversee the arbitration; how many arbitrators shall hear the matter and how they shall be selected; where the arbitration shall be held; what governing law shall apply; how and where arbitral awards shall be entered with the relevant court or government; whether there is a time period by which the arbitration must be completed (and what happens if the process is delayed beyond this date); and if desired, what limits there will be on the number of witnesses, depositions or documents each party may present or subpoena.

338 Where the survival clause specifies the time period of survival, it may break this down according to particular provisions (*i.e.*, representations survive indefinitely, warrantees survive for a specified period after the signing or termination of the contract, *etc.*).

TIP
ARBITRATION CLAUSE

Owing to the need for a high level of detail on many issues, the arbitration clause is usually based on one of the standard forms available in the country in which the arbitration will be held or a model or standard provision offered by the arbitration body named in the contract.[339]

8.6 Parties that Are Not Parties: Other Persons or Entities that Might Seek Enforcement

In many cases, a contract between parties results in some benefits for persons who are not parties to the contract. There are detailed laws regarding which of these "third-party beneficiaries" (TPBS) have rights under the contract.[340] In an agreement to build a new factory, for example, the contract may benefit all of those who live in the neighbourhood of the factory (because they may find jobs there) and all local businesses (whose receipts may increase as the number of people coming to the area increases.) In general, however, the only TPBS who have the right to enforce the contract are those whose benefit is "intended" by the contract's parties. Thus, where A pays B to provide an education for C, C is the intended beneficiary and may enforce the contract. On the other hand, where A and B contract to build a house, and later agree to use C as their contractor because he is the best contractor in the area, C is only the "incidental beneficiary". A & B's intent is to build the house, not to benefit C. If A decides to violate the contract, and the house is not built, C has no legal right against either A or B.[341]

339 There are a nearly infinite supply of standard clauses. In the United States, for example, jams, Inc (formerly Judicial Arbitration and Mediation Services) provides a range of elements and options for possible clauses.

340 Some aspects of the application of Third-party Beneficiary concepts to ABS are examined in ¶ 4.4.2.

341 The determination of intention in these cases can be challenging – a problem that is normally addressed in contractual practice by inserting a provision that specifically states the name of the third-party beneficiary and explains the benefits intended. An excellent and detailed discussion of the rights of third parties in contract law, is found in Markesinis and Unberath, 2002.

Third-party beneficiary issues often arise where a governmental agency, community, charitable institute or academic institution is one of the parties to the contract. Arguably, these types of entities are, by definition required to take actions that protect, regulate and benefit a specific (often large) group of people. In the context of ABS, the TPB issue raises three as-yet unanswered questions, as discussed below.

8.6.1 *TPBs in ABS Contracts between Users and Provider Governments*

First, of course, where the provider government negotiates ABS agreement, it is often assumed that the provider government is acting on behalf of certain citizens or communities, and that when benefit-sharing occurs the benefits will flow to these TPBs, whether directly or indirectly. It does not matter whether the contract says that they are TPBs or even states that there are no TPBs. They could have, *inter alia*, the legal right to compel performance of the contract, to seek interpretation of benefit-sharing provisions, or possibly even to compel that the user make payments to them directly. Clearly, it is in the interest of all parties to be clear about the TPBs of an ABS contract, and what rights are intended.

8.6.2 *TPBs in ATK Contracts, Community-held Genetic Resources and Farmers' Rights*

The rights of an individual holder of the ATK or genetic resource may be legally tied to the community welfare, whenever the contract involves indigenous knowledge, locally derived varieties and subspecies or farmers' rights, For example, where a community's traditional medicinal knowledge is traditionally passed down from one designated shaman or other healer to his/her successor, sometimes within a single family line, the critical question is whether that knowledge "belongs" to the individual healer or family, or constitutes a traditional knowledge resource of the entire community. A similar challenge would arise where a farmer in an ILC raises varieties derived from a long process of local development. Are the current specimens the property of the individual farmer, or does he act for the entire community that developed the variety or subspecies when he "provides" these specimens to a user under an ABS contract?

8.6.3 *International Bodies and National Governments as "Third-party Obligees"?*

The TPB concept was deliberately invoked by the ITPGRFA negotiators, in the Standard Material Transfer Agreement (SMTA), which provides "that FAO, ... is the third party beneficiary under this Agreement."[342] This is an abnormal use of the TPB concept – the SMTA states that its intent is only to ensure that FAO has the right to request that the parties provide the required monitoring information.[343] Unlike most TPB provisions, the SMTA does not provide a particular benefit to FAO itself. All that this clause does or intends to do is (in essence) to make FAO a party for purposes of its exercise of administrative oversight, but not a party against whom an enforcement action can be taken.[344] The same result could have been achieved by a "contract administration contract" between FAO and the CGIAR centres. This approach (and this view of the meaning of the term "third-party beneficiary") is rather clearly not in accordance with the prevailing legal principles governing the TPB concept.[345] Parties are strongly advised not to imitate this approach in their ABS contracts, because, in an enforcement action, a court might declare it to be void.[346]

One interesting aspect of this clause has not been fully analysed, however. FAO's status as a TPB may imply that FAO has a legal responsibility to protect the rights of the "actual TPBs" – the ABS providers.[347] This question is particularly important, in light of the fact that the only direct "benefit sharing" under the ITPGRFA occurs through the SMTA, under which the "recipient" of seeds

342 ITPGRFA Governing Body Resolution 2/2006.

343 ITPGRFA Arts. 4.3 and 4.4 referring to Arts. 5e, 6.5c, 8.3, and Annex 2 paragraph 3.

344 It is not possible, at this point to know why the negotiators chose this path. Some suggest three possible reasons (i) FAO could not legally become a party to the SMTAs when signed; (ii) the seed collections that must use the SMTA would not agree to enter into a contract with FAO as a party; or (iii) FAO did not want responsibility or liability in the event that the contract was breached or that not properly enforced. None of these would explain why the drafters chose not to use a more conventional arrangement.

345 One reading of the law on TPBs is found in UNIDROIT Principles 2004 (and 2010) at §§ 5.2.1–5.2.6. This approach is complicated by national and international ABS regime instruments, which state or imply that genetic resources and ATK are special assets with special limitations on their use and approval of that use.

346 Such a holding would not only deny enforcement of the ABS contract, but might raise doubts about the legality of the entire SMTA system.

347 This theory would be based on the idea that the UN Specialized Agency sponsored the negotiations of the Treaty as part of its overarching mandate to ensure that utilization of genetic resources for agricultural purposes would not interfere with the rights of provider countries as to those resources. There is, however, another possible interpretation – that the duty of FAO is limited to monitoring and securing the rights of the international collections of plant genetic resources for food and agriculture, *i.e.*, that FAO's status as a TPB is intended to protect the collections. This approach would deny the rights of provider countries, and as such seems less likely to accord with FAO's mandate.

or other plant germplasm from a collection, pays a specific benefit-share into a fund administered by the ITPGRFA Governing Body and Secretariat, which operate under the FAO umbrella. Thus, the original providers of the genetic resource do not share in the benefits unless FAO acts in their interests.[348]

In this vein, it may be possible to infer a similar responsibility for user countries. Some commentators, for example, have opined that the Netherlands' failure to adopt ABS user measures accounts in part for the failure of the Teff Agreement. In light of the fact that an Ethiopian governmental unit was an identified party to the Agreement, and the Embassy of the Netherlands participated, to a limited extent in the negotiations, some have argued that the Netherlands had some obligation to protect the provider, when it became clear that the user company was intentionally defaulting on its commitments, and that Ethiopia could not take legal action.[349]

The argument here is that the ABS contract might also create a new type of "non-party party" – the "third party obligee."[350] The users' and providers' rights and obligations under their ABS contract are arguably linked to the existing

348 The literature circulated in connection with the negotiation of the SMTA and ITPGRFA noted that the entire world benefits from food security, new variety development, and access to the international seed collections. This fact, while true, is not relevant. The entire world benefits from medicinal and pharmaceutical discoveries as well; however, benefit-sharing under the NP and CBD is focused, not on the fact that there is a general benefit, but rather on the fact that some company, researcher or individual derives *specific* (monetary or non-monetary) benefits from *utilization* of the genetic resource or ATK. ABS focuses on the sharing of *that specific benefit*, and in the case of the ITPGRFA, that occurs when the recipient pays into the ITPGRFA's multilateral fund.

349 Dr Tewolde Berhan Gebre Egziabher stated his country's situation succinctly: "[In the Teff Agreement, w]e said that Ethiopian law would apply for compliance and we agreed on a procedure but we know it is feeble. If there is no international law on compliance, it is a matter of a gentleman's agreement." Quoted in Wynberg, 2008, at p. 67.

350 As noted in Andersen and Winge, 2012, at p. 112: "An important question in this context is whether the Netherlands had any obligations with regard to the Teff Agreement. This is a much-discussed topic among the involved stakeholders in Ethiopia, and many think that the Netherlands had an obligation in this regard. ...The Teff Agreement was an agreement between the Ethiopian state and a Dutch company. Nevertheless, the Embassy of the Netherlands did interact with the IBC, in providing the IBC with information and through some meetings. A question in this regard is whether the diplomatic channel could have been used to a greater extent, *e.g.* as an instrument for mediation. It is also worth noting that the last letter about mediation from the IBC was sent after the HPFI had been declared bankrupt: the IBC was evidently not aware of the bankruptcy process that was taking place in the Netherlands, and here the Embassy of the Netherlands could have had a role to play."

legal relationship between the user and provider countries under the CBD and NP. Among other commitments, the CBD and NP specifically require all States to take legislative, administrative or policy measures "with the aim of sharing in a fair and equitable way the results of research and development and the benefits arising from the commercial and other utilization of genetic resources,"[351] ATK,[352] and "genetic resources that are held by indigenous and local communities."[353] In the NP, States commit to ensuring that providers have "an opportunity to seek recourse under their legal systems, consistent with applicable jurisdictional requirements, in cases of disputes arising from mutually agreed terms."[354]

These options and practices give rise to inquiry: Does an ABS contract between a provider in country X and a user in country Y cause countries X and Y to have an obligation to ensure that the contract is fulfilled? Does it make them, in effect, third party obligees? Although the CBD and NP clearly require user measures, they are ambiguous regarding what those measures must include. The NP's provision regarding enforcement of MAT resembles a "gentlemen's agreement" in that they are only effective if and to the extent that the user country is behaving "like a gentleman" – adopting measures that meet the overall expectation of that clause, rather than simply adopting the bare minimum necessary to avoid a legal action.

351 CBD, Art. 15.7. This language is mirrored in, but not superseded by, NP Art. 5(1), 5(3) and 5(5) (see NP, Art. 4(1), 4(3), and 5(1).).

352 NP, Art. 5(5).

353 NP, Art. 5(2).

354 NP, Art. 18.2.

CHAPTER 9

"Protect Contractual Expectations to Minimize the Need for Litigation": Guarantees, Incentives, and Other Security Arrangements

As noted throughout this book, the functionality challenge of ABS contracts, and indeed of the entire ABS regime, lies in the basic fact that formal contract enforcement (in courts or arbitration) of international contracts[355] is so difficult and expensive that ABS providers normally cannot attempt it without financial and other help.[356] As noted in Chapter 7, the likelihood of a party walking away from a contract in this way decreases significantly where the contract is legally enforceable. Still, however, the parties to an ABS contract[357] should not rely solely on formal legal enforcement as the primary method of ensuring the parties' compliance.[358] If a party's interest should change in the months following the completion of the negotiations, it may well wish to eliminate or ignore its contractual responsibilities. If such a breaching party were somewhat unscrupulous, he may even have entered into the contract *on the assumption* that it will become meaningless in this way.[359]

This chapter focuses on an important, second basic question: If they cannot enforce it in the courts, what can the parties *really* do in case of an unresolved

355 As explained in Chapter 2, a contract is often considered "international" if its parties, the components of the *res* or any activities are located in more than one country.

356 In the words of one developing country official (after explaining that neither his country nor the providers would be practically able to take action against a user who had violated the ABS contract): "We said that Ethiopian law would apply for compliance and we agreed on a procedure but we know it is feeble. If there is no international law on compliance, it is a matter of a gentleman's agreement." Andersen and Winge, 2012, at p. 113, quoting Dr Tewolde Berhan Gebre Egziabher.

357 This paragraph is generally true of all contracts. In ABS contracts, the risks to a defaulting user may be higher because of the bad publicity that would occur, if its breach and the resulting impact on rural and indigenous communities were to become known.

358 Even when the contract is clearly enforceable, many commercial parties will engage in a "cost/risk vs. benefit" analysis, to determine whether its costs and risks from breaching the contract are outweighed by the benefits that it will recognize.

359 Even where all parties signed the contract in good faith, this result may be inevitable, especially in ABS situations involving providers with no intent or possibility of taking legal action against a larger institutional user from a developed country.

 | DOI 10.1163/9789004356573_010

conflict or breach of contract? It is divided into five discussions. It begins with a brief summary of the reasons that "non-judicial remedies" (contractual remedies that can be applied without going to court) are valuable (¶ 9.1), turning next to the "balance" of contractual benefits and responsibilities and the role of non-judicial remedies (¶ 9.2), followed by an explanation of how non-judicial remedies function, so that the negotiating parties can understand the pitfalls of improper drafting and know what to look for (¶ 9.3). Section 9.4 then introduces various types of non-judicial mechanisms (direct asset transfer, escrow arrangements, pledges of assets as "security," liquidated damages clauses, self-executing measures, insurance and other assurances) and discusses how to use them, giving examples in some cases. The two final sections focus on non-judicial issues of the substantive aspects of the contract: ¶ 9.5 looks at how the specific details of key provisions, such as the nature of payment and the long-term nature of the relationship among the parties, might enhance the likelihood of compliance by creating other incentives. Section 9.6 then returns to the issue of balance, considering various legal challenges involved in making sure that the contract's non-judicial mechanisms are able to protect the parties against a range of legal and practical challenges.

9.1 The Advantage and Disadvantage of Non-judicial Remedies

The most important aspects of most non-judicial remedies for ABS contracts are (i) they are entirely localized, and are usually designed so that they be exercised in the provider country; and (ii) they provide the protected party with a remedy "up-front," so that any litigation or arbitration will happen after the remedy has been paid. This means that the burden of enforcement effectively shifts. The "secured party" (the party to whom a payment or future action is promised; usually the provider, in ABS transactions) receives his remedy promptly and non-judicially. It is then up to the party that gave the security to bring any action he thinks necessary, if he feels that the remedy has been obtained in violation of the contract.

The main disadvantage of non-judicial remedies is that they are, by nature, limited in size and specific in coverage. If the secured party's injury is greater than the value of the collateral or outside the scope of the remedy, he must either absorb the additional loss or take legal action (lawsuit or arbitration) to obtain the additional remedy needed.[360]

360 If he brings such an action for additional remedies, then the secured party will again have the burden of proof.

9.2 The Contractual Balance and the Role of Non-judicial Remedies

In essence, every contract is a balancing process in which each party seeks to ensure that its own interests will not be lost, and to find ways that the contract can be amicably interpreted, even in the event of a change of circumstance that causes one or all parties' interests to change. Every day, nearly every one of the more than eight billion people and the estimated 1.5 billion companies and businesses on the planet enters into at least one (and maybe a great many) contracts, spanning a broad range from the purchase of one's morning cup of coffee (an oral/implied contract) to multimillion dollar international stock transactions. It has been estimated that more than 20 billion written contracts are executed every year.

Fortunately, only a tiny fraction (less than 0.0001%) of contracts are ever litigated or arbitrated. The critical question for this book is "why?" What factors increase the likelihood that the parties will comply with the contract, without the need for litigation or other formal action? The answer is twofold: "balance" and "incentive." In a good and effective contract, each party obtains something they desire, in exchange for giving something they are willing to give. Or phrased in the negative, for each party the consequences of failing to complete the contract are greater than the costs (in time, money and other demands) of complying.

The challenge for ABS contract drafters is to find the appropriate balance. They must make sure that the costs and consequences are not so great that they cannot be balanced by benefits, but to ensure that the other party will not consider them insignificant (*i.e.,* to ensure that they are not too small). This challenge is complicated by the fact that the contract deals with the future, so that many aspects of that balance may change for a variety of reasons. If the contract's basic balances were initially correct, such changes normally result in communication among the parties, leading to compromise or other goodwill based solutions. Where the contract is not balanced, change often results in breach that may require litigation or arbitration and even then may not achieve a positive solution.

9.3 How Non-judicial Remedies Function

In general, non-judicial remedies, which are sometimes called "secured transactions," operate by providing the secured party with a right to obtain "collateral" (a sum of money or some asset(s) of value) directly, in the event that the party giving the security should fail to make the promised payment or take the required action. The first step in any such clause, is for the parties to agree on who will provide the security; what is being secured; and the nature of the assets that are to be used as security. Once these have been agreed, the mechanism to be used must be agreed. (There are many different types of non-judicial remedies, described in ¶ 9.4.)

A full discussion of all of the operational and legal issues related to commercial security arrangements is certainly well beyond the scope of this book. This section focuses on the three main elements of commercial non-judicial security arrangements that are most important to ABS contract draftsmen: How the collateral is pledged and held (¶ 9.3.1); how the secured party's right is "exercised" in case of a breach of contract (¶ 9.3.2); and how termination of the contract may impact the security (¶ 9.3.3). All three of these elements apply to all types of non-judicial security arrangements.

9.3.1 *Holding/Pledging the Collateral*

Once the nature of the collateral has been agreed, the parties must determine how it will be pledged. There are several different ways of pledging collateral. These include direct transfer into the full possession of the secured party subject to requirements; establishment of a fund or other arrangement to hold a payment of money; conditional transfer of title through a third party (using a "mortgage" or "deed of trust" arrangement); or the purchase of an insurance policy or letter of credit.[361] Each of these options has positive and negative elements, which must be separately considered in every transaction.

The type of pledge used is a critical issue for all parties. For the party pledging the security, the pledge must be arranged in a way that ensures that the secured party may only obtain it in the event of a breach (*i.e.,* that he may not use or spend it unless he does so in conformity with the agreement.) Conversely, the secured party is primarily interested in ensuring that he may exercise his right to the security directly and locally, and that he will not be forced to go through litigation or arbitration in order to obtain the remedy.

In general, the existence of a security arrangement must be documented in a written instrument, except that an oral contract is allowed where the secured party is actually holding the collateral.[362] Where the collateral is pledged in a

361 There are many other types of security arrangements, however, they are used in types of transactions that are not apparently relevant to ABS contracts. For example, special secured rights (liens) may apply to transactions in which a business borrows operating capital, secured by a mortgage or lien on its merchandise, or where a contractor works on, builds or repairs on another's property which property is collateral for his payment for that work.

362 The requirement that most secured transactions be written down is derived from a general legal concept of commercial law called, in common law countries, the "statute of frauds." Where collateral is given directly (for example, where the user's vehicles and

way that does not directly transfer it to the secured party, or where it is intangible, then the pledge must include everything necessary to completely transfer the asset to the ownership of the secured party in the event of a breach. Specifically, the agreement must clearly state of the intent to transfer, all transferring documents and titles must be signed,[363] and any other necessary forms must be completed. As explained in ¶ 9.3.2, the transfer documents and other forms (and sometimes the security itself) are often held by a third party (bank, trustee or escrow holder) pursuant to an agreement, until a breach occurs.

In order for the security agreement to be valid, the party pledging the collateral must usually have rights in it. If a party pledges his neighbour's car as collateral and the neighbour does not endorse this pledge, then the security agreement is ineffective. It is possible, however, to specify in the agreement that it includes "after-acquired property." For example, a pledge of "all automobiles owned by [the party] at any time during the term of this agreement" would include the neighbour's car if the party later buys it from the neighbour.

The final component of the pledge is "perfecting" the security. This is automatic where the pledge involves direct transfer of the security to the secured party or to a third-party escrow, subject to the terms of the contract, or where the security is provided by insurance, letter of credit or other money transfer.[364] In pledges of assets that continue to be held by the pledging party it may be necessary to formally file a record of the transfer in an appropriate public office. This is done to ensure that the pledging party cannot eliminate the secured party's rights by selling the collateral to a third-party who does not know of the security interest, or using it as security in another transaction with such a party. In that case a "good-faith purchaser" may receive the property free

---

equipment are used for bioprospecting and initial testing, on the understanding that they may be retained by the provider if the user defaults under the contract) then that agreement may be oral. In general, however, oral agreements are not recommended, where the parties are not long-time neighbours and/or friends.

363 Increasingly, the law of some countries is recognizing "electronically marked" documents in place of signatures. If the secured party is not certain as to whether an electronically marked document will be upheld by the court or arbitrator that might be called to interpret it, it is preferable to obtain an appropriately attested or notarized signature from a person formally authorized to bind the company or individual giving the security.

364 As discussed in ¶ 9.4, these kinds of security operate without perfection, because they cannot be transferred without the express approval of all interested parties.

of the unrecorded obligation. In many countries, however, if there is a public record of the security interest, the purchaser would be considered to know of it.[365] Then, the secured party could still exercise his right to take the collateral in the event of breach.

9.3.2 *"Exercise" of the Secured Party's Rights*

Where a contractual security arrangement exists, the manner in which the secured party's rights are exercised is determined by the contract. In some cases, however, the main contract is supplemented by a second agreement, which may be known as a "mortgage," "trust-deed," "security agreement" or some other term.[366] Such security agreements are commonly used in several situations, for example:

- Where the law requires a separate instrument;
- Where there is concern that the parties' rights might be affected by termination of the contract (see ¶ 9.3.3, *infra*);
- Where a third party (a trustee, bank, escrow holder or insurance company) is involved, who will be bound by the procedures for exercise of the security; or
- Where the security interest must be "perfected" by recording in public records (see ¶ 9.3.1, *supra*) and either party wishes to keep the main contract confidential.

No matter what type of security arrangement is used, it is absolutely essential that the parties agree on the basic elements of the security agreement, whether their security arrangement is documented as a clause of their contract or as a separate security agreement. Given the strong likelihood that all or part of any ABS contract will be "international" in nature, it is usually preferable that this arrangement should be documented in writing and should address all aspects of the exercise of the secured party's rights, including matters that are governed by applicable law or local practice.[367] Specifically, the security clause or agreement should include:

365 In law, this is called "constructive notice" – the party is assumed to know of all matters that are duly recorded in the proper legal office.

366 This chapter will use "security agreement" to refer to all of these, except where specifically stated otherwise.

367 Example of the kinds of issues that might be covered may be found in the Uniform Commercial Code (UCC), which has been adopted in some form by every state in the United

- A clear statement of the rights of the secured party and of the party granting the security (including rights and duties regarding care and maintenance of the collateral); and
- Concrete and detailed information on exactly what the secured party must do in order to obtain the collateral in the event of breach of the secured obligations (with forms annexed, if necessary).[368]

Thus, the contract or security agreement, and the manner in which it is drafted, may have a significant impact on the effectiveness of the non-judicial remedy. In ABS, these issues are critical in any clause in which any party makes a statement or commitment, especially clauses that involve direct promises to take action in future, and any clause that states that one party "indemnifies," "guarantees," "represents" or "warrants" anything (see below.) In addition to being very concrete about what each party is obliged to do (see Chapter 5, *supra*), these provisions should be very clear about when the obligation is triggered and, specifically, what constitutes a breach or default.

Often the coverage of these clauses is limited. For example, a party may warrant that it has not misrepresented itself and that one statements made by that party are true and correct. The warrantee clause would only apply in the event of a misrepresentation, but when is it triggered – on discovery of the misrepresentation, or when it results in damage to another party? And if the latter, what constitutes "damage?"

All of these questions are important for two reasons. First, obviously, they define the parties' obligations and rights with regard to the contract. Second, however, for purposes of non-judicial remedy, it is critical to have a clear understanding about when the non-judicial remedy is triggered. If there is a bank, trustee or insurance company involved, how will the secured party prove that he may exercise his rights? To protect itself from liability, such an institution will only transfer the collateral when it is absolutely certain that it is doing so in compliance with the agreement. This means that if the security agreement is ambiguous, it may not operate. The only effect of the security agreement will be that secured party will be forced to engage in litigation against the bank, trustee or insurer, rather than against the party providing the security. This is a poor trade-off.

States. Cornell University UCC access. The UCC provisions regarding the rights of parties with regard to asset security are set out in Article 9.

368 As noted below, it is essential that any trustee, bank, insurer or other third party that might be involved should specifically agree on this information.

TIP
SECURITY, INDEMNITY, GUARANTEE, REPRESENTATION OR WARRANTEE

Typically, the contract should include indemnities, warranties, guarantees and representations, supported by non-judicial security, to cover every necessary aspect of the transaction, which one party cannot verify for himself, but which he feels is essential in order for the contract to function. As noted in prior chapters, ABS contracts include a range of such issues, including the legal status of the parties (Chapter 4); This is the nature of the user's business (Chapter 5); the user's commitments limiting the types of use he will undertake(*id.*); the user's assurance that he will exert R&D efforts with regard to the genetic resources and ATK (*id.*); the user's financial and other ability to meet his obligations (*id.*); the promises made regarding or restricting transfer (Chapter 6); *etc.*

It is important for the security clause or agreement to be very specific about which action, indemnity, guarantee, representation or warrantee clause is covered by the security; to what extent; and what is secured. For example, does the security guarantee payment to cover losses occasioned by the breach? Does it include a duty to "hold harmless" – *i.e.*, to undertake (and/or pay all costs of) defence, if the protected party is sued by one of the persons that expected payment or benefit-sharing under the ABS contract?

9.3.3 *Surviving Contract Termination*

The possibility that the contract will terminate before it has been fully performed is potentially problematic, because it may mean that the parties' respective rights under the contract have also terminated. For example, ¶¶ 6.3, 6.4 and 8.3.2, *supra*, discuss the possibilities that particular actions or breaches may cause the contract to terminate, and suggest the drafting of an enforcement provision that allows the parties to take action on a breach of contract without terminating the contract and the rights thereunder. Similarly, ¶ 8.4.7 discusses the use of a "survival clause" which specifically states that certain provisions of the contract will "survive" (remain in force and continue to be actionable), even after the termination of the contract.

In ABS negotiations, when a party is planning and drafting non-judicial remedies, it is essential to ensure that those remedies survive in the event of specified types of termination or other conclusion of the contract. Whether the security arrangement is documented in a separate "security agreement" or only in a clause of the contract, it is strongly advisable that the parties specifically (re)state that the security rights and collateral arrangements contained therein survive, in the event of any termination of the contract as a result of breach by either party. They need to state that these arrangements continue until either the security rights have been fully executed and no claim regarding them remains, or until the secured obligations under the ABS contract have been fully performed to the satisfaction of all relevant parties.

9.4 Non-judicial Remedy Mechanisms for Use in ABS Contracts

Based on the general "pledge – exercise – survival" format described in ¶ 9.3, there are many variations in the mechanisms through which non-judicial remedies may function. The following seven examples are presented in the following manner: each will begin with an extremely brief description of the particular mechanism, followed by a short discussion of the special challenges that arise in using that mechanism in the context of ABS contracts.

9.4.1 *Direct Asset Transfer Subject to Conditions*

The simplest form of security arrangement is the "direct transfer of collateral, subject to conditions subsequent." In using this mechanism, the party giving security transfers all of his interest in the collateral to the secured party, who has full possession and/or title to the collateral. The contract states that this transfer is only made as security for the transferring party's specified performances under the contract, and that the assets shall be returned following full performance.

The challenge in using this method in ABS contracts relates to the "balance" issue described in ¶ 9.2, *supra*. Traditionally, most international conservation projects include as one element that the project shall bring vehicles and equipment into the country, with the expectation that they will be left behind after the project ends. The parties to an ABS contract that uses this type of security must confirm that the value of such equipment will be enough to satisfy their expectations from the contract, since the other party may already assume that the transfer of this equipment is an "up-front" cost of the contract, and thus be more-than-usually willing to walk away from these assets.

For the party giving security in this manner, if he expects it to be returned, it may be necessary to record a security interest (*see* ¶ 9.3.2, *supra*) in the transferred assets to protect this expectation.

9.4.2 *Escrow Arrangements, Letters of Credit and Other Monetary Security*

In most other types of international contracts, the most common form of secured transaction amounts to prepayment of a specified amount of money, in one form or another. For example, a party may simply agree to open a bank account in a specified amount[369] which may be used only as security for the party's obligations under the contract. As another option, if its credit rating allows, it may pay the necessary fee to a specified bank, so that that bank will provide a "letter of credit" ("LOC")[370] assuring payment in such instances.

International LOCs and escrow arrangements are normally used in purchase and sale transactions, and usually apply to the rather straightforward question of whether a specified payment of a stated amount of money is made on schedule. In those cases, the financial institution will generally be willing to sign a relatively standard agreement, detailing what the secured party must do in order to draw on the LOC. Typically it will require the secured party (or its designated representative) to appear in person at the institution, with a legally sufficient declaration[371] specifying how and in what respects the other party has failed to fulfill its obligations.[372] Upon compliance with all necessary requirements, the secured party receives a check for the appropriate amount.

In attempting to use these mechanisms, the ABS parties should pay close attention to the fact that an ABS contract is markedly different from a straight purchase/sale or commodity contract in a large number of ways. As a result, the security contract that applies an LOC to an ABS transaction cannot function properly if the parties use a standard form LOC agreement or clause. Instead, they will need to be carefully craft a document that both addresses the unique needs of ABS contracts, and meets the strict requirements of the institution issuing the LOC. Although they may use a relatively standard approach

---

369 See "liquidated damages," as discussed in ¶ 9.4.4, *infra,* and in ¶¶ 8.2.2(b) and 8.3.4, *supra,* and in other parts of this book.

370 A "Letter Of Credit" is a document issued by a bank or similar financial institution guaranteeing that, in the event the party providing the security fails to make full payment or take other action on time, that financial institution must cover the full amount of any overdue payment, or make specified payment in the event of other breach.

371 This may be called a "notarized statement," a "declaration under penalty of perjury" or some other name. Often the financial institution will provide a sample or form showing exactly what will be required.

372 Where the arrangement used is an LOC, the financial institution and the party giving the security enter into a separate "backstopping agreement" under which the latter agrees to repay the former, in the event that the LOC is drawn. The party giving security pays a fee to the financial institution for this service.

where discussing the provider's right to draw on the security after the user fails to make timely payment of money in response to a clear trigger (date or externally obvious event),[373] it will also be important to specify the exact mechanism and amount to be paid with regard to each type of non-monetary breach that is covered by the security.[374] This recommendation is intended to indicate that parties should apply the lessons regarding specific and careful drafting of obligations and rights, as discussed in Chapter 5, to this provision. They must also recognizing the need to understand and address the complex of laws governing financial institutions and their activities.

Subject these caveats, escrows and LOCs are relatively common. This may mean that it could be relatively easy to find an institution willing to perform these services, although it may be slightly more difficult to find institutions willing to alter these mechanisms to accommodate the ABS contract. The uncertainty inherent in ABS contracts, coupled with the financial institution's lack of experience can be obstacles to this approach. Here also, the amount of funds escrowed or the maximum payout on the LOC must be carefully balanced, so that either: (i) the amount paid will satisfy the expectations and contractual needs of the secured party; or (ii) the party giving security will find that it is preferable to comply with the contract, rather than lose the money pledged.

9.4.3 *Assets Pledged as Security: Mortgages and Other Commitments*

The most common form of collateral is the pledge of assets, where the title and/or possession of the asset stays in the name of the party pledging the security, to be automatically transferred to the secured party in the event of a breach. This mechanism is well known, where a person borrows money to buy something of high value (land, a building, a car, *etc.*) and, by signing a mortgage or similar document, arranges to automatically transfer that property to the lender if he fails to repay the loan in full.

373 Even this clause must be carefully drafted, to ensure that it will always be clear to the financial institution exactly how much money it is obligated to pay. Recalling that many benefit-sharing clauses have been somewhat ambiguous (see, Chapter 5, *supra*), it is important for the security clause or agreement to leave no doubt in the mind of the financial institution regarding how much it may/must pay out.

374 As noted in Chapters 5, 6 and 8, many concepts, such as notification to the provider of particular events, are much more critical in ABS contracts than they might be in other contracts. Given the number of ABS contract terms that may be ambiguous or difficult to draft concretely, such failure of notice may be one of the few key provisions that a user can rely on in seeking to enforce his contract, whether judicially or non-judicially.

This same mechanism is often used in other transactions as well.[375] The pledging party agrees to a mortgage of property he owns, in favour of the secured party, as security for his promise to perform under the contract. If the pledging party breaches the contract, the secured party may "foreclose" (take possession of the mortgaged property), either through the courts or through non-judicial processes (in countries that allow them), in the country where the mortgaged property is located. In either case, a mortgage places the title documents and other forms and material necessary to transfer the asset in the hands of a trustee, financial institution or other person/company. That institution is bound by the agreement and by law to complete the transfer when the secured party has complied with all specified procedures to foreclose on the collateral.

In drafting such a "performance mortgage," however, it is important to be very specific and concrete about the required actions that are secured by the collateral for the same reasons mentioned in ¶ 9.4.2. Specifically, a the trustee, financial institution or other mortgage holder will not agree to administer a mortgage unless it is absolutely clear how and in what circumstances the secured party will be entitled to exercise his rights of foreclosure. Using the terms of CBD and NP will not be sufficiently precise for this purpose.

The use of a formal mortgage might also have potentially beneficial impact in bankruptcy situations that may arise (see ¶¶ 6.6.1 and 6.6.2.) In many countries, bankruptcy laws include special rules and priorities for any of the bankrupt's property that has been formally pledged as security. When the bankruptcy trustee sells that property, the proceeds of the sale go first to the secured party, and only after the secured party is fully paid is the excess added to the fund used to pay other creditors. This doesn't guarantee that the secured party will receive full payment, but at minimum it might ensure that he will receive more than the other creditors.[376] In addition, the fact that most mortgages are formally recorded in public records may make it easier for the provider to know about and participate in the bankruptcy procedures.

375 In many countries, the parties may use a mortgage/trust-deed mechanism to secure non-monetary obligations (including, potentially the obligations to engage in R&D and other actions required under ABS contracts).

376 Normally, if the secured party is not paid in full, then the rest of his debt is considered an "unsecured debt," entitling him to a share of the final payment out of the bankruptcy estate.

9.4.4 *The Role of "Liquidated Damages"*

It is probably obvious that the above mechanisms could all be tied in with the "liquidated damages" clause in the contract. As discussed in ¶ 8.3.4, the drafting of a liquidated damages clause is very similar to a non-judicial remedy. Such a clause must also be very detailed in itemizing the potential amount that should be paid in the event of each particular type of breach. Similarly, if the liquidated damages clause is well drafted, it may prompt the breaching party to resolve the dispute without going through litigation – *i.e.,* to simply pay the liquidated damage amount. In drafting non-judicial security clauses or agreements, it may be useful to specify the relationship between the two clauses. One could perhaps note that the non-judicial security will involve a lower payment (either a percentage discount or the fact that no attorneys' fees and court/arbitration costs will be added), unless some litigation or arbitration is necessary after the secured parties have exercised their non-judicial of the rights.

9.4.5 *Self-executing Protective Measures*

For the parties to an ABS contract, there may be other measures that the parties would prefer to take, in the event of a breach or default of the contract. For example, the provider may wish to confiscate samples, bar the defaulting user from future access to the genetic resources or bioprospecting area, cancel relevant permits, inform government oversight bodies, formally file a cancellation of any "internationally recognized certificate of compliance" and/or refuse to acknowledge the user's rights in the genetic resources or ATK. Any of these actions may be appropriate in the event of a breach or default, but unless they are specifically mentioned in the ABS contract and/or security agreement, it is possible that the user may view them as actionable violations of law.

TIP
SPECIFYING SELF-EXECUTING MEASURES

To maximize the provider's rights in the event of a breach by the user or some other party to the ABS contract, it is strongly advised that all such powers and potential actions be specifically mentioned in the contract itself.

9.4.6 *Insurance*

Insurance is common to nearly every country and industry. The purchase of insurance to protect against future injury is also common. In many contracts, the obligation to purchase and maintain insurance is specifically allocated to one of the parties, who shall have the duty to make certain that losses to the other part[ies] are covered by that insurance.

In general, however, there are many reasons that insurance may not be a useful option in an ABS contract, three of which (discussed below) are as follows: (a) collection on insurance policies is often only a different form of litigation; (b) most types of liability insurance specifically excludes liability arising out of contract violations; and (c) there is no current insurance product that can easily be adapted to ABS.

a) Collecting on Insurance

Increasingly, insurance companies find themselves in a difficult position. They must compete with other insurers to provide the lowest rates, but at the same time, they must make a profit in an industry that is, in effect, gambling on the possibility that certain future events will or will not occur. As a result when the insured seeks to collect on a policy, the insurance company may often use every argument it can think of in an effort to avoid paying. For this reason, the specific language in the policy is very detailed. The secured party is frequently forced to take legal action against the insurer to collect the amount due under the policy. In current practice, the time, cost, complexity and ill will involved in trying to collect a payment owed under an insurance policy is no less difficult than litigating the liability issue directly against the breaching party.

For ABS contract parties, however, there may be two advantages to the use of insurance to protect the parties' rights. First, in most countries reputable insurance companies must meet regulatory standards, including financial solvency. This means that the insurance company may be able to pay, even if the user has become bankrupt. In addition, in many cases, insurance companies based in the user country may also have offices authorized to represent the company in the provider country. This could mean that a legal action against the company may often be prosecuted locally. This will normally be preferable to the task of bringing a lawsuit or arbitration against a user in a distant country.

Thus, the question of whether to include an insurance clause involves a careful situation-by-situation balancing process. It will be useful to get the advice of an insurance law expert in the countries of the provider and of the user to make sure that the insurance clause in the contract requires all of the protections the parties desire and expect, and also to confirm that any policy actually purchased[377] conforms to those requirements.

377 In general, where a contract requires the purchase of insurance, it is strongly recommended that the policy be bought before the transaction closes, and that all parties receive a copy confirm that it satisfies the contract.

b) Exclusion of Contract-based Liability

Another ABS contract challenge arises out of the basic principle that liability insurance is not intended to allow a party to shift his voluntarily undertaken contractual obligations to the insurer. In most basic liability policies, including so-called "D&O policies" (the standard type of policy used to insure corporations, corporate directors and officers, and corporate activities) there is an "exclusion" which states that liabilities arising out of contract violation are not covered by the policy.[378] Often, instead of an exclusion, the policy coverage description will be specific and limited.[379] This means that the insurer may refuse to pay off on a breach of contract claim, and the only remedy for the provider will be a direct action against the user and/or its individual directors and officers. In that case, the insurance clause will not change the provider's level of security at all. Similar exclusions may also apply to "criminal" acts.

Thus, in negotiating an ABS contract that includes insurance provisions, it will be essential to review both the insurance policy in question and the law governing it, to ensure that the policy will provide the expected level of protection.[380]

c) Insurance "Products"

The above challenges strongly suggest that standard types of liability insurance would not provide a non-judicial solution to the risks of an ABS contract. There may, however, be other insurance options. There are many other kinds of insurance products currently available, including mortgage insurance, surety bonds and operational insurance coverage. Any of these might possibly be configured to address bioprospecting and other ABS activities. Beyond this,

---

378 Such an exclusion will normally speak in terms like the following: "[This contract precludes coverage] for claims based upon, arising from, or in consequence of any actual or alleged liability of an Insured Organization under any written or oral contract or agreement provided that this exclusion ... shall not apply to the extent that an Insured Organization would have been liable in the absence of the contract or agreement." (This language is directly quoted from a current D&O policy issued to a major US corporation. A relatively recent case upholding this approach in the US is *Spirtas Company v. Federal Insurance Company*.)

379 It is common, for example, for D&O policy coverage to be limited to protecting against the claims of shareholders.

380 See, *e.g.* *GE HFS Holdings, Inc. v. National Union Fire Insurance Co. of Pittsburgh, Pennsylvania*, in which a corporation misstated its financial status in negotiating a contract, leading the other party ("lender") to extend credit because it did not realize that the first company was bankrupt. The exclusion was upheld with regard to the corporation and all of its directors and officers, and as a result, the lender was forced to seek remedy from the individual directors and officers.

insurance companies are regularly developing new types of insurance products, to meet specialized needs.

One example of this kind of development is in the area of business casualty insurance products, such as "credit insurance," a special product that is often divided into narrower categories such as "trade credit insurance," "business credit insurance" and "export credit insurance." Each of these is carefully crafted for a particular type of business situation. As such, the parties might meet resistance in attempting to convince the financial institution to adapt them to an ABS contract. Credit insurance, for example, combines property/casualty insurance and a risk management, and usually focuses on protecting the "accounts receivable" of the insured from loss due to credit risks such as protracted default, insolvency or bankruptcy. In some instances, trade credit insurance can cover the political risk of non-payment by foreign buyers due to currency issues, political unrest, expropriation *etc.* As such it seems potentially adaptable to ABS situations.

Although it is currently doubtful that any existing insurance product could address the potential liability/damage issues relevant to ABS contract without substantial amendment, the insurance industry is extremely flexible and willing to cooperate in the development of new products. Early on, insurance on ABS contracts will have to be individually and specifically negotiated, both with the other parties to the ABS contract and with the would-be insurer.[381] Over time, however, if ABS contracts regularly require insurance, the industry is likely to develop standard policies and predictable coverage and rates.

9.4.7 *Return of the* Res

Unfortunately, there is no apparent non-judicial remedy for the most obvious challenge in ABS enforcement – that is, for the fact that a defaulting user will have genetic material, genetic information and traditional knowledge that will not or cannot be returned. Once a company has obtained samples of genetic material, the provider has no way of confirming whether that material has been multiplied. Similarly, where research has resulted in a mapped genetic sequence or other information, there is no way to "un-ring the bell" and prevent the user from using the information obtained after his right to do so has expired or been terminated. The same challenge exists regarding ATK. The material and information in the hands of the company may, in some cases, be used to defeat the provider's right and ability to obtain benefit-sharing in future

381 The contents of insurance policies, and the applicable law are extremely complex, suggesting that the parties may want to acquire the services of an expert who specializes in insurance matters, to help them with this part of the negotiations, and ensure that their needs are properly met.

on ATK or a genetic resource that has been the subject of a failed contract in the past. Lacking the option of effective restitution, the parties will usually need to rely on other financial and practical incentives and requirements, in order to maintain the balance in the ABS contract.

Commercial law generally assumes that the parties will still want to go forward with a unidirectional contract, even if some needed remedies may not be available.

> TIP
> BALANCING THE CONTRACT
>
> It is the obligation of the parties to balance the contract, prior to signing, to ensure that the contractual remedies that are available are sufficiently valuable and available so that, in case the contract fails after the *res* has changed hands, they will not be in a worse position than if they had never entered the contract in the first place.

9.5 How ABS Contractual and Legislative Requirements Can Enhance Future Remedial Options

There are many ways in which the contract terms can improve the non-judicial effectiveness of the ABS contract. In addition, although the drafting and contents of national ABS legislation is beyond the scope of this book, there are legislative provisions, too, that can help.

In essence, the most effective remedy in any contract is to avoid the need for a remedy. This can be done by considering the nature of the particular challenges posed by ABS contracts, and the balance and incentives of the contract (*see* ¶ 9.2, *supra*) as perceived by both sides, and then re-building the contract in a manner that helps to avoid the challenges and sets a new and clear balance. This section will discuss a few examples of how this has been done, focusing on contractual terms and provisions.

9.5.1 *Advances and Prepayments*

From the earliest prototypes of ABS contracts, the parties have been aware that the only moment when providers can claim to truly control an asset desired by the users is before the contract begins.[382] By the time the genetic material

382 In some instances, this claim is illusory. Experience has shown that biological materials have often been legally purchased and removed from the provider country as seed, food,

or ATK is in the laboratory and/or removed from the country, the user's compliance with ABS responsibility depends almost entirely on the good faith behavior of the user, without which, the provider may not know what has been done with the samples or whether any benefit (research results, commercial products, interim product or derivative) has arisen.

As a result of this concern, early ABS contracts focused significant attention on getting at least some remuneration to the provider at the "front-end" of the transaction, whether as a pre-bioprospecting "payment for access" or as a pre-sampling payment at the time samples are collected. Those early payments were often relatively small, based on three factors: (i) there was no assurance that any samples taken would actually lead to useful results, products or derivatives; (ii) the providers were often given to expect a range of non-monetary benefits to be shared after closing; and (iii) the users placed significant emphasis on their obligation to either pay negotiated benefit-shares or return and negotiate for such payment, in the event that utilization of the resource produced benefits. More recent experience has cast some doubt on the second and third of these factors, leading many ABS negotiators to suggest that up-front payments should include a much broader scope (*i.e.*, transfering samples, establishing in-country testing facilities, providing relevant training of local personnel in a broader range of activities,[383] conducting seminars, providing scholarships, *etc.*) ensuring that the required payments are all made or formally committed at a point at which the party making the commitments is also motivated to comply.

9.5.2 *Requiring the Establishment of Local Operations*

One approach that is designed to improve the providers' ability to monitor and enforce its ABS relationships is to impose a requirement that all bioprospecting and all R&D relating to genetic resources and ATK obtained under an ABS contract must be undertaken by a domestic company formed and operating in the provider country. One example of this approach is found in the previous Brazilian law.[384]

While this type of requirement does not resolve all enforcement problems, it may solve many of them. For example, it may ensure that the user remains

---

pets, ornaments or other types of commodities, and later utilized as genetic resources without permission. After removal to another country, the purchaser may either utilize the genetic components of the biological material himself or sell/transfer the material to another entity which does so. Cases in which such issues have arisen in ABS are documented in Young, 2006.

383 It has been common for ABS contracts to involve training of local workers in field collection techniques, sample preparation and labelling, but less common to help the country develop its abilities in the fields of genetic and ATK research and development.

384 BRAZIL, Provisional Act No 2,186-16, dated August 23, 2001.

within the jurisdiction of the provider country. If so, then the provider country's laws on access and benefit-sharing will continue to be enforceable against that user, and the provider country can enforce more detailed and long-term provisions of any ABS permit. Normally, at present, if the user's activities occur outside of the provider country, they will not necessarily be subject to the provider country's laws and permit requirements. In such situation the provider would need special help from the country in which those activities occur. Even with that help, the provider and provider country may not receive any benefit from foreign enforcement.[385]

By keeping the user's "utilization" activities in the provider country, the ABS process can ensure that any penalties and liability are paid to the provider or used by the provider country in accordance with its national ABS laws. This can only happen, however, if the user's in-country activities and assets are sufficiently valuable. If not, the user would be willing to leave them behind, in the event of a breach. In theory, this might operate to provide a non-judicial remedy to the provider. Once again, however, if the user's in-country assets are of low value, the provider may not feel adequately compensated by taking them over, although it may not have the practical ability to obtain any other remedy for the breach.

TIPS

REQUIRING SUFFICIENT LOCAL ASSETS

When requiring the user to conduct all "utilization" and R&D activities through a new domestic company or venture in the provider country, it is important to ensure that the domestic company is fully capitalized and holds all relevant assets in its own name. It may be necessary to specify the amount and type of locally available capital that must be held in the name of the new company. Where assets are viewed as security for the company's compliance with the ABS contract, it may also be appropriate to impose escrow and/or mortgage requirements, as well, or to require the purchase of insurance or bonding to protect the providers' interests (see ¶ 9.4, *supra*).

In addition, if the ABS contract will require any action, payment or other performance by the original user[s] (which will become "parent," shareholder or other type of related person/entity of the new domestic ABS company), it is important to ensure that these original user[s] are clearly obligated under the ABS contract, in addition to the obligation of the new domestic company (see ¶¶ 4.1–4.3).

385 See generally, Tvedt and Young, 2007, at § 2.7.

> If the formation of a new company is required by national ABS law, the ABS contract should specifically assign responsibility for undertaking this task, for payment of any filing costs, and for annual reporting or other national legal requirements imposed on such companies under national law of companies and other regulations. It should also specify what must be done if any necessary filing or formative application is denied.

9.5.3 *Payment in Shares of Stock*

One option that may sound like an easy and attractive solution is to specify that benefit-sharing payments be made in shares of stock in the user company. The synergies of this approach are generally obvious. As shareholders in the user company, the providers would gain a share in the increased profitability of the company, as the company itself benefits.

Unfortunately, corporate financing arrangements are so complex that this solution is not very simple, and may not actually function as desired, unless the contract contains very detailed and specific legal provisions, which must be closely overseen and monitored. Without them, there is a real possibility that payment will be in a separate "class" of shares that do not rise in value or produce returns, that the genetic resources will be "sold" to a related corporation, and/or that a corporate bankruptcy may occur. Even if the contract is sufficiently detailed to avoid the risk of these intentional violations, there may be many non-intentional events that impact the value of shares received in this way. Specific legal advice on these points is normally necessary.

9.5.4 *Regulatory and Contractual Incentives*

One other approach should be mentioned – the linking of ABS to specific incentives and motivating factors. It has long been noted that the use of commercial mechanisms (such as private or public-private contracts) to achieve social objectives is only effective where there is an appropriate motivation for the commercial parties to comply.[386]

Such motivations may span a wide range. Certain types of users (NGOs and aid agencies, for example,) are motivated by the desire to provide assistance to developing countries, rural and indigenous communities, and protected areas. They may also be strongly motivated to link that assistance to conservation and sustainable use objectives in the manner that ABS does. Non-commercial researchers may share in many of these objectives, but also be motivated by personal objectives relating to their planned research and how it will promote

386 See, Tvedt and Young, 2007, at § 6.2. See also, Young, 2004.

their plans for their future careers. Commercial users (including collectors and other middlemen), while possibly sharing in the desire to help and to promote conservation and sustainable use, are motivated by commercial objectives as well. In some instances, this commercial focus may overwhelm the potential user's other concerns. A rather different range of motivations may apply to various providers.[387] The major challenges for ABS functionality are to develop incentives that strongly motivate commercial users and user countries to obtain and comply with ABS contracts and permits and to clarify the motivations driving providers.

To understand these challenges, consider the nature and components of commercial and regulatory incentives. At base, a successful incentive offers some person or entity (the target) something desirable that it could not otherwise obtain (the incentive), in exchange for an action that it might not otherwise take (the desired behaviour). For example, it is common in many countries to offer owners of agrarian land special tax rates if they will promise not to develop that land.[388] The target (the landowner) receives an incentive with cash value to him (lower taxes) in exchange for a desired behaviour (refrain from developing the land) that he is not otherwise required to undertake. In some cases, even where the desired behaviour is required by law, incentives are used in recognition of the fact that direct enforcement may not be possible in many or most cases.[389]

Clearly in ABS, the desired behaviours – compliance with national ABS laws and with ABS contractual obligations – are difficult or impossible to enforce, so that many users have specifically said that they consider such provisions to be (at most) optional. It is necessary, then, to find something that is desirable and within the control of the provider countries (individually or collectively)

387 Although it is sometimes ignored, the reality is that there is a relatively broad range of motivations driving providers as well. National level motivations may be very broad, encompassing both the desire for benefit-sharing and the national environmental and social welfare objectives of protecting the environment and ensuring that benefits are received and shared equitably. For individual communities and institutions, these motivations continue, but may be focused more narrowly on their own members, without consideration of the rights and resources of neighbouring communities or other indigenous groups that hold similar or identical ATK. Where the provider's decisions are made individually, they may often narrow further, becoming much more focused on the individual's own monetary and other financial situation, with less concern for the environment or for the wider needs of community and country.

388 See, *e.g.,*. California Government Code, § 65864, et seq. (the "Williamson Act.").

389 In the 1990s, for example, the United States took advantage of the national attention to environmentally harmful fishing practices, adopting legislation regarding the labelling of all tuna marketed in the country as "dolphin-safe." UNITED STATES 16 U.S.C. § 1385.

to use as an incentive that will motivate commercial users to obtain and comply with ABS contracts and permits. Many of the suggestions of possible ABS incentives are either not sufficiently controlled by the provider,[390] or not of sufficient value to be desirable to the user.[391]

To create a useful incentive for ABS, provider countries need to identify some benefit that they can tightly control, and find a means of linking it to ABS compliance status.[392] One possible example would involve the provider agreeing to give ABS-compliant users priority status in the processing of other key permits, so long as the user remains in compliance with his ABS contract and/or permit. For example, many commercial users of genetic resources are seeking to develop GMOs, which will ultimately need permits under the country's national biosafety framework, in order to be marketed in the country. It may be possible to give GMO applications priority processing status, where the GMO applicant can demonstrate that he has an ABS contract and/or permit and that he is in compliance with it. It may be possible to create similar links to other types of importation and/or marketing permissions.

For a large country with a sizeable level of commercial importation, it may be possible to make this kind of incentive operate on a purely domestic level. For example, a large developing country (Brazil or China) may choose to give priority on domestic GMO and/or other marketing permissions only to users who have ABS contracts in that country. For other developing countries, it may be more appropriate to band together, agreeing to give priority status of this type to any user who has obtained and is in current compliance with an

390 For example, there are often many ways to legally obtain and/or remove samples of biological material without ABS compliance, and many samples have been removed and placed in foreign genebanks, zoos, herbariums and other collections without permission from the provider country. As a result, access to the genetic material is relatively easy to obtain without ABS compliance. In addition, personal communications to the authors by collectors, researchers, customs officials and others have noted that it is relatively common for legally collected genetic resources and ATK to be "shared" by researchers and others without permission from the provider.

391 Frequent suggestions that the user will get positive publicity if it complies with ABS are clearly specious, particularly in light of the fact that there are, at most, only several thousand people, worldwide, who actually know what ABS is. Examples of this kind of flawed approach have been and continue to be prevalent, however, whenever commentators seek oversimplified answers to ABS challenges. See, *e.g.*, Glowka (undated) and Tobin 2012. The possibility of linking ABS to international certification schemes such as Fair Trade International (http://www.fairtrade.net/), while it may potentially become a useful incentive when those schemes begin to have a major commercial impact, is presently of relatively minimal value as a commercial incentive.

392 See Young, 2004.

ABS contract or permit, duly issued by any of the other countries that are members of the alliance.

9.6 Avoiding the Draconian – "Reasonable and Streamlined" Mechanisms

The use of non-judicial remedy mechanisms can provide a major benefit to ABS contracts, improving the balance of mandates between the parties. It is important to stress that the name "non-judicial remedy" does not mean that commercial law does not apply. The opposite is, in fact, true. The law of contracts governs *every* provision of a contract. A non-judicial mechanism may be exercised without first going to a court, arbitrator or enforcement agency, but if it is legally "unfair" (inequitable) or "unreasonable," the law may later overturn it, or may even impose penalties against the party who exercised the mechanism.

Beyond this like all contracts, ABS contracts depend on "mutuality." Unless the user and the provider *both* feel that it is "worth the effort" to negotiate, draft and implement an ABS contract, then no such contract will ever exist.

Up to now, the balance of ABS contracts have more often appeared heavily weighted in favor of the users, because the world was perceived to be a "buyer's market" in which the resources are plentiful with many sellers, but the number of purchasers were few. As a result, the perception of competition among providers led to pressure to complete ABS agreements quickly, and led providers to seek to undercut each other by offering lower prices, fewer controls and a more "streamlined" process.[393] Often the result was a situation in which little or nothing was paid "up-front", communications often diminished to nothing following removal of the *res,* and post-access payments were rare and small.

More recently, discussions have turned to the idea that providers should band together to raise the market, sometimes even suggesting that relatively standard percentages should apply to all ABS contracts. Elaborate models have sometimes been proposed to utilize existing legal frameworks in new ways that accommodate ABS,[394] leading to a range of criticisms from researchers

393 See, *e.g.*, Vogel, 2007.

394 *Ibid.* at p. 130.

complaining that those models are too vague, to developing country representatives who argue that they are too specific in deleting major provider protections such as PIC and MAT. A few more moderate proposals address the application of ABS to conservation and other research, in one instance seeking to find and apply a generally accepted principle on the public domain.[395]

In general, commercial law assumes that judicial enforcement and arbitration are the mechanisms that best protect the parties and ensure the "rule of law." The availability of non-judicial mechanisms is generally recognized as a convenience to the parties, especially to parties for whom the cost and complexity of courts and arbitrators in distant lands would be prohibitive. In order for remedies to be obtained in without judicial involvement, however, the law generally includes some exception, stating that, where a non-judicial remedy is excessive (the payment too high, the compelled actions or loss of assets too draconian), then such remedy is invalid, regardless of how perfectly drafted the clause.

Thus, at a minimum,[396] non-judicial remedies clauses must be designed in a way that a court will probably view them as "reasonable."[397] Although often ridiculed by non-lawyers, the legal concept of known as the "reasonable" standard is well established. Over hundreds of years, in dozens of different legal areas, the courts and lawyers have honed this concept, so that it is often relatively clear whether a particular clause, action or requirement will be found "reasonable." In the context of non-judicial remedies for breach of contract, the simplest measure is whether the outcome following exercise of the remedy will be equitable. That is, the remedy's availability will depend upon whether the losses to the breaching party caused by exercise of the non-judicial remedy balance properly with the damage or injury to the other party or the losses of its agreed expectations. If, for example, the secured party obtains assets and money with a total value many times the amount that either party expected or stated would be paid under the contract, the extreme result might well be considered too draconian, giving the breaching party the basis of a claim for reimbursement.

395 See, *e.g.*, Kamau, *et al.*, 2015.

396 Some countries (*e.g.*, Norway) impose this type of requirement on ALL clauses of a contract, and may even re-write the contract if it does not provide an equitable outcome otherwise.

397 Recall that the advantage of non-judicial remedies is that the parties will prefer to pay them rather than go to court. A party making this decision is less likely to pay if he assumes that a court will invalidate the non-judicial remedy by finding it "unreasonable."

It is important, therefore, for providers to balance their ABS financial, procedural and other demands, both in order to make ABS participation attractive to users, and to ensure that their ABS contract and especially its non-judicial remedy provisions are legally justified. On the other hand, the use of appropriate non-judicial remedies can be a major tool for providers seeking to plug "loopholes" that enable/encourage some users to breach the ABS contract.

CHAPTER 10

"Avoid Making Legal Assumptions": The Perils of Relying on a "Governing Law" Clause and/or "Private International Law"

The challenges of ABS contracts are not easily resolved. One of the greatest of these challenges is the need to eliminate misunderstandings borne of mistaken legal assumptions. In international contracts,[398] the three most common mistaken assumptions are as follows:

> Mistaken Assumption 1: a party's legal uncertainties about foreign contract law can be eliminated if that party insists that his own country's law be designated as the "governing law" of the contract;
> Mistaken assumption 2: most legal concerns relating to international contracts can be easily resolved under "private international law" (PIL); and
> Mistaken assumption 3: there is a body of "international commercial law" to resolve problems in international contracts and their enforcement.[399]

Throughout the negotiations of the NP (and earlier during the negotiations of Article 15,) poorly informed participants often opposed the idea that the negotiators should address the legal issues relating to ABS contracts, stating one, two, or all three of these mistaken assumptions. Their arguments often appeared to sway the delegates, and in the end, the NP includes no provisions that can clarify the most important challenges preventing implementation

---

398 As noted in Chapter 2, in many negotiations, the phrase "international contracts" is used to mean any contract that is not entirely functioning within a single country – that is, any contract where one or more of the parties or potential transferees are from different countries, or where any of the assets, activities or obligations occur in a different country from the one in which the contract is established/signed. Most ABS contracts involve some foreign participation, and as such are essentially "international contracts". This even applies if the national law requires the foreign user to form a local company or joint venture to undertake the obligations of the contract, because the foreign user must be bound to use and/or capitalize that company or joint venture. This obligation is imposed on a foreign party.

399 As detailed in Chapter 2, in ABS, there is a fourth mistaken assumption about contract law – that there is no need to worry about ABS contracts, because all problems with them can be solved by applying existing contract law or law of property.

 | DOI 10.1163/9789004356573_011

and enforcement of ABS contracts. In light of the fact that there is no other law that clarifies these challenges either, the misunderstanding regarding PIL and international commercial law can be seen as the primary cause of the ABS framework's non-functionality.

It is certainly true that greater certainty regarding which body of law governs would make it much easier to negotiate, draft, implement and enforce an ABS contract. Beyond that, if there were a single body of law that always applied to all ABS contracts, the prospects for a speedy resolution of ABS disputes would improve. Unfortunately, however, as explained in this chapter, it is not possible to ensure that all aspects of the contract will be decided only by the designated "governing law." Moreover, there is no single accepted body of "private international law" or "international commercial law."[400] The false beliefs – that a governing law clause will solve legal problems, that "PIL" is a body of law that can be used to decide international cases, and/or that some body of "international commercial law" exists – can lead contract negotiators and draftsmen to make errors that may affect the contract's validity and functionality in many negative ways.

This chapter briefly discusses the use of governing law clauses, emphasizing the reasons that such clauses may obscure critical challenges (¶ 10.1). At ¶¶ 10.2 and 10.3, it presents the basic concepts of PIL, explaining why and how those concepts are misunderstood. At ¶ 10.4, it lays out the current status of efforts to create a single body of internationally agreed commercial law; and at ¶ 10.5, takes a look the consequences of identifying PIL or particular international principles as the governing law for an ABS contract. These discussions are not comprehensive.[401] The authors' goal is only to give those negotiating and drafting ABS contracts a "heads up" about the above mistaken assumptions, and to illustrate the rule "Avoid Making Legal Assumptions," which applies across the full range of ABS contract issues.

10.1 The "Governing Law" Clauses

In general, the "Governing Law" or "Applicable Law" clause in a commercial document simply states that in the event of a dispute or the need for legal

400 Although there have been international efforts to develop conventions on the law of contracts that are "international" in scope, those efforts have largely been unsuccessful up to now.

401 For the reader interested in a deeper knowledge of PIL and international commercial law, the authors recommend the following textbooks and other sources: Briggs, 2008; North and Faucett, 2004; Collins, 1996 and Reimann and Zimmermann, 2006.

interpretation of the contract, the law of Country X [selected by agreement of the parties] shall apply. Although not all contracts designate governing or applicable law, most do, especially where the contract has some international element.[402] There are many other types of clauses that are linked to this governing law clause, including especially a choice-of-court clause that states that any action to enforce or interpret the contract must be brought in Country Y (specified by agreement of the parties.) As discussed in ¶¶ 10.2 through 10.4, in a few cases, the governing law clause will identify a particular international instrument, or may simply designate that it is governed by "international commercial law" or "private international law."

10.1.1 *Mistaken Assumptions – Why "Governing Law" Clauses May Not Add Certainty*

To understand how a "governing law" clause can improperly mask a hidden problem, it is necessary to consider how such a clause may be used or negotiated. In essence, this clause is intended to select the legal framework that will be used in interpreting or implementing the contract. The interpretation or implementation may be very different under one country's laws than under another's. As a result, the choice of governing law is thought to be strategic. In most negotiations, each party will try to select as governing law, the country whose courts are more likely to support that party's viewpoint. Or if one jurisdiction has a particular law or policy that would increase the chance that a party will receive a better verdict, that party will prefer that country. At its simplest, a party may simply prefer that his own country's law be designated, because then he will not need to hire additional lawyers or undertake additional research – his current commercial lawyer will already know the law applicable in his own country. With these ideas in mind, the parties' negotiation over governing law involves each hoping to obtain an advantage over the others. All assume that the selection of governing law will have this impact.

In fact, however, there are reasons why this approach is not advisable, including some that are specific to ABS and some that are more general. Taking the ABS issues first, as frequently discussed, there is virtually no law in any country that addresses the contractual aspects of ABS. No country's courts have comprehensively ruled on any contract issues regarding genetic resources, ATK or their utilization. This means that the results of any enforcement action or request for judicial interpretation of an ABS contract will be difficult to predict. Even though there may be some advantage for the provider who puts his case to a court in a provider country, it must be recalled that the court will, in any case be deciding commercial law questions, even if he is also addressing

402 See ¶ 1.1.1, *supra.*

ABS. Few judges would be comfortable coming to a decision on a contract law issue that might affect other contracts, since they are aware of the importance of commercial law, and more knowledgeable in that area. As a strategic matter, parties hoping for a ground-breaking decision on an ABS contract may be more likely to get that result from a liberal judge in a user country than from one in a provider country. In ABS, many providers attempt to avoid the need to negotiate difficult issues relating to transfer and enforcement by seeking to have their home country named as the contract's governing law.

The general problems with governing law clauses, however, are more serious. Governing-law clauses and choice-of-court clauses are rather easy to avoid. Although most academic texts on commercial law will tell you that a governing law clause is "usually be upheld by courts and arbitral tribunals in countries with developed legal systems," that statement is misleading. Statistically, a court in the jurisdiction that has been designated as governing law of the contract will normally rule that the governing law clause is valid, even if it has to overrule other precedents to do so.[403] Where a case is brought in a different country, however, the court will often prefer applying its own law.[404] It is statistically more likely to rule against application of the governing law clause.[405]

The main justification used to do this is a claim that the contract is not valid. On the surface, it appears that, when a party brings an action in a court in a

---

403 See, *e.g.*, *IRB-Brasil Resseguros, S.A. v. Inepar Investments, S.A.*

404 Not only does it know its own law better, but it will not have to deal with inconveniences, including (i) the need to obtain copies of relevant law from the governing law country and (ii) the need to obtain and interpret official translations from the language of the governing law into the language of the deciding court. In addition, most countries' courts operate under rules and guidelines for statutory interpretation. It is not always clear whether or how a court will apply those rules and guidelines in interpreting and applying the governing law.

405 Formal discussions about addressing the role of choice of law/governing law clauses in contracts. These make it clear that, where a court is construing a contract that contains a choice of law clause that identifies the law of the country/state/province in which that court is located, the court will nearly always accept that clause at face value and apply its own law. Where a court in another country/state/province is asked to rule on the contract, most commentators indicate that there is a substantial possibility that such a court will decide not to apply the selected law, for any one of a variety of reasons. Clearly, since each country's national legal system is unique, it is not possible to provide a comprehensive analysis of this issue. For a deeper understanding of some of the most critical elements of this topic, the reader is referred to the following: McClean and Beevers, 2005, at 13–012–13–025; North and Fawcett, 2004, at Chapter 18; Lookofsky, 1996, at 1.4; Allan and Hiscock, 1987, at Ch. 1; and Reimann and Zimmermann, 2006, at 902–905. As noted in Furmston, 2001, at 28–31, these matters are often integrally interlinked with questions of national public policy and other national restrictions on what may be included in a contract.

different country, the governing law clause would appear to require that other court to apply the designated governing law. Any party to that case, however, may avoid this result by alleging that the contract is invalid. The court will then have to begin by ruling on the validity question. For this ruling, it will use its own national law, because if the contract is found to be invalid, then the governing law clause, too, is invalid.

In ABS, this loophole presents a serious risk, because most ABS users are based outside the provider country and their assets are located outside the provider country as well. Thus, in many cases, an enforcement action may need to be filed in the user's country. Even if the original case is filed in the "governing law" country and the provider obtains a judgment against the user, the provider will usually have to seek enforcement of that judgment in a country where the user has operations and assets. The same argument (that the contract is invalid) can be used in the enforcement action to avoid the need to apply the contract's designated governing law.

The circumvention of the governing law clause can be very problematic, particularly where the parties decided not to adopt detailed enforcement and remedy clauses in their contract, instead relying on their governing law country's courts to take a particular view of the contract.

10.1.2 *Legal Analysis Required*

There is also a strategic reason to be wary of governing law clauses. In selecting one country's law as "governing" the contract, the parties are not selecting only that country's contract/commercial law. Many other national laws may impact the parties' rights and duties under the contract, such as laws on intellectual property, trade, social responsibility and torts, to name a few, as well as the laws governing access to justice and civil procedure. These will all be settled under the laws of the governing-law country. Thus, it is not advisable to select governing law on the basis of a single legal issue. Significant research and analysis may be needed to decide between governing law options, especially if the available options are not the country whose laws you are most familiar with.

10.2 "Private International Law" – A Misunderstood Concept

Closely related to the "governing law" question is the mistaken belief that there is a body of "private international law" – a single body of international law – that can apply to resolve legal challenges. Unfortunately, this is not correct. Even where a contract is "international,"[406] any legal or practical question

406 Footnote 398, *supra*.

regarding that contract is still decided by the national contract law of some country. "PIL" is essentially academic shorthand – it refers to the study of the manner in which each country comes to a decision about which country's national contract law will apply in a given contract lawsuit.[407] Where an action is filed in a European country's court regarding a Nigerian contract that designates Nigerian law as the "governing law," for example, the European court might choose to apply Nigerian contract law, or by applying its national principles of PIL, might conclude that it may apply its own law. It will not apply some body of internationally recognized law, because there isn't one. Thus, as emphasized throughout this book, there is really no legal "safety net" for a contract that has omitted a basic point, or drafted it in ambiguous terms.

Thus, PIL is not the study of a single body of law, but an examination of the rules, standards and exceptions that apply where hundreds of different legal systems attempt to determine whether and how each will give effect to the other, in transboundary situations. As one might guess, there are as many different ways of handling transboundary legal situations as there are countries. Every country comes to its own conclusion on these issues, based on its own national laws and policies. Indeed, if parties to a contract file separate lawsuits on the same point, in two different jurisdictions, it is highly likely that the two judges will each rule that a different body of law applies to the contract.[408] The more one studies PIL, the more complex it becomes because in most countries, the principles regarding which law applies are primarily unwritten, requiring a judge to undertake detailed analysis and logical construction in order to come to a decision.

Various types of PIL principles arise in contract-related cases in many situations. One of these, noted above, is the situation in which a party to a contract lawsuit alleges that the contract is invalid (whether there is a "governing law clause" or not.) Other PIL issues arise when the case alleges that one of the parties committed a commercial tort (fraud, mistrepresentation, non-disclosure,

---

407 In legal circles, PIL is actually a relatively new term, used to describe a very old set of legal issues – the manner in which a judge who is interpreting an international contract or deciding an international contract dispute decides which country's national law should apply. In the past, this area of study was called "Choice of Law" – a term that conveys its meaning much more accurately. See *e.g.*, Briggs, 2008; North and Faucett, 2004; North, 1982; Collins, 1996; and Reimann and Zimmermann, 2006.

408 For example see the Australian case, *Armacel Pty Ltd v Smurfit Stone Container Corporation*: "In case of parallel litigation where parties' contract contained clause designating Australian court as proper forum, Federal Court of Australia rules that, where defending U.S. party's challenge to its jurisdiction is still pending, Australian party's request for notices for U.S. party to produce documents is premature." Description provided by Hi-beam Research (online). Accessible from https://www.highbeam.com/doc/1G1-186273890.html.

unfair trade practices, *etc.*) In addition, another strain of PIL cases will arise where any part of the action addresses issues of compliance with national ABS law or permit requirements.

In sum, PIL is an attempt to develop a taxonomy of national approaches to these questions, and to see if it is possible to discern commonalities, trends and standards that appear to apply in all or nearly all cases. At most it can provide the parties to ABS contracts with a level of understanding regarding the uncertainties of their contracts, and help explain why it is not advisable for those contracts to rely on ABS terminology and concepts.[409]

10.3 The Basic Questions Considered by "Private International Law"

Even the shortest basic texts on PIL are around 100 pages in length, and most run to several hundred pages. All of these sources generally agree that, with regard to contracts, the concept of PIL addresses *only* one, two or all three of the following questions:

- Jurisdiction of the national court considering the contract (*i.e.*, that court's legal ability and authority to consider the contract); and/or
- The court's ability and/or responsibility to "recognize" (*i.e.* apply or enforce) a foreign judgment relating to that contract; and/or
- The determination of which body of law should apply in order to determine the legal questions raised in or related to the contract.[410]

The great challenge of PIL lies in the fact that there are over 200 individual countries (or protectorates with separate national law) in the world, which means that there are over 40,000 possible combinations of countries that may be involved in a two-country international contract. Given that most ABS

409 As detailed in Chapters 3 through 10, contract implementation and enforcement depends on concrete drafting so that the concepts are clear, certain and mutually agreed. This means that the current use of ambiguous ABS terminology is not appropriate in a contract, because there is no clear, concrete understanding of those terms. The Parties in the negotiations had very different views on, for example, specifically what a "genetic resource" or "traditional knowledge" is, what activities are considered to be "utilization" or either of them, what benefits arise from that utilization and when that happens. As a result, the CBD and NP definitions were designed to accommodate that ambiguity and the various Parties' differing interpretations, rather than to clear it up or achieve a unified view. Contracts cannot live with that level of ambiguity.

410 See, *e.g.*, North and Faucett, 2004, at p. 7 and Chapter 18.

contracts involve multiple countries, the number of possible combinations is astronomical.[411] Added to that, every different type of contractual clause or legal issue may lead to a different decision regarding which country's law governs the interpretation or application of that clause or issue, so that a single contract can produce hundreds of different opinions.[412] Over the years, the study of PIL has come to resemble the biological quest for concrete taxonomic nomenclature – slowly it has become much more clear and certain, and been able to focus more clearly on details, but it may never produce "certainty," even as to the very basic questions it seeks to answer.

PIL is only a mechanism that might help the judge, arbitrator and parties to a contract to determine which national law should apply, when deciding a question relevant to the interpretation, implementation and/or enforcement of that contract. It is not a binding set of rules, and offers little help in addressing even the most basic challenges facing international contracts.

10.4 International Commercial Law

For more than two centuries, international contracts have been rendered uncertain and potentially unenforceable due to the lack of a single body of stable, agreed international law on contracts and related commercial matters. Thus, the desire for greater stability in international contracts has existed for decades, maybe centuries. While a few efforts have been mounted, however, they have met with little success because countries are generally unwilling to agree to externally imposed changes to their most basic body of law. As noted in Chapters 1 and 2, commercial issues were addressed in some of the world's earliest legal codes and recorded legal decisions. Modern countries' wellbeing relies heavily

---

411 Virtually all modern contracts involve more than two parties, and even a two-party contract may potentially involve more than two countries. (See Chapter 2, *supra.*) In ABS, for example, if a two party contract were negotiated between the provider and a collector or other user, not only would their respective countries be considered, but so would any country through which the resources are taken *en route* to the final user, the country of any transferee, any country that possesses the same subspecies *in situ,* and the country of any designated arbitrator.

412 As noted in preface to the original (first edition) of *North & Cheshire,* PIL is "not overloaded with detailed rules; it has been only lightly touched by the paralyzing hand of the Parliamentary draftsman; it is … fluid not static, elusive not obvious; it repels any tendency to dogmatism; and above all, the possible permutations of the questions that it raises are so numerous that the diligent investigator can seldom rest content with the solution that he proposes."

on the stability and strength of commercial activities and relationships that were built on the basis of the currently applicable commercial code or acts, many of which have been in place for decades or centuries. Although such laws are amended, the amendments are normally minor "tweaks" or clarifications, leaving the overall system in place. The entire system of business in most countries operates in the expectation that the national commercial system will remain essentially the same from year to year. Thus, for many countries, the advantage of a single global system of commercial law is outweighed by the possibility that the country's own domestic commercial foundation will be impacted and forced to make changes. This is why it appears impractical to attempt to adjust commercial principles in order to better enable ABS contracts. Although many countries are interested in improving the implementation of ABS contracts, none are willing to experiment with significant alteration of their commercial code.

If a single worldwide commercial code could be created, it might provide a mechanism to resolve most of the ABS contract issues mentioned in this book. Solutions adopted could then be universal, without the long process of slowly integrating ABS into national law and then slowly unifying the national laws. Unfortunately, for the reasons described above, most global codification efforts have not received general acceptance. Many formally adopted commercial conventions have never entered into force, some garnering only three or four ratifications.

More recently, as general agreement on an overall code was seen to be nearly impossible, less ambitious efforts were attempted. International commercial negotiations were undertaken on individual agreements that focused on particular, narrow details of commercial practice. This narrowing of focus did not help countries get past the deadlock. Few of the narrower international negotiations have produced instruments that are in force, and those that have entered into force usually have few parties.

In an attempt to provide something of use to the parties to international contracts, efforts have eventually focused on creating non-binding guidance and best-practice-style documents, including in particular the UNIDROIT Principles of International Commercial Contracts ("UNIDROIT Principles 2010"),[413]

413 Available online at http://www.unidroit.org/english/principles/contracts/principles2010/integralversionprinciples2010-e.pdf. Between the completion of this draft and its publication, UNIDROIT adopted a newer version of these principles. As described in UNIDROIT's website, "At its 95th session (Rome, 18–20 May 2016), the UNIDROIT Governing Council adopted amendments and additions to the 2010 UNIDROIT Principles of International Commercial Contracts and authorised the Secretariat to prepare and publish a new edition to be known as the '2016 UNIDROIT Principles of International

discussed below. These principles take advantage of the basic rule that the text of the contract can, if properly drafted, settle most legal issues[414] in a manner that does not rely on legislation. Unfortunately, however, the Principles are extremely long, so that it is not possible to analyse their impact in detail. As noted below, however, they do not address the points on which ABS contracts need to rely on governing law.

The following sections begin by looking briefly at the three main efforts directed at creating a comprehensive body of international commercial law. The international commercial conventions that may be relevant to ABS contracts and their implementation are next briefly analysed in ¶ 10.2.2. Other international instruments are briefly discussed in ¶ 10.2.3; and relevant concepts from international trade law are summarized in ¶ 10.2.4.

10.4.1 *Status of Attempts to Establish International Contract/Commercial Law*

As noted above, the basic principle underlying international contracts is that they are governed by national law, and that the choice of which country's law governs is complex and can be only partially resolved by the contract parties. The resulting uncertainty has become increasingly problematic, as a result of the great increase in the number and variety of contracts and other commercial instruments with international elements. Beginning more than 100 years ago, the commercial and legal communities were eager to develop a unified body of international commercial law, assuming that it would make such transactions more certain and enforceable and minimize the number of problems that arose in them. As such, it was hoped, international commerce would be stimulated, to the benefit of all. With these goals in mind, three major initiatives sought to develop relatively comprehensive international codes of commercial law, with very limited success.

(a) UNIDROIT

The first of formal effort to develop an international code was UNIDROIT (the International Institute for the Unification of Private Law), which was originally conceived in the 1920s, as a part of the League of Nations. When the League fell apart, UNIDROIT was re-created as an independent international body, whose membership currently consists of 63 States.[415] Although the avowed purpose

Commercial Contracts.'" Reported at http://www.unidroit.org/english/governments/councildocuments/2016session/cd-95-15-e.pdf. At this writing, that new edition is not yet available online.

414 Apart from validity issues discussed in Chapter 4, *supra*.

415 A State becomes a member of UNIDROIT by formally ratifying the UNIDROIT Statute.

or UNIDROIT is to promote the creation of a single international body of private law,[416] the States that sign/ratify the UNIDROIT Statute are not required to adopt, recognize or even recommend any of the documents produced by UNIDROIT. In essence, UNIDROIT's operational design and mandate is focused on the studying private law, rather than changing it.[417] Over the years, UNIDROIT has produced over 70 drafts, approximately 50 of which are no longer mentioned on its website.

Although initially focused on creating a unified body of commercial law, the sheer size of that objective was obviously too great to be handled at once. Accordingly, UNIDROIT's efforts generally focused on narrow "pieces" of the overall issue.[418] For many years, UNIDROIT's working groups soldiered on, developing international agreements, despite a very low rate of uptake. UNIDROIT's most recent convention development has focused on very narrow areas such as chattel financing (as in the "Convention on International Interests in Mobile Equipment," and its three protocols[419]) and on issues that are not, strictly speaking, matters of commercial law (albeit financially related), such as the *UNIDROIT Convention on Stolen or Illegally Exported Cultural Objects* and the *Convention Providing a Uniform Law on the Form of an International Will*.[420]

---

416 According to Article 1, "The purposes of the International Institute for the Unification of Private Law are to examine ways of harmonising and coordinating the private law of States and of groups of States, and to prepare gradually for the adoption by the various States of uniform rules of private law."

417 The Statute describes UNIDROIT's actions as follows: "The Institute shall: (a) prepare drafts of laws and conventions with the object of establishing uniform internal law; (b) prepare drafts of agreements with a view to facilitating international relations in the field of private law; (c) undertake studies in comparative private law; (d) ake an interest in projects already undertaken in any of these fields by other institutions with which it may maintain relations as necessary; [and] (e) organise conferences and publish works which the Institute considers worthy of wide circulation."

418 See, *e.g.*, the UNIDROIT Convention on Agency in the International Sale Of Goods; UNIDROIT Convention on Substantive Rules for Intermediated Securities; and UNIDROIT Convention on Stolen or Illegally Exported Cultural Objects

419 The protocols are the "Protocol [To The Convention On International Interests In Mobile Equipment] On Matters Specific To Aircraft Equipment," "Luxembourg Protocol [To The Convention On International Interests In Mobile Equipment] On Matters Specific To Railway Rolling Stock" and "Protocol [to the Convention on International Interests in Mobile Equipment] on Matters Specific to Space Assets." Only the first of these is in force.

420 The UNIDROIT Conventions that are in force that are most directly related to contract practices are the International Convention on Travel Contracts (8 Parties); the Convention on the Contract for the International Carriage of Goods by Road (55 Parties), UNIDROIT Convention on International Financial Leasing (10 Parties) and the UNIDROIT

Beginning in the mid 1990s, UNIDROIT appears to have increasingly altered its approach. Rather than focusing only on the development of conventions that enable countries to slowly harmonize their commercial law, it has begun to direct much of its effort to developing and publishing "principles," which do not require State ratification. These principles were intended to benefit the persons drafting contracts, skipping over entirely the original goal of eventually superseding PIL and the desire to eliminate the choice of law problems, by creating a single harmonized approach.

Currently, the centrepiece of UNIDROIT's products is the UNIDROIT Principles 2010,[421] a 498-page document, which aims to provide a basis for international contracts. Unfortunately, as discussed in ¶¶ 10.2.3, 10.3 and 10.4, below, despite its size, the UNIDROIT Principles 2010 do not provide answers to the critical contractual questions facing ABS contracts. In addition, by focusing on individual contract negotiators, the new UNIDROIT offerings fail in the original goal of eliminating the "choice of law" problem. As discussed in ¶10.4, a contract that adopts one or more of the UNIDROIT principles as its governing law can still find those principles overturned by a court under PIL/choice of law rules.

UNIDROIT's website lists 26 documents, of which 8 are binding commercial instruments in force, two are binding commercial instruments not in force, nine are nonbinding commercial instruments, one is a binding instrument related to commercial enforcement and two others (one binding and one not) are potentially relevant instruments addressing national interests in "cultural objects."[422] In this connection, however, two points are notable: First, five of the eight binding commercial conventions that are in force have fewer than 10 Parties. Second, the issues covered by the commercial instruments are very narrow, including commercial practices that have little or nothing to do with ABS (factoring, commercial leasing, international interests in mobile equipment, close-out netting, franchising, leasing and carriage of goods by road.) As a result, of its existing commercial binding and non-binding instruments, only 12 of UNIDROIT's binding and non-binding instruments appear on the surface to have any relevance to ABS. These instruments are briefly discussed in ¶¶ 10.2.3, below.

Convention on International Factoring (9 Parties). These are also accessible at the UNIDROIT website.

421 Footnote 413, *supra.*

422 http://www.unidroit.org/news. Chose "Instruments" in the left-hand menu.

(b) The Hague Conference on Private International Law

The second major initiative was the Hague Conference on Private International Law. Although the Hague Conference describes itself as having commenced in 1893, its formation as an intergovernmental body appears to have happened much later, with the first state signatures to the Hague Statute dated in the 1950s. Apparently, it was initially a conference of experts from 16 countries (15 in Europe, plus Japan), which declared itself a membership body of States in 1955, opening its membership to other States/individuals in addition to those that had already been participating.[423] The Hague Conference website reports that the Conference currently has 81 States as members, although this characterization is not completely clear, since a State does not have to ratify the Conference Statute to be considered a member.[424] The Hague Conference specifically allows the EU (and any other Regional Economic Integration Organizations that may become Parties to it) to ratify its various documents on behalf of its members.[425] As a result, in three of its most recent conventions 25 to 28 of the listed member States are EU Members that have not actually ratified the instrument, but are bound because the EU has done so.[426]

Like UNIDROIT, the Hague Conference is essentially a study mechanism, mandated to "prepare draft Conventions or to study all questions of private international law which come within the purpose of the Conference." In this connection its stated purpose is "to work for the progressive unification of the rules of private international law." As such, its purview extends far beyond

423 From Hague Statute: Art 2: "(1) Members of the Hague Conference on Private International Law are the States which have already participated in one or more Sessions of the Conference and which accept the present Statute. (2) Any other State, the participation of which is from a juridical point of view of importance for the work of the Conference, may become a Member. The admission of new Member States shall be decided upon by the Governments of the participating States, upon the proposal of one or more of them, by a majority of the votes cast, within a period of six months from the date on which that proposal is submitted to the Governments."

424 The list of members is based on signatures, and does not give the name or affiliation of the signatories. It is available at https://www.hcch.net/en/instruments/conventions/status-table/?cid=29. The earliest signatories, in the 1950s were primarily European States and Turkey, with Israel, the US and Canadian signatures dated in the 1960s.

425 *Ibid.* Art 3.

426 Clearly, as to some matters, EU member States are automatically required to implement EU legislative instruments, while in others the EU's legislative action only acts as a mandate that they adopt conforming legislation. Each of the three instruments mentioned in text has fewer than 33 Members, even after adding the 28 EU members, suggesting that the net result might not make much difference beyond the EU.

commercial matters, so that its primary activities appear to address legal aspects of domestic and family matters. Of its 31 conventions in force, a total of 17 were developed by the Hague Conference to address marriage, divorce, parental responsibility, protection of children, protection of dependent adults, wills and decedents estates, domicile and related matters. By contrast seven Conventions in force were developed by the Hague Conference to address commercial law issues, and another six on litigation and tort matters.[427] (There are many Hague Conference conventions that are either not in force or not open to ratification, including six on commercial topics.)

Among the Hague Conference's commercial conventions in force, there are six that have 15 or fewer Parties (some having entered into force with as few as three parties); and another five with fewer than 33 parties, even after application of the rule that allows the Conference to count all EU Member States as Parties on the basis of the EU's ratification. Twenty Hague Conference instruments are potentially relevant to ABS. These are examined at ¶10.2.3, below.

(c) Other International Commercial Conventions and Instruments

In combination with the above overarching systems, a few international commercial conventions have been adopted that address specific aspects of international contracts. The main existing conventions on international commercial contracts that appear relevant to ABS are the UN Convention on Contracts for the International Sale of Goods (CISG);[428] the New York Convention on the Recognition and Enforcement of Foreign Arbitral Awards (NYC);[429] and the "Incoterms" (a set of standard provisions developed for international use by the International Chamber of Commerce (ICC.))[430] These instruments have widespread acceptance among countries.[431] Although their titles might

427 The 31st is the Hague Conference Statute.

428 United Nations Convention on Contracts for the International Sale of Goods. Vienna. 1980.

429 Convention on the Recognition and Enforcement of Foreign Arbitral Awards. New York. 1958.

430 International Chamber of Commerce (ICC) *Incoterms 2010 English Edition*. The ICC publishes the Incoterms and provides them for sale at http://store.iccwbo.org/incoterms-2010, along with a range of publications to assist in their use and interpretation.

431 As of April 2016, the NYC had 156 member States, and the CISG had 84. The Incoterms are not a convention and thus not ratified, however the ICC states that it has "hundreds of thousands of member companies and associations in over 120 countries." ICC website at http://www.iccwbo.org/worldwide-membership/.

suggest that these instruments might solve many ABS-contract problems, there are factors (see ¶ 10.2.3, below) that sharply limit their usefulness.

Even though they do not help with the primary contractual challenges described in this book, however, these three instruments may include many provisions that could help the drafter. As discussed in ¶ 10.2.2, they also provide a lesson in the level of detail needed in order to create an agreed international commercial law. They demonstrate why experts counselled the CBD and NP negotiators to give greater attention to commercial issues and not simply dismiss identified problems as "issues that will be addressed under commercial and/or property law." The challenges facing ABS are still unsolved in international commercial law after centuries of effort.

As a practical matter, even though the CBD and NP negotiators did not invest in understanding and coordinating with international commercial law, the parties to ABS contracts must do so. At a minimum, they must determine whether any existing international convention or set of principles would be useful to them or would make their contract more effective.

10.4.2 *Important Issues and Issues Agreed or Near Agreement*

For purposes of negotiating and drafting an international contract, the most important questions relating to international commercial conventions are "What issues and problems have been addressed by international commercial conventions?" and "Can this help our contract?" In this section we identify the main contractual issues on which there is international agreement, noting, unfortunately, that they provide little or no help in ensuring that an ABS contract can be properly interpreted, implemented and enforced.

(a) The ICC Incoterms

The ICC's "Incoterms" provide an excellent example of the reasons current commercial conventions are of little use to ABS contracts. First published in the 1930s and regularly updated since then, the current set (Incoterms 2010) are the eighth revision. The ICC describes them as follows:

> The Incoterms® rules have become an essential part of the daily language of trade. They have been incorporated in contracts for the sale of goods worldwide and provide rules and guidance to importers, exporters, lawyers, transporters, insurers and students of international trade.[432]

432 ICC website at http://www.iccwbo.org/products-and-services/trade-facilitation/incoterms-2010/.

Although this sounds rather hopeful, the reality is that there are relatively few Incoterms (only 11), and these are focused on providing standard approaches relative to shipping the *res*, and the most common approaches to allocation of particular tasks related to shipping and transit.[433] Thus, for example, they focus specify the moment at which the ownership of goods is transferred from seller to buyer in commercial situations involving the shipment of goods. Their purpose is to help alleviate a common question that has plagued many

433 The 11 Incoterms are divided into two main groups, general rules and rules for water transport (it is sometimes challenging to determine which category applies): (General Rules:) **EXW** ("Ex Works": the seller makes the goods available at his own premises or at another place named by him, so that the buyer's responsibility begins from there, including loading, transporting, customs documentation, *etc*); **FCA** ("Free Carrier": the seller must deliver the goods at a specified place of delivery in the seller's country. Until they get there, the goods are the responsibility of the seller. After that, no matter whether further transport is needed to get them where the buyer wants them, they are the responsibility of the buyer. This incoterm is a modern, adjusted version of the old term "FOB" ("free on board") when applied to non-water transport); **CPT** ("Carriage Paid To": This term addresses the separate issue of who pays the costs and freight charges for transport to the named place. Even where one party has agreed to take responsibility for the goods during transport, the other party may have the duty to pay these costs); **CIP** ("Carriage and Insurance Paid to": This is an alternative to CPT where the seller is required to obtain insurance for the goods while in transit. The CIP incoterm specifies the value that must be insured and the currency in which the insurance should be defined); **DAT** ("Delivered At Terminal": the seller must deliver the goods, unloaded, at the named terminal, covering all the costs of transport (*e.g.,* export fees, carriage, unloading from main carrier at destination port and destination port charges) and assuming all risk until that point); **DAP** ("Delivered At Place": the seller retains responsibility until it places at the disposal of the buyer for unloading at the named place of destination); **DDP** ("Delivered Duty Paid": Seller must deliver the loaded goods to the named place in the buyer's country of the buyer, paying all costs such as import duties and taxes. This is a parallel of the common term "Free In Store (FIS)"); (Water transport (shipping) Rules:) **FAS** ("Free Alongside Ship": the seller's delivery is complete when the goods are placed alongside the appropriate vessel at the named port of shipment. The buyer will normally have to have export clearance in order to get the goods to that point); **FOB** ("Free on Board": the seller bears all costs and risks up to the point the goods are loaded on board the vessel); **CFR** ("Cost and Freight"; the seller pays for the carriage of the goods to the named port, transferring risk to the shipper, but only when the goods have been loaded on board the ship); **CIF** ("Cost, Insurance & Freight"): similar to CFR, but the seller is required to insure the goods while in transit. In addition, the Incoterms 2010 also define some old incoterms which have been deleted, in case some parties or contracts might still use them. Those terms are *DAF* ("Delivered at Frontier"); *DES* ("Delivered Ex Ship"); *DEQ* ("Delivered Ex Quay") and *DDU* ("Delivered Duty Unpaid.").

conventional international contracts for the sale of goods – Where goods are injured and destroyed in transit from the seller's country to the buyer's, which party must bear the loss? ABS contracts deal with the rights to collect and remove samples and the location of and manner in which research and development activities are conducted. Few ABS contracts have involved bulk transport of goods, but only these would benefit from the use of the Incoterms.

For the parties to ABS contracts the Incoterms are instructive in a different way. Even though every conventional contract for the sale of goods involves the delivery of the goods and their transportation to the buyer's chosen location, the Incoterms show 11 different "standard practices" regarding that delivery. Parties can include an incoterm in their contract by simply specifying the three-letter code. Legally, however, those three letters incorporate the entire Incoterm in the contract. Incoterms themselves are not short. In fact, each Incoterm specifies not only the delivery procedures, but also allocates 12 separate types of costs between buyer and seller.[434] None of the Incoterms mentions ABS, PIC, MAT, governmental ABS permits, or international certificates of compliance, although many of them discuss the duty to obtain customs permits and similar governmental approvals.

In 1936, when the first Incoterms were developed, global commerce had been in existence for more than 2 centuries and regional commerce between countries had existed for millennia. The development of the Incoterms was based on clear and detailed understanding of the possible areas of uncertainty that must be addressed with regard to various shipping and delivery options in a contract for the international sale of goods. Despite that knowledge, the Incoterms are very long and detailed, requiring most contract parties to use a lengthy and detailed guidance document. The Incoterms and guidance have been revised seven times. Despite this high level of attention and guidance, litigation over international transport of goods still occurs. The foregoing description may help the parties to ABS contracts to understand why their contractual provisions have not functioned and why it has proven difficult to develop models within the few years since the NP was adopted.

(b) CISG

The international sale of goods is another international contract area in which there is thought to be general agreement. The UN Convention on Contracts

434 Costs discussed include those related to export customs, carriage to port, unloading of truck in port, loading on vessel/airplane; sea/air carriage, insurance; unloading after import; loading imported goods onto a truck, carriage to final destination; import customs, import duties and taxes.

for the International Sale of Goods (CISG) has been ratified by 84 countries, making it one of the most successful of the international commercial conventions.[435] Unfortunately, the UN currently includes 193 Member States, plus two permanent observers (Palestine and the Holy See). The CISG specifically applies only "to contracts of sale of goods between parties whose places of business are in different States: (a) when the States are Contracting States; or (b) when the rules of private international law lead to the application of the law of a Contracting State."[436] This initial point is interesting for ABS contracts in two ways.

First, it demonstrates one reason that there are many contracts to which the CISG does not apply. Specifically, the CSIG will not apply to contracts in which any party is from one of the 102 States that are not CISG members, unless the court chooses to involve PIL rules under which a CISG Member State's law applies. Thus, the CISG does not eliminate the uncertainties relating to the application of different countries' contract law, nor does it eliminate the need to understand the PIL rules.

Second, it means that the nationality of the parties to a contract is irrelevant if the parties' places of business are in different States.[437] In this connection however, the CISG goes on to say that the location of the parties' place of business will not be inquired into in applying the CISG, unless it is specifically stated in the contract.[438] At first glance, this does not seem very important. Virtually all contracts, including all ABS contracts that the authors have seen, name the parties in detail and identify their place of business. The lesson of the CISG is that, if the parties are expecting any participation from offices or officials of a business or government that are located outside of the provider country, they need to specify those persons and offices, as well.

---

435 Compare for example the similarly named UNIDROIT instrument: the Convention relating to a Uniform Law on the International Sale of Goods. It has only 9 ratifications (but has entered into force because it required only 5.) In addition, the Hague Conference developed its own Convention of 22 December 1986 on the Law Applicable to Contracts for the International Sale of Goods, which has been ratified by only 2 countries and is not in force.

436 CISG, Article 1(1). This issue (and those referenced in the next three footnotes) is also found in other instruments that have attempted to develop uniform contractual laws on the sale of goods. See, the Hague Convention relating to a Uniform Law on the Formation of Contracts for the International Sale of Goods; and the Hague Convention relating to a Uniform Law on the International Sale of Goods.

437 CISG Article 1(3).

438 CISG Article 1(2).

Beyond that first step, the CISG's application to ABS becomes even less clear. By definition, it covers the "sale" of "goods," but it does not define either term except by stating particular types of action and *res* that are excluded from its coverage. Specifically, the following are excluded from the "goods" covered by the CISG: (i) goods known at the time of the transaction to be bought for personal, family or household use; (ii) ships, vessels, hovercraft or aircraft; (iii) electricity; or (iv) stocks, shares, money, investment securities or negotiable instruments.[439] Similarly, the following activities are not covered: auctions; foreclosure and other acquisition of property by operation of law; certain contracts that under which one party agrees "to supply of goods to be manufactured or produced" where the other party agrees "to supply a substantial part of the materials necessary for such manufacture or production," contracts in which "the party who furnishes the goods" is also supplying labor or other services.[440]

It is difficult to come to any conclusion about whether genetic resources are "goods" under a convention that was finalized and adopted before the CBD. Currently, for example, there is little agreement on what a "genetic resource" is (the physical sample, the genetic information contained in the sample or both.)

Even if genetic resources and/or ATK are "goods" under the CISG, one must inquire closely into other possible controversies to determine if they might lead the contract to be excluded from the application of the CISG. Even then, the CISG's coverage is limited to the buyer and seller, so that it does not cover any rights of others (*e.g.*, the community or country, if the national law allows individuals to be "providers" (in essence, sellers) of genetic resources, or *vice versa.*)[441] In addition, the CISG expressly excludes questions of validity or the impact of the sale on property rights, leaving these to be decided under national law.[442] Parties to a contract can agree in their contract that the CISG does not apply.[443] The CISG specifically states that all matters outside of its coverage must be settled either by PIL or by governing law and principles. Thus, the parties to an ABS contract governed by the CISG would be no better off than if the CISG did not apply.[444]

439 CISG, Article 2.

440 CISG, Articles 2, 3 and 4.

441 CISG, Art. 4.

442 *Ibid.*

443 CISG, Art. 6, and see Chapter 8, *supra.*

444 CISG, Art. 7.

Ignoring the doubts regarding whether it can apply to an ABS contract, a review of the CISG's terms suggest that the CISG would not be very helpful, even if it did apply to ABS contracts. For example,

- It is built on the unwieldy "offer-acceptance" model,[445]
- It uses terms like "substantial detriment," "fundamental breach," "contract avoidance," "specific performance," "reliance" and "modification" in generic clauses, without defining them. This means that national law and PIL principles must be used to determine what these terms mean;
- Its remedy provisions are very focused on a certain category of remedial issues (*e.g.*, remedies that apply if goods are late or arrive in spoiled condition.) These points are not very helpful in most ABS situations.

Like the Incoterms, the CISG focuses on transfer issues such as transfer of risk, although it also addresses other common contractual interpretation questions including the time of delivery of the goods; remedies for late delivery and/or payment; and the quality of goods received (*e.g.,* who bears the responsibility to ensure the quality of the goods and ensure that they arrive in tact.)

At Articles 41 through 44, the CISG considers ownership issues, including possible lien and intellectual property situations. They include provisions that would be inordinately complicated and place demands on all parties, when applied to bioprospecting or other ABS situations. They could, potentially, enable the establishment of third-party liens against genetic resources or ATK transferred by the contract. Given the uncertainties regarding the *res* in ABS contracts, such liens could render an ABS contract completely unworkable. The providers, provider governments and users might all find themselves mired in complex litigation as a result. The only possible mechanism for protecting themselves would be for the providers to give the users notice of the possible lien. Such a notice would almost certainly scare off potential users with any awareness of business risk issues.

Most problematic of all, the clauses which discuss breach of contract and damages are phrased in a way that assumes that the value of the "goods" is known and/or knowable. As such these provisions appear particularly inappropriate for addressing ABS situations, in which perceptions of the value of the genetic resources may vary widely.[446]

---

445 CISG, Arts. 8–24. Note that major headings include "obligations of seller," "obligations of buyer" and "provisions common to the obligations of seller and buyer." See discussion in Chapter 2, *supra*.

446 Among the different views of the value of genetic resources and traditional knowledge are the following: The researcher/developer's view (the potential value of the resource

(c) New York Convention

With over 150 Member States, New York Convention on the Recognition and Enforcement of Foreign Arbitral Awards (NYC)[447] is the most successful international commercial convention. Its purpose is to address the "enforcement problem," which is widely agreed to be the most glaring problem caused by the lack of a single unified international commercial code.

Basically, the enforcement problem can be simply explained. Given that all contractual violations may only be redressed under national law, that means that enforcement of judgments and arbitration awards relating to a contract is a legal issue to be addressed under the law of the country in which the award will be enforced.[448] This enforcement decision is complicated by the enforcing court's right to review certain aspects of the judgment or award, applying its own law and to refuse to enforce the award on that basis.[449] This means that, even after the plaintiff has completed a legal or arbitral action and gotten a judgment, he will have to essentially try the entire case again, in order to obtain enforcement of that judgment by a court with jurisdiction over the defendant and its assets.

Many international efforts have been made to improve the enforcement of court judgments, but these have been generally unsuccessful.[450] The situation regarding arbitral awards is much better, thanks to general acceptance of the NYC, which represents a major agreement among States. It is now much easier to enforce arbitral awards in NYC Member States. The inclusion of an arbitration clause, however, is not some type of universal cure for the enforcement problem. Even the NYC authorizes the enforcing court to review the original award under its own national law and policy, before deciding whether to enforce it.[451]

---

as an input into a future discovery or product); the external view (the money value of the samples themselves – i.e., the price of a few beans, seedlings, blood samples, *etc.*); the environmental / social welfare view (the value of the resources within the ecosystem or community in which they are found); the providers'-rights view (the value of the provider's continued ability to control access to and obtain benefits from the utilization of the species); *etc.*

447 Footnote 429, *supra.*

448 See Chapter 8, *supra.*

449 Every year a great many actions are recorded under the NYC's oversight process, in which one party to a contract has been forced to take legal action to enforce an arbitral award in the country of another party. See UNCITRAL database.

450 For example, the Hague Convention of 1 February 1971 on the Recognition and Enforcement of Foreign Judgments in Civil and Commercial Matters has received only 5 ratifications (Albania, Cyprus, the Netherlands, Portugal and Kuwait.).

451 Among the situations in which the enforcing country can refuse to enforce the award, one of the most important arises where the award is incompatible with the public policy of

The possibility that a costly arbitral award obtained relating to a contract violation might still not be enforceable presents a major obstacle to building a functional ABS system. Consider, for example, the fact that all international instruments on ABS are expressed in very vague and ambiguous language. As a result, the parameters of national NP implementing legislation are relatively unrestricted. Each country's interpretation of the meaning of ABS concepts will be very different from the others. As a result, when the provider brings a judgment or arbitration from Country X to a court or official in Country Y, it is very likely that the Country Y court could apply some portion of Country Y's ABS legislation as a basis for refusing to enforce the judgment or arbitration.

This is one of the reasons that this book recommends that contracts relating to the access to and use of genetic resources and ATK should be written as enforceable contracts, and should not rely on ABS legislation, terminology or concepts. Even then, however, the enforcement challenges are significant, in light of the major differences among the various countries' national commercial law.

As further discussed in Chapter 7, the success of the NYC has led many experts to state that, if one has a grievance with regard to an international contract, it is easier and more effective to arbitrate than to seek and obtain a legal judgment, because in international situations the enforcement of arbitrations is more dependable than the enforcement of court judgments.

(d) Agency

In international commercial laws, there is little consensus regarding "agency" – the duties of one who holds intangible assets or negotiate contracts as an agent, on behalf of another.[452] This is unfortunate, because these issues have proven to be very important in ABS contracts.[453] It is common, for example, for a person

---

the enforcing country. For example, in many countries, enforcement will not be granted against a party that had no adequate opportunity fairly to present his case before the judgment was issued; where the award was obtained by procedural fraud; or where current proceedings between the same parties about the same situation are ongoing or have produced an inconsistent result. See ¶ 7.3.3, *supra*.

452 Even relatively conventional points have failed to garner more than a few ratifications. See, *e.g.*, the following Hague Conference conventions: Convention of 5 July 2006 on the Law Applicable to Certain Rights in Respect of Securities held with an Intermediary, which has received only two ratifications, the Convention of 14 March 1978 on the Law Applicable to Agency (four Contracting Parties) and the Convention of 1 July 1985 on the Law Applicable to Trusts and on their Recognition (12 Contracting Parties.) Convention on Agency in the International Sale of Goods, Geneva, 17 February 1983. According to the UNIDROIT website, this convention has been ratified by 10 countries.

453 They were, for example, extremely relevant to the Teff agreement, as discussed in ¶¶ 4.1, 5.4.5(c) and 8.1, *supra*.

or entity in the provider country to negotiate or even enter into a contract on behalf of a foreign person or company. For example, when person X negotiates with provider Y on behalf of user Z, what is the legal relationship of Y to Z and what responsibility and liability applies to X? In general, the existing instruments relating to this topic focus on protecting Z from any responsibility for matters agreed by the agent X. None of these instruments have received more than a few ratifications. For ABS contracts, the lesson to be learned is that the Parties must take extra care to ensure that each party is directly bound by the contract.[454]

In addition, these conventions underscore the possibility that Z might later "ratify" the contract by action or by written statement.[455] Thus, it will be extremely important for the parties to an ABS contract to maintain careful records of everything that happens under the contract; once it has been signed.

10.4.3 *Other Specific Instruments on Contracts and Their Status*

As noted in ¶ 10.4.1, a large number of international instruments have been developed relevant to international contracts via UNIDROIT and the Hague Conference. Unfortunately, only a few of them have been successful in entering into force and obtaining more than a small number of ratifications. For this section, the authors reviewed all of the commercial instruments developed by these two processes, as well as the UNIDROIT Principles 2010, other UNIDROIT model instruments[456] and UNIDROIT's instrument and guidance on cultural heritage.[457] Ultimately, this research has shown that most of the presently available binding instruments are very narrowly focused on particular details related to contract enforcement. Most of these are not very relevant to ABS.

With regard to the principles and models that are less narrow and focused on contractual development, as explained in ¶ 10.4.1, reliance on these instruments offers no greater assurance than simply relying on national commercial law and standard commercial practice. Indeed, in light of the fact that they have not been formally applied in many countries, international commercial conventions are actually less dependable or predictable.

Our review of the UNIDROIT and Hague Conference instruments on commercial law, however, has indicated a few areas in which these might provide some assistance to the parties to ABS negotiations. First, some ABS contracts are focused on multiplication of native species with valuable properties.[458]

---

454 See generally, ¶¶ 4.4–4.6, *supra*.

455 NYC, footnote 429, *supra*, at Article 15.

456 The UNIDROIT Principles 2010, Model Clauses and Legal Guide on Contract Farming are all provided on the UNIDROIT website.

457 *Ibid.*

458 For example, in China, recent discussion of ABS implementation is focused on altering the processes by which species of national or traditional origin are multiplied and used

Contracts for this kind of ABS implementation closely resemble farming contracts. One of the international commercial instruments reviewed is a guide to international farming contracts produced by UNIDROIT, in conjunction with FAO and other international bodies.[459] Although it does not mention ABS, it does discuss biosafety and a range of issues that need to be addressed in such contracts.

Second, some of the instruments underscore the challenges arising with regard to language. Where the parties speak different languages, it may be important to specify the language in which various communications will be made, in addition to other details related to how communications are sent and documented.[460]

Third, it is important not to be deceived by the titles to conventions. For example, conventions on "access to justice" are sometimes misunderstood. These conventions generally appear to focus entirely on legal aid issues and on ensuring that national laws do not make it impossible for foreign nationals to file suit, or impose discriminatory fees.[461]

Finally, we note that UNIDROIT's Convention on Stolen or Illegally Exported Cultural Objects,[462] offers little value to the ABS process. We reviewed it in the hope that it might provide something useful for ATK contracts. Unfortunately, that Convention does not define "object"; however, it uses the term in a way that suggests that it probably does not include ATK or locally developed genetic resources.

10.5 Impacts of PIL and International Commercial Law on ABS Contracts

The mistaken belief that there is some unified body of international commercial law can impact the contract under negotiation in many ways. It can lead the parties to accept unsupported statements by opposing negotiators that

---

in the production of essences, traditional medicines and other ingredients. GEF Project 5533, China.

459 UNIDROIT, FAO, IFAD, 2015.

460 See, *e.g.*, Convention of 1 March 1954 on Civil Procedure, at §§ 1–16. Despite its broad title, this Convention addresses only communication, security for costs, free legal aid, access to court records and physical detention. (The Hague Conference's Convention of 25 October 1980 on International Access to Justice covers an almost identical list of topics at about the same level of detail.)

461 See *e.g.*, Convention on International Access to Justice (Hague Conference, 1980).

462 Rome, 1995.

some particular clause is "standard practice" and need not be explained. It can create a "false sense of security," leading the parties to believe that, if they fail to cover an essential issue, the omission will not matter, because existing commercial law will apply in a fair and predictable way, serving as a basis for a reasonable compromise if a problem arises in future.

Moreover, the only existing international commercial conventions that are widely accepted are quite narrow in scope and coverage, limited to a few specific points on which there is already widespread consensus in the commercial world. There are still many other conventional practices that have existed for decades or centuries on which the States of the world have been unable to agree.

For negotiators and parties in ABS contracts, this situation is extremely problematic, because ABS is a new type of commercial relationship. As a result there are no legal and practical commercial principles that are parallel to ABS, on which the new system will be based. It may be unrealistic to expect new developments in international commercial law to address matters like ABS on which there is no long history of international commercial practices.

The following sections note some of the potential pitfalls of attempting to rely on PIL or international commercial law to govern an ABS contract.

10.5.1 *Implications of PIL and International Commercial Conventions on Governing Law*

Many negotiators have stated that, even though the international commercial conventions have not been generally ratified, the parties to a contract are free to designate them as the "governing law" of their contract. For example, Article 7 of the Standard Material Transfer Agreement (SMTA) of the ITPGRFA provides, "The applicable law shall be General Principles of Law, including the UNIDROIT Principles of International Commercial Contracts 2004, the objectives and the relevant provisions of the Treaty, and, when necessary for interpretation, the decisions of the Governing Body." There are two main reasons why it is not advisable to follow this example, whether naming the UNIDROIT Principles or any other instrument.

First, this provision does not eliminate the problem described in ¶ 10.1. All of the international commercial instruments described in ¶¶ 10.4.1 and 10.4.2, above specifically state that their terms do not apply to the determination of whether a contract is valid or not under national law. Thus, in the event of a breach or an action to interpret a contract naming an international convention or principles as applicable law, a lawsuit may be filed in any country and that court's first deliberation will be to determine whether the contract was "a valid contract" under that court's own national law. If it finds that the contract is not valid, it may apply its own law to all remaining deliberations, including the nature and availability of a remedy, without any reference to the designated international convention or principles.

Second, the contents of the international law may not provide any basis for fair determination of the issues of an ABS contract. One example is the SMTA, as mentioned above, which incorporates the UNIDROIT Principles 2004. Like the more current version (the UNIDROIT Principles 2010) the Principles 2004 state the obligation of the parties with regard to all government approvals as follows:

> Where the law of a State requires a public permission affecting the validity of the contract or its performance and neither that law nor the circumstances indicate otherwise (a) if only one party has its place of business in that State, that party shall take the measures necessary to obtain the permission; (b) in any other case, the party whose performance requires permission shall take the necessary measures.[463]

The UNIDROIT commentary on this Principle states that it embodies the usual practice, however, in the authors' experience, this is far from being standard practice. This clause might easily be missed, however, by a negotiator who is reviewing the nearly 500 pages of the Principles in order to determine whether to designate them as governing law in his ABS contract. Indeed, it might well have been missed by the SMTA negotiators. This principle is potentially problematic in ABS, as well as the SMTA. In ABS, national ABS legislation in provider countries often conditions PIC and MAT and other permits and certificates on major input from the user. If the above quoted principle applies, the provider would bear the risk and responsibility in case the PIC, MAT, permit or certificate were not granted, even if that decision were the user's fault for failing to participate in the regulatory processes. Similarly, the SMTA is essentially a contract between the middleman and the user. Most of the time, neither party to the SMTA has any direct contact with the provider country, or any awareness regarding whether and how ABS requirements of the provider country will apply to the SMTA.

Thus, the main consequence of designating the UNIDROIT Principles 2010 as "applicable" or "governing" law is that it may impose obligations the parties would not accept if they knew of them. And given that the Principles are a 500 page document that is not the law of any country (and thus is not necessarily within the essential knowledge of any commercial lawyer's experience), it is

463 UNIDROIT Principles 2010, Article 6.1.14(a).

very likely that the parties will not know of many of these provisions. It is not very likely that a plant breeder getting access under the SMTA knows any of the articles in the UNIDROIT Principles.

For all ABS contract negotiators, this example should underscore the need to specifically include contract provisions addressing key requirements, such as the obligation to obtain all necessary governmental permissions, and comply with all PIC, MAT and certificate requirements.

10.5.2 *Legal Analysis Required*

As with any "governing law" choice, it is important to undertake or obtain a careful legal analysis of the impact of the choice. Unlike a decision to choose a national legal system as governing law, however, the choice of an international instrument is more problematic, for several reasons.

First, the document selected as "governing law" may not cover ABS contracts. For example the CISG specifically covers contracts for the "sale of goods." It is clear that the CISG recognizes that there are many kinds of sale contracts that are not "sale of goods." It is not at all clear that an ABS contract providing access to genetic resources in exchange for benefit sharing will be considered a "sale of goods" contract. Thus, if the ABS contract selects the CISG or some other instrument as its "governing law," that instrument may be inapplicable, meaning that there is no designated "governing law."

Second, of course, contracts and their implementation are governed by many other kinds of law, in addition to commercial law. The parties' concerns may bring in a range of laws, including laws on intellectual property, trade, social responsibility and torts, to name a few, as well as the laws governing access to justice and civil procedure. Designation of an international commercial instrument as "applicable law" does not provide any guidance as to these areas of law.

10.5.3 *Reliance on PIL or International Commercial Law to "Fill in the Blanks"*

One final problem with relying on international law as the "applicable law" for your contract arises if your contract fails to address some points. As explained in Chapter 4, where a contract omits any mention of some essential question, or is ambiguous about it, there is a possibility that the contract will be declared to be invalid or the court will refuse to consider it.[464] It is often difficult to predict which issues a court will find to be "essential" for this purpose, or how much uncertainty will be permitted, especially in an international contract. For example, where an international contract for the sale of an undetermined

464 See, *e.g.*, the Australian case of *Vetreria Etrusca srl v Kingston Estate Wines P/L.*

number of units of a particular product called for a payment equal to $XX per unit, the price was not ambiguous. Even though the final total was not specified, the mechanism for calculating it was clear.[465] In another case, the court ultimately found the pricing provision insufficient where it didn't specify (i) which currency would be used to pay the price or (ii) where the price would be paid.[466] In ABS contracts, many concepts (genetic resources, ATK, derivative, *etc.*) are still rather ambiguous even where they have been defined in the CBD, NP, ITPGRFA and/or national law, so that some ABS contracts have included payment/valuation clauses that were much less specific than this example. The lesson for negotiators/drafters of ABS contracts is that it is important to pin down as many points as possible in concrete details in the ABS contract.

Most countries' national commercial law and experience might be broad enough to enable courts to fill gaps of this type. The challenge in using international instruments is that they normally provide no basis for "filling in the gaps" in a contract. As such, it may be more likely that an incomplete contract will be declared invalid, if that contract relies on international instruments as its governing law.

In this connection, we note that it is common for agricultural contracts to address the purchase of an entire harvest. Since such contracts are usually signed well before harvesting time (usually before the crop is planted), it is not possible for the parties to know how much produce will be harvested, if any; or whether the quality of the produce will be satisfactory. Over the years, contractual practices have developed dealing with most aspects of these uncertainties. With regard to uncertainty regarding the volume of the harvest, the contract will be considered sufficiently concrete, if it provides a very specific formula for determining how much to pay per unit, and specifies the maximum volume the buyer will agree to purchase. The contract may also address the possibility that some other factor will intervene that prevents the harvest (a storm or fire that destroys the crops, for example.) The question of quality is more difficult. In some cases, where the contract includes a provision that the buyer's duty to pay is conditional on the buyer's satisfaction with the quality of the produce or product, it is possible that the contract will be deemed invalid. It could be regarded as only a "pre-contract" that is not binding unless/until the buyer approves the product quality.

465 See *e.g.*, SWITZERLAND: *Kantonsgericht Zug*.

466 UKRAINE: Chamber of Commerce and Trade Arbitration proceeding.

CHAPTER 11

Contract-related Provisions of ABS Regime Instruments

ABS is a network of instruments, which in turn call for the creation of additional international and national instruments and institutions, and for coordination among them. Together, they are intended to create and clarify the ABS regime and to enable individual ABS transactions to function. International instruments (conventions, treaties, protocols, *etc.*) focus on the obligations of States to each other. To this end, they focus most of their attention on structural development, and mandating national legislative action. These international instruments are not directly applicable to the individual ABS contract. They may, however, have a role in making ABS-contracts functional.

As noted in Chapters 2 through 10, the authors recommend that, the parties to an ABS contract must make every effort to ensure that their contract is a binding and enforceable instrument under basic contract law. This approach will ensure application of well established contract principles to the contract, rather than forcing any person, court or other official to attempt to interpret it under "ABS law." This is important because the concept of ABS does not formally exist in the laws of most countries.

The use of the contract approach, however, does not exempt the contract's parties from the obligation to comply with national PIC and MAT requirements and other ABS laws of the countries involved.[467] Thus, the parties to an ABS contract, need to understand all of the various elements of national ABS law, as well as the provisions of the global ABS framework that affect ABS contracts and their negotiation, drafting and implementation.

There are already innumerable relatively complete overviews of the various international instruments within the international ABS regime. This chapter will not reiterate that effort, but instead will focus attention on those provisions within that regime that are specifically relevant to ABS contracts. It will begin with a discussion of the role of contracts within the ABS regime (¶¶ 11.1 and 11.2), followed by a very basic outline of the agreed aspects of the manner in which the ABS process is expected to function and a listing of the international instruments that address issues relevant to the ABS regime, and a caveat regarding other international instruments and regimes that may also be

467 Contract provisions relating to compliance with these laws are discussed in Chapter 8.

 | DOI 10.1163/9789004356573_012

potentially relevant (¶¶ 11.3 and 11.4). It will then examine the contract-related provisions contained in the various international instruments that comprise the ABS regime, divided into five subject areas. (¶ 11.5).

This chapter is closely linked to the discussion in Chapter 2 of this book. There it explains the legal fallacy of presuming that ABS contracts should be based on the terms and contents used in the ABS regime and the problems that arise when one attempts to do so.

11.1 Contracts as Tools of the ABS Regime

Since the earliest CBD negotiations, the parties universally agreed that contracts would be the core operative mechanism by which ABS would be implemented. The accepted view still assumes that private contracts (as supplemented by permits, certificates, PIC and MAT) will be the legal tool by which ABS is implemented in practice.

The primary advantage of this contractual approach is the involvement of the private sector. Even in 1992, financial and other support for conservation and sustainable use was becoming difficult. The CBD negotiators recognized the need to look to the private sector to implement these goals in the context of biological diversity. Thus, the aim of ABS was to secure private-sector support for future progress toward these goals. From those days to this day, one of the strongest motivations driving the development of the international ABS regime was the hope and expectation that private funds can be marshalled to promote social welfare, environmental conservation and other recognized sustainability issues.[468]

Regarding these objectives, the ABS regime negotiators faced many difficult challenges. Not least among these were the many legal issues discussed in this book, related to the ambiguity and functionality of ABS contracts. To date, most theoretical analysis of these points has failed to produce suggestions that can function under conventional contract law. CBD Parties have discovered, however, that it is nearly impossible for the environmental/social welfare sector to force changes to national and international contractual laws and practices. As a result, national ABS implementing measures are each based on the country's own individual interpretation of the ambiguous international ABS instruments, in the context of that country's unique framework of contractual/ commercial law. These interpretations will differ markedly, not only in the

468 As has been noted, international processes have been singularly ineffectual at gaining a large number of signatories to international instruments addressing even long understood and relatively simple commercial issues. See discussion in ¶¶ 10.2–10.4.

manner of implementation,[469] but in the most basic view of the contents and operational objectives of ABS.[470]

Some have suggested that ABS contracts simply will not work. This book takes the position, that ABS contracts can function if the parties draft their ABS "stand alone" contracts. That is, they will function if they are "legally binding" documents that can be interpreted and implemented under contract law, without the need to resolve any of the ambiguities and terminology of the international ABS regime (see Chapters 2 through 7). The contract must also be carefully drafted to ensure its compliance with all relevant national ABS laws and regulations (as discussed in Chapter 7).[471]

11.2 Components of the ABS Regime

Although there are still some who dispute the basic framework of the ABS regime, most people agree that the following components of the ABS process are generally accepted: access; benefit-sharing; terms / requirements (PIC, MAT, ABS permits and ABS contracts[472]); compliance; capacity building; and streamlining (See box).

469 International instruments are designed with the intent to allow each country to apply its own system to implement the agreed commitments, so it is positive and expected that the manner of implementation varies.

470 International instruments are normally designed to provide a shared view of the overall operational issue that the instrument addresses, the varying systems of national implementation are directed toward fitting the national actions into the overall international framework. The NP does not include such basic agreement on the essentials (scope, definitions, and other basic operational concepts,) so that national systems have no basis for integration. Like a dance recital in which each of the dancers on stage is wearing headphones and a personal stereo that is playing that dancer's favourite music, even where the individual performances are excellent, the overall effect is chaotic and fails to achieve the recognized goals.

471 The distinction between negotiating/implementing an ABS contract, on one hand, and complying with ABS regulatory requirements on the other, and the importance of keeping these concepts separate, is discussed in more detail in ¶ 2.1 of this book.

472 Unlike the PIC and MAT requirements (which normally involve participation and approval by the government and or other local communities regardless of who is the authorized provider of the genetic resources or ATK) or the (governmental) ABS permit, the ABS contract has a role in the regime that goes beyond that of complying with national ABS legislation – its job is to create a binding instrument, enforceable under contract/commercial laws and principles, governing the specific rights and duties of the specific parties directly involved.

BOX: BASIC ABS TERMINOLOGY

"Access": the mechanism(s) and process(es) by which users obtain genetic resources of other countries.
"Benefit-sharing": either a negotiated payment or "the sharing of benefits arising from utilisation of a provider's genetic resources."
"Prior Informed Consent" (*PIC*): unless waived by the country, the process of obtaining administratively required approval of access from the CBD/NP Party (or its formally authorized person/agency).
"Mutually Agreed Terms" (*MAT*): terms agreed between the CBD/NP Party that is providing access (or its formally authorized designee) and the user or other person who is obtaining access.
"ABS permit": Permit issued by the provider country regulating/allowing access and possibly also addressing benefit-sharing.
"Compliance": Depending on context, either the user's and provider's compliance with national ABS law, or the user's and provider's implementation of the ABS contract.
"Capacity Building": the duty to resolve the legal and technical challenges which have interfered with ABS functionality in the past.
"Streamlining": processes that may allow certain types of ABS permits, approvals, documents and practices to be more accessible in certain situations.

Each of these components includes elements that directly impact the negotiation, drafting and implementation of ABS contracts. The following discussion will focus only on the most directly relevant provisions, and those that create the most significant challenges to parties seeking to negotiate an ABS contract. Parties negotiating and drafting ABS contracts should be warned that the entire regime may impact their work, and should make the effort of reading all of the instruments mentioned in this chapter.

11.3 Global ABS Regime Instruments Addressing ABS Contracts – The Broadest View

Given its role as guidance/assistance to drafters of ABS contracts, this book obviously need not provide an in-depth study of the entire ABS regime. Instead, as noted above, the goal of this chapter is to do what many other analyses have not done – to analyze the regime provisions most relevant to contract drafting and discuss their relevance. In order to do this appropriately, however, it is necessary first to determine which instruments are part of the ABS regime, and to note that those involved in ABS contracts should make every effort to become familiar with the entire regime as it exists at the time of their negotiations.

Thus, we are not suggesting that you limit your understanding to our analysis. In addition, we offer two caveats. First, this chapter provides a snapshot of an evolving regime at a specific point in time. In a few instances, we have mentioned work that is ongoing at present, but we cannot provide any guidance on that work, until critical provisions have been agreed and adopted. Second, as discussed in greater detail in ¶ 11.4, there is a much broader range of other international instruments that may be relevant to some ABS transactions, including the international bodies of commercial law (briefly discussed in Chapter 10) and intellectual property law.

In selecting the instruments that we will consider as part of the "Global ABS Regime," the authors have been challenged by the lack of agreement among negotiators regarding which international instruments should be included.[473] This chapter attempts to include all international instruments that include or regulate at least one direct aspect of ABS, as such, in four categories:

- The ABS-related elements of the following instruments adopted under the auspices of the CBD:
  - the CBD;[474] which establishes legally binding ABS obligations on all CBD members directly in Article 15, and includes other sections that have direct impact on ABS contracts;[475]
  - the NP;[476]
  - the Bonn Guidelines;[477] and
  - the Cartagena Protocol on Biosafety.[478]

---

473 These discussions were very briefly summarized in http://www.iisd.ca/vol09/enb09544e.html. Other commentators have described them in more detail, albeit possibly focusing on their own positions regarding which instruments should be considered part of the ABS regime. See Singh Gan, 2012, at p. 78–79.

474 The Convention on Biological Diversity. UNTC I-30619, 5 June 1992 (Rio de Janeiro) in force. In all, 195 countries plus the European Union (separately from its individual Member States) are currently listed as CBD Parties. CBD website.

475 Some commentators on ABS limited their focus to three CBD Articles: Articles 1, 2 and 15. It is axiomatic in law, however, that an international instrument should be interpreted in its entirety. It is a serious mistake to apply a single clause, without having a complete understanding of the entire instrument, and how that single clause fits within it.

476 As discussed throughout this book and in Morgera, *et al.*, 2014.

477 The Bonn Guidelines were and remain a non-binding instrument.

478 The Cartagena Protocol addresses the development and introduction of "living modified organisms" (a term which essentially means "genetic modified organisms" or GMOs.)

- Non-CBD-related instruments that have been adopted or overseen by other bodies, which intend that these instruments will coordinate new and/or pre-existing institutions and legal systems with the Global ABS Framework:
  - the ITPGRFA, adopted under the UN Food and Agriculture Organization (FAO), addressing the plant agricultural sector (including the Standard Material Transfer Agreement (SMTA), which is the format used in a large number of transfers of plant genetic resources);[479]
  - the World Intellectual Property Organization's (WIPO's) work is also felt to be relevant to the ABS regime particularly, the ongoing negotiation or discussion in the Intergovernmental Committee on Genetic Resources, Traditional Knowledge and Folklore (IGC).[480]
  - the World Health Organization's Pandemic Influenza Preparedness (PIP) framework, addressing a specific range of genetic-resource activities;[481]
  - the Micro-Organisms Sustainable use and Access International Code Of Conduct (MOSAICC) Regulation;[482]
  - The ongoing negotiations under the UN Convention on Law of the Sea (UNCLOS)[483] regarding access to marine genetic resources or marine bioprospecting in the areas beyond national jurisdiction.
- Regional instruments, adopted to enable ABS implementation, including
  - the revised African Union initiative;[484] and

GMOs have been recognized by to be one of the main groups of products of the utilization of genetic resources.

479 The ITPGRFA converted the former International Undertaking on Plant Genetic Resources for Food and Agriculture (the "Undertaking"), with significant revision, into a binding instrument. Its adoption represented an important step for the global ABS regime – the adoption of a mechanism to apply the ABS concept to a specifically defined sector.

480 At this writing, a number of ABS-related documents are apparently still on the table, including, for example, the "Consolidated Document Relating to Intellectual Property and Genetic Resources," "The Protection Of Traditional Knowledge: Draft Articles," "The Protection of Traditional Cultural Expressions: Draft Articles," and the "Joint Recommendation on Genetic Resources and Associated Traditional Knowledge."

481 Pandemic Influenza Preparedness Framework for the sharing of influenza viruses and access to vaccines and other benefits.

482 This is a voluntary code of conduct.

483 United Nations Convention on the Law of the Sea.

484 This document was intensively promoted at CBD events.

- the Andean Community's Decision No. 391 Establishing the Common Regime on Access to Genetic Resources.[485]

and

- National ABS Implementing Measures.[486]

For purposes of negotiating and implementing ABS contracts, the last of these groups (National ABS Implementing Measures) has the most significant impact on the contract, and the first group (CBD Family) currently is the main source of international input to individual ABS contracts. Clearly, given that many items on the above list are "ongoing negotiations" it will be necessary for the parties to undertake updating research, before applying any of the lessons of this chapter to a new contract in the years to come. In seeking guidance in addressing disagreements or conflicting claims, the contractual parties, mediators, arbitrators and judges will be most likely to consider the instruments in these two groups. Obviously, the other instruments may take on added relevance when named in the contract or in the relevant national law.

485 At least one Community Member (Ecuador) has attempted to adopt Post-NP amendments to its national legislation implementing Decision 391. See *Reglamento Nacional al Régimen Común de Acceso a los Recursos Genéticos en aplicación a la Decisión No. 392 de la Comunidad Andina (Decreto Ejecutivo N° 905 de 3 de octubre de 2011.)*

486 Since the first adoption of the ABS concept in the CBD (1992), commentators have stated that a number of countries are in the process of developing and adopting national ABS laws. Following the NP's entry into force, this may be true, although relatively few such laws have been listed in the ABS Clearinghouse's database of national ABS legislation. As of this writing, the database proclaims that 123 legislative documents have been published, however 56 of these are duplicates of the EU ABS Regulation and Implementing Regulation, which was already posted against the EU, which is separately a party to the NP. Moreover 22 of the 28 countries posting this regulation have not at this writing posted national implementing legislation, required for EU Regulations. Of the remaining instruments, 30 are generic biodiversity and species conservation instruments not mentioning ABS, and at least seven others are one page ratification decrees, which do not specify implementing information. This indicates that there are only approximately 30 national laws which directly address at least one substantive requirement of ABS. Most of these focus only on identifying/establishing a regulatory institution, but leave the task of clarifying national law on ABS for the future. The drafters of national ABS legislation could provide major positive support to the ABS regime, if they applied a contract-perspective to the drafting and implementing of such legislation.

Additional developments may occur in any part of the global regime that facilitate, guide or otherwise affect ABS contracts.

11.4 Caveat: Other International Instruments and Regimes of Potential Importance to ABS Contracts and Their Parties

As noted throughout this book, all ABS contracts and all parties to them are subject to all relevant laws. The creation of a functional and binding ABS contract does not insulate the parties from the obligations to comply with law, nor does it eliminate the relevance of other legal systems. This is clearly true at the national level, but is equally true with regard to international laws. The main difference, of course is that relatively few international laws are directly relevant to private contracts.

As noted in Chapter 10, there is no globally functional international body or law on contracts and commercial transactions. International instruments are not binding on individuals except to the extent that applicable national law exists to implement the international instrument. There are, however, many international legal regimes that may impact ABS contracts in other ways, even though those regimes do not directly consider genetic resources or any other ABS concept. Thus for example, an ABS contract that addresses the development of new and innovative products and processes must clearly accommodate the possibility that a patent or other intellectual property right might be granted. Similarly, ABS contracts related to marine species, even if found or collected within national EEZs should be cognizant of the impacts of relevant parts of the UNCLOS regime.

The prospect that a user might patent genetic-resource-based or traditional-knowledge-based innovations or processes has been widely addressed since the beginning of the ABS concept.[487] At present, as noted above, the WIPO-IGC is engaged in addressing particular intellectual-property-related questions of ABS directly, although the authors are not presently optimistic that these efforts will produce useful guidance or tools for the functionality of ABS contracts. It is important, however, for the parties to an ABS contract to keep in mind

487 One of the earliest expert research initiatives related to ABS was the formation of the Crucible Group – a group of intellectual property professionals who had expressed concerns about the assumptions underlying ABS. It produced three books, which examined many IPR-related issues within the context of ABS. Thereafter, WIPO took on the task of further analysis, producing a number of detailed documents, still available on the WIPO and CBD websites.

that the national and international regime on these issues may also impact their work, and to be aware of the instruments and tools available through that regime, particular the WIPO-administered the global search system for patent applications under the Patent Cooperation Treaty.

As noted above, another global legal regime of potential importance for ABS contracts is the UN Convention on Law of the Sea (UNCLOS).[488] Here also, as noted above, there is ongoing work toward the development of some type of document that will directly link to and be a part of the ABS regime, clarifying the roles of UNCLOS and the NP with regard to "marine genetic resources beyond national jurisdiction."[489] It is not yet clear which marine genetic resources will be included within this concept, when/if these processes produce some result.[490] In the meantime, however, it is clear that many resources that may be included within an ABS contract are already within the scope of UNCLOS. For example, UNCLOS Part XIII (Articles 238 through 265), which addresses "Marine Scientific Research" (MSR), applies to research in all ocean areas, including those clearly within national jurisdiction (territorial seas, contiguous zones and continental shelf areas). As such, it may apply to any marine-related ABS contract, involving either genetic resources or ATK, even where those resources and research are conducted entirely within the undisputed national jurisdiction of the provider country.

Part XIII operates like PIC in the sense that it authorizes coastal States "to regulate, authorize and conduct marine scientific research in their exclusive economic zone and on their continental shelf" through the mechanism of formal consent from the coastal State.[491] Given that they, too, relate to a State's consent to the use of resources over which it has sovereign rights, these provisions may be useful and instructive for countries when implementing ABS. Notably, they include specific requirements regarding the information

488 In force.

489 Ongoing negotiations regarding a possible UNCLOS implementation instrument, potentially addressing access to marine genetic resources or marine bioprospecting in the areas beyond national jurisdiction have gained momentum recently, following a 2015 mandate regarding these negotiations from the UN General Assembly. UNGA Resolution, A/RES/69/292 "Resolution adopted by the General Assembly on 19 June 2015 [without reference to a Main Committee (A/69/L.65 and Add.1)]" Sixty-ninth session, Agenda item 74 (a).

490 UNCLOS is relatively vague on the meaning of "national jurisdiction" as applied to national ownership over resources.

491 UNCLOS, Article 236. Part XIII places some limits on the States' right to refuse consent with regard to the extended portions of the State's continental shelf.

that must be provided to the country, in connection with the application for consent.[492] In addition, they provide a range of measures regarding the relationship between the private research projects and the coastal State. These provisions also parallel some parts of the NP's listing of non-monetary benefits.[493] UNCLOS's MSR provisions go further than the NP, providing a basis for assuming that the coastal State has consented, if it has failed to act within four months of receipt of the application by the proper authority, and also providing a mechanisms for coastal State decision to terminate or suspend the research, including for failure to comply with the above mentioned benefit measures.[494]

Similarly, even before any other instrument is developed, ABS contracts related to the ocean floor beyond each country's outer continental shelf[495] must consider the relevance of UNCLOS's provisions governing each country's OCS, as well as Part XI (Articles 133 through 191) and the so-called "Part 11 Convention,"[496] which addresses the natural resources of "the Area"(UNCLOS terminology for referring to the ocean floor beyond the limits of national jurisdiction.) These provisions are particularly important, because they seek to create a commercially functional mechanism controlling the use of specific resources attached to the Area.

Unfortunately, the potential application of these provisions and the Part 11 agreement to genetic resources[497] is far from clear. States' rights in their

492 UNCLOS, Article 248.

493 UNCLOS, Article 249.

494 UNCLOS, Articles 252 and 253.

495 The "outer continental shelf" (OCS) concept is also difficult to interpret for ABS and other purposes, for two reasons. First, under UNCLOS, the OCS appears to be within "national jurisdiction" in the sense that each country has one, regardless of whether they declare it. Unfortunately, UNCLOS also requires countries to declare their OCS and submit to a process for clarifying any conflicts between one declaration and that of other countries. This makes the application of CBD national sovereignty over genetic resources a bit unclear, even for genetic resources from the OCS of countries that are party to the CBD, particularly if those countries have not yet completed the OCS processes. Second, of course, there are a few coastal countries that have refused to become Party to UNCLOS, specifically because they claim a larger OCS than UNCLOS allows. These outliers make it difficult to consider UNCLOS's practices regarding the OCS to be definitive enough to be the basis of a contract or commercially reliable law.

496 The Part 11 Agreement is in force.

497 It is generally assumed that little or no ATK will apply to areas beyond national EEZs (200 miles from shore) and beyond the OCS (often very deep and more than 350 miles from shore).

continental shelf areas beyond their EEZ specifically include both "mineral and other non-living resources of the seabed and subsoil" and "living organisms belonging to sedentary species, that is to say, organisms which, at the harvestable stage, either are immobile on or under the seabed or are unable to move except in constant physical contact with the seabed or the subsoil."[498] Currently, Part XI applies only to mineral resources. Even if the living resources of the seabed are eventually included among resources of the Area,[499] the only UNCLOS controls on access to the living resources beyond national jurisdiction that are not affixed to the seabed (*i.e.*, resources of the "water column" beyond national jurisdiction) are its rules on fishing, a practice that is generally thought to be distinct from bioprospecting.[500]

Although they currently are not directed to biological resources, these provisions and the body established to implement them (the International Seabed Authority or "ISA"),[501] have been cited as the logical body to have oversight regarding utilization of the genetic resources of the seabed, and possibly also of the marine resources beyond national jurisdiction. Particularly if the current work on marine genetic resources beyond national jurisdiction does not produce an instrument, process or other document, Part XI, the Part 11 Convention and the ISA may be very important to an ABS contract or activity involving resources outside national jurisdiction.

In addition, the "Fish Stocks Agreement" (FSA),[502] is the currently the only UNCLOS instrument that directly refers to the biological resources of the ocean

498 UNCLOS Article 77.4. UNCLOS Article 11, which discusses international rights to exploit (and receive benefits from exploitation of) the "resources of the Area," covers only minerals, UNCLOS Articles 1(1) and 133.

499 Many international diplomats believe that, after years of discussion of the issue, the UN Member States will soon enter into negotiations for the establishment of a new UNCLOS-family instrument addressing "the Biodiversity of Marine Areas Beyond National Jurisdiction." See, *e.g.*, Kohona, 2015.

500 The various regional fisheries bodies and instruments do not appear to address bioprospecting issues. Although the Fish Stocks Agreement's general provisions address all "impacts of fishing, other human activities and environmental factors on target stocks and [other] species," Its overall approach focuses on fishing and fisheries. Even its provisions on scientific and technical research are limited to the "collect[ion] and exchange [of] scientific, technical and statistical data with respect to fisheries for straddling fish stocks and highly migratory fish stocks." UN FSA Article 14 and Annex I. Its provisions regarding the States' duties to comply with conservation and management measures are limited to "straddling fish stocks and highly migratory fish stocks." *Ibid*, Articles 18–22.

501 The International Seabed Authority.

502 The Fish Stocks Agreement is in force.

beyond national jurisdiction that are not attached to the Area.[503] Although it does not discuss "genetic resources" or any other ABS concept, it addresses/ regulates the taking of biological resources, and as such appears to be relevant to ABS contracts and other bioprospecting in these areas.

All of this has relevance for contracts involving the utilization of marine genetic resources – providing a reason why the parties need to make it clear whether such resources are being obtained from an area within national jurisdiction or sovereign rights pursuant to a binding contract with the proper provider, and to take care that this activity also complies with both national ABS laws and relevant procedures for marine scientific research. The uncertainty of the future situation with regard to marine genetic resources of the Area and/or of the water column beyond national EEZs suggest a potential mine field that could be much more difficult than the challenges of compliance with multiple relevant legal regimes. Based on Part XI, however, one thing appears clear: If the marine genetic resources beyond national jurisdiction are considered as international resources similar to the minerals of the Area, the user will be required to enter into well-scrutinized contracts or joint ventures with an international body, with no option to enter into a private contract governed by modern contract principles and no enforcement in national courts.[504]

11.5 Specific Provisions Directly Relevant to Drafting ABS Contracts

This section looks at the specific provisions within the international ABS Regime that might have legal relevance for ABS contracts. It is divided into five categories reflecting the most important elements of the global framework from a practical, ABS-contract perspective: sovereign rights (¶ 11.5.1); scope and definitions (¶ 11.5.2); contractual content (¶ 11.5.3); ATK (¶ 11.5.4); and international mechanisms that may impact contractual negotiation and/or implementation (¶ 11.5.5). This overview is clearly not exhaustive, and does not address how any of these international provisions has been implemented at the national level in any country.

503 UNCLOS legal experts refer to the oceans above "the Area" as the "water column."

504 See especially, the Part 11 Agreement. Annex, Section 1, Articles 5 and 6; Section 2; and Section 8. See also Section 5, Article 1(b), indicating that the Enterprise (part of the International Seabed Authority established under Part 11) may have the power to call on parties to such contracts to transfer technology and States to support this action.

11.5.1 *Sovereign Rights (Oversight, National ABS Procedures and User Measures)*

The ABS regime appears to give individual national governments three major roles for each in implementing the ABS process. The first of these roles relates to sovereign rights. Each country has the sovereign right to its genetic resources. This means that all countries have sovereign rights to legislate on all aspects concerning genetic resources. As explained below, however, there are differing views among countries regarding these provisions, suggesting that a country that intends to control access to its genetic resources (through PIC, MAT, permits, certificates and ABS contracts) is advised to adopt legislation clearly stating this intent.

The second national government role is a procedural role, regarding the genetic resources over which the country has sovereign rights. As always, in the exercise of those sovereign rights, countries are expected to adopt procedural systems to regulate access.

The third role relates to the country's obligations with regard to users of another country's genetic resources or ATK. Every country is potentially a user country and specifically obligated under both the CBD and the NP to adopt measures relating to ensuring that the user side of the ABS concept is properly implemented and functional.

In the following paragraphs, the authors discuss these roles and the ways in which each country's commercial and contract law and principles govern not only how contracts are made, but how they interact with ABS.

(a) Sovereignty Issues and the Waiver of PIC

Each State has unquestioned sovereign rights over its genetic resources. These rights form the basis of the entire global biodiversity regime, of the ABS concept,[505] and of many provisions on ATK.[506] Sovereign rights include the

---

505 CBD, Article 3. This was specifically reiterated with regard to genetic resources in both the CBD (CBD, Article 15.1.) and the NP. (NP Article 15.1).

506 NP Article 16.1, Sovereignty issues with regard to ATK are somewhat difficult to interpret legally. For example, the CBD is only open to States to sign. Hence, indigenous communities are not Parties, and all provisions of the CBD discussing the rights and activities of those communities are subject to the States' interpretation and implementation. That said, the NP does appear to presume that particular indigenous communities have their own type of "sovereignty," not only with regard to ATK, but also with regard to their recognized lands and resources. This is clearly an important development in international law, but its meaning scope and import can only be determined by either legal action or the development of a consistent body of international practice. Over the coming years, it

country's internationally recognized authority to unilaterally regulate certain questions concerning its own land, people and resources, without the need for any other country's or institution's approval. Sovereign rights must be enforced by the country. The CBD and NP provisions relating to these sovereign rights do not include any exception for situations in which the user is attempting to gain access to genetic resources in a country has not adopted a law labelled "Access to Genetic Resources and ATK." The authors are not aware of any type of sovereign right that ceases to exist if a country has not adopted legislation addressing it.

As a legal matter, with or without a specific ABS law in any of the countries involved, contracts for access to genetic resources would be governed by existing and relevant national commercial law. As enumerated in ¶ 2.3.2(d), *supra*, the bodies of national law that already exist to address these matters include, for example, the national laws governing various types of property, contractual/commercial law, trade law and the interpretations of equitable principles that have been adopted by the country's courts.[507] These laws, however, merely govern contractual processes. Their application does not alter the question of the provider country's sovereign rights over any type of resources.

The NP partially clarified two important aspects of national sovereign rights with regard to genetic resources: the fact that a country may waive its right to require PIC, and the fact that it may delegate the responsibility/authority to grant PIC. These clarifications, however have led to other controversies.

With regard to the country's right to waive PIC, the issue was initially somewhat equivocally addressed in the CBD Article 15.5, which said that PIC was required "unless otherwise determined by that Party [*i.e.*, the country providing the resources]." The NP specifically provides more clearly, that access to genetic resources "shall be subject to the prior informed consent of the Party providing such resources that is the country of origin of such resources or a Party that has acquired the genetic resources in accordance with the Convention, *unless otherwise determined by that Party*."[508]

---

will be interesting to see how national governments interpret and implement this aspect of the NP.

507 As discussed in Chapter 6, *supra*, the manner in which each country designates and governs the various categories of property will have a significant impact on the validity of ABS contracts. In this respect, international agreements are subordinate to national law, particularly in the context of individual transactions.

508 NP Article 6.1 (*emphasis added.*) The comparable provision on ATK is unequivocal, in that it does not reference any right of either the indigenous/local community holding the knowledge or the country in which it is located to waive PIC with regard to ATK.

Another NP provision identifies specific legislative obligations of countries that have not waived PIC.[509] That clause, however, does not mean that a country that has not formally adopted such legislation can be presumed to have waived PIC.[510] Most international delegations would agree in wishing to avoid any international interpretation that held that sovereign rights are lost through inaction. The lack of measures clarifying the PIC process in the would-be provider country is thus not an implied waiver of that country's right to require PIC. At most, that lack may render it more difficult for the user to obtain PIC and thereby discourage potential users. It cannot alter the Party's sovereign rights regarding its genetic resources and the ATK of communities under its jurisdiction.[511]

The NP and the Bonn Guidelines specifically state that a country may delegate its responsibility to grant PIC and/or to establish MAT. This type of delegation, however, requires a formal decision, whether the country makes a separate decision for each ABS transaction or adopts legislation that applies to all ABS transactions.

TIP

Regardless of whether the provider country has adopted any formal "ABS legislation," the parties to an ABS contract should (i) always comply with the property, contract and commercial laws of the provider country (including laws on the protection of consumers and other contractual parties); and (ii) ensure that the country's government is formally

509 NP Article 6.3.

510 The would-be provider country's lack of measures clarifying the PIC process may render it more difficult for the user to obtain PIC, and thus discourage potential users, but it cannot alter the Party's sovereign rights regarding its genetic resources and the ATK of communities under its jurisdiction.

511 One of the authors adds that: One need only reflect on the legal chaos that would result if this position were upheld and later applied to all types of sovereign rights (in all countries) to realize how potentially harmful this approach would be, and that international jurists would be unlikely to uphold it. Any interpretation that allowed any other sovereign right to be ignored if it weren't specifically addressed in legislation would be quickly rejected. In ABS, such a view would be very unbalanced, given that no country has fully met its user-side obligations under CBD Article 15.7 (As noted in other writings of the authors, Japan, Norway and the EU have adopted attempts at comprehensively meeting those obligations, but have not fully met them.) The failure of a country to adopt user measures has had no negative impact on their users. It appears somewhat unfair to indirectly penalize provider countries for failure to adopt newly required PIC legislation, when no penalty (direct or indirect) applies to user countries that fail to adopt the user-side measures that have been mandatory since the CBD's entry into force in 1992.

informed in the event that any part of the *res* might be considered to be either a genetic resource or ATK, within the scope of that country's sovereign rights, as it interprets them.

(b) Procedural Access Controls (PIC, MAT, ABS Permits) and Participation

The regulation of access is the ABS element about which the greatest number of national laws have been adopted. They range in scope from the simplest provisions which simply repeat the CBD language (calling on the designated agency to adopt regulations and stating the overall goal of enabling "access to genetic resources for environmentally sound uses") to more complex frameworks specifying more demanding implementation requirements. Relatively few countries have adopted full, detailed regulatory requirements, and some of these have proven to have potential for improvement and are, at this writing, being reconsidered or revised.[512] As a result, it is not currently productive to detail the manner in which current national access requirements may impact a transaction. Instead, we briefly consider how the international regime instruments have described the procedural and access elements of national access measures, in particular, PIC, MAT, public participation and the issuance and use of ABS permits/certificates. The contractual relevance of these administrative requirements is discussed below, followed by some explanation of how they could be reflected in the text of the contract.

PIC: In its substantive operation, the PIC concept is similar to the concept of full and fair disclosure, as applied in all contract negotiations (under which, as briefly discussed in ¶ 7.3.3(c), *supra*, a contract is not binding on a party that did not have a full and fair ability to know all relevant facts prior to agreeing to the contract.) There is one major difference between PIC and contractual disclosure: Although full and fair disclosure only refers to the parties to the contract, PIC requires that the provider country's government, (or the agency, community, entity or person designated by that government[513]), should also be informed and give consent. Thus, in some countries, PIC is simply another

512 See, *e.g.*, GEF Projects 5760: Brazil; 3801: India; 5593: Malaysia; and 4962: Costa Rica.

513 The Bonn Guidelines (a non-binding guidance instrument) underscore the fact that PIC is a governmental power, so that if anyone (the provider, a community, or a particular agency or official) is to grant PIC a formal designation is needed. Bonn Guidelines, Annex, §§ 29 through 31.

way to refer to contract negotiation principles. In countries that have decided that ABS contracts should be directly negotiated with particular individuals or communities, however, PIC adds a level of regulatory oversight to the negotiation of contracts involving genetic resources or ATK.

PIC is mentioned briefly in the CBD (Article 15.5), but more frequently referenced in the NP, where it is not only a prerequisite to access (Article 6.1), but also specifically waivable.[514] It is also mentioned in connection with the Global Multilateral Benefit-sharing Mechanism[515] and is considered a critical trigger point of compliance provisions and of the global monitoring regime.[516] Other ABS-related international instruments mention PIC, as well, see particularly, the MOSAICC.[517] Unfortunately, none of these clauses provides any guidance on the nature of PIC. For example, none of them sheds any light on whether the word "informed" implies that the user must provide more than information than would normally be required under contract law.[518]

Although not binding, the Bonn Guidelines, attempted to provide a more detailed discussion of the possible contents of a transparent PIC process, providing for example an outline of the legislative/regulatory outline of a "PIC system."[519] Regarding the actual disclosure (the substantive element of PIC, most relevant to contracts), the Guidelines suggest that PIC should be limited in scope to the specific use disclosed by the applicant, so that a "second PIC"[520] will be required where a different use is proposed or other changes occur.[521] They also provide an "indicative" list of a large number of disclosure items that are suggested as possible required content of PIC. They specifically state, however, that this list is not set in stone, and that it "should be adapted to national circumstances.[522]

Another key aspect of PIC that is important to contract negotiations and drafting relates to the manner in which the consent is actually given. The Bonn Guidelines specifically recommend that both access applications and either the grant or denial of should be "documented in written form."[523]

514 NP, Article 10, see ¶ 11.5.1(a), *supra*.

515 See ¶ 11.5.5(d), *infra*.

516 NP, Articles 13 through 17. See Chapter 8 in this book.

517 MOSAICC, §§ 1.1 and 1.2.

518 See discussion of contractual disclosure issues in ¶ 7.3.3(c), *supra*.

519 Bonn Guidelines, at para 27, *et seq*.

520 See ¶ 3.6, *supra*, for a discussion of the problems with return obligations.

521 Bonn Guidelines, at para 34.

522 Bonn Guidelines, at para 37.

523 Bonn Guidelines, at para 38.

In comparison with ABS contracts, PIC is primarily an administrative/regulatory duty, conferring no contractual rights, and not usually enforceable in other countries.[524] Although the NP contains provisions relating to PIC enforcement, those provisions are quite limited,[525] and do not impose any obligation to enforce another country's PIC requirements.

TIP

In order for a contract clause relating to fulfilment of the PIC requirement to function properly, it must be specific and detailed. It must clarify each party's responsibilities relative to PIC. It should also include a specific mechanism by which the other parties can confirm that PIC requirements have been met. This last need is easily met where national law states that any decision granting or denying PIC must be in writing. The party responsible for complying with PIC need only provide the written consent as received from the authorized person or entity, and the other party need only verify its authenticity.

The MOSAICC, in light of its early establishment, includes "model" forms of PIC, presumably for use in countries that do not have PIC formats of their own.[526] Certainly, it is up to the country to choose the proper PIC format, although the parties may suggest a format, if the country is finding it difficult to do so.

MAT: MAT operates in generally the same manner as the "mutuality" aspects of contract validity (¶ 7.3.1, *supra*). Here also, national implementing legislation may either retain all ABS authority within government, or explain which individuals or communities are authorized to enter into ABS contracts. Where such legislation is adopted, it will determine whether MAT is simply another way to say "ABS contract" (where the government is a party to all ABS

524 As noted in Tvedt and Young, 2007, at ¶ 3.3, it is not usually possible to enforce one country's regulatory instruments and permits in another country.

525 NP Article 15 requires only that "[e]ach Party shall take appropriate, effective and proportionate legislative, administrative or policy measures to provide that genetic resources utilized within its jurisdiction have been accessed in accordance with prior informed consent" and "take appropriate, effective and proportionate measures to address situations of non-compliance"; and "as far as possible and as appropriate, cooperate in cases of alleged violation of domestic access and benefit-sharing legislation."

526 MOSAICC, "Examples of Prior Informed Consent (PIC) documents." The authors have chosen to refrain from commenting on the adequacy of these models, in light of the fact that the format of PIC is a matter of national sovereignty, to be determined by national law, regulation, or other measures.

contracts) or an additional regulatory requirement (where contracts may be entered into with individual or community providers, but the government retains the responsibilities relating to establishing MAT). As noted with regard to PIC, it will then also be necessary for the contract to specific address the parties' responsibilities regarding MAT. The NP includes a provision requiring States to "ensure that an opportunity to seek recourse is available under their legal systems, consistent with applicable jurisdictional requirements, *in cases of disputes arising from mutually agreed terms*."[527] It does not discuss ABS contracts, however, given that it has always been expected that ABS contracts will be enforced under the law of contract, whereas PIC and MAT obligations are designed as regulatory matters, implemented by national law of the providing country.

In theory, MAT should follow the rule explained in Chapter 4 of this book and "BE SPECIFIC AND CONCRETE," if the provider country hopes to utilize foreign courts to enforce it.[528] Unfortunately, where national ABS law uses the ambiguous ABS terminology, or relies on the vague and unspecific "definitions" that were adopted in the CBD, NP, ITPGRFA and SMTA (See ¶ 11.5.2, *infra*), MAT will probably also use these terms.

Public Participation: "Participation"[529] is not required under CBD Article 15. It became a part of the ABS process through the efforts of numerous countries, commentators and consultants, who interpreted the CBD's requirement of "prior informed consent of the Contracting Party [country] providing the resource"[530] to constitute a requirement of public participation.[531] The Bonn Guidelines took a variety of inconsistent positions regarding participation issues,[532] providing little guidance – at most suggesting possible approaches for national legislation. The NP, too, appears to avoid the issue, including only one mention of participation – in the context of the participation of indigenous and local communities in the establishment of mechanisms

527 NP Article 18.2, *emphasis added.*

528 The basic rule that a contract's terms must be sufficiently concrete or the court cannot enforce them applies to virtually all court actions. A court that is petitioned to enforce a foreign administrative instrument, such as MAT or an ABS permit, may conclude that the terms are too non-specific to be enforced. See ¶ 7.3.2, *supra*.

529 The authors are using this term in the sense of the "public participation processes" that is generally recommended as elements of good governance.

530 CBD Art 15.05. In the CBD, the term "Contracting Party" refers to a country that is a Party to the CBD, and is not a reference to ABS contracts or their parties.

531 See, *e.g.*, Swiderska, 2001. Swiderska's work on this issue was generally thought to be definitive and followed by a large number of countries.

532 Bonn Guidelines, Part III "Participation of Stakeholders" §§ 17–21, as well as §§ 16.b.vii, and 14.g and h.

to inform potential users of ATK about their ABS obligations.[533] As such the regime documents offer little useful guidance to contract parties, apart from the lesson that it is essential to be certain that their actions comply with the provider country's legislation and established practices on this issue.

ABS Permits and Certificates: One of the most important changes adopted in the NP process was the concept of the "internationally recognized certificate of compliance" (IRCC).[534] The IRCC is discussed in ¶ 11.5.5, *infra,* in terms of its role in the international monitoring system being developed for the ABS regime. At the national level, however, the IRCC clauses are important for another reason – they formally has recognize the ABS permit.[535] Like all other nationally required and issued administrative approvals, the ABS permit is only legally enforceable within the issuing country. In general, countries have adopted legislation that allows a foreign government to *request* that the country's courts or agencies prosecute a violator of that foreign country's regulations or permit. In general, however, those provisions do not obligate any country to accede to this type of request.[536] Even where enforcement is granted, it provides little benefit to the requesting country. The penalty imposed is normally a fine, rather than an order of compliance. The fine does not benefit the requesting country either, given that all penalties collected are retained by the country in which the action was prosecuted.[537]

Within the issuing country, however, ABS permits have significant potential, because the entire weight of the country's enforcement arm is available. In addition in most countries administrative agencies have powers to take action on permit in a manner that is much more quick and effective than most actions available to parties seeking enforcement of or compliance with a private contract.

---

533 NP Article 12.2.

534 NP Article 17.3.

535 See NP Article 17.2. Article 6.3 (mentioned in 17.2) imposes no obligation on the parties to an ABS transaction, nor does it automatically create national legislation. Presumably, the NP is simply opining that a permit is only effective if it was granted pursuant the legislation adopted in accordance with this paragraph and made available to the Access and Benefit-sharing Clearing-House.

536 This is a long existing issue. See, *e.g.,* Houghton, 1929. ABS commentators in the US frequently cite the Lacey Act, which was originally enacted to address traffic in illegally obtained wildlife. It was found to be non-functional in the manner described in text, however, and that non-functionality was one of the main motivations that drove the negotiation and adoption of the Convention on International Trade in Endangered Species of Fauna and Flora (CITES.) See discussion in Tvedt and Young, 2007, at 3.2.1.

537 Tvedt and Young, 2007, at 3.2.1.

(c) User Measures

As noted in Chapter 1, lack of international agreement on the composition, scope and/or interpretation of a clear legal framework for individual ABS contracts seriously compromises the enforceability and implementability of ABS contracts that rely on that framework for functionality. The *res* of a contract, even if it is regulated by the ABS laws of the provider country, may be outside of the scope of the ABS laws of the user country.[538] Such uncertainties add doubts to any ABS contract, because

(i) the genetic information may be taken to or transferred to other countries besides the provider country, even where the user is required to form a company in the provider country and conduct utilization activities there;[539] and
(ii) a foreign user (even one required to conduct operations or maintain assets in the provider country) will normally have its primary offices and holdings in another country.

Other sources have discussed the basic CBD requirement of "user measures" (Article 15.7) and the legal misunderstandings that have built the ABS system on an unrealistic expectation that such measures can be expected to make the regime functional.[540] Although these issues were well canvassed in the NP negotiations, the Protocol does not address them (apart from extending the user measures obligation to make it clear that it also applies to ATK).[541]

As noted in ¶ 11.5.5(b) and (c), *infra,* the NP's new monitoring system imposes additional, but equally vague, user-side requirements on NP Parties. Specifically the NP imposes an obligation to designate "checkpoints" and adopt relevant procedures. Although the checkpoint requirement is mandatory and

538 See ¶ 11.5.2, *infra,* for a discussion of the manner in which the NP negotiations' lack of agreement on scope and definitional issues affects the stability and predictability of ABS contracts.

539 See Chapter 6, *supra.*

540 Tvedt and Young, 2007, was among the first direct commentaries on these matters.

541 NP Article 6. Apart from the addition of references to ATK, the NP does not move beyond the wording of CBD Article 15.7, and is in some cases reusing the exact language. This is interesting because, as of the final NP negotiating session, 18 years had passed since CBD Article 15.7 had imposed the original user measures requirement, in which time none of the nearly 200 CBD Parties had fully implemented that requirement. During this long time, only a few countries had made any noticeable steps to even partially implement it.

unequivocal,[542] only fifteen countries (eleven of which are in Europe) have designated checkpoints at the time of this writing.[543] It is unclear whether this requirement in the NP will be observed and complied with more fully than the "user-measures" required in the CBD Art. 15.7.

Although some countries had included certificate provisions in their ABS legislation prior to the NP,[544] none of those provisions had functioned. As a result, when adopted in the NP (and still today), the provisions relating to the use of certificates and check-points are entirely experimental in nature. These uncertainties underscore the importance of ensuring that the ABS contract is a fully enforceable commercial contract, completely independent of the (global and national) ABS regimes. Its implementation and enforcement should not be impacted by the vagaries of various interpretations of ABS.

(d) Integrating ABS with Other National and International Law

Another NP legislative issue is the ability to apply many different legal instruments and regimes at the same time, with minimal conflict. This issue (sometimes called "legal integration") is critical for the future of ABS. Every country already possesses a comprehensive body of national laws applicable to all types of commercial transactions. Those long established laws are well understood by all parties, arbitrators, judges and advisors, and are thus more reliable, consistent and predictable than ABS concepts and laws.

By the time that the ABS regime is finally and comprehensively established, it will have found ways to integrate the ABS concept with the well-established body of commercial law. At that point, it is assumed that

542 NP Article 17.1. A full discussion of the checkpoint requirement as well as the legal and practical reasons that it is difficult to implement is beyond the scope of this book. The authors are aware of a book in progress, that focuses on providing guidance for NP Parties seeking to implement their various legislative, regulatory or administrative obligations to adopt "measures, as appropriate." As of this writing, however, production details are not currently available.

543 CBD-Nagoya Protocol website (ABS-CH), last consulted on 5 August 2017. The countries are Belarus, Denmark, Dominican Republic, Finland, Germany, Hungary, Kenya, Malta, Peru, Slovakia, South Africa, Spain, Sweden, Switzerland and the UK.

544 *E.g.*, Costa Rica, *Normas Generales para el Acceso a los Elementos y Recursos Genéticos y Bioquimicos de la Biodiversidad* Arts. 6(f) and 19 ("*...se certifica la legalidad del acceso a elementos o recursos genéticos o bioquímicos de la biodiversidad y el cumplimiento de los términos en los que fue autorizado al interesado el permiso de acceso correspondiente*"); see also Decreto No. 31 514, 2003, issued pursuant to the Organic Law on the Environment (N° 7554 of 4 Oct. 1995) §§ 46–47; and the Biodiversity Law (N° 7788 of 30 April 1998). In 15 years of active ABS application in the country, no user ever sought a certificate. Cabrera Medaglia, Jorge, Personal communication, 26 March 2007.

the national interests in supporting the rapid development and flourishing of contractual relationships will ensure that pre-legislation ABS contracts should still be a valid and enforceable, and will specify how and to what extent new legislation will apply to such contracts.[545] Until then, integration with all relevant national law is an issue that should be addressed in each ABS contract.

11.5.2 *Scope and Definitional Issues*

As noted, the primary task of eliminating ambiguity in the ABS concepts must be addressed by each CBD or NP Contracting Party in its national law.[546] Given that CBD and NP could not come to agreed meanings and methods, countries will undoubtedly develop their own national interpretations and processes. This is likely to increase the variability and uncertainty of ABS for contract purposes. As noted in Chapters 3–9, individual ABS contracts can and should avoid these scope and definitional issues through careful drafting. The body of ABS contracts may ultimately do what the NP negotiators could not. Specifically, it may eventually coalesce into a recognized "standard approach" to ABS contracts. It is important, however, for this body of practical law to integrate unequivocally with the legal requirements of ABS. For this latter reason, we include the following very brief discussion of the contractual issues and the legal hazards embodied in the scope and definitional provisions of the NP.

(a) Geographic, Temporal and Activity-Based Scope

The NP negotiators' were unable to agree on any scoping choices and, as a result were unable to adopt any scope-defining provisions.[547] Thus, the only binding scope provisions regarding ABS are those found in CBD Article 4, which states that the Convention applies within the limits of each Party country and to activities under its control "within the area of its national jurisdiction or beyond the limits of national jurisdiction." As noted in ¶ 11.4, *supra*, this provision is particularly relevant to marine genetic resources, especially those in States that are Party both to the CBD and to UNCLOS.[548]

545 See Tvedt and Young, 2007.

546 Of the other Instruments in the Global ABS regime several (especially the ITPGRFA and its SMTA, and the various drafts prepared under the WIPO negotiations) either copy the CBD/NP definitions or include new ambiguous terminology or both.

547 Legally, it is considered a major error to interpret an international instrument on the basis of items that are omitted, unless the instrument specifically discusses those omissions. Thus, there is only one point that can be inferred from the NP's failure to address critical unanswered scope questions: The Parties were unable to agree.

548 UNCLOS imposes its own system with regard to certain activities outside national jurisdiction. Negotiations are currently ongoing regarding the manner in which "genetic resources in areas beyond national jurisdiction" will be accessed in future.

After final adoption of the NP, there remain many open questions regarding scope. Most of these open questions relate to undefined concepts such as the location of genetic resources or ATK, its country of origin, and/or the time at which it was "acquired in accordance with the [CBD]," "accessed" or "utilized." For example,

- What is the legal the meaning of "acquired in accordance with the Convention"?
- How does one identify the "country of origin"?
- Must the precise origin of every specimen be traced to a specific "country of origin"?
- As of what date is origin or acquisition-in-accordance-with-the-Convention determined?
- Are there genetic resources or ATK that do not come from either a country of origin or a country that acquired them in accordance with the CBD?
- What happens if a user obtains biological samples from a local collection/propagator who had not properly obtained the rights to access/utilize the genetic resources?
- What if different users obtain identical genetic resources from different countries?
- How are patent principles applicable to and/or affected by ABS?[549]

These areas of ambiguity pose a difficult problem for those attempting to make ABS contracts work through application of the ABS regime instruments. The number and importance of such un-resolved questions underscores the need to make every effort to ensure that your ABS contract is interpreted and enforced under contract law, rather than these unpredictable concepts.

(b) *Definition-based Scope Issues*

Given the number of articles and chapters that have been written regarding the ambiguities and vagueness of the CBD's ABS-related definitions, it is not necessary to detail them here. Parties negotiating ABS contracts, however, may find it useful to identify key terms that might create contractual problems and should be avoided.

---

549 Commentators have suggested that granting a patent to an invention based on biological material that occure in more than one country could devalue the source country's interests in its genetic resources, see, *e.g.*, Oh, 2016.

The term "genetic resources" is a good example. As discussed in Chapters 2 and 5, the ABS regime's ambiguous terminology is a problem for those drafting ABS contracts. It is often not possible for the parties to a proposed contract to determine, on the basis of the CBD definition, if their proposed contract involves "genetic resources". After the NP negotiations, efforts to alleviate the problem by concretely adopting other terms were unsuccessful. In the end, countries only adopted similarly unhelpful and vague definitions using different names for the terms,[550] and failed to adopt others.[551] To use any of these terms in a contract would essentially bring the ambiguity of the Nagoya Protocol into that contract, and thus either prevent a judge or arbitrator from ruling on the contract, or cause him to "re-form" the contract, based on his own views of what the parties wanted or should have agreed.[552]

The ITPGRFA provides a useful example of this kind of ambiguity. It defines "plant genetic resources for food and agriculture" to mean "any genetic material of plant origin *of actual or potential value for food and agriculture*."[553] Given that modern biotechnology inserts plant genes in animals and vice versa, and that bioprospecting (under the heading "plant germplasm collection") in the wild has been ongoing for many years,[554] it is difficult to use this definition as a means to differentiate which specific genetic resources are covered by and for the purpose of the ITPGRFA.[555] This is important for ABS contracts, because the NP includes a possible exclusion for resources that are covered by other instruments within the ABS regime.[556]

---

550 "Utilization of genetic resources" and "derivative" are examples of NP terms whose definitions are too ambiguous for contractual use.

551 The negotiators did not attempt definition of many key terms. In particular, despite intensively using the term "traditional knowledge associated with genetic resources," the negotiators did not even attempt to define it.

552 See Chapters 3 and 7, *supra*. Many ABS contracts and national ABS laws compound this problem by not only using these terms, but specifically adding the phrase "as provided in the CBD" (and/or in the NP.) This phrasing will render any contractual clause ambiguous, in light of the ambiguity in the international ABS documents.

553 ITPGRFA Article 2, *emphasis added.*

554 See FAO's "International code of conduct for plant germplasm collecting and transfer"

555 This challenge is underscored by the fact that the IARCs use the non-negotiable SMTA for transfers of species not listed in the Annex to the ITPGRFA.

556 Under NP Article 4.4, "Where a specialized international access and benefit-sharing instrument applies that is consistent with, and does not run counter to the objectives of the Convention and this Protocol, this Protocol does not apply for the Party or Parties to the specialized instrument in respect of the specific genetic resource covered by and for the purpose of the specialized instrument." Thus, it is important to delineate the

By contrast, an example of a clearer delineation for this purpose is found in the WHO Pandemic Influenza Preparedness (PIP) Framework (*supra.*) It defines "PIP biological materials" for purposes of the WHO-SMTAS as follows: "includes human clinical specimens, virus isolates of wild type human H5N1 and other influenza viruses with human pandemic potential; and modified viruses prepared from H5N1 and/or other influenza viruses with human pandemic potential developed by WHO GISRS laboratories, these being candidate vaccine viruses generated by reverse genetics and/or high growth reassortment."[557] This definition tends towards being specific.

Consequently, it is clear that, where a proposed contract involves plant genetic resources, the drafters will need to clarify the parties intentions as to whether the relevant regime is the NP, the ITPGRFA or both.

11.5.3 *Content and Negotiation of ABS Contracts*

In the CBD, national ABS legislative obligations were divided into two categories – access-related measures[558] and benefit-sharing measures.[559] The NP continued this division.[560] Every CBD Party is required to adopt both access measures[561] (including measures for granting PIC[562] and establishing MAT[563]); and benefit-sharing or "user" measures[564] (including measures to recognize PIC and MAT.[565])

Although a number of countries have attempted to regulate access to their own genetic resources effectively and comprehensively, few countries adopted measures that satisfy the benefit-sharing obligation The measures that exist generally address only part of that obligation. A range of legal obstacles are thought to have prevented countries from identifying or developing mechanisms that involve enforcing a provider country's regulatory provisions that impose benefit-sharing obligations.

---

particular nature of the GR, in order to determine whether it is covered by the NP and NP implementing legislation, or by an instrument that qualifies for an Article 4.4 exception.

557 PIP, § 4.1 The PIP also defines "clinical specimens" equally specifically. This enable a clear identification of which specimens/species are covered by the WHO-SMTA and which are not. See, *especially.*, footnote 1 to the PIP framework.

558 CBD Arts. 15.1, 15.2, 15.4, 15.5 and 15.7.

559 CBD Art. 15.7 (directly) and Arts. 15.1 and 15.6 (indirectly.)

560 The NP addresses access-related measures in NP Arts. 6 and 7 and benefit-sharing in NP Arts 15 and 16.

561 CBD Art. 15.2.

562 CBD Art. 15.5.

563 CBD, Articles 15.4 and 15.7.

564 CBD, Article 15.7.

565 CBD, Articles 15.4, 15.5 and 15.7.

In negotiating the NP, States were unwilling or unable to achieve agreement on the key legal issues that had, long prevented implementation of benefit-sharing requirements.[566] In this respect, as discussed in ¶ 11.5.4, *infra,* the NP's most important change was its direct addition of ATK to the ABS regime. The following paragraphs discuss other particular contract issues, in terms of the ABS regime.

(a) ABS Contract Clauses that Address Compliance with National ABS Laws and Regulations

It is important that the parties to individual ABS contracts take pains to ensure that the vagueness and controversies of the ABS regime are not "imported" into their ABS contracts. At the same time, the parties seeking to enter into an ABS contract clearly must comply with these laws.[567] The challenge is to ensure that actions taken for compliance with these laws do not invalidate the contract or prevent it from functioning.

Obviously, to achieve the objectives of an ABS contract, it will be important to ensure that all proposed actions under the contract are in compliance with relevant law. To ensure this, the terms of the ABS contract must specifically address the practical aspects of national ABS legislation. Specifically, it must

566 NP Article 5 reiterates the benefit-sharing obligations; while Articles 6, and 7 provide more details of national access legislation. They give particular attention to more details regarding the relatively simple regulatory concept of the procedures for PIC and MAT in the CBD. None of these provisions addresses in any way the various legal issues that had long prevented ABS from functioning. Article 8 discusses, but does not require, streamlining some access requirements, only asking that the parties "create conditions to promote and encourage research which contributes to the conservation and sustainable use of biological diversity," and noting possible options: "[p]ay due regard to cases of present or imminent emergencies," and "[c]onsider the importance of genetic resources for food and agriculture." MOSAICC (art. 1.2) includes an actual approach for streamlining the PIC process.

567 Under NP Article 15 and 16, the user country also has responsibilities to promote compliance with the laws of the country of the provider. Under NP Articles 15.1 and 16.2, the obligations of the user countries have been less strictly stated, and only require that users prove that PIC have been obtained and MAT have been established. NP Articles 15.2 and 16.2, however, require user countries to "take appropriate, effective and proportionate measures to address situations of non-compliance" with those laws; and NP Articles 15.3 and 16.3 include an (admittedly very soft) obligation to "as far as possible and as appropriate, cooperate in cases of alleged violation of domestic access and benefit-sharing legislation or regulatory requirements." The latter four cited clauses limit the provider country's responsibility to ensuring compliance with *the user country's* laws requiring proof of initial compliance with PIC and MAT.

assign each the various responsibilities that the parties must undertake in order to ensure that they obtain consent and approval for the actions that are required under the contract. The contract must also specifically consider what will happen in the event that the relevant legally authorized person or agency decides not to grant PIC, establish MAT or issue the permit. It must also clarify related issues such as how the costs and time needed for this work affects the contract.

EXAMPLE

a. As a necessary pre-condition of any transfer of all or any part of the res under this contract, or the granting of any rights or incurring any other obligations hereunder, [Party X] agrees to obtain all necessary consents, instruments and permits and to undertake all other governmentally mandated activities necessitated under [name of relevant law] and other national measures relevant to access to, utilization of or benefit-sharing related to genetic resources and/or ATK. [Note, if appropriate, the foregoing sentence may assign particular responsibilities to particular parties.] In the course of this activity, Party X may rely on the reasonable cooperation of all parties, with regard to providing information, executing verifications and all other activities required, including the correction deficiencies identified by the person or agency to whom the application is submitted.
b. Not less than XX days prior to submitting any application or other document to the relevant agency or individual, Party X shall deliver to all other parties copies of the proposed submissions, and shall not address any party's concerns regarding such document, before it is submitted.
c. Party X shall provide all other parties with certified and verifiable copies of all final documents submitted, as well as of all consents, instruments and permits granted and all correspondence leading to or accompanying the grant of each consent, instruments or permit.
d. The costs of obtaining the necessary consents, instruments and permits shall be paid by [specify party or parties]. If the total of these costs exceed $XXX, the parties shall, within XX calendar days from the determination of said costs, mutually agree in writing on how the excess shall be paid and by whom. If the parties fail to reach an agreement on the payment of the excess, this contract shall never commence, and any all deposits held on behalf of either party shall

be returned to that party, less that party's agreed share of settlement costs pursuant to paragraph XX of this contract.

e. The requirements of this paragraph shall be satisfied, and this contract shall commence upon the earlier of the following dates: (i) the date on which all parties have received copies of all necessary consents, instruments and permits, and agree that the requirements of this paragraph XX have been met; or (ii) XX days after the date on which all parties have received copies of all necessary consents, instruments and permits, if no party has objected.

(b) Access Measures

Prior to the NP, the access side of the ABS system was already broadly developed.[568] Although the CBD did not mandate them, nearly all national ABS measures that were adopted were, in fact access measures.[569] The CBD's provisions with regard to access stressed that countries should "not to impose restrictions that run counter to the objectives of this Convention."

The NP's discussion of access measures focuses on PIC. It calls on parties to "take the necessary legislative, administrative or policy measures, as appropriate" and provides general descriptions of the objectives of such measures, without explaining how these measures must (or could) work.[570]

For purposes of ABS contracts, however, the most interesting of these provisions is the NP's call for "clear rules and procedures for requiring and establishing mutually agreed terms." This legislation does not suggest any limit on what may be included in national MAT legislation, nor does it identify any mandatory elements. It merely identifies a list of possible provisions : "(i) A dispute settlement clause; (ii) Terms on benefit-sharing, including in relation to intellectual property rights; (iii) Terms on subsequent third-party use, if any; and (iv) Terms on changes of intent, where applicable."[571]

---

568 "Access" has never been formally defined, and discussions of it range from those that view "access to genetic resources" to mean the scientific and/or commercial utilization of genetic resources to those that assume it refers simply to "physical access" – the right to collect samples.

569 This contrasts vividly with user-side/benefit-sharing measures, which are expressed in mandatory terms binding all 198 CBD Contracting Parties, have only but rarely and incompletely been adopted in 22 years.

570 NP Article 6.3.

571 NP Article 6.3(g).

While the first two of these are relatively standard (see Chapters 8 and 5, respectively), the fact that the NP does not address the legal obstacles to the latter two is unfortunate, as these two issues pose significant problems for ABS contracts (*see* Chapters 5 and 6.)[572]

In addition, these provisions use a number of terms that are not used or clarified elsewhere in the NP.[573] They suggest the existence or relevance of legal standards,[574] despite the fact that no such standards have been agreed or determined (*see* Chapter 12.)

As discussed in ¶ 11.5.1(b), *supra*, MAT can often be a separate concept from the ABS contract. Even so, the NP's discussion of national MAT legislation provides a clear indication of the issues on which the provider country is willing to commit to enforcement (see Chapter 8.)

(c) Fair and Equitable Benefit-sharing

Throughout the ABS regime, reference is made to the fact that benefit-sharing should be "fair and equitable."[575] Although it has a clear legal meaning to some countries, the concept of "equity," is not commonly used in the legal systems of most of the CBD/NP parties. Even in the countries that recognize it as a legal construct, "equity" has very different meaning from country to country.[576] Accordingly, if an ABS contract were evaluated under ABS principles rather than basic contract law, it is not clear how the regime's "fair and equitable" terminology will be applied. In some countries, for example, the idea of equity might serve as a justification for the court's alteration or redesign of the

572 There are contractual provisions on these points that are simple on the surface, however, the national goal in adopting provider-side measures is not "to find the most simplistic legislative provisions," but rather, "to make ABS work properly." To do this, the clause must be externally verifiable, implementable and enforceable – a difficult task.

573 Phrases like "change of intent" and "transparency," for example, are entirely undefined in the NP, and have dozens of potential legal meanings.

574 Although not specific, "within a reasonable period of time" is thought of as an established legal standard, but still must be interpreted in each legal field. To date, there is no basis for knowing how this phrase will be applied in ABS. To add certainty more quickly than waiting for a standard practice to become legally recognized, the Parties should have agreed on an outside time limit (see, *e.g.*, the Cartagena Protocol, Articles 9 through 12.) Since they did not, each country's law must separately come to their own determination.

575 CBD Preamble and Articles 1, 8(j), 15.7 and 19.2; NP Preamble and Articles 5, 8(b), 10, 12.2, 22.5(b).

576 Most textbooks and sourcebooks on international law discuss this issue. An excellent comparative discussion, although limited to comparing the primary European systems, is found in Beatson and Schrage, 2003.

contract, to ensure that its payments and sharing provisions are "equitable." In others, a court might assume that any payment that is agreed "at arms length" (*i.e.*, in a fair negotiation) is equitable by definition, absent allegation of fraud, misrepresentation, nondisclosure or related improprieties, discussed in ¶ 7.3.3, *supra*.

The concept of what constitutes a benefit, and how an "equitable share" is determined is yet another difficult issue on which the international regime instruments shed little light. The CBD and Bonn Guidelines stated only that the parties should share equitably in the "benefits arising from the utilization of genetic resources,"[577] and the latter provided a list of the forms in which payments could be made in ABS transactions, *de facto* choosing not to address the phrase "sharing in a fair and equitable way benefits arising from the utilization of genetic resources," but rather to assume that it actually says "making negotiated monetary or non-monetary payments."[578]

Although it retained the form of words used in the CBD, the operational approach of NP essentially appears to have interpreted the Bonn Guidelines' approach to that phrase.[579] It uses, for example, the Guidelines' indicative list of the various means of payment/sharing that could be used.[580]

With this provision, the NP appears (or at least attempts) to shift responsibility for ABS's conservation impact (which the CBD imposes on all States) to the specific parties to individual ABS contracts. This is a welcome change, especially for researchers, many of whom would be happy if their conservation activities will be considered to be benefits shared under their contract. A similar view of the ABS capacity-building requirement could also be applied to researchers, who are also generally happy to provide capacity-building (workshops, seminars, scholarships, *etc.*), but normally lack the financial ability to provide other types of negotiated benefits.

Other major controversies regarding benefit-sharing were not resolved by the NP negotiators. For example, the NP touched on but did not address the sometimes controversial question of whether and to what extent the user has any right to control or decide the manner in which benefits are distributed

---

577 CBD Articles 1 and 15.7.

578 See Bonn Guidelines, Appendix 2.

579 NP Article 5.4.

580 NP Annex. That list includes the results of research regarding genetic resources and/or ATK; financial, informational, technological and other benefits arising out of the R&D, utilization and commercialization of genetic resources and/or ATK; and "subsequent applications" of genetic resources and/or ATK.

within the provider country.[581] On one hand, its strong support for the national regulation of PIC and MAT processes, in which benefit distribution is included, suggests that the NP recognizes that such distribution choices are generally a matter of the provider country's national sovereignty. On the other, its strong language regarding ATK and genetic resources of indigenous and local communities is somewhat ambiguous. The ABS regime instruments also leave many open questions regarding the confidentiality of data, samples and other information.

(d) The SMTA and Other Contract Guidance from the ABS Regime

The ITPGRFA is frequently identified as a potential model for ABS, but equally often its approach has been described as inapplicable or irreproducible. The authors, although noting that many aspects of the ITPGRFA do not appear useful for ABS implementation, also note that some particular details and elements of the Treaty may provide useful guidance. Specifically, the Treaty is among the first attempts to address ABS sectorally. Ongoing efforts (although sometimes unsuccessful) to ensure that the ITPGRFA meets its stated goal of operating "in harmony with the CBD"[582] have taught the Parties to both instruments a great deal about how inter-instrument cooperation will work,

With regard to ABS contracts, the most relevant aspect of the ITPGRFA is its "standard material transfer agreement" (SMTA). This form contract has met with approval from many commentators who have even suggested that, the SMTA should become the model for all ABS documentation. Unfortunately, the SMTA's creation and use involved numerous formative issues that are totally unique to the SMTA and not relevant to other sectors. Consequently, the authors generally do not agree with the suggestion that all ABS contracts should use the SMTA. We do, however, feel that the SMTA is worth discussing, because it is already one of the best known ABS contracts. The following brief summary focuses both on clarifying which elements should definitely not be copied or imitated and pointing out the elements that provide useful lessons and/or are worth emulating.

---

581 See, for example, the MOSAICC provision regarding monetary benefit-sharing: "MOSAICC recommends that monetary compensations to those that provide or enable access to MGRs should be dedicated to technical and scientific co-operation programmes." MOSAICC, Art. 1.7.

582 See NP Article 4.4. As noted in ¶ 11.4.2(b), *supra,* it is not clear to what extent the Treaty meets this clause's requirements.

Unlike other models that have been prepared or proposed, the SMTA has been formally put in place in a way that mandates its widespread use.[583] Unfortunately, because its use is mandatory under the ITPGRFA and its terms may not be changed in any way, its desirability as a "model ABS contract" is doubtful. Moreover, some commentators have noted that the SMTA was negotiated by persons and entities that will not be parties to the individual contracts, when used.[584] They suggest that models created in this way are rarely appropriate for use in negotiated contracts.

There are many legal uncertainties relating to the SMTA, including how it triggers benefits. At the time of this writing, the ITPGRFA Governing Body has authorized work on revising the SMTA to enable users to unilaterally withdraw from their commitments (with the objective of making the use of PGRFA through the Treaty's Multilateral System more desirable to users.) Such revisions may increase uncertainties. Consequently, it appears that the ITPGRFA is not an appropriate model for ABS contract negotiators who are hoping that their contract will be enforceable.[585]

11.5.4 *ATK Contract Issues*

Undoubtedly, the most important change that the NP made to the ABS concept was its specific inclusion of ATK within the ABS framework. Unfortunately, in

583 Initially, the Treaty's Governing Body required that all genetic resources transferred through the Treaty's Multilateral System (MLS) must be addressed only through the SMTA, and specifically allowed the International Agricultural Research Centres (IARCs) to make use of the SMTA mandatory for all genetic resource transfers, even those involving specimens of species that are not included in the Annex to the ITPGRFA (the Annex lists all crops and forages that are included within the MLS), and thus not "transferred through the MLS.

584 Even if the motivations underlying the negotiation of another ABS contract are identical to your own, it is not advisable to copy a clause from a final contract (See ¶ 3.5.1, *supra*.)

585 Among other legal uncertainties, there are many doubts about the impact of the SMTA's use of the so-called "click-wrap" and "shrink-wrap" mechanisms on the contractual rights of the parties to the SMTA. This is particularly problematic, because according to the ITPGRFA, even though the SMTA is pre negotiated and unchangeable, in case of a contractual dispute under a particular SMTA, enforcement obligations rest exclusively with the parties to that SMTA (SMTA Article 8). In addition, the relevant law is problematic where the SMTA is applied to species not listed in the ITPGRFA Annex, and specifically how ABS benefit-sharing requirements apply where there is no specific indication that the provider country agreed to inclusion of such specimens in the collection that is entering into the SMTA. Finally, as discussed in Chapters 3 and 7, *supra*, the legal obligations implied by the special role given to FAO (using a new interpretation of the term "third-party beneficiary") is uncertain.

making this change, the negotiators did not define ATK or explain the legal mechanisms by which ABS can function when applied to ATK.[586] In many instances, the NP includes strong and mandatory language regarding ATK and the genetic resources of indigenous and local communities. These obligations, however, are rendered quite ambiguous for purposes of implementation and contracts owing to NP's failure to address the essential differences between ATK and genetic resources. The NP's provisions are phrased in a fashion that makes it almost impossible to even imagine how an ABS contract regarding ATK be negotiated, regulated, adopted, implemented and/or enforced.

The NP also broke new ground in recognizing another separate concept: "genetic resources held by indigenous and local communities."[587] Closely related to these discussions is the ITPGRFA concept of "farmers' rights," which clearly must be integrated into any ABS contractual work involving traditional varieties and farming methods. In addition to briefly describing these concepts, this section considers the additional special challenges contract parties may face where their ABS contract involves ATK or the genetic resources held by ILCs.

(a) Failure to Address the Difference between ATK and Genetic Resources

Despite significant differences in the nature of the resources,[588] the nature of the providers, the types of protection and other restrictions already provided under the law, and the motivations of the parties involved, the NP essentially treats ATK identically to genetic resources. In doing so, the NP provides no guidance on how the regime should actually function with regard to ATK.[589] Its ATK provisions parrot the general clauses from the genetic-resource-related provisions, adding only a few uncorrected grammatical differences and a rather unspecific statement that PIC requirements must be delegated to the indigenous/local communities involved.

---

586 The term is not defined in the CBD either. For almost 20 years, the IGC under WIPO has been discussing the need for a legal definition of "traditional knowledge" as a term usable in a system for intellectual property rights, without any agreement.

587 NP Article 5.2.

588 Genetic resources are very different from ATK in many dimensions.

589 In many instances, the NP includes separate provisions regarding ATK. For example, following its provisions on "access to genetic resources" (NP Article 6), benefit-sharing relating to the utilization of genetic resources (NP Article 5.1 and 5.3), and compliance with the provider country's access requirements and MAT (NP Article 15). The NP includes separate provisions on "access to traditional knowledge associated with genetic resources" (NP Article 7); benefit-sharing related to ATK (NP Article 5.2 and 5.5) and compliance relating to ATK (NP Article 16.)

The NP omitted the "ATK phrase" from several other key provisions.[590] Many of the NP's more detailed efforts to clarify ABS concepts mention only genetic resources. As a legal matter, this suggests two possible interpretations – (i) that the more detailed provisions apply (possibly *mutatis mutandis*) to ATK as well; or (ii) that the NP Parties did not intend to apply these provisions to ATK. In negotiating ABS contracts relating to ATK, it does not necessarily matter which of these is true. What matters is the lack of certainty: One cannot predict which of the two positions will be upheld if a particular ATK contract or permit were tested in the courts. As a result, the parties to an ATK contract cannot be certain that it will be legally enforceable, or that the permit received will be legally considered to be a "final decision."[591] It is thus essential to tread carefully within contracts addressing this range of issues, ensuring that their enforceability depends on contract law, rather than the NP or national NP implementing legislation. It is also critical, however, to take special care to ensure that no part of the contract triggers or violates national ABS measures related to ATK.

(b) Genetic Resources of ILCs

Another important separate provision discusses benefit sharing with regard to genetic resources held by indigenous and local communities.[592] This provision speaks of the genetic resources that are "held" by ILCs, and of "domestic legislation regarding the[ir] *established rights*" (emphasis added). Once again, these phrases raise legal questions. The term "held" implies a legal right. The phrase "established rights" has an important legal connotation – suggesting that rights over the resources must be formally established either under the country's general legal system, or under a traditional system that is legally recognized under national law.[593] Both of these issues are extremely uncertain of interpretation, once again indicating that the parties to an ABS contract involving indigenous and local communities should exercise care and obtain

590 Its omission is most notable in Article 1 ("Objective"), which is nearly identical to the third objective of the CBD. Coupled with the lack of definitions, and the fact that operative provisions on ATK do not consider in any respect the key differences between ATK and other resources, these omissions (and indeed the entire Protocol) constitute an intense and wide-ranging challenge for the field of traditional knowledge protection.

591 The question of when and whether a country has come to a "final decision" on an ABS application is a critical component of "legal certainty." It is extremely important to building a binding ABS contract, given that it is critical for the contract to specify how the parties will divide the responsibility for ensuring that all requirements of national ABS measures have been satisfied. See ¶ 11.5.3(a), *supra*.

592 NP, Art. 5.2.

593 NP Articles 5.2 and 6.2.

governmental and legal advice, to ensure that their contract is not later subject to challenge.

(c) Farmers' Rights

Although not specifically addressing ATK, the ITPGRFA includes strong commitments in this area, under the heading of "farmers' rights." As in the case of ATK under the NP, the ITPGRFA does not include any concrete mechanisms for protecting and supporting those rights. It does however including the specifically enunciate the farmers' "right to equitably participate in sharing benefits arising from the utilization of plant genetic resources for food and agriculture,"[594] a statement that is generally stronger than any comparable statement in the CBD.[595] It specifically identifies the rights under discussion, to include the right "to equitably participate in sharing benefits," but does not directly discuss this right in the context of farmers' rights. It also extends beyond the NP, by using the verb "protect" in relation to traditional knowledge held by farmers.[596] These substantive provisions are somewhat ambiguous, however, and the ITPGRFA places the duty of figuring out how to resolve those ambiguities on the countries themselves.[597]

(d) Contractual Negotiation and Drafting Involving ATK

Although it does not clarify or provide guidance on what ATK is and how a contractual approach to access to ATK would actually function, some of the provisions of the NP do suggest the need for caution in any transaction involving ATK or genetic resources of ILCs. One of the clearest examples is Article 12.4, which states,

> Parties, in their implementation of this Protocol, shall, as far as possible, not restrict the customary use and exchange of genetic resources and

594 ITPGRFA Article 9.2b.

595 The general view of the Treaty as more conservative and less protective than the CBD, is partly belied by its extension of farmers' rights beyond the range of the CBD's protection of ILCs and Traditional Knowledge. The Treaty's benefit-sharing, however, which occurs through a broad-dissemination "facilitated access" system for distribution of benefits (the MLS), does not require identification of (or direct sharing with) the precise source or provider, making this "right" easier to adopt.

596 ITPGRFA Article 9.2a.

597 Article 9.2 leaves the realizing Farmers' Rights up to national governments who may protect Farmers' Rights "in accordance with their needs and priorities ... as appropriate, and subject to national legislation."

associated traditional knowledge within and amongst indigenous and local communities in accordance with the objectives of the Convention.

As guidance for parties drafting a contract, this provision is not clear. For example, what would constitute a "restriction"? How will the law interpret "community"?[598] If an ABS contract with one community transfers ATK that is also held by a neighboring community, does this restrict the second community's customary use and exchange of genetic resources and associated traditional knowledge?[599]

In the past, the ambiguity and lack of functional guidance or substantive agreement regarding the basic factors relating to ABS contracts for ATK were often cited by users who had adopted their own rule – "avoid any situation involving traditional knowledge."[600] For most providers and provider countries, however, the goal is to avoid scaring off possible users, and to encourage them to enter into contracts. This latter goal is best achieved where the ABS/ATK laws are clear, and/or where the contracts are unambiguous under relevant contract law.

Finally, it is possible that many of the NP's provisions may be interpreted as international "public policy" in favor of protecting – and sharing the benefits from utilization of – ATK.[601] As discussed in ¶ 7.3.3(e), contracts are normally interpreted in accordance with the "public policy" of the country where the law is being interpreted. If that country is a Party or signatory to the NP or participated on record in other negotiations on these issues, the NP's protection of ATK and ILCs may be found to be public policy of that country and applied by the courts in interpreting ABS contracts.

598 For example, is any group of local residents a "community" for this purpose and able to enter into an ABS contract for its resources, or must the term only apply where the community and its leadership are formally recognized?.

599 The problem of identical genetic resources in the possession/ownership of multiple users permeates the entire ABS regime. The NP focuses this point with regard to ILC situations, but these provisions address only international (transnational) shared resource situations (Article 11.1.) In addition, Article 10 call for a "global mechanism" to be developed in future.

600 As discussed in several sessions of the Norway/UN Conference on Technology Transfer and Capacity Building, commercial companies generally avoid entering into negotiations where the legal situation is unclear, especially where there is a possibility that they might be subject to liability or bad publicity or labelled as a "biopirate."

601 See, *e.g.*, NP Article 12, which focuses on mandating the development of national domestic law on ATK, informing and protecting the rights of ILCs, and providing various aspects of capacity building.

TIP

As a result of these uncertainties, the task of negotiating and drafting an ABS contract involving ATK continues to be as problematic after the NP as it was before. Clearly, each ATK contract will need to be as specific and formal as possible in confirming that the persons purporting to act for the community are properly authorized. It should also give special attention to demarcating the extent to which other persons within and outside the community are restricted by that contract. To the extent possible, it is recommended that the parties make every effort to obtain governmental clearance before drafting the contract. Finally, as discussed throughout this book, it will be advisable to avoid making specific reference to the NP or using any ABS-regime terms (especially "traditional knowledge" "genetic resources," "farmer's rights" and "indigenous community") in the contract. Throughout the drafting, however, in order to make sure that the contract is clear and concrete enough to be enforceable, the negotiator will need to be aware of the NP provisions and open questions that could potentially lead to misunderstandings.

11.5.5 *International Elements Affecting Contract Negotiation and Drafting*

Although not relying on the international regime, ABS contracts should be drafted with awareness of the various international mechanisms within it. Their relevance to the contract may be simply described: Either they impact contract formation, or they may, in the future, impact contract implementation. This section very briefly discusses the possible impacts of four of the primary global ABS mechanisms on ABS contracts.

(a) Institutional Connectivity: Focal Points and Other Linkages

The Bonn Guidelines and the NP both mandate and discuss the designation of national focal points (NFPs) and competent national authorities (CNAs) with specific responsibility for ABS.[602] As nationally designated ABS resource persons, it is important to know whether the advice given to ABS contract parties by the NFP and/or CNA can be binding, so that it will impart legal certainty for

602 NP, Article 13; Bonn Guidelines, §§ 13–16.

any party that follows such advice. This question is not answered in the NP and thus is left to national law.

(b) The ABS Monitoring System: Checkpoints and Certificates

The ABS experience between 1992 and 2010 demonstrated the recognized need for a durable international operational ABS framework for monitoring and supporting the function of ABS. Many negotiators believed that such a monitoring system would need to be certificate-based and global in scope.[603] In addressing these points, the negotiations were hobbled by lack of experience. During the first 18 years of ABS under the CBD, no country had adopted a certificate process that was functionally able to address these needs.[604] Hence there was no practical method of determining whether such a system would work, how certain elements would affect its functionality or what provisions would be needed.

Ultimately, the NP adopted some elements of a monitoring system, which it describes in text as a tool "to support compliance." The monitoring system is also expected to "enhance transparency about the utilization of genetic resources."[605]

The three primary components of the NP's monitoring system are (i) checkpoints, (ii) documentation (either the "internationally recognized certificate of compliance" (IRCC) or the ABS permit) and (iii) the ABS Clearinghouse (ABS-CH). The first two components are discussed below. Owing to its broader scope, the ABS-CH is separately discussed in ¶ 11.5.5 (c), *infra.*

Overall, the monitoring system will focus only on the proof of three facts regarding genetic resources and/or ATK that is being utilized outside of the provider country:

- That PIC has been properly obtained;
- That PIC was granted by the proper country (the "source of the genetic resources"); and
- That MAT has been established.[606]

---

603 Fernández-Ugalde, 2005; Fernández-Ugalde, 2004.

604 Some national laws included a certificate option, but there is no evidence that it functioned as a monitoring system (or even that it functioned at all.) In Costa Rica, for example, in two decades of such a clause, no transaction participant had ever sought a certificate, and no country adopted user measures that would make one necessary or useful. A more recent certificate process in Australia appears to have neither external application, nor a monitoring purpose.

605 NP, Article 17.

606 NP, Articles 17.1(a)(i).

Each country is required to establish checkpoints. Apart from stating that they "should be relevant to the utilization of genetic resources," the NP does not provide any indication of what a "relevant" checkpoint might be.

Checkpoints must address each of the three bullet points listed above, but they will not necessarily receive a copy of the MAT. They are not required to know or review the contents of the MAT nor to oversee or confirm how the resources are being utilized.[607] The checkpoint's primary activity involves receiving the IRCC.

The permit/certificate aspect of the monitoring system calls for the checkpoint to receive either the IRCC or "a permit or its equivalent" that is issued in accordance with NP Article 6.3(e).[608] The checkpoints are to be mandated to receive "relevant information related to prior informed consent, to the source of the genetic resource, to the establishment of mutually agreed terms, and/or to the utilization of genetic resources, as appropriate."[609] Where used, the IRCC is supposed to "serve as evidence that the genetic resource which it covers has been accessed in accordance with prior informed consent and that mutually agreed terms have been established, as required by the domestic access and benefit-sharing legislation or regulatory requirements of the Party providing prior informed consent."[610] The NP specifies the minimum information that must be included in such document (to the extent that such information is not confidential).[611] Specifically, the IRCC must name the issuing authority and must include the date; identify the provider "person or entity to whom prior informed consent was granted"; the "subject-matter or genetic resources covered." Finally it must include a unique identifier (certificate number); "confirmation" of PIC and MAT; and "commercial and/or non-commercial use."

As of this writing, the NP's checkpoint/certificate system is not functional. Only fifteen countries have thus far declared a total of 33 checkpoints.[612] It is relatively clear that the international ABS monitoring system will not be

607 Article 17's requirement that national ABS measures "shall include... encouraging users and providers of genetic resources to include provisions in mutually agreed terms to share information on the implementation of such terms, including through reporting requirements," provides no basis for user-side oversight of MAT compliance.

608 NP Article 17.1(c).

609 NP Article 17.1(a).

610 NP Articles 17.3.

611 The NP's incomplete and poorly drafted clauses on confidential information (NP Articles 17.4, 14.2 and 17.1(a)(iii)) do not address any of the key legal points necessary for a contract or clause to be identified as confidential. Confidentiality clauses in legislation are very difficult, and if not carefully overseen, their use can essentially eliminate the effectiveness of any reporting or other information-based provision.

612 According to the ABS CH, when consulted on 5 August 2017.

established or be free from controversy in the near future. Until that system is actually in place and functioning, it is not possible to make a comprehensive legal analysis of it or give clear advice as to how best to draft contract provisions with regard to its requirements.

> TIP
>
> In drafting, it will be essential to clarify which party is responsible (on a continuing basis) for compliance with the global monitoring requirements, which countries the utilization will occur in, and what information, if any, is confidential. It will be important to work with the provider country's designated officials, as well, to ensure that all persons or entities that might be involved in the process are "on the same page" with regard to the monitoring system.

A further gloss on the monitoring issue is the MOSAICC monitoring provision, which calls for the use of a Global Unique Identifier (GUID), as an aid in the monitoring and tracing of genetic resource movement.[613] It is not yet clear whether and how a GUID system could apply to track not only the movement of samples but the utilization of all genetic resources and/or whether a comparable process could apply to ATK.

(c) The ABS-CH

Although it is a key part of the monitoring system, the ABS-CH has a much broader role.[614] By their use of this mechanism the negotiators' indicated their commitment to information-sharing at the broadest level.[615] For contract parties, the most important aspect of the ABS-CH is its role in the monitoring system – the publication of IRCCs and ABS permits. The NP does not state who (user, provider, user-country, or provider-country) is authorized to make the choice between submitting an IRCC and submitting a permit or its equivalent, nor does it state who is authorized to submit the selected instrument to the ABS-CH.[616] In implementing the Protocol, however, the apparent decision was

613 See footnote 482, *supra*.

614 NP Art. 14 ("The Access and Benefit-sharing Clearing-House and Information-sharing.").

615 On the other hand, however, this blithe acceptance of the CHM approach ignores the fact that neither the CHM nor the Biosafety Clearing-House (BCH, adopted by the Cartagena Protocol on Biosafety) functions in a reliable way. See Young, 2013.

616 NP, Articles 17.1(a)(iii) and 17.2. There is no requirement in this clause that the "permit or equivalent" contain the information listed in the IRCC.

made to place this among the types of filings that may only be made by national governments.[617] So long as the accepted practice is that only the original provider country posts certificates, contract parties will have some level of certainty regarding what information is posted and made generally available.

Another important aspect of the ABS-CH for those seeking to negotiate ABS contracts is informational. Under the NP, the ABS-CH may also be a source for accessing each Party's "legislative, administrative and policy measures on access and benefit-sharing";[618] designation of its national focal point (NFP) and competent national authority (CNA);[619] and (optional) "model contractual clauses;... (c) methods and tools developed to monitor genetic resources; and ... codes of conduct and best practices,"[620] (discussed in Chapter 11, *infra.*) These may all be very useful to the contract parties.

The ABS-CH's mandate is to "provide access to information made available by each Party relevant to the implementation of this Protocol."[621] In this connection, it could be particularly useful to the parties to ABS contracts if the parameters are set in a functional way. It is also, however, potentially subject to the problems created by the NP's failure to explain the meaning and standards of its use of the phrase "confidential information."[622] Although the other clearinghouses[623] have not been used in this way, it is possible that the ABS-CH (and the rules applied in implementing it) could become a mechanism for resolving these problems.[624]

(d) The Global Multilateral Benefit-sharing Mechanism

NP Article 10 is one of the most legally challenging aspects of the Protocol. It calls on the NP Parties to consider developing a global mechanism to address "the fair and equitable sharing of benefits derived from the utilization of genetic resources and traditional knowledge associated with genetic resources that occur in transboundary situations or for which it is not possible to grant or obtain prior informed consent." The legal challenges involved in this question were obviously too complex to be addressed by the NP negotiators.

617 There are two categories of filings: "national records" and "reference records." ABS-CH on 10 October 2015.

618 NP, Article 14.2(a).

619 NP, Article 14.2(b).

620 NP Article 14.3(b), (c) and (d).

621 NP, Article 14.1.

622 NP, Article 14.2.

623 The CBD's Clearinghouse Mechanism or "CHM," and the Cartagena Protocol's Biosafety Clearinghouse (BCH.)

624 See, Morgera, *et al.*, 2014, at 451–505.

At this writing, these issues are the subject of intensive negotiation in an expert group, charged with making a recommendation on the implementation of Article 10.[625] Many commentators have been drawn to the possibility that Article 10 implementation will clarify some of the immense ambiguities of ABS. If this happens, the results may be of great value for contract parties. Apart from that, however, the most important aspect of Article 10 For parties to an ABS contract is the possibility that the particular resource or ATK that is the subject of their contract might be found to be in a "transboundary situation," or that it might be considered a "genetic resource ... for which it is not possible to grant or obtain prior informed consent." If either of these possibilities should arise, the creation of the Global Mechanism could be extremely significant to the contract negotiations. For this reason, it will be important for all ABS contracts to be as specific as possible about their subject matter and how it is defined.[626]

---

625 Just a year after the agreement of the NP, an informal group discussion about Art. 10 was held at the Fridtjof Nansen Institute. A number of core questions that will need to be clarified were discussed in that session. Tvedt, 2011.

626 See *Chapter 5, supra.* The MOSAICC system may offer some insights into the type of clarification that may be needed, useful or accepted by courts, in order to address the challenge of "shared" genetic resources and/or ATK. It formally includes a "regularizing" mechanism for microorganisms into the system, which involves recording an "electronic tag." MOSAICC describes this as a "correcting measure [that] will fulfil the need to identify the *in situ* origin of the strains by recording and transferring the adequate information. This measure must remain exceptional. It is intended to get back into the regular circuit MGRs that have for any reasons bypassed the standard procedure."

CHAPTER 12

The Risks and Benefits of Shortcuts: Models, Forms, Guidelines and Existing-contract Examples

Anytime a complex legal issue applies to contracts, there is a call for the development of "model contracts" or "model clauses" to help the parties address those issues properly. "Standard forms" may also sometimes be developed or proposed. When neither models nor forms are available or satisfactory, the parties to contract negotiations may often attempt to use a contract from another transaction as a pattern for their current negotiating draft.

In many cases, the use of models, forms, and pre-existing contracts is an excellent idea, beneficial to all parties. There are, however, many risks and pitfalls, if these tools are used improperly or indiscriminately. This chapter offers advice regarding the use of models, forms and pre-existing contracts to shortcut past some ABS legal and negotiating challenges. It begins with a brief summary of the reasons that models, forms and other recent contracts are attractive ABS options (with particular attention to the Nagoya Protocol's provisions that refer to models and/or specific format matters) (¶ 12.1). This is followed by a description of the basic types of ABS model instruments (¶ 12.2) and a brief discussion how to select and evaluate models, forms and examples for use in your own negotiation and drafting processes (¶ 12.3). It ends with a brief look at the future work in the development of model clauses in ABS, as well as the related work on guidelines and community protocols (¶ 12.4).

12.1 The Desire for "Model Contracts," "Model Clauses" and Other Examples in ABS

Whenever a complex legal issue affects a contract under negotiation, the parties and their advisors wisely search for all available help. Often they will turn to copies of other contracts that have addressed the same problem, standard forms that may apply to it, and model provisions that have been developed. In light of the number of challenging and often unresolved legal complexities in ABS, it is not surprising that the Nagoya Protocol negotiators, too, expressed a desire for such tools. The following paragraphs begin by looking at the relevant elements of the Nagoya Protocol (and other instruments in the global

 | DOI 10.1163/9789004356573_013

ABS regime), then lists the possible benefits to the parties if competent models are eventually developed.

As noted above, studies have indicated that if a party's obligations under a contract are highly detailed and clear, the possibility of a legal problem that cannot be solved by compromise and negotiation actually decreases. Thus, a legally competent model may greatly improve the likelihood that an ABS contract will be fully implemented.

12.1.1 *The Call for Forms and Models in the Global ABS Regime*

In reviewing the NP's provisions regarding models, it is important to recall that there are two distinct types of models considered in that instrument: model legislation and model contracts. These calls came primarily from users, for a simple reason. Negotiation of ABS contracts often takes a rather long time. Users want "easy access" to genetic and ATK resources. Their need to streamline the process is even more intense when they are working in countries that do not have current or complete ABS legislation, and when negotiating with officials or individuals with limited experience with contracts. In those countries, users face the added concern that they might later be accused of "biopiracy."[627] Since it is not a book about legislation, this book does not include any further discussion of the proposals for "model legislation" and/or "model legislative provisions."[628]

627 Throughout the negotiations, many delegations noted that in many developing countries no legislation had been adopted governing ABS, and that often, when it did exist, such legislation was so general that it could not be formally applied in the courts of a developing country or international tribunals. (In 2009, although many national legislative documents were filed in the Convention Clearinghouse Mechanism's database of national ABS legislation, fewer than 25 countries had actually adopted basic operational elements of provider-side ABS operations.) Some delegations even proposed that these models be adopted as "default provisions" – *i.e.*, when a country had no ABS law, or a user had not obtained MAT, then the courts in the user country could apply the model provisions to fill the gaps.

Earlier commentators had claimed that the lack of legislative implementation of ABS in developing countries was indicative of those countries' lack of interest in ABS (still affirmed by Scott, 2006). By 2009, however, it was clear that this was not the case. It was agreed, however, that the lack of clear ABS legislation could create undue stresses on users and that model or default legislation might be offered in a way that did not interfere with the Parties' sovereign rights (Young and Tvedt, 2009.)

628 Arguably, that issue is now dead, given that none of the States that are Party to the NP agreed to give up any part of their sovereign right to determine which legislation applies to activities and assets in their countries.

The discussion of model contractual provisions, however, had a different source.[629] This chapter examines several practical aspects that did not arise in the NP negotiators' discussion of models. The following is a brief history of the concept of model contracts and model provisions in ABS.

Throughout more than 20 years of genetic resource contracts, the problem with ABS contracts, as seen from a providers' perspective, was the user's lack of compliance. This was a serious problem. Even the most successful contracts produced only "up-front benefits," with none of the users identifying any result as a basis for sharing the benefits that "arose out of their utilization" of those resources.[630] Often the earliest contracts were essentially irreproducible. Another country would, for numerous reasons, find that its position was too different from the position of the country involved in the prior contract.[631]

Although, by 2009, many contracts had been completed and signed and made publicly available, most of them were not enforceable for some reason, most commonly lack of concretely stated rights and obligations.[632] In a few cases, ABS contracts were well publicized as excellent examples of how the ABS

---

629 As finally adopted, the NP does not even discuss model legislation, although it clearly indicates the need for governmental measures (including legislative, administrative and other measures) and clearly indicates that other national laws apply to govern issues and activities that are addressed in ABS legislative measures. In three provisions, it calls for particular action, but limits that call with the words "[i]n accordance with domestic law." (NP §§ 6.2, 7, and 12.1.) Ten other provisions require only "measures," modified the words "as appropriate." (NP §§ 5.2, 5.3, 5.5, 6.2, 6.3, 7, 16.1, 16.2, 17.1 and 18.3) Given that this phrasing was used in the CBD with regard to "user measures" that were to be adopted by all CBD Parties, and that after more than 30 years no country has fully complied with this provision, there is little expectation of compliance with these measure, unless the ABS regime becomes desirable enough that States choose to comply, in order to solidify their participation in the regime. Finally, in several clauses (compliance, awareness-raising and capacity-building) provisions, measures are required without the softening language of "as appropriate" or in accordance with domestic law. (NP § 15.1, 15.2, 21 and 22.3.) It remains to be seen how these requirements will be interpreted in national legislation.

630 As of 2000, the benefits receive via Costa Rica's highly publicized ABS system, which had been in place with at least one major contract since 1998, were characterized as (i) vast amounts of foreign AID and services invested in the development of that national ABS system and institutions and a significant (ii) numerous pieces of used laboratory equipment provided by users as front-end payments for access to genetic resources and used in that national ABS system. Global Biodiversity Forum, 2000, at CBD fifth Conference of Parties (COP V).

631 The investment of foreign AID in the development of another system like Costa Rica's is manifestly unlikely. Consequently, the early practice of writing ABS contracts that are virtually identical to the published versions of Costa Rica's contract was clearly inadvisable.

632 Young and Bhatti, 2009.

concept should work. Only later, when they failed did the parties consider the reasons for the failure (such as bankruptcy,[633] bad faith,[634] and poorly drafted contractual protections[635]) that may not have been noticed in the original negotiations. In the meantime, between all of the publicity and the realization of failure, such contracts were sometimes copied by others, who thus incorporated the same failings into their own relationship. As a result of this history, there was a strong call from developing countries for model instruments and clauses. User companies and organizations that use models quickly joined in this discussion, preferring that models be negotiated at the international level with them at the table.

The SMTA example offered hope. But in the end, all it proved was that negotiating a contract between diplomats at an international level does not guarantee that the end product is actually a workable contract. Moreover, the situation of the parties to the SMTA could not be more different from that of most ABS contract negotiations. The provider under the SMTA is mostly an international collection (a "middleman," in effect), which has acquired genetic resources from many persons, but primarily from foreign collectors, rather than provider countries or their nationals.

The collections' intent was to continue to provide the resources essentially free of charge. The SMTA supports this goal, but as a result of having been diplomatically negotiated by a group numbering in the dozens or hundreds, it ultimately reduced the benefit-sharing obligations to an unchangeable "gentleman's agreement."[636] In such situations, when the text is not a functional contract, one cannot expect it to deliver the level or type of results on benefit sharing that developing countries expected. Unfortunately, having agreed to a negotiated model, the parties are stuck with a non-enforceable model. This is

633 One of the earliest Hoodia contracts, between a now-defunct company and a group of San People in Southern Africa failed due to the bankruptcy of the company formed with well publicized social-welfare and profit motivations. See generally, Young, 2005.

634 The Teff Agreement between Ethiopia, a Dutch company, which later declared bankruptcy after transferring its Teff patent to another company owned by the same holding companies, is often reckoned an instance of bad faith, although the core persons continues to allege that they acted within the contractual and legal rights. See Andersen and Winge, 2012.

635 Exemplified recently by an as-yet-not-publicly-available multiparty contract involving a Swiss academic institution, a US pharmaceutical company and a Zimbabwe-based organization.

636 The text as it stands practically eliminates monitoring and tracing. Having declared itself to be both mandatory and unchangeable, it provides no flexibility to adapt it to the concrete situation.

far from an optimal outcome. It has been suggested that the Treaty would be better off with no model at all. Currently, there is an ongoing negotiation of ammendments to the SMTA. Negotiators are, however, very focused on the existing text of the SMTA and changes in few articles can be expected. Model contract development for ABS should hope to have greater success.

In the end, the NP neither requires nor excludes the possibility of developing model contracts and/or contract clauses. The Parties adopted only a series of general clauses calling on parties to take the following actions with regard to the need for and use of model and form contracts and clauses:

- "encourage, as appropriate, the development, update and use of sectoral and cross-sectoral model contractual clauses for mutually agreed terms";[637]
- "encourage, as appropriate, the development, update and use of ...voluntary codes of conduct, guidelines and best practices and/or standards";[638]
- "periodically take stock of the use of sectoral and cross-sectoral model clauses";[639]
- "periodically take stock of the use of voluntary codes of conduct, guidelines and best practices and/or standards";[640]
- "consider the adoption of specific codes of conduct, guidelines and best practices and/or standards";[641] and
- "support, as appropriate, the development by indigenous and local communities ... of model contractual clauses for benefit-sharing arising from the utilization of traditional knowledge associated with genetic resources."[642]

Clearly, although the NP looks kindly on the possible development and use of model clauses, it neither requires their creation nor authorizes parties to make them mandatory. Its model-related provisions are stated very generally and flexibly and not imposed as requirements.

Other instruments in the global ABS regime have also addressed models. They can be divided into three categories: The first, consisting of the ITPGRFA and the World Health Organization's Pandemic Influenza Preparedness (PIP) framework,[643] has formally adopted one or more mandatory form instruments (SMTAs) that must always be used with little or no alteration. A second

637 Nagoya Protocol Article 19.1.

638 Nagoya Protocol Article 20.1.

639 Nagoya Protocol Article 19.2.

640 Nagoya Protocol Article 20.2.

641 *Ibid.*

642 Nagoya Protocol Article 12.3(c).

643 Pandemic Influenza Preparedness Framework for the sharing of influenza viruses and access to vaccines and other benefits ("PIP Framework").

category is exemplified by the Micro-Organisms Sustainable use and Access International Code Of Conduct (MOSAICC) Regulation,[644] which has developed a model "material transfer agreement," but does not mandate its use or prohibit alterations.[645] The third category is exemplified by the Bonn Guidelines, which do not mandate anything with regard to models,[646] but do include suggestions that they may be useful.[647]

12.1.2 *Potential Benefits from the Development of Model Instruments*

The desire for model contracts and contractual provisions is entirely understandable, when one considers two factors:

- The many legally complex and uncertain issues in drafting an ABS contract; and
- The nature of the persons drafting and negotiating ABS contracts.

With regard to the first factor, as this book has shown, the validity of an ABS contract depends on many elements, some of which can be addressed through careful legal drafting. Experience has shown that many persons who are expert in domestic contract law cannot be confident that their ABS contract will be legally valid, enforceable and fully implemented. There are many possible ways for such a contract to fail – and some of them depend on complex areas of law. Models are sometimes seen as (and may be) a solution.

As for the second factor, it is clear in most ABS contract negotiations that both user and provider are represented by individuals who have had very little, if any, experience with the negotiation and drafting of written commercial contracts. The providers are often either rural residents/indigenous persons with little business or commercial experience of any kind, or governmental

644 MOSAICC Micro-organisms Sustainable Use and Access Regulation International Code of Conduct (as updated June 2011).

645 *Ibid.*, at p. 18.

646 Upon adoption, and throughout both the guidelines and the adopting resolution, it is repeatedly stated that the guidelines are only offered as suggestions and a source of information on lessons learned as of that date (2002). It was expected that they would be revised, however, the negotiation of the NP may have eliminated that expectation.

647 Bonn Guidelines § 42.d (suggesting the "[d]evelopment of different contractual arrangements for different resources and for different uses and development of model agreements.") The Bonn Guidelines took essentially a "mix and match" approach to contract negotiations, providing, for example, three lists of possible terms that could be included in model provisions (Bonn Guidelines §§ 43 and 44.) They also made general suggestions about how ABS contracts should be documented, executed, overseen and enforced (Bonn Guidelines §§ 52–54, 57–58 and 61.).

officers whose expertise and knowledge is primarily in the fields of science, social welfare or environmental management. These negotiators are keen to do a good job, and also to ensure that their work does not result in a minor error that eventually invalidates the entire contract or makes it unenforceable.

On the other side of the transaction, users are often represented by field-level employees – researchers, and national representatives – most of whom also lack experience with commercial contracts of this nature, although often they have worked with more conventional types of contracts. Where a user's representative has a more sophisticated knowledge of commercial issues and contract law, he is often held to a different standard where negotiating with inexperienced persons, especially indigenous groups and rural residents. User's representatives often feel (correctly in many cases) that their job and career can be lost if they commit an error in the negotiations that negatively impacts their employer.[648]

For both groups of negotiators, the use of an agreed form or model may provide protection. If the negotiator has approval to use the form, then he may be protected from blame, in the case where the document negotiated does not result in a binding, enforceable and fully implemented contract. Thus, the use of models may help with the second of the two factors discussed above. As noted below, however, the mere fact that a contract is drafted on the basis of a form or model will not ensure that it is valid, enforceable or implemented – inevitably, this depends on the competence of the model and its adaptation to the concrete situation.

12.2 Types of Models and Examples and Their Associated Risks

In general, there are four main types of instruments that are sometime used as a basis/example for the drafting of a new ABS contract: standard forms, model contracts, compendiums of model clauses, and previously negotiated contracts. Each type is different from the others in many ways, particularly in the nature of risks arising from its use.

12.2.1 *"Standard Forms"*

Standard "form contracts" are often preferred where the contract will be negotiated by a specific individual or officer who is acting on behalf of the

648 As noted in Chapter 4, it is also possible that a negotiator who believes that he is acting as a representative of the user may be held personally responsible, if the contract is ultimately found not binding on that user.

whole country, community or company. If that individual or officer is not an experienced commercial lawyer, he faces the somewhat frightening possibility that he might make a mistake that causes a negative result. In some cases, that mistake might indicate (in fact or only in external appearance) that he had used his position illegally with the goal of furthering his own interests. In others, the mistake might result in a loss of expected benefits for his entire company, community or country. In either case, he may face controversy and even the loss of his job. A form contract, with clear and concrete rules about how it must be used is essentially a protection for these negotiators. If they follow the rules, they cannot be accused of favoritism or error.

Another common reason for using form contracts is that they can often be processed and finalized very quickly. This is especially true when the form is almost completely pre-written and leaves only a few blanks to fill in and where the rules say that the rest of the form may not be changed.[649] In essence, the processing of these form contracts may be a simple secretarial task, if the form is strict enough. This frees the time of professional staff to address other matters.

There are three significant risks of the use of standard forms. First, as discussed in Chapters 4 and 7, *supra*, the use of any unalterable form contract carries the risk that the contract will be declared invalid, under basic principles of unconscionability and contracts of adhesion. Where a government adopted the form, the finished document would still be domestically enforceable as a regulatory permit, but might not be enforceable in a foreign country.[650] Second, in most cases, only one standard form has been adopted, creating the significant risk (as enumerated in ¶ 12.3, *infra*) that the form will not be appropriate in most of the various kinds of ABS situations. Third, is the possibility that a provision in the form will be interpreted by a court or arbitrator in a

---

649 The most explicit example of this approach is the SMTA, which insists that no changes may be made in the use of the form. The parties may only fill in the blanks (name, institution, resources changing hands, *etc.*) A different approach is taken in the form instrument in Costa Rican legislation, which specifically allowed parties using the form to adopt other clauses that they consider advisable, although the form identifies a large selection of specific matters whose content must be addressed.

650 As noted in §§ 2.3.2(c) and 3.5, if the user country has adopted NP-required measures to enforce MAT (NP, Article 18), there is a chance that the MAT will be enforceable there as a permit, even if the provider does not have access to broader, more effective contractual enforcement tools. In the 24 years since the CBD made user-side legislation mandatory, however, few countries have adopted any actual user measures, and no country has fully complied with the user-measure requirement. Hence, the chance is very small that provider-country form MAT will be enforceable in the user country, unless it is, or is combined with, a valid and enforceable ABS contract.

manner that negatively impacts not only the contract being litigated, but all other contracts that use the form or the particular clause.[651]

12.2.2 *Model Contracts*

Models are essentially "hypothetical contracts." Models are often written or promoted by academics or by industry associations or other bodies which will not actually become parties to the contracts themselves. Given that no party or entity commits itself to their use, models development processes are often unilateral or based on limited input from other sectors. While models sometimes offer innovative solutions to contractual development challenges, their primary value is that they provide insight into the objectives or perspective of the sector or entity proposing the model. Forms and models are most effective when they are (i) focused very narrowly on a specific type of situation between very specific categories of parties;[652] (ii) negotiated in a process that reflects the interests of all stakeholders that would otherwise negotiate an individual instrument; and (iii) negotiated under surveillance of the actual parties and their legal or other representatives, rather than diplomats taking care of more strategic national interests.

The greatest difficulty with models is the first point. A model that purports to be usable for all ABS contracts is usually subject to one of the following errors, either

- It so general that it does not address the needs of the actual contract parties. Instead, it requires the parties to develop all of the individual clauses of their contract, without assistance; or

651 Although this possibility exists whenever a contract written in one country is evaluated in another country, it is increased where standard form language is used, because the language may not be properly applicable to the particular contractual situation. The court or arbitrator may have an obligation to interpret it in a way that makes it work in that situation. If so, when another case arises in which the same clause is at issue, the court/arbitrator may be obligated or otherwise inclined to use the same interpretation.

652 In many countries, legal disputes over agreements based on "model contracts" are plentiful. In general, forms and models have been most successful in legal areas that have developed over a long time. For example, the law governing the ownership and transfer or lands and buildings has evolved over many centuries; the particular issues and formalities of this type of transaction are well understood. Consequently, in many countries, a variety of forms and models (*e.g.*, sale contracts, leases, mortgages) are a primary tool of commercial practice. In California, for example, there are well over 100 standard model real estate contracts that have been adopted by recognized state agencies.

- It was developed by a sector or organization that is not aware of or interested in the broad range of ABS situations, believing that its own concerns are the only ones that matter.

Consequently, in order to be effective, there must be a very broad range of models that address a range of different ABS situations, and address a range of different types of commercial law options and issues.

At the most basic level of analysis, there are three primary risks involved in the use of models, forms, guidelines and examples as the basis for your ABS contract: (1) the content risk (that the model chosen will be inappropriate, that it will be legally deficient or come from a biased source); (2) the risk that the model will be used incorrectly; and (3) the risk that the model will not have the necessary legal status to enable enforcement. (These issues are detailed in ¶ 12.3, *infra.*)

12.2.3 *"Model Clauses": Picking and Choosing*

Over the course of the NP negotiations, it was increasingly recognized that a single model could not cover all types of resources, contracts, parties, activities and sectors that might need to be reflected in an ABS contract. Moreover, the SMTA example was proving that implementation and functionality were problematic, even in the rare situation in which a homogenous group of providers was using an identical contract with regard to a specifically limited type of utilization of genetic resources.

At that point, most discussions of models and forms added the option of developing "model clauses,"[653] to assist parties in addressing particular and difficult legal and practical challenges in their ABS contracts. Although this change was welcome and rational, the possibility of it working is dubious. Consider, for example, the NP itself. Despite a generally shared desire of most delegations to include some practical elements relating to MAT, in the end they could not agree on anything that actually had practical or contractual relevance. In negotiating Article 6.3, which discusses the contents of MAT,[654] they were only

653 The NP specifically mentions the development of model clauses in Article 19 (a call for non-mandatory development of "sectoral and cross-sectoral model contractual clauses for mutually agreed terms") and separately in a provision on "for benefit-sharing arising from the utilization of [ATK]" (Article 12.3(c).) It also mentions the Parties rights to include model clauses in the ABS-CH (Article 14.3(b).) See more detailed discussion in ¶ 12.1, *supra.*

654 As discussed in ¶¶ 2.3.2 and 11.4.1(b), *supra*, MAT are essentially a regulatory requirement, but potentially built like an ABS contract (possibly with different parties) and potentially enforceable in foreign courts as a contract. In addition, in some countries, the national

able to state that States may (but are not required to) include four types of provisions in their MAT.

Of these four recommendations, one – a dispute settlement clause – is commonly included in virtually every contract. Thus, its inclusion in an "ABS Contract" is conceptually non-controversial. The other three are simply statements of points that are problematic in ABS: "Terms on benefit-sharing, including in relation to intellectual property rights; Terms on subsequent third-party use, if any; and Terms on changes of intent, where applicable."

It has always been expected that any MAT or ABS contract should include all four of these. The CBD parties and NP negotiators, however have long recognized that the lack of definitions and regime clarity has made the last three items difficult or impossible to address in a legally functional way. The negotiators were aware of this. Ultimately, they were not even able to agree on a complete list of the clauses necessary to make MAT enforceable, much less to provide any suggestion of how the various regime deficiencies would be repaired.

The great risk of using a set of "model clauses" is that they are often provided without adequate information and explanation. The parties are forced to decide on whether to use a particular clause on the basis of whether it "looks like something we should include in our contract." The result is often a contract that contains legal contradictions, irrelevant clauses of uncertain impact, and other legal problems. A provider who is faced with a large number of unexplained "model clauses" is often at the mercy of a more legally sophisticated user who may easily convince him to add or drop certain clauses for legally questionable reasons. For this reason, it is recommended that every model clause be accompanied by explanatory material. In addition, providers need to have access to unbiased legal advisors to help them make these choices, rather than relying on the advice of persons on the other side of the transaction

12.2.4 *Other Contracts Used as Examples*

An existing contract's usefulness as an example or template for a new contract depends on a combination of factors. The first group of factors that must be considered before deciding to use an existing-contract example relate to making sure that the model is appropriate. As detailed in ¶ 12.3, *infra*, this involves determining the situational factors: which types of parties and uses was it intended for, and how was it intended to function? The only time that using an

---

MAT requirement provides simply that the designated government agency or official must approve any ABS contract in order for it to be valid and effective.

example is beneficial is when it's contours are extremely similar to the proposed contract under negotiation.

As noted above, another group of factors involves obtaining a competent evaluation of the quality and functionality of the contract. Using as your example a contract that has failed or will fail can easily lead to a similar failures for your contract.

The third group of relevant selection factors is how that template is used. As detailed in ¶ 3.5.3, *supra*, it is often inadvisable to start from the finally agreed positions of a previous contract. By the time the parties have agreed on a contract, each side has made numerous compromises – normally giving the most ground on particular issues that are non-essential to them in that deal, and perhaps fighting harder for other points. In your deal, the matters that you feel are essential may be quite different. It is important, then to use an existing-contract example only as a "skeleton" of your draft, assuming that you will need to address each of the issues in the example, but recognizing that each one may need to be altered significantly. Such an example should present a series of ideas of which clauses should be included in your first draft, but its compromise-developed clauses should not be offered as a "point of departure for the negotiation." Moreover, no matter how complete your example contract may be, you should not forget that there may be additional points that are important to you that were deleted or never even considered for the example contract.

Perhaps the most important group of factors involves the basic recommendation to "trust but verify." Like models and forms, existing contracts are only useful and effective if they were competently drafted and designed to address all of the problems and concerns that might have an impact on whether they will be implemented and/or enforceable. With models and forms, the drafting process by which the instrument was created is generally known. For the best models and forms, the drafters usually have prepared detailed explanatory materials, to help the parties identify which issues were addressed and how they were concluded. When you are using a pre-existing contract as your example, this is rarely the case. Most other contracts are not supported by interpretative information. The drafters may have omitted or forgotten to address one or more issues. Another possibility, as noted above, is that they consciously deleted such a point, because it was not relevant to their particular situation. If your own negotiations that rely on such a contract, you too may omit the point, even though it is highly relevant to your situation.

Finally, factors related to the passage of time may also be important. Since the time that your example was negotiated, there may have been new the developments of law and practice. This places you in a difficult situation in choosing an example. As noted above, it is often a mistake to use a very recent contract or model as the basis for your negotiations, because you cannot predict how that contract will fare in the future. The converse, however, is also true. If relying on a very old contract as a template for your negotiations, you will need to carefully evaluate it, in terms of the new legal and practical factors that did not exist when the old contract was completed. For example, all of the instruments listed in ¶ 11.3, *supra*, as parts of the current "international ABS regime"[655] were adopted after the famous *Merck-InBIO* contract in Costa Rica.[656] In addition, many scientific developments have occurred affecting the way that genetic resources and ATK are utilized. Countries have adopted legislation which defines or applies the international regime terminology in many different ways over the years. Cases and experience involving the implementation of ABS contracts have provided new lessons over the intervening years as well. Conventional contract law has also continued to evolve, so that even the contract's more conventional clauses may be out of date. Thus, if using the *Merck-InBIO* contract as an exemplar for your negotiations, you should reconsider virtually *every* clause to determine whether and how it should be altered in light of later developments. Contract law is a moving target. This must be reflected in the use of examples as a basis for drafting new contracts.

12.3 Finding the Best Model, Form or Example for Your Needs

Although models, forms and examples may be desirable to inexperienced negotiators, there is a simple motto for all ABS parties using models to remember: If the wrong model or example is used, or if it is used improperly, the result may put the parties in a worse position than if none had been used at all.

In each ABS contract, the approach taken must depend on the "diagnosis" of the specific needs, issues, conditions, nature and attitudes of that contract's unique combination of parties, activities and *res*. A provision, model, form or guidance document that was very effective in one set of circumstances can lead to problems in another. The legal context may add additional challenges. A contract that has been enforced under one user country's legislation, could be declared void or unenforceable in another.

655 See ¶ 11.3, *supra*.

656 This contract was publicized through Reid, *et al.*, 1993, and was subsequently used as a template for many ABS contracts around the world.

Where the parties have no choice (*i.e.*, where one party insists that another party must use a specific standard form without deviation), the key question that the parties must ask is whether they would be better off agreeing to the standard model or simply walking away from the transaction. Although this is a rather simple question, many parties never ask it. They become so deeply involved in and committed to the transaction that they never consider whether it continues to offer them anything they need. Since no negotiation is allowed, it is not necessary to evaluate the form's appropriateness as a model, only to determine what it requires and provides to you, in your particular contract.

Where there is a choice of whether to use particular model or example as a starting point for negotiations, more questions arise. Each proposed model/example should be considered in detail, asking "Is this model/example a useful and appropriate starting point or basis for our negotiation and/or contract?" and "Is there a better starting point for our transaction?"

In answering, it will be necessary to consider the source (who developed it); the type and sector of activities covered; the nature of the intended parties; the countries and legal issues involved; and the "track record" for each model or example. In general, we can consider each of these factors in terms of its comparability (similar situation and general structure to the proposed negotiation) and functionality (similar underlying factors that motivate effectiveness). The following sections discuss choosing a suitable model or example for use in your negotiations.

12.3.1 *Source of the Model/Example*

The first factor to consider is the "source" of the model or example. One should investigate, to find out who prepared the model, how it was prepared and what was the preparer's objective in preparing it. Often models prepared by particular users or organizations are unfairly criticized as attempts to convince providers to agree to "model" contracts that do not protect their interests. Although most models are designed with the intent to be fair, the party suggesting it may be doing so because they feel it protects their interests. In some instances, even though one or more "provider representatives" participated in the model development process, they were too few to represent the diverse concerns of the entire range of possible providers.

12.3.2 *Type of ABS Contract*

Models are often prepared in ABS, assuming that all ABS situations are basically similar. In 2009, however, one of the authors of this book undertook and in-depth analysis of approximately 75 ABS contracts and models (which constituted all of the ABS contracts and models in existence to which the author could obtain access).[657] They ranged rather widely, including the following (in order of frequency):

- "Downstream" contracts between the original collector or researcher who obtained genetic resources and a subsequent user;
- Classic "material transfer agreements" (provider transfers of specific germplasm to user);
- Research contracts;
- Bioprospecting contracts;
- IPR transactions and other intangible property instruments;
- Domestic contracts (in which the user of genetic resources based in the provider country);[658]
- Agricultural seed multiplication contracts; and
- A genetic resource repatriation contract (a contract in which contract, under which an *ex-situ* collection agreed to repatriate genetic resources to communities in the country of origin.)

Predictably, the nature of the *res,* and the parties respective rights and obligations under the contract were very different for each of these types of ABS contract. In deciding to use a model or example, then, the first question is "What type of ABS contract are we negotiating, and does the proposed model/example address that type?" This question may be relatively easy to answer where the proposal is to use a previously negotiated contract. Such an example (if it is good enough in quality to be proposed as a good basis for a new contract) will probably be relatively clear about exactly what types of genetic resource or ATK are involved and what activities are covered, mandated or prohibited. Many proposed "models" are less clear about these matters, seeking to encourage parties to use them for all ABS transactions. Clues to the type of contract that the model envisions may be found by considering which entity or organization developed the model and where else it has been used.

In this connection, the particular sector involved in the contract is also important. The laws, objectives and common practices in the forest and

657 Young, 2009.

658 This was less that 10% of the ABS contracts reviewed. All other contracts in that study involved a user from a different country than the provider. Within this category are included domestic contracts addressing bioprospecting, material transfer, research and product development (use of genetic material as a component in a product), where all parties, the *res*, and all activities are in the same country, even where the user was a domestic company formed by a foreign user.

agricultural sectors, for example, are very different. Contractually speaking, research that is focused on conservation issues is very different from commercially oriented research, and within the commercial research sector, pharmaceutical research is very different from agricultural. Finding a model or example within the particular sector of your own contract can make a significant difference. Therefore, if models are to be developed, it is clearly important to develop a range of them, each addressing a different type of ABS contract.[659]

12.3.3 *Specific Activities and Sectors*

There is a wide range of significant differences among sectors and particular types of activities, in terms of how contracts are used and interpreted. As a result, the models, forms and examples used in the negotiation of an ABS contract should also consider these factors. In governmental sectoral areas (forestry, marine, agriculture, natural resources, *etc.*), the use of a sectoral model may mean that the model uses sectoral terminology. Often it can use particular mechanisms in a manner that supports and clarifies the more unusual aspects of the ABS contract, thus minimizing disagreements born out of a misunderstanding.

Where negotiating parties can find no appropriate model or example for the particular sector of their transaction, it is sometimes useful to compare models in terms of the particular activities being discussed. For example, where "taxonomic" activities[660] (*e.g.*, collecting, identifying, labelling and preserving/conserving samples) are planned, another sector's contract for this type of activities may provide more value to the negotiations than a sectorally appropriate contract for a different kind of activities. Similarly, a non-commercial research contract may often offer little value as a model for a commercial research contract. The converse is not always true, however. In contracts in which a non-commercial researcher wishes to ensure that he has the future right to transfer or use his samples and/or results for commercial purposes, the parties may be strongly advised to consider the use of a commercial research model.

659 As noted in ¶¶ 3.2–3.4, *supra,* the parties should develop a strategy and map of the ABS contract they desire. A key factor in this process will be maximizing knowledge about the other parties to the negotiation.

660 Normally, taxonomic contracts will be broader in biological scope, including a wider range of specimens and species than R&D/analysis contracts. In addition, the taxonomy contracts will normally grant the parties broader powers and greater flexibility to choose which specimens to collect or analyse.

12.3.4 *Nature of the Parties*

There are many other factors that would alter the nature of the contract significantly enough to make it inappropriate as a model. These revolve around two primary factors – the type of parties involved and the type of activities they will undertake. Simply put, different types of parties have different contractual objectives and necessitate different types of provisions.

For example, in the early years of ABS, a lot of attention was focused on the contracts used by the US National Institutes of Health (NIH) and the National Cancer Institute (NCI) when they undertook bio-analyses of local germplasm in developing countries, as part of their search for medicinal properties that might be beneficial to all.[661] The "form contracts" used in these transactions were sometimes suggested as potential models for all ABS contracts. These suggestions forgot or ignored a basic fact – the goals and obligations that motivate a nonprofit organization that is dedicated to the public benefit and social welfare are generally quite different from the objectives that motivate large companies, academic researchers and others. The proposals to use them as models focused on the fact that the NIH and CIC are developed-country institutions. They did not mention the more critical legal issue. These contracts could be written in a relatively "soft" manner in light of the fact that those organizations had strong public benefit motivations. Their mandate included both fostering the development of medicines and strongly promoting social-welfare by providing benefits to the residents of localities in which genetic resources were being collected. Relatively few commercial entities are as unselfishly committed to the welfare of their suppliers. For this reason, it would be unwise to use these same soft and non-concrete clauses in dealing with such entities.[662]

This is only one example, there are many other types of parties, including bioprospectors (middlemen), academic institutions, researchers and others, each of which is driven by a different mixture of mandates and objectives.[663]

661 See, *e.g.*, Rosenthal, *et al.*, 1999.

662 Commercial users' contracts typically assume that the providers' goal is individual profit (if the negotiation is with an individual) or community profit (if the negotiation is with a community.) This is entirely understandable, since a company or commercial venture normally has a profit-oriented mandate, and may be legally prevented from taking charitable actions that divert profits away from shareholders. One cannot measure a commercial user by the yardstick that is used to measure the performance of aid agencies, research agencies, collections or NGOs.

663 For example, an agency whose objective is foreign aid may focus more attention on helping the provider community or country to develop its own research capacity and/or ability to develop the results of that research. By contrast, the first objective of a user country's national health agency is the promotion of its own R&D capability, with a secondary desire to achieve social purposes in the provider country. Research agencies

For most of these, especially commercial entities, it may be difficult to obtain copies of contracts or models, which they may consider to be "confidential," refusing to make them public. As a result the majority of contracts that are publicly available are either from non-profits or from parties seeking to present their preferred approach as a "model."

When drafting a contract, the characteristics, mandates and objectives of the parties form a major component in deciding what contractual risks may exist and how they should be addressed. A model or example designed for a contract with a non-profit organization may not include key provisions that would be essential in a contract with a commercial entity, for example. It may also not address the issues relating to a contract with an academic researcher in the ways that are most appropriate and acceptable for that type of contract.

Even within the category of non-profit social-welfare-oriented institutions, there is significant variation from one non-profit to another. In the NCI-CIC example above, for example, in addition to their social welfare mandates, the NCI and CIC had strong obligations to the US companies that might ultimately utilize the materials and information obtained through the NIH/NCI programs. These concerns were reflected in strongly worded clauses ensuring that those companies would receive clear IPRs related to the germplasm and research results, with no long-term obligation to the provider country. A non-profit agency with a different set of objectives might not intend or desire that type of provision.

Although less frequently discussed, it is also clear that there are significant differences among the different types and level of providers, as well. The goals or objectives addressed in the ABS contract differ markedly, depending on whether the person or entity negotiating the provider side of the contract is representing (i) central government,[664] (ii) some agency or institution within

---

and academic institutions may have both individual interests (to ensure that they may later publish or sell their discoveries without limit) and global scientific objectives (to ensure that other researchers, conservation experts and governments have access to information), which are paramount over any particular interest in social welfare or livelihoods within the particular provider country or community. The user, although usually very sympathetic to the needs of the provider, will perceive those needs very differently.

664 Normally, when negotiations are lead by the national level, the contract will have a broader view, placing a greater emphasis on benefits applicable to the entire country and its citizenry. Benefits that are focused too narrowly on a single individual or community may overlook the country's sovereign duty to all of its citizens (to ensure proper use of the country's resources and proper benefits to the country). Benefits may also focus on increasing national capacity, providing new industrial or technical opportunities and/or employing local citizens.

the government,[665] (iii) a local community, or (iv) an individual.[666] None of these options is *per se* either negative or positive.[667] The designation is a matter of law of the provider country (see Chapter 3), which is often misunderstood by parties on both sides who assume that an individual landowner, shaman, institution or official has the authority to contract as the provider.[668]

Accordingly, it is important to select any examples and models that you will use in your negotiations to ensure that the parties and their situation addressed by the model or example are as close as possible your own parties and situation. It is important, however, to realize that no matter how similar your parties are to the parties in an example, there is a very good chance that some part of their motivation will differ from yours. This means that even a carefully chosen model/example may not address all issues you need to address, or may adopt provisions that you do not want or need.

---

665 Where a government agency, research institute or university is "the provider," negotiators may focus on benefits to their own sector or institution, but sometimes perceive these benefits in terms of an institutional mandate to provide long-term value to the country. They may value "national benefits" like training, scholarships, equipment, *etc.*, as well as research rights, rights to publicize research results, and access to information.

666 Where the provider is an individual landowner or small community, negotiations are normally focused on the narrowest view of the term "benefit" – specific value transfers to that particular individual or group.

667 In each country, the decision to centralize the negotiations or to devolve those rights to other levels may reflect a particular national strategy, indicating that ABS has been integrated into a larger national framework (such as the national strategy for conservation, for rural development, for agriculture, *etc*).

668 An early ABS case example (no longer available on any of the CBD databases) documented a case in Cameroon, in which the user negotiated with a particular academic institution, and the ABS contract, PIC and MAT were later invalidated because that institution was not authorized to negotiate as a provider of the genetic resources under the agreement. Based on information in the ABS-CH and also information obtained through the CBD's ABS measures database before it became inaccessible, the authority to negotiate as a provider is treated very differently from country to country. In some countries, the authority to negotiate as "provider" of the country's genetic resources is a duty of the central government. Several others delegate rights and responsibilities of the provider to specific agencies, ministries or to individual protected areas, which operate as separate "providers." In a small number of countries, individual landowners are authorized – usually those who own or control the land on which specimen-collection activities occur. Delegation of authority may be made by statute in some countries, or determined on a case-by-case basis, in others. Most existing ABS laws embody a combination of these approaches, with separate approvals needed from various agencies, individuals and communities.

12.3.5 *Jurisdictional Situation*

As detailed throughout this book, the combination of countries whose national law applies to the contract (*i.e.*, the country of the provider, the country of the user, the countries into which some part of the *res* may be transferred, the country in which a legal action or arbitration will be brought, *etc.*) has a great impact on the contents of the contract. In essence, every such combination is legally different. In its effort to be functional in all legal situations, a model may attempt to ensure that its provisions are enforceable in all countries. In general, an existing-contract example will have been negotiated on the basis of a particular mix of national laws.

As noted throughout this book, it is difficult or impossible to be certain that any contract provision will be enforceable in all countries. The best solution, when choosing models or examples, is to determine the mix of countries most relevant to your transaction, and to measure each model or example in terms of whether it will function in those countries.

12.3.6 *Track Record*

Although it is frequently ignored, the "track record" of a particular model or example is extremely important to the decision whether to use that model/example in your transaction. Throughout the ABS regime, it has been common for countries, organizations and/or contractual parties to publish their recently completed ABS documents (legislation, models, forms, contracts, *etc.*) on the assumption that these documents should be considered as models for future work simply because they have been completed. This assumption has contributed to many legal and practical problems.

By copying a new document before that document has produced results, however, the negotiating parties are effectively multiplying their risk of failure. The parties that initially drafted the contract will normally have tailored it to their unique situation, accepting the risks that it may not function as well as they hope. The parties using that contract as a model will be not only accepting those risks, but adding the risks that the different situation and factors of the new contract might increase the risk of contractual failure.

Similarly, where a model instrument has not yet successfully produced benefits, use of that model is essentially a gamble on its functionality. For example, between the ITPGRFA's 2006 adoption of the SMTA and the publication of a 2013 Report to the Governing Body, no benefits had been received under the nearly 45,000 SMTAs that had been signed.[669] This fact should provide a

669 ITPGRFA "Report on the implementation of the Multilateral System of Access and Benefit Sharing," at § 52. As that report noted, there have been numerous contributions from

clarion call to those negotiating ABS contracts, suggesting that the SMTA may not be the best possible model/example for their contract.

Unfortunately for the CGIAR Collections (the "providers" in SMTAS,) the ITPGRFA does not give them a choice – they must use the SMTA with no alteration unless/until the Governing Body of the ITPGRFA can agree on an amended version.[670] For others, however, it would appear inadvisable to use the SMTA as a model, until it has demonstrated that its benefit-sharing arrangement can actually produce benefits.

12.4 Future Developments

As noted in ¶ 12.1, *supra*, there are many international calls for the development of ABS model contracts and clauses,[671] and such models could be beneficial to ABS in many ways. Other clauses suggested that documents such as guidelines and "community protocols" may also be developed. It seems likely, then, that a key future activity within the ABS regime will be the production and assessment of model contracts and clauses.

12.4.1 *Development of Model Clauses*

As this chapter has shown, however, it is not enough that "a bunch of model contracts and model clauses" should be created. Instead, it is important that the models be developed in a systematic way, which maximizes their accessibility and also the contractual parties' ability to select and use the options most appropriate to their individual situation. This suggests that the first step will be to identify a list of different types of ABS contracts, in terms of the contractual objectives and specific activities addressed, the nature of the parties and the sector governing the resources.

The second step will be to identify the governmental and legal jurisdiction options. As noted above, the success of any ABS contract is tightly connected to the national commercial/contractual law, ABS law and other types of law

national aid budgets and other comparable sources, but no actual payments under any SMTA.

670 As noted in ¶ 11.5.3, *supra*, the negative experiences, particularly the lack of benefit-sharing under the SMTA have triggered its renegotiation. This clearly shows that it was far too early to recommend SMTA as a model before it had produced and benefit sharing as intended.

671 The Protocol specifically left several key areas of controversy (compliance, model instruments, emergency and special cases, *etc.*) for future negotiation and/or action. It is clear that all of these need to be resolved concretely, in order for the regime to function.

in all countries potentially involved in the transaction. In the first 28 years of ABS, it became clear that ABS contracts would only be functional, if and to the extent that all countries agreed to enforce them. This is still one of the most important and effective ways for achieving a functional ABS regime. If an international model development process had been undertaken in connection with the NP negotiations, all countries could have specifically agreed that the resulting models would be enforceable in their own courts.[672] Without such agreement, however, an internationally driven model development process will have only limited success. For example, even though it was internationally drafted, the SMTA is not a useful model. There has been no global agreement that all courts of the ITPGRFA member countries will enforce the SMTA, if it should ever be challenged in their courts.[673]

The third step will be to identify a list of issues that must be addressed in each transaction. For each issue, it will then be necessary to determine if a model clause or clauses would be useful or whether each negotiation must determine whether and how to address the issue in an individual way.

The final step will be to develop the draft model contracts clauses through an expert-driven process that assesses the contractual needs and risks of each clause. It is necessary that any such model clause should be is inclusive in addressing the full range of perspectives – not only government officials that may have ABS responsibilities, but also all types of users and all types and levels of providers.[674]

Once the models are completed, they need to be made accessible through an indexed database that is built on and provides relevant explanatory material.

---

672 Chapter 10 notes many of the challenges faced by those attempting to develop a uniform body of international contract law. The ABS model process could avoid these challenges, if countries simply agreed that the specific ABS models would be enforceable in their courts.

673 Moreover, its "governing law" provision is highly confusing, listing three sources of governing law, two of which ("general principles of law" and "decisions of the [ITPGRFA] Governing Body [on contract interpretation]") do not exist, and the third, the UNIDROIT Principles 2004, has not been formally adopted, interpreted or approved by any country or court.

674 In this process, however, many of the countries would face financial constraints that could prevent them from participating in the model development process, if there are too many of these negotiations. The SMTA development process showed that such negotiations are time consuming and may be expensive, at a time when little interest remains among funding agencies. The importance of an effective model development process indicates a need to avoid an imbalanced process or a process that is forced to adopt an ineffective instrument due to deadlines and lack of funds.

12.4.2 *ABS Contractual Guidelines*

Although the concept of formal guidelines for ABS contracts has often been suggested, it offers little potential to assist parties. In general, commercial companies, larger academic institutions and nonprofit organizations are unwilling to accept anything but existing contract law as a limit or restriction on their contract practices. Where sectors are subject to limits and guidelines, they arise, in most cases, through permit requirements and other laws. Only a few voluntary certification systems have been successful at imposing guidelines without legislative requirements. These successes are attributable to specific factors. In some, the "volunteers" realize that if they do not comply then legislation will be adopted that is much more stringent than the voluntary certification system.[675] In others, there is a financial incentive (*e.g.*, a large segment of the population is sufficiently aware of and concerned about the issue, so that it is willing to commit to purchasing only products that qualify for certification.)[676] In general, only a small percentage of the target population participate in voluntary certification systems, unless the benefit of participation is something they cannot get any other way and of significant value.[677]

To date, it appears that users have been relatively uniform in calling for guidelines for providers, but have not indicated any willingness to abide by general guidelines themselves.[678] Although many providers have asked for assistance with ABS contracting challenges, few have been willing to accept the idea of unilateral guidelines that apply only to providers, without comparable provisions regarding the behavior of responsible users.

Thus, although ABS guidelines exist that discuss ABS contracts, many of them are of doubtful relevance. The Nagoya Protocol's provisions regarding

---

675 One common example of this is the so-called "Comics Code," adopted by publishers of comic books in the US in the 1950s to alleviate "inappropriate content" (sex, violence, *etc.*), which the ultra-conservative majority in that country felt should be eliminated from reading material for children. That voluntary system was adopted because comic-book producers were aware that, if they did not act, the government would impose stricter controls on their products. The Comics Code alleviated that risk, and continued to operate until well after the 1970s, by which time national opinions had altered dramatically. See, Hajdu, 2008. See other examples, analysed in Börkey, *et al.*, 1999.

676 Several certification systems, including especially "Fair Trade" certification, have achieve significant coverage in Northern Europe and elsewhere.

677 Young, 2004.

678 Exceptions exist, of course, especially in the case of Botanic Gardens Conservation International (BCGI), which has produced a range of "ABS information and tools targeted towards botanic gardens and academic researchers," which are generally believed to have a wide following among BGCI member organizations.

MAT (a contractual aspect of national ABS legislation) provide a good example of this phenomenon. Those provisions are expressed in non-binding language and make no effort to be comprehensive, listing only a few possible clauses.[679] Beyond them, the NP gives no guidance in how to deal with those topics or how to draft the recommended types of clauses.

12.4.3 *Community Protocols and ATK MAT*

In addition to its direct discussion of model provisions, the Protocol also specifically encourages parties to "support, as appropriate, the development ... of community protocols and minimum requirements for MAT related to the use of associated traditional knowledge."[680] Although some efforts to create these instruments have been undertaken, to date the use and value of these options have not yet been demonstrated. The most important challenge of both of these processes is the need to create something with functional value, and to avoid over-inflating the expectations of the communities or holders of traditional knowledge.

When the concept of "community protocols" was first mentioned at a meeting focused on enabling and supporting user participation in ABS transactions, the reaction was immediate and positive – but only until the participants were told the description of the community protocol concept that was then being circulated. The user and developed country participants in that meeting were in general agreement that the development of community protocols would benefit both sides of the transaction, if it accomplished the following goals:

- Clearly designated the community members who would be authorized to negotiate ABS contracts and/or which persons or groups would be considered the "holders" of various types of genetic resources or ATK, and what their "established rights" in those assets might be;
- Specified the exact processes that must be completed in order for a user to obtain a binding ABS contract and/or permit, MAT, *etc*;
- Listed the precise information that the user must provide in those processes;

679 In Articles 5, 6, 7, 13, 15, 16 and 18, the Protocol only calls for the "establishment" of MAT, and in Article 12 it identifies the objective of "developing minimum requirements" for MAT as an option, but not a requirement. In Article 6.3(g), the NP identifies four types of provisions that might be, but are not required to be, included in MAT.

680 Nagoya Protocol Article 12.3.a-b. It is also useful to consider Nagoya Protocol Article 18.2 calling on parties to ensure that an opportunity to seek recourse is available in disputes arising from MAT.

- Clarified how the analysis of that information will be undertaken and whether the user would provide or pay for those analytic services;
- Listed the specific criteria that would be applied in the decision-making process, including guidelines on the nature and amount of benefit-sharing, and the listing of any elements that are "off-limits" or cannot be a part of any ABS transaction; and
- Specified how long the overall process would take.

The meeting's participants noted their ongoing concern that, in most of their attempts to negotiate ABS contracts with indigenous and local communities and individuals, it took a long time before any contact person was designated, and the authority of that individual was never clear. The overall process was generally unclear. Moreover, in most negotiations, the community had no fixed idea of what their negotiating objectives were – as one community meeting described it, they wanted to "keep their options open and see what they could get." The result was that commercial negotiations, and even non-commercial negotiations generally foundered, because someone in the community would reject a proposal, without offering a counterproposal. Negotiations, which sometimes took months or years, often ended in failure – no contract ever agreed.

Also attending the meeting were community ABS advisors, who also noted that a community protocol that specified the procedural issues mentioned above would be of inestimable value. They pointed to another problem that frequently arises in connection with ABS community processes – over-inflated expectations. Communities that avidly use the community protocol process to state their view of the value of their assets and the amount they expect each ABS contract to produce run the significant risk of excluding themselves from the market. Users will avoid these communities, especially if their protocol has not clarified the administrative and procedural issues listed above.

CHAPTER 13

Conclusion

The ABS concept was not created by consistent legal practical and theoretical design. Rather, it grew "like topsy" – originating in CBD provisions that make statements about the desired outcome (CBD Article 1), and the apparent belief that a few lines of additional explanation (CBD Article 15) would be sufficient to enable and mandate the creation of an entirely new legal concept and regime. Over the 18 years between the adoption of the CBD and the adoption of the NP, practical experience and analysis has added more detail in some aspects, but divergences in the way the ABS concept came to be perceived and implemented rendered many of the most basic ABS provisions and approaches uncertain. The Nagoya Protocol, while again adding details in particular areas, contributed to the increase in the general ambiguity of ABS especially for ABS contracts. We were still essentially attempting to use a few words negotiated by a committee of environmental negotiators to guide the creation and implementation of an entire new commercial concept.

These few words, however, were supplemented by one of the few concrete statements on ABS that the CBD negotiators agreed – their statement that ABS would be implemented by the contract mechanism.

The decision to tie ABS functionality to the contract mechanism was, in many ways an excellent choice. Contracts and the contract concept exist in the practical and legal frameworks of every country and indigenous culture. The contract mechanism has existed for millennia. As such it is well defined in detail. The business world relies on it to enable commerce to function in a way that is both effective and efficient. If any agreement, in any walk of life, possesses all of the elements that promote contractual functionality (Chapter 1), that agreement will probably operate effectively for all parties. If that agreement meets the relevant legal standards of contract law (*i.e.*, if it is valid, binding, implementable and equitable), it will be considered "enforceable." Enforceability offers two benefits to the parties to the agreement. First, in the event of a breach of contract, an enforceable contract can be enforced by a court. Second, however, if a contract is enforceable, the parties are less likely to breach it, *even if they know that the other party would be unlikely to take any formal action to enforce it.*

The challenges facing ABS contracts are equally troubling to both users and providers. For both, the fact that a contract is unenforceable creates both risk

 | DOI 10.1163/9789004356573_014

and uncertainty. Neither side is protected if the legal document they rely on is unenforceable or invalid.

Unfortunately, 25 years of ABS contracts have demonstrated our original point – that ABS was not designed with the objective of making a system that could be easily implemented using existing contract law, its goals were environmental protection, social welfare and benefit-sharing. After 21 years of international ABS negotiation,[681] however, it is clear that the negotiation of the ABS concept is ended. From this point onward, we must recognize that the development of a fair, balanced, effective international ABS regime is a matter of implementation – the power to make it work is in the hands of national legislators (drafting national ABS laws of all types and setting up the institutions that will implement the relevant governmental processes); of regional and sectoral groups (developing agreements to better enable implementation in each particular region or sector); and most importantly, of the parties negotiating ABS contracts (negotiating and drafting contracts that are functional and effective.)

This book has focused on the latter. Through the negotiation, drafting and implementation of effective ABS contracts, the parties that are most directly affected by ABS can bring about two important consequences: They can make their own contracts balanced, functional and effective; and they can help build an internationally operational ABS framework that works and becomes progressively more effective, more broadly accepted and easier to use.

13.1 Contracts and ABS

13.1.1 *Contracts: A Useful and Flexible Tool*

The contract mechanism has developed over many centuries into a tool that is very flexible. Its principles can be successfully applied to a very wide variety of situations and relationships. This mechanism, however, is not *infinitely* flexible. In order to apply the contract mechanism to your desired agreement, it is necessary to design your agreement in a way that meets the minimum

---

681 ABS was a major element of the CBD negotiations, which began in about 1989. Even after the adoption of the CBD, it was recognized that additional work was needed to realize the ABS concept, with a long series of negotiations in biannual meetings of the CBD Conference of Parties, eventually leading to a series of Expert Group meetings, Ad-hoc committee sessions, the adoption of the Bonn Guidelines, and rather immediately thereafter the beginning of negotiations that led to the adoption of the Nagoya Protocol in 2010, which has been thought of as the completion of the international ABS negotiations.

standards of functionality and enforceability. Your agreement must follow the legal rules.

Even then, however, the success of a contract depends on functionality, which is, primarily, a matter of design. Specifically, as considered in Chapter 1, in order to be functional, your agreement needs to (i) be designed around the particular type of relationship that the parties have with one another (a contract with a stranger is built in a different way from a contract with a friend or neighbour); (ii) recognize and address differences (in culture, country, industry or social factors, for example) and similarities of the parties; and (iii) support (or supplement) the incentives that will drive these specific parties to comply with and fully implement the contract.

Similarly, as discussed in Chapter 7, in order to be enforceable, the contract needs to meet the standards of the applicable legal system (the national law of the country in which the contract will be enforced and/or the provider country) which determine whether that contract is "valid," "binding" and "implementable." If it does not pass this bar, no court will enforce it, and the parties to the agreement may well view their obligations as voluntary, and decide not to implement them.

13.1.2 *The Contracts Used in ABS Transactions*

The law and practice of negotiating, drafting and implementing contracts includes elements that address both functionality and enforceability. Even though the body of contractual law has been in place for many centuries, it is constantly evolving. It has evolved one contract at a time, and different areas of contracts are at different stages. When a contract functions and is enforceable, it forms a part of the growing library of "best practices." When it fails, its failure can provide a bit of information about what went wrong and why. Particularly if one can gain access to the actual information regarding how implementation happened or failed to happen. It is potentially multiplication of errors to use an existing ABS contract as a template for a new contract before it has proven its effectiveness in the real world.

Even a quick perusal of ABS contracts demonstrates that a large percentage of them are both non-functional and unenforceable. Even focusing only on the few that have functioned well, most of them were legally unenforceable – the parties complied with the contract for reasons unrelated to contractual obligation. For example, they may have viewed compliance as an ethical responsibility or felt that there were non-legal reasons (such as the desire to build goodwill to support future transactions) to comply.

Legally unenforceable contracts are ineffective to protect the parties' rights and bind them to their obligations. They also offer no contribution to the development of a durable and effective ABS system. They may even pose a threat to the functioning of the contract (or indeed the entire ABS system) by giving the parties the false impression that the user is bound. It is thus essential to find ways to make ABS contracts both functional and enforceable. This requires the adaptation of established contract mechanisms to a kind of relationship that is very different from any previously recognized commercial arrangement – a task that takes effort and hard work.

13.1.3 *The Uniqueness of ABS Contracts*

Throughout the contractual negotiations, drafting and implementation, it is important to remember the three primary ways in which an ABS contract is different from other types of contracts:

- "Genetic resources" and "benefit-sharing" are new and different types of subject matter, possessing legal and practical characteristics that have not been addressed in other contracts. A primary challenge facing ABS implementation is the need to find mechanisms and approaches that create a legally enforceable and functional range of options and means of implementing ABS.
- Even though they rely on national legislation and other national factors, most ABS contracts are "international." There is, however, no body of generally agreed "international contract law." National contract law regimes vary widely. Most important, current practices among uses suggest that it is very likely that genetic resources and/or ATK will be transferred to third parties, perhaps outside of either the user or provider country. Taken together, these facts create a major challenge for ABS contracts.
- ABS contracts often lack the factors that make other contracts functional (reiterated in 13.1.1).

This uniqueness is the source of the challenges that this book has endeavoured to address. In addition to these, many of the unique challenges facing ABS contracts are reflected in the web of international instruments that are often thought of as the "international ABS regime" (Chapter 12.)

13.1.4 *The Reasons That ABS Contracts to Date Have Failed*

One of the most frequent questions about ABS asked in COP-13 was "Why do ABS contracts fail?" From a legal/practical perspective, one can discern at least seven reasons:

- *Lack of pre-contract preparation.* If parties do not undertake the necessary pre-negotiation investigation, they miss many opportunities to protect against common causes of contract failure.
- *Lack of a contractual strategy.* Without a specific strategy, applicable to the particular actions and relationships under negotiation, parties develop their proposed ABS contracts in a random fashion that virtually guarantees that the resulting document will be unenforceable and potentially non-functional.
- *Meeting of different worlds.* ABS contracts embody the development of a relationship between persons who are negotiating a contract for environmental/social purposes on one hand, and other parties who view the contract as a business/commercial mechanism and seek business/commercial results on the other. This gap widens still further where the commercial entity is negotiating with indigenous peoples or communities.
- *Simplification.* The widespread promotion of the view that ABS Contracts can and should be "simple" is a major disservice to both providers and users. One cannot say the magic words "ABS is simple to implement" and make it so. In general the desire to simplify ABS contracts has produced documents that are completely unenforceable and that can only be functional if both parties agree to work together to resolve the ambiguities and unaddressed matters that arise on a daily basis. It is certainly possible (and recommended) for ABS contracts to be written in a way that does not use "legalese" and "fine print," It is impossible, however, to document a legally certain and enforceable ABS relationship in a few simple pages that have been written without considering the basic legal requirements of contract enforceability.
- *Ambiguity and Lack of Concrete Specificity.* As a result of the pressure for simplification, in light of the "meeting of worlds" phenomenon, the parties to ABS contracts have, up to now, typically had very different perceptions of their respective obligations and expectations under the contract. This leads to ambiguity, which will often become a source of disagreement. When it does, given that ambiguous contracts are unenforceable, the "simple" clause becomes a direct cause of non-compliance.
- *Structure of the "ABS approach."* The CBD's brief statement of ABS was built around a the general picture of timing/structure (access granted to users; then if "benefits arise" from utilization, and finally those benefits are shared.) This commercially improbable model is often reproduced in the ABS contracts themselves. That is, the user/collector obtains the genetic

resource at the commencement of the contract, while his obligations under the contract do not arise until "benefits of utilization" have arisen. This type of timing in any contract encourages the "user" parties to have "second thoughts". That is, leading the user to ask whether the contract is enforceable, and if not, to walk away from the remaining contractual obligations. Thus, the design of ABS inhibits basic contract functionality, by reducing the incentives that encourage user compliance.

It is certainly possible to negotiate and draft ABS contracts that address all of these factors. While one can never say that a contract is "iron-clad" or provides complete protection to its parties, by addressing all of these issues and focusing on making the contract legally enforceable, the parties can minimize the risks and challenges that they face.

13.2 The ABS Challenges and the Seven Rules of Contracts

This book has been built around describing the problems and challenges of ABS contracts. It began by digging into the reasons that ABS contracts have not met the expectations up to now (Chapters 1 and 2). The main body of its discussion focuses on key practices and basic rules for negotiating and drafting.

13.2.1 *The "Golden Rule"*

This book's primary message can be thought of as the "Golden Rule" of contract drafting: AVOID AMBIGUITY. This rule applies to all types of contracts, and every clause of every contract, because ambiguity *kills* contracts. By definition, if a contract is ambiguous, it is unenforceable. To achieve the negotiation and drafting of every aspect of an unambiguous and externally verifiable contract, it is necessary to ensure that all of its operative provisions are concrete and specific. For example, it is generally advised that the parties should not use any of the very general and imprecise terms that have been "defined" in the CBD and NP (Chapter 5).

13.2.2 *Preparation and Strategy*

The process of creating a functional and enforceable ABS contract begins with a preparatory process (Chapter 3), which includes both research and strategic development. The success of any contract is a direct result of how well this planning process is completed.

13.2.3 *The Seven Rules of Drafting Successful* ABS *Contracts*

The main focus of this book has been structured around seven "rules of drafting." Each issue is discussed with a goal of making sure that the reader has a basic overall understanding of why the issue is important, supported by an explanation of a few key details that might arise in negotiations as well as some annotated examples of the manner in which the reader might start to think about particular provisions. To briefly reiterate the seven rules:

The first rule's instruction to "make sure you contract with the right parties" addresses the need to be sure that the right parties are named in the contract, and that they are legally recognized entities that can be bound by and perform the contract (Chapter 4);

The second rule is that ABS contracts should "be specific and concrete regarding all substantive obligations and processes." This rule reiterates the critical need to ensure that all aspects of the contract are unambiguously clear. It is best exemplified by the importance of defining the material transferred under the contract and clearly stating the specific responsibilities of the parties so concretely that they are legally recognized as "enforceable" (Chapter 5);

The third rule's call to "manage and address major risks" is discussed in the context of an important ABS risk – the risks and impacts of third-party transfers (Chapter 6);

Rule 4's statement that one should "know the possibilities and limitations of contract law" focuses on taking all possible measures to ensure that the contract is legally valid and enforceable (Chapter 7);

Rule 5's call on parties to "expect the best; plan for the worst" focuses on the need to make sure that the contract imposes real, legal consequences on parties that violate their obligations, and gives the non-violating parties the tools they would need should they ever decide to take the matter to court to enforce their legal remedies (Chapter 8);

Carrying this idea further, the statement in Rule 6 that parties should "protect their contractual rights/expectations" recognizes that in the vast majority of cases, the most effective protections against breach of contract are private measures that can be exercised without going to court (guarantees, letters of credit and other tools). All of these measures must be addressed in the contract, if they are to be used (Chapter 9); and

Finally, Rule 7 cautions the parties to "avoid mistaken legal assumptions." This rule arises out of the myriad of misunderstandings and myths about contract law that have cropped up in the international ABS negotiations. It notes, for example, that reliance on concepts such as "governing law," "private international law" and "international commercial law" can often lead the parties to believe that they have solved a problem, when they have at best ignored it, and at worst added more complications (Chapter 10).

13.3 The Quest for Shortcuts

At Chapter 12, this book considered the most common solution sought by non-lawyers seeking to avoid the challenges facing those who negotiate and draft ABS contracts, the desire to find a quick solution either by

- adopting an agreed "model contract," or
- using a prior another contract (between other parties and/or involving other activities/resources) as a template (changing the names, *etc.*, but keeping the prior contract's wording.)

While these ideas are not necessarily bad, they are often risky; so models and templates should be used with caution.

Models carry the risk of forcing parties to accept terms that are not appropriate for their particular combination of factors (the mix of party categories, nationalities, objectives, resources and other factors varies widely from contract to contract). Similarly, efforts to use an existing contract as a template face this problem as well as many others.

It is a critical error to assume, simply because a contract has been signed, that it is an effective/successful contract. If the contract is already proven to have been successful in the past, it is probably old enough that it might no longer function, in light of recent developments.

13.4 Making ABS a Functional and Effective Tool for the Future

Clearly if ABS is going to be implemented, it will be necessary to resolve these challenges. Simply put, our attitudes and practices with respect to ABS contracts must undergo a major paradigm shift, with the goal of making ABS contracts functional and enforceable. If we fail to do this, the next generation of ABS contracts, too, will prove (too late) to be unenforceable. At that point, it is likely that the world will give up on ABS, and a major opportunity to develop a new approach to international environmental and social development will be lost.

In this endeavour, we must not lose sight of the need not only to increase capacity to negotiate, draft and implement ABS contracts, but also to make that process evolve into something that is easier to engage in and more frequently undertaken. In short, the work of making and using ABS contracts needs to become easier with time.

There are several concrete steps toward that goal that we can begin taking now: First, as explained in this book, we need to stop perpetuating the use of bad and unenforceable ABS contracts. Effort, attention and indeed innovation is required to create functional and enforceable (successful) ABS contracts, but those efforts will pay off, both for the contract being created and for the international ABS concept.

Second, we need to encourage openness about ABS contracts. Although confidentiality about some facts and provisions may be necessary to one or both parties, the practice of requiring secrecy concerning the entire contract is preventing the development of recognized standards of ABS contractual practice. Once such standards develop, they make it easier to negotiate, draft, implement and enforce all ABS contracts from that point onward. In the meantime, openness helps us identify positive practices and share experiences.

The third important step that must be taken now is to encourage every country to adopt legislation that enables better implementation and enforcement of ABS contracts, from both the user and provider perspective. Clearly, this process will have to include not only the administrative ABS provisions mentioned in CBD Art. 15.7 and the Nagoya Protocol, but also provisions of procedural and commercial law that address the special challenges of enforcement that arise from the unique nature of ABS and from the need to ensure that providers and provider countries have fair access to the justice mechanisms of provider countries, including adequate remedies.

It has long been recognized that a complete failure to make ABS work could pose a threat to the entire global collaboration represented by the CBD. Full functional implementation of ABS is long overdue. There is an urgent need to build and fully enable high-quality, enforceable and functional ABS contracts. The authors hope that this book provides a meaningful step in this process.

Resources Cited[1]

International/Multinational Instruments

Andean Community's Decision No. 391 Establishing the Common Regime on Access to Genetic Resources.

Bonn Guidelines on Access to Genetic Resources and Fair and Equitable Sharing of the Benefits Arising Out of Their Utilization. 2002. Annexed to CBD COP Decision VI-24. Available online from the CBD website, at https://www.cbd.int/decision/cop/default.shtml?id=7198. Non-binding instrument.

Cartagena Protocol on Biosafety to the Convention on Biological Diversity. UNTC A-30619 29 Jan 2000 (Montreal) in force.

Convention on Biological Diversity Adopted 5 June 1992, UNTS vol. 1760, p. 79, entry into force 29 December 1993, in force (herein "CBD").

Convention on Contracts for the International Sale of Goods (Vienna, 1980), entry into force on 1 January 1988 (herein "CISG"). Available online at http://www.unidroit.org/, at the "Instruments" tab. UNCITRAL publishes the convention in book form, along with some interpretative material, online at https://www.uncitral.org/pdf/english/texts/sales/cisg/V1056997-CISG-e-book.pdf.

Convention on International Trade in Endangered Species of Fauna and Flora (CITES).

Convention on the Recognition and Enforcement of Foreign Arbitral Awards. New York. 1958. UNCITRAL has posted the text of this convention online at http://www.uncitral.org/pdf/english/texts/arbitration/NY-conv/New-York-Convention-E.pdf.

European Patent Convention, 5 October 1973, as amended on 17 December 1991, 21 December 1978, 13 December 1994, 20 October 1995, 5 December 1996, 10 December 1998 and 27 October 2005 and 29 November 2000 (herein "EPC").

1 As explained in ¶ 1.3, supra, with virtually no established law directly on the point of how the ABS process will interact with contract laws and implementation, it has been necessary to consider virtually the entire body of global contract jurisprudence, legislation and analysis. The intention of this book, however, was to make it possible for the parties negotiating, drafting, implementing and enforcing ABS contracts to avoid the need to become experts in international contract law and practice. Accordingly, this list is not a complete bibliographic listing of all of the documents used in the production of this book, but only a list of the formal citations of those documents that were cited, whether as examples or as sources of additional information. The authors will be happy to provide additional references to anyone who takes the time to ask.

European Regulation (EC) No 593/2008 of the on the law applicable to contractual obligations, (herein "Rome I").

FAO International code of conduct for plant germplasm collecting and transfer, adopted by the 27th FAO Conference, 1993, online at http://www.fao.org/docrep/x5586e/x5586e0k.htm.

FAO International Undertaking on Plant Genetic Resources for Food and Agriculture (the "Undertaking"), adopted 1983.

Hague Convention of 22 December 1986 on the Law Applicable to Contracts for the International Sale of Goods, is not in force. (All Hague Conventions are available online at the website of the Hague Conference on Private International Law, at https://www.hcch.net/en/instruments/conventions.

Hague Convention of 1 February 1971 on the Recognition and Enforcement of Foreign Judgments in Civil and Commercial Matters.

Hague Convention of 5 July 2006 on the Law Applicable to Certain Rights in Respect of Securities held with an Intermediary.

Hague Convention of 14 March 1978 on the Law Applicable to Agency.

Hague Convention of 1 July 1985 on the Law Applicable to Trusts and on their Recognition.

Hague Convention of 1 March 1954 on Civil Procedure.

Hague Convention of 25 October 1980 on International Access to Justice.

Hague Convention on Agency in the International Sale of Goods, Geneva, 17 February 1983.

Incoterms 2010 English Edition. International Chamber of Commerce (ICC) The ICC publishes the Incoterms and provides them for sale at http://store.iccwbo.org/incoterms-2010, along with a range of publications to assist in their use and interpretation. ICC website at http://www.iccwbo.org/products-and-services/trade-facilitation/incoterms-2010/.

International Treaty on Plant Genetic Resources for Food and Agriculture. UNTC I-43345, 4 November 2001 (Rome) in force.

Nagoya Protocol on Access to Genetic Resources and the Fair and Equitable Sharing of Benefits Arising from Their Utilization to the Convention On Biological Diversity, UNTC A-30619 (29 October 2010: UNEP/CBD/COP/DEC/X/1), in force.

Rome Convention on the Law Applicable to Contractual Obligations, 1980 (OJ C 27, 26.1.1998, pp. 34–46), not in force.

Statute of the Hague Conference. (Available on the website of the Hague Conference, at https://www.hcch.net/en/instruments/conventions.

UNCLOS Agreement relating to the implementation of Part XI of the United Nations Convention on the Law of the Sea of 10 December 1982, 28 July 1994 (New York), in force.

UNCLOS Agreement for the Implementation of the Provisions of the United Nations Convention on the Law of the Sea of 10 December 1982 relating to the Conservation and Management of Straddling Fish Stocks and Highly Migratory Fish Stocks, 4 August 1995 (New York), in force.

UNIDROIT Principles of International Commercial Contracts 2010 (herein "UNIDROIT 2010"). Available online at http://www.unidroit.org/english/principles/contracts/principles2010/integralversionprinciples2010-e.pdf.

UNIDROIT Principles of International Commercial Contracts 2004 (herein "UNIDROIT 2004"). Available online at http://www.unidroit.org/instruments/commercial-contracts/unidroit-principles-2004.

UNIDROIT Convention relating to a Uniform Law on the International Sale of Goods (The Hague, July 1, 1964), in force.

UNIDROIT Other Conventions cited: Convention on Agency in the International Sale Of Goods; UNIDROIT Convention on Substantive Rules for Intermediated Securities; and UNIDROIT Convention on Stolen or Illegally Exported Cultural Objects. International Convention on Travel Contracts; the Convention on the Contract for the International Carriage of Goods by Road, UNIDROIT Convention on International Financial Leasing (10 Parties) and the UNIDROIT Convention on International Factoring. All are available online at http://www.unidroit.org/, at the "Instruments" tab.

United Nations Convention on the Law of the Sea, UNTC I-31363, 10 December 1982 (Montego Bay) in force.

WIPO Consolidated Document Relating to Intellectual Property and Genetic Resources, Document WIPO/GRTKF/IC/28/4. Available at http://www.wipo.int/meetings/en/details.jsp?meeting_id=32091 (click on the document number.) WIPO has not yet formally adopted this document.

WIPO The Protection Of Traditional Knowledge: Draft Articles, Document WIPO/GRTKF/IC/28/5. Available at http://www.wipo.int/meetings/en/details.jsp?meeting_id=32091 (click on the document number.) WIPO has not yet formally adopted this document.

WIPO The Protection of Traditional Cultural Expressions: Draft Articles, Document WIPO/GRTKF/IC/28/6. Available at http://www.wipo.int/meetings/en/details.jsp?meeting_id=32091 (click on the document number.) WIPO has not yet formally adopted this document.

WIPO "Joint Recommendation on Genetic Resources and Associated Traditional Knowledge," Document WIPO/GRTKF/IC/28/7. Available at http://www.wipo.int/meetings/en/details.jsp?meeting_id=32091 (click on the document number.) WIPO has not yet formally adopted this document.

International Bodies, Reports and Decisions

ASTM International website.

BioTrade website.

Botanic Gardens Conservation International, "ABS information and tools targeted towards botanic gardens and academic researchers." Available online at https://www.bgci.org/policy/abs_links.

CBD Bodies and Reports

COP decisions available on the CBD website: https://www.cbd.int/information/parties.shtml.

COP 5 Decision V/26.

COP 6 Decision VI/24.

COP 7 Decision VII/19.

CBD Secretariat (2007) "Report on the Legal Status of Genetic Resources in National Law, Including Property Law, Where Applicable, in a Selection of Countries." UNEP/CBD/WG-ABS/5/5.

CBD INF, 2009. "Report of a Workshop on Access and Benefit-Sharing in Non-Commercial Biodiversity Research" UN Doc: UNEP/CBD/WG-ABS/7/INF/6.

Various "Report[s] of the International Negotiating Committee for the CBD" (available in hard copies at IUCN Environmental Law Centre).

Various "Report[s] of the Ad-hoc Working Group on Article 8(j)," including UNEP/CBD/WG8J/8/INF/10/Add.1.

Various "Report[s] of negotiations that led to the adoption of the Nagoya Protocol" in 2010.

Fair Trade International. Online at http://www.fairtrade.net/.

FAO-ITPGRFA Bodies and Reports

Governing Body Resolution 2/2006.

Report of the Expert Panel, 2016, "Options for Introducing a Termination Clause"; FAO Document IT/OWG-EFMLS-3/15/Inf.7 at http://www.planttreaty.org/sites/default/files/OWG%20EFMLS%203-15-Inf7%20Termination%20Clause.pdf.

"Report on the implementation of the Multilateral System of Access and Benefit Sharing," ITPGRFA Document IT/GB-5/13/5. Available online at http://www.planttreaty.org/content/fifth-session-governing-body.

Global Biodiversity Forum, 2000, at CBD Vth Conference of Parties.

Global Environment Facility Projects (documents available on line at https://www.thegef.org/gef)

5760: Brazil – Capacity Building and Institutional Strengthening on the National Framework for Access and Benefit Sharing under the Nagoya Protocol.

3801: India – Strengthening the Implementation of the Biological Diversity Act and Rules with Focus on its Access and Benefit Sharing Provisions.

5533: China, "Developing and Implementing the National Framework on Access to and Benefit Sharing of Genetic Resources and Associated Traditional Knowledge."

3801: India – Strengthening the Implementation of the Biological Diversity Act and Rules with Focus on its Access and Benefit Sharing Provisions.

5593: Malaysia – Developing and Implementing a National Access and Benefit Sharing Framework.

4962: Costa Rica – Promoting the Application of the Nagoya Protocol through the Development of Nature-based Products, Benefit-sharing and Biodiversity Conservation International Institute for the Unification of Private Law.

Others

International Seabed Authority. website

International Standards Organization (ISO) website.

Norway/UN Conference on Technology Transfer and Capacity Building. 23–27 June 2003 (Fourth Trondheim Conference on Biodiversity)

UNIDROIT, FAO, IFAD. 2015. Legal Guide on Contract Farming. Accessible online at http://www.unidroit.org/instruments/contract-farming/legal-guide.

WIPO took on the task of further analysis, producing a number of detailed documents, still available on the WIPO and CBD websites.

International Databases and Mechanism

ABS Clearinghouse (ABS-CH). Online at https://www.cbd.int/abs/theabsch.shtml.

ABS Clearinghouse's database of national ABS legislation (https://absch.cbd.int/search-new/nationalRecords?schema=measure).

Cartagena Protocol on Biosafety, Biosafety Clearinghouse (BCH). Online at https://absch.cbd.int/search/national-records/CP.

CBD's Clearinghouse Mechanism or "CHM."

International Chamber of Commerce (ICC) website on Incoterms at http://www.ic-cwbo.org/products-and-services/trade facilitation/incoterms-2010/.

International Chamber of Commerce (ICC) see also http://store.iccwbo.org/incoterms-2010 (Incoterms book, along with a range of publications to assist in their use and interpretation).

UNCITRAL database of international contract enforcement cases and other records, at http://www.uncitral.org/uncitral/en/case_law.html.

UNCITRAL database of NY Convention cases at http://www.uncitral.org/pdf/english/texts/arbitration/NY-conv/New-York-Convention-E.pdf.

UNCITRAL websites at http://www.uncitral.org/uncitral/en/uncitral_texts/arbitration/NYConvention_status.html and http://www.uncitral.org/uncitral/en/uncitral_texts/sale_goods/1980CISG_status.html.

UNIDROIT All versions of the UNIDROIT Principles are online at http://www.unidroit.org/publications/unidroit-publications, under “instruments”/ “commercial contracts.”

UNIDROIT the Model Clauses are online at http://www.unidroit.org/instruments/commercial-contracts/upicc-model-clauses;

UNIDROIT The Legal Guide on Contract Farming are online at http://www.unidroit.org/instruments/contract-farming/legal-guide.

WIPO database of ABS contracts.

Expert Commentary, Opinion and Analysis

Ahrén, M., Ali, N., *et al.* 2012. *An explanatory guide to the Nagoya Protocol on access and benefit-sharing.* IUCN Environmental Law Centre (ELC).

Allan, D. and Hiscock, M. (1987) *Law of Contract in Australia.* CCH Australia Limited.

Allen & Overy LLP, 07 January 2009 “Hardship and anticipatory breach revisited. Belgian civil law concepts?” Online at http://www.allenovery.com/publications/en-gb/Pages/Hardship-and-anticipatory-breach-revisited--Belgian-civil-law-concepts--.aspx.

Andersen, R. and Winge, T. 2012. *The Access and Benefit-Sharing Agreement on Teff Genetic Resources: Facts and Lessons.* Lysaker: Fridtjof Nansen Institute.

Angerer, K. 2011. “Frog tales – on poison dart frogs, epibatidine, and the sharing of biodiversity.” *Innovation: The European Journal of Social Science Research.* 24(3): 353–369.

Arlt, A., Bervoets, C., Grechenig, K.R. and Kalss, S. 2002. “The Societas Europaea in Relation to the Public Corporation of Five Member States (France, Italy, Netherlands, Spain, Austria).” 3 *European Business Organization Law Review,* 4: 733–764.

Bavikatte, K. and Meienberg, F. 2014. “The Ambiguous March to Equity: A Commentary on the Limitations of the European Union Regulation on Access and Benefit Sharing.” Berne Declaration (BD), Natural Justice and UNU-IAS.

Beatson, J. and Schrage, E. 2003. *Cases, Materials and Texts on Unjustified Enrichment.* Hart Publishing.

Bhatti, S. *et al.* (Eds). 2007. *Contracting for ABS: The Legal and Scientific Implications of Bioprospecting Contracts.* IUCN

BioTrade Verification Framework for Native Natural Ingredients, § 3, Union for Ethical BioTrade, International Standard 1, Proposed Draft 3 – Clean 2007-06-20 (http://www.biotrade.org/ResourcesPublications/BT_Verification_framework_NI_June07_en.pdf).

Blackstone, W. 1765. *Commentaries on the Laws of England.*

Börkey, P., Glachant, M. and Lévêsque, F. 1999. *Voluntary Approaches for Environmental Policy: An Assessment.* OECD

Briggs, A. 2008. *The Conflict of Laws.* Oxford University Press, Clarendon Law Series.

Cabrera, J. 2009. "The Role of the National Biodiversity Institute in the Use of Biodiversity for Sustainable Development: Forming Biopropsecting Partnerships." In Kamau, E.C. and Winter, G. (Eds) *Genetic Resources, Traditional Knowledge and the Law: Solutions for Benefit-sharing*, 244–269. London and Serling, VA: Earthscan, at 244–269.

Cohen, F. 1945. (4th printing.) *Handbook of Federal Indian Law.* United States Government Printing Office.

Collins, L. (1996) *Essays in International Litigation and the Conflict of Laws.* Clarendon Paperbacks.

Corbin on Contracts. (Multi-volume text – regularly updated.) West Publishing Company.

The Crucible Group. 1994. *People, Plants and Patents. The Impact of Intellectual Property on Trade, Plant Biodiversity, and Rural Society.* IDRC; Available at www.idrc.ca/booktique.

The Crucible Group. 2000. *Seeding Solutions, Volume 1: Policy Options for Genetic Resources (People, Plants, and Patents Revisited)* IDRC and the Dag Hammarskjold Foundation); Available at www.idrc.ca/booktique.

The Crucible Group. 2001. *Seeding Solutions, Volume 2: Options for National Laws Governing Control Over Genetic Resources and Biological Innovations.* IDRC, the International Plant Genetic Resources Institute and the Dag Hammarskjold Foundation. Available at www.idrc.ca/booktique.

Davies, P.L. 2008. *Gower's Modern Company Law* (8th ed.) Sweet and Maxwell, London.

Feldman, S.W. and Keyes, W.N. 2011. *Government Contracts in a Nutshell*, (5th ed.) West Nutshell Series, Minneapolis.

Fernández-Ugalde, J.C. 2005. "The Feasibility, Practicality and Cost of a Certificate of Origin system for genetic resources: Economic considerations." In *Proceedings of the Yokohama Roundtable: Towards Fair and Equitable Benefit-Sharing – Instruments for the Effective Implementation of the Bonn Guidelines under the Convention on Biological Diversity.* UNU-IAS, JBA.

Fernández-Ugalde, J.C. 2004. "Elements for the Design of a Certificate of Legal Provenance." In *Proceedings of the International Expert Workshop on Access to Genetic Resources and Benefit Sharing, Final Report.* Environment Canada and CONABIO. Available at http://www.canmexworkshop.com/papers.cfm.

Furmston, M. 2001. "Chapter 16: The Voluntary Assignment of Contractual Rights and Liabilities." In *Cheshire, Fifoot and Furmston's Law of Contract* (14th ed.) Butterworths LexisNexis.

Gen Goto. 2013. "The Outline for the Companies Act Reform in Japan and Its Implications"; University of Tokyo – Graduate School of Law and Politics. Online at http://papers.ssrn.com/sol3/papers.cfm?abstract_id=2348554.

Glowka, L. 1998, *A Guide to Designing Legal Frameworks to Determine Access to Genetic Resources*, IUCN Law and Policy Series No. 34, Gland: IUCN.

Glowka, L. (undated) *Towards a Certification System for Bioprospecting Activities.* Swiss State Secretariat for Economic Affairs.

Gollin, M. 2002. "Elements of commercial biodiversity prospecting agreements," Chapter 10 in Laird, S. *Biodiversity and Traditional Knowledge: Equitable Partnerships in Practice.* Earthscan.

Hajdu, D. 2008. *The Ten-Cent Plague: The Great Comic-Book Scare and How It Changed America.* New York, NY: Farrar, Straus and Giroux.

Houghton, N.D. 1929. "The Position of Unrecognized Governments Before the Courts of Foreign States." Republished republished online *Indiana Law Journal* 4(8). Online at http://www.repository.law.indiana.edu/cgi/viewcontent.cgi?article=4236&context=ilj.

Papers and Studies of The ABS Project. IUCN. 2000–2007. Project website no longer maintained, but all documents available from IUCN Environmental Law Centre, Godesberger Allee 108–112, Bonn, DE 94175. Five of the five formally published (ISBN listed) books of this project are included in this Bibliography.

Jacur, R. (ed.) 2015. *Natural Resources Grabbing: An International Law Perspective.* Brill/Nijhoff.

Jonas, H., Makagon, J.E. and Shrumm, H. 2013. *The Living Convention: A Compendium of Internationally Recognised Rights That Support the Integrity and Resilience of Indigenous Peoples' and Local Communities' Territories and Other Social-Ecological Systems.* Online at http://www.forestpeoples.org/guiding-principles/free-prior-and-informed-consent-fpic.

Kamau, E.C. and Winter, G. (Eds) (2009) *Genetic Resources, Traditional Knowledge and the Law: Solutions for Benefit-sharing*, London and Serling, VA: Earthscan.

Kamau, *et al.* "The Nagoya Protocol on Access to Genetic Resources and Benefit Sharing: What Is New and What Are the Implications for Provider and User Countries and the Scientific Community?" *Law, Environment and Development Journal* 6: 3.

Kamau, E.C., Winter, G. and Stoll, P-T. 2015. *Research and Development on Genetic Resources – Public Domain Approaches in Implementing the Nagoya Protocol.* Earthscan, Routledge.

Kohona, P. 2015. "The Multilateral Treaty Framework – An Abiding Achievement of the UN." *Environmental Policy and Law*, 45(6): 246.

Laird S. 1993. "Contracts for Biodiversity Prospecting," in Reid W.V., *et al. Biodiversity Prospecting: Using Genetic Resources for Sustainable Development*, Washington, DC: World Resources Institute.

Laird, S.A. 1999. *Equitable Biodiversity Research Relationships in Practice: Written Agreements Between Communities and Researchers*. Waterbury Center, VT: World Wildlife Federation.

Laird, S.A., Cunningham, A.B. and Lesinge, E. 1999. "One in Ten Thousand: The Cameroon Case of *Ancistrocladus korupensis*." In Zerner, C., ed. *People, Plants, and Justice: The Politics of Nature Conservation*. Columbia University Press.

Lookofsky, J.M. 1996. *Consequential Damages in Comparative Context*. Jurist-og Økonomforbundets Forlag.

Markesinis, B.S. and Unberath, H. 2002. *The German Law of Torts: A Comparative Treatise*. Hart Publishing.

McClean, D. and Beevers, K. 2005. *Morris: The Conflict of Laws*, (6th ed.) Thomson/ Sweet & Maxwell.

Mgbeoji, I. 2005. Mgbeoji, I. 2006. "Analysis of Four Claims of Unauthorised Access and Misappropriation of Genetic Resources and Associated Traditional Knowledge." Circulated in pamphlet form at CBD-COP-8. The ABS Project (IUCN-ELC.)

Moore, Gerald and Timowsky, Witold. 2005. *Explanatory guide to the International Treaty on Plant Genetic Resources for Food and Agriculture*. IUCN Environmental Law Centre (ELC).

Morgera, E., Buck, M. and Tsioumani E., 2013. *The 2010 Nagoya Protocol on Access and Benefit-sharing in Perspective: Implications for International Law and Implementation Challenges* (*Legal Studies on Access and Benefit-Sharing*), Martinus Nijhoff.

Natural Justice. 2013. "Access or Utilisation – What Triggers User Obligations? A Comment on the Draft Proposal of the European Commission on the Implementation of the Nagoya Protocol on Access and Benefit Sharing." Natural Justice/Berne Declaration. Available online at https://www.bernedeclaration.ch/fileadmin/files/documents/Biodiversitaet/130618_Access_or_Utilisation.pdf.

North, P.M. and Faucett, J.J. 2004. *North & Cheshire's Private International Law* (13th ed.) Oxford University Press.

North, P.M. (ed.) 1982. *Contract Conflicts*. North-Holland Publishing Company.

Oh, C. "IPRs and Biological Resources: Implications for Developing Countries," Third World Network. Online at http://www.twn.my/title/iprharare.htm. Last consulted 10 June 2016.

"Overview of the San Hoodia ABS Experience." Online at https://www.evb.ch/fileadmin/files/documents/Biodiversitaet/060330_Umsetzung_der_CBD_Overview_of_San_Hoodia_Experience.pdf.

Park, W.W. 2009. "Non-signatories and International Contracts: An Arbitrator's Dilemma." Oxford. Online at http://www.arbitration-icca.org/media/0/12571271340940/park_joining_non-signatories.pdf.

Pollock, F. 1886. *The Law of Torts: A Treatise on the Principles of Obligations arising from Civil Wrongs in the Common Law* (4th ed.). Stevens and Sons, Limited.

Price, J. 1982. "What You Didn't Learn About Contracts in Law School: Orientation of New Attorneys to the Demands and Challenges of Domestic and International Contracts." Buchman, Kass, Morgan & Miller. Oakland, CA, USA.

Reid, Walt, *et al.* 1993. *Biodiversity Prospecting: Using Genetic Resources for Sustainable Development*, World Resources International.

Reinmann, M. and Zimmermann, R. 2006. *The Oxford Handbook of Comparative Law.* Oxford University Press.

Rosendal, G.K., *et al.* "Balancing ABS and IPR Governance in the Aquaculture Sector." In *Global Governance of Genetic Resources Access and Benefit Sharing after the Nagoya Protocol.* Edited by Oberthür and Rosendal. Routledge, 2014.

Rosenthal J.P., D. Beck, *et al.* 1999. "Combining high-risk science with ambitious social and economic goals." *Pharmaceutical Biology* 37:6–21.

Ruiz Mueller, M. 2015. *Genetic Resources as Natural Information.* Abbingdon: Routledge.

Ruiz Mueller, M. and Lapeña, I. (Eds). *A Moving Target: Genetic Resources and Options for Tracking and Monitoring their International Flows*, IUCN/SPDA. 2008. (IUCN Environmental Policy and Law Paper, no. 67/2).

Schei, P.J. and Tvedt, M.W. 2010. "'Genetic Resources' in the CBD: The Wording, the Past, the Present and the Future." Lysaker, Fridtjof Nansens Institutt (FNI Report No. 4/2010).

Schloen, M., *et al.* 2011. *Access and Benefit-sharing for Genetic Resources for Food and Agriculture – Current Use and Exchange Practices, Commonalities, Differences and User Community Needs – Report from a Multi-stakeholder Expert Dialogue. Rome,* CBGRFA no. 59.

Scott, P. 2005. "User and provider country measures in the context of the international regime: Some thoughts and observations." Presentation at the International Expert Workshop on Access to Genetic Resources and Benefit-Sharing, Cape Town, South Africa, September 20–23, 2005.

Shelton, D. 2014. "The Human Security of Endangered Peoples: Indigenous Groups Living in Isolation and First Contact." *Environmental Policy &Law* 44 (1–2: 218. IOS Press, Amsterdam.

Singh, A. 2015. *Company Law* (16th ed.) Lucknow: Eastern Book Company

Singh Nijar, G. and Gan Pei Fern. 2012. *The Nagoya ABS Protocol: A Record of the Negotiations.* University of Malaya Press, at 78–79.

Swiderska, K. 2001. *Stakeholder Participation in Policy on Access to Genetic Resources, Traditional Knowledge and Benefit Sharing. Case studies and recommendations.* IIED. Biodiversity and Livelihoods Issues, No 4.

Tobin, B. 2012. "Bridging the Nagoya Compliance Gap: The Fundamental Role of Customary Law. In LEAD, *Protection of Indigenous Peoples' Resource and Knowledge Rights.*

Ten Kate, K. and Wells, A. (undated, circa 2001) "Preparing a national strategy on access to genetic resources and benefit-sharing." Kew. Circulated at CBD-COP-5.

Tvedt, M.W., Eijsink, V., Steen, I.H., Strand, R. and Rosendal, G.K. 2016. "The Missing Link in ABS – The Relationship between Resource and Product" in *Environmental Policy and Law* 46 (3–4): 228–237.

Tvedt, M.W. and Schei, P.J. 2014. "The Term 'Genetic Resources': Flexible and Dynamic while Providing Legal Certainty?" In Oberthür and Rosendal (eds). *Global Governance of Genetic Resources Access and Benefit Sharing after the Nagoya Protocol.* Routledge.

Tvedt, M.W. and Young, T.R. 2007. *Beyond Access: Exploring Implementation of the Fair and Equitable Sharing Commitment in the CBD*. IUCN. (IUCN Environmental Policy and Law Paper, no. 67/2).

Tvedt, M.W. 2011. "A Report from the First Reflection Meeting on the Global Multilateral Benefit-Sharing Mechanism." Fridtjof Nansens Institutt (FNI Report 10/2011).

Tvedt, M.W. 2013. "Disentangling Rights to Genetic Resources Illustrated by Aquaculture and Forest Sectors." *Law, Environment and Development Journal* 9(2): 129–140.

Tvedt, M.W. 2015. "Changes in the Plant Treaty – How Can Benefit Sharing Happen and the Link to Intellectual Property Rights – Assessing the Mutually Supportiveness." *Law, Environment and Development Journal* 11(1): 23–34.

Vogel, Joseph *et al.* 2011. "The Economics of Information, Studiously Ignored in the Nagoya Protocol on Access to Genetic Resources and Benefit Sharing." *Law, Environment and Development Journal* 7: 1.

Vogel, J.H. 2007. "From the 'Tragedy of the Commons' to the 'Tragedy of the Commonplace': Analysis and Synthesis through the Lens of Economic Theory." In McManis, C.R. (ed.) *Biodiversity and the Law*.

Williston on Contracts (4th ed.) 2002–2018. Multi-volume treatise, updated regularly. Lawyers Cooperative Publishing.

Witkin, B. 2005. *Summary of California Law: Contracts*, (10th ed.). Volume 1 of an annually updated multivolume treatise. Thomson-West.

Young, T.R. and Tvedt, M.W. 2009. "Balancing Building Blocks of a Functional ABS System." Published as UNEP/CBD/WG-ABS/8/INF/2 (CBD).

Young, T.R. and Bhatti, S. 2007. "ABS Contracts and Contract Law: The 'contractual side' of the international ABS negotiations and implementation." In Bhatti, S., *et al.*, 2007, *supra*.

Young, T. 2013. "The Biosafety Clearinghouse in Practice." In Cordonier Segger, M., Perron-Welch, F. and Frison, C. (Eds). *Legal Aspects of Implementing the Cartagena Protocol on Biosafety*. Cambridge University Press.

Young, T. (Ed.) 2009. *Covering ABS : addressing the need for sectoral, geographical, legal and international integration in the ABS regime: papers and studies of the ABS project*. IUCN Environmental Law Centre (ELC).

Young, T. 2007, "Contract Provisions and Experience," and "Applying Contract Law to ABS." In Bhatti *et al.*, 2007, *supra*.

Young, T. 2006. "Analysis of Claims of 'Unauthorised Access and Misappropriation of Genetic Resources and Associated Traditional Knowledge'" UNEP/CBD/WG-ABS/4/INF/6, Reprinted in Young, 2009, *supra*.

Young, T.R. 2004. *An Examination of the Pros and Cons of IUCN Involvement in Environmental Certification Systems and Standards Development*. Situation analysis and scoping paper prepared under the IUCN Programme for Innovation, Integration, Information, and Communication (III-C) Fund. IUCN.

National Instruments/Examples

Andean Community Online at http://www.wipo.int/wipolex/es/details.jsp?id=9446, or search "Decisión No. 392 de la Comunidad Andina."

Australian Government Response to Notification 2011–216; Access to Genetic Resources and Benefit-sharing; Ref.: SCBD/ABS/VN/SG/74553.

Australia: Environment Protection and Biodiversity Conservation Regulations 2000 (Cth) ("the EPBC Regulations") made under the Environment Protection and Biodiversity Conservation Act 1999, Part 8A. Available online at http://www.austlii.edu.au/au/legis/cth/consol_reg/epabcr2000697/.

Bayh-Dole Act, 35 U.S.C. 200–212 (PL 96–517), Patent and Trademark Act Amendments of 1980.

Brazil: Provisional Act No 2,186-16, dated August 23, 2001.

California Corporations Code.

California Government Code.

Cornell University, Legal Information Institute, which provides links to all relevant state-law regulation in the US at https://www.law.cornell.edu/wex/table_corporations; free searchable access to the UCC, at https://www.law.cornell.edu/ucc/.

Contract Act of Norway § 36. Act no 4 og 31. May 1918 LOV-1918-05-31-4.

Ecuador: Reglamento Nacional al Régimen Común de Acceso a los Recursos Genéticos en aplicación a la Decisión No. 392 de la Comunidad Andina. Decreto Ejecutivo No 905 de 3 de octubre de 2011.

Idaho Annotated Code.

JAMS, Inc (formerly Judicial Arbitration and Mediation Services) provides a range of elements and options for possible clauses at http://www.jamsadr.com/files/Uploads/Documents/JAMS-Rules/JAMS-ADR-Clauses.pdf.

Uniform Commercial Code (UCC), (see Cornell Universirty).

United States: Dolphin-safe tuna legislation, 16 U.S.C. 1385.

United States: Lacey Act, enacted as Pub. L. 97–79, Sec. 3, Nov. 16, 1981 (last amended 2003), codified in the US Code at 16 USC §§ 3371–3378. Available online from http://www.Thomas.gov.

National Caselaw

AUSTRALIA *Thornton v Shoe Lane Parking Ltd.* (1971) 1 All ER 686.

AUSTRALIA *Armacel Pty Ltd v Smurfit Stone Container Corporation* [2008] FCA 592:

AUSTRALIA *Vetreria Etrusca srl v Kingston Estate Wines P/L*, [2008] Supreme Court of South Australia 75, 14 March 2008.

COSTA RICA, Normas Generales para el Acceso a los Elementos y Recursos Genéticos y Bioquimicos de la Biodiversidad Arts. 6(f) and 19.

COSTA RICA, Decreto No. 31 514, 2003, issued pursuant to the Organic Law on the Environment (No 7554 of 4 Oct. 1995) §§ 46–47; and the Biodiversity Law (No 7788 of 30 April 1998).

SWITZERLAND: Kantonsgericht Zug; Case law on UNCITRAL texts (CLOUT) abstract no. 629.

UKRAINE Chamber of Commerce and Trade Arbitration proceeding, 23, CLOUT Case 1023 September 2004.

UNITED KINGDOM *Federal Commerce & Navigation Co v Molena Alpha Inc* (the 'Nanfri') [1979] AC 75 7 at 778–9.

UNITED KINGDOM *Hong Kong Fir Shipping v Kawasaki Kishen Kaisha* [1962] 2 QB 26.

UNITED STATES *Avery v. Hughes*, 661 F.3d 690 (1st Cir. 2011).

UNITED STATES *Davis v. Jones*, 254 F.2d 696 (10th Cir. 1958).

UNITED STATES *Forrest Associates v. Passamaquoddy Tribe*, 2000 ME 195, 760 A. 2d 1041 (Me. 2000).

UNITED STATES *GE HFS Holdings, Inc. v. National Union Fire Insurance Co. of Pittsburgh, Pennsylvania*, 520 F. Supp. 2d 213, 217 (D. Mass. 2007).

UNITED STATES *Henderson v. Henderson Investment Properties*, L.L.C., No. 35138, 2010 WL 569890 (Idaho Feb. 19, 2010).

UNITED STATES *IRB-Brasil Resseguros, S.A. v. Inepar Investments, S.A.*, No. 08669; 2012 WL 6571286 (N.Y. 2012).

UNITED STATES *Narragansett Indian Tribe v. RIBO*, Inc., 686 F. Supp. 48 (D.R.I. 1988); *Taylor v. Grant*, 204 Or. 10, 279 P. 2d 479 (1955), *decision clarified on rehearing*, 204 Or. 10, 279 P. 2d 1037 (1955);

UNITED STATES *Penobscot Indian Nation* v. *Key Bank of Maine*, 112 F.3d 538 (1st Cir. 1997).

UNITED STATES *Spirtas Company v. Federal Insurance Company*, 81 F. Supp. 2d 993 (E.D. Mo. 2007), aff'd, 521 F.3d 833 (8th Cir., 2008).

UNITED STATES *Taylor v. Grant*, 204 Or. 10, 279 P .2d 479 (1955), *decision clarified on rehearing*, 204 Or. 10, 279 P. 2d 1037 (1955).

UNITED STATES *U.S. v. Ahtanum Irr. Dist.*, 236 F.2d 321 (9th Cir. 1956).

Publicly Available Contracts, Forms and Similar Instruments

Ethiopia. The Teff Agreement. Reprinted in its entirety in Andersen and Winge, 2012, *supra*.

ITPGRFA, *Standard Material Transfer Agreement* [SMTA], ITPGRFA Governing Body, 16 June 2006, Resolution 1/2006 Annex 2, Art. 6.7. (emphasis in original).

Swiss Academy of Sciences document entitled "Agreement on Access and Benefit Sharing for Non-Commercial Research: Sector specific approach containing Model Clauses" (available online at http://www.naturalsciences.ch/organisations/biodiversity/abs/publications/36817-sample-abs-agreement-for-non-commercial-research-2010-).

MOSAICC Micro-organisms Sustainable Use and Access Regulation International Code of Conduct (as updated June 2011), online at http://bccm.belspo.be/documents/files/projects/mosaicc/code2011.pdf. This is a voluntary code of conduct.

MOSAICC, "Examples of Prior Informed Consent (PIC) documents."

MOSAICC Micro-organisms Sustainable Use and Access Regulation International Code of Conduct (as updated June 2011), online at http://bccm.belspo.be/documents/files/projects/mosaicc/code2011.pdf.

Pandemic Influenza Preparedness Framework for the sharing of influenza viruses and access to vaccines and other benefits ("PIP Framework"). Adopted the Sixty-fourth World Health Assembly, 24 May 2011. Online at http://apps.who.int/gb/ebwha/pdf_files/WHA64/A64_8-en.pdf.

WHO-SMTAs. Available online at http://www.who.int/influenza/pip/en/.

Index

Ability to Perform
  corporate entities 95–96
  in general 205–206
Administrative law 49, 91
African Union 326
Agriculture 156, 161, 267, 381, 384
Amendment or Re-formation 185–190, 252–254
Allocation 174, 310
Ambiguity
  "creative ambiguity," inappriateness of 24
  in general 23–29, 72–73, 114–116, 126, 136, 178, 211, 232, 235, 299, 322, 343–345, 357–358, 389, 393–394
Arbitration/Mediation 262–263
Areas (and resources) beyond national jurisdiction 44, 328, 331–333, 345
Australia 15, 76, 77, 78, 150, 249, 300, 321, 361
Authorized Representatives
  corporate entities 103–104
  agency 104–105, 314–315
  in general 103, 105–106
  governmental entities 105

Bankruptcy 64, 82–85, 89, 95, 98, 104, 109, 110, 158, 180, 191–195, 221, 227, 232, 241, 242, 252, 256, 266, 279, 281–283, 287, 367
Benefit-sharing 123–128
Biological diversity. *See* Convention on Biological Diversity (CBD)
Biosafety. *See* Cartagena Protocol
Bonn Guidelines 1, 73, 325, 335–339, 351, 358, 369, 390
Brazil 287, 291, 338

Cartagena Protocol 289, 316, 325, 350, 361, 362
Calculation of payment 124–126, 257–259
Casual Sharing/Transfer of Genetic Resources, Samples, Data and ATK 174–175, 181–182
CGIAR. *See* Collections
Change of Use/Intent 146–156
China 291, 317, 318
Civil law. *See* Legal systems
Classification of contracts 224–226
Collateral and security 271–273
Collections 25, 59, 68, 153–156, 159, 160, 218, 265–266, 289, 354, 363, 367, 378, 380, 384
Collectors and Transferees 138, 151–156, 157–196
Common law. *See* Legal systems
Commercial use 148–150
Compensation (remedy) 104, 182, 223, 236–240, 243, 250–254, 286
Concreteness 4, 22–33, 35–36, 42, 73, 86, 113–157, 172, 175–177, 179, 198, 198–200, 207–209, 211–212, 223, 224, 237
Confidentiality 53, 58, 60, 61, 63, 64, 79, 132, 212, 221, 261, 273, 351, 360–362, 381, 397
Conservation 1, 2, 30, 68, 101, 150, 278, 289, 293, 324, 329, 333, 349, 353, 383, 384
Contracting parties 316, 351
Contracts of Adhesion 215–220
Contractual Scope
  in general 128–129
  limitations on 129–132
  exclusivity 131–132
  expiration 132
Convention on Biological Diversity (CBD) 1–2, 6, 9, 12, 19, 24–25, 27–30, 38, 43, 45–46, 48, 73, 75, 82, 102, 115, 119, 126, 135, 138–139, 160, 203, 222, 226–227, 276, 279, 299, 307, 311, 320, 321–363, 366, 371, 374, 382, 389–393, 397
Costa Rica 12, 13, 128, 338, 344, 361, 368, 373, 378
Crops 28, 37, 227, 322, 355
Customary use 356, 357

Databases
  ABS Clearinghouse 47, 361, 363, 364, 367
  CBD Clearinghouse Mechanism 365
  WIPO contracts database 15
  potential value of 387
Derivative 24, 25, 29, 128, 156, 190, 245, 258, 287, 322, 347
Default 245–247

Definitions
of ABS terms in international instruments 24–25, 31, 83, 114, 119, 127, 139, 155, 299, 323, 324, 332, 339, 344–345, 346, 354
in contracts 25, 29, 31, 33, 55, 114, 119, 125, 127, 139, 177–178, 193, 195, 196, 343, 354, 374
of contractual terms
anticipatory breach 260–261
binding contract 201
breach of contract 242–247
conditions 243–244
contract classifications 224–225
contract of adhesion 215–216
disclosure 220
elements of a contract 5
enforceable contract 202–203
estoppel 259–260
implementation of a contract 202
international contract 3–4
intention 209–210
legal certainty 204
legal personality 80
legally recognized capacity 80, 96–97
level playing field 96
minor breach 243
mutuality 208–209
repudiation 260–261
rules of construction 72
silence 143, 157–165
standards and commercial practices 226
survival 261–262
transnational contract 3–4
unconscionable contract 215–216
waiver 259–260
Delay 244–245
Developing country 13, 16, 30, 66, 67, 68, 81, 178, 220, 270, 289, 291, 293, 367, 369, 382
Disclosure 220–221
DNA 138, 147, 178

Enforceability 197, 229–267
Enforcement
filing, standing and other issues 255
in general 241–254
burden of proof 255–257

Equity 197, 201, 208, 212–221, 352
Exclusion 247–248
Exclusivity 131–132, 178–179
Exercising Security/Foreclosure 273–275
Exempt use 148–150

FAO 133, 219, 266–268, 318, 328, 355
Farmers' rights 101, 266, 356, 358
Food, genetic resources in 113, 156, 161, 267, 268, 286
Food security 268
Forest 72, 380
Foreclosure. *See* Exercising Security/ Foreclosure
Fund 152, 273, 281

Gentleman's agreement. *See* Soft obligations
Global Multilateral Benefit-sharing Mechanism 32, 38, 339, 364
Good governance 341
"Governing Law" 293–294, 294–297

Heritage 317

IARCs (International Agricultural Research Centers) 347
ICC Incoterms 306, 307–309
Incentives 287–290
Influenza 219, 220, 328, 348, 370
In situ 24, 79, 302, 326, 365
Intellectual property rights (IPR) 12, 15, 50, 132, 134, 136, 200, 226, 243, 254, 299, 314, 321, 327, 330, 351, 356, 376
Intention 209–211
Interim users 138
International commercial law 300–316
International law 23, 27, 49, 50, 51, 111, 139, 268, 270, 320, 321, 330, 344, 352
Invalidation 222–223
ITPGRFA 73, 130, 132, 139–140, 155, 159, 160, 218, 264–266, 317, 320, 326, 339, 343, 345, 346, 352–356, 368, 383–385
ITPGRFA Fund 140, 268

Knowledge 10, 14, 17, 26, 29, 30, 65, 101, 102, 116, 119, 129, 138, 174, 214, 223, 236, 259, 296, 311, 321, 372, 381, 389

Legal Authority to Act on Behalf of a Party 101–106
Legal Certainty 203–205
Legal Personality 87–94, 97, 98, 101–103, 105, 107
Legally Recognized Capacity 96–100
Liquidated Damages 247, 248–252

Mediation. *See* Arbitration/Mediation
Mergers and Corporate Restructuring 195–196
Middlemen. *See* Collectors and Transferees
Monitoring 132–133
MOSAICC 326, 337, 338, 347, 352, 361, 363, 369
Multilateral 97
Multilateral system 140, 141, 160, 268, 355, 385
Mutuality 207–209

National authority 47, 130, 364
Necessary Parties 106–112
New York Convention on the Recognition and Enforcement of Foreign Arbitral Awards 306, 313–314
Non-ABS use 147–148
Non-commercial use 148–150, 151–153
Non-exempt use 148–150
Non-Judicial Remedies
  advances and prepayments 284–285
  assets pledged as security 278–279
  direct transfer subject to conditions 276
  escrow arrangements, letters of credit and other monetary security 277–278
  in general 268–292
  insurance 280–283
  liquidated damages as non-judicial remedies 280
  mortgages (*see* Assets pledged as security)
  payment in shares 287
  prepayments (*see* Advances and prepayments)
  requiring establishment of local operations 285–287
  self-executing Protective Measures 280
  return of the Res 283–284
Norway 104, 153, 242, 243, 293, 337, 359
Notification 183–184

Objective/Purpose Clauses 143–146
Obligation/Action Clauses
  in general 123–133
  triggers 138–143, 183–184
Operative Provisions 116–118

Patents and other IPRS 133–137
Pandemic 219, 220, 328, 348, 370
Patent 37, 43, 58, 84
Peru 344
Plant breeding 27, 83
Plant breeders' rights 84, 141
Private International Law 297–300, 316–320, 397
Protected areas 289, 384
Protected Classes 214–215
Public Policy 222

"Reasonable" standard 290–292
Remedies 229–262
  compensation for loss, harm or damage 246–247
  costs/fees reimbursement 248–249
  coercive ("equitable") remedies 239–241
  declaratory judgment 235–236
  interpretation 235–236
  liquidated damages 247
  punitive damages 247–248
  reformation 240–241
  specific performance 239–240
Res 118–122, 283–284
Reciprocal 33
Risk 7, 11, 28, 59, 71, 80, 89, 106, 108–110, 159, 165, 171, 174, 176, 193, 203, 206, 245, 250, 270, 285, 289, 299, 310, 314, 320, 366, 372, 375, 376, 383–380
Rules of Contract Construction/ Interpretation 72, 233–235

Scope. *See* Contractual Scope
Seed 27, 137, 267, 268, 286, 315, 380
Soft contractual obligations 223–224
Sources of law governing international contracts 50–51
Standards 226–228
Statutory 6, 9, 97, 298
Subject matter of the contract. *See Res*
Survival 261–262, 275–276

Taxonomic collections. *See* Collections
Teff 110, 120, 134–138, 138, 141, 153, 180, 218, 231, 273, 330, 331, 346
Termination 165–166, 169–170, 275–276
Third-party Beneficiaries 100–101, 263–264
Third-party Obligation 264–267
Third-party Transfers. *See* Collectors and Transferees
Timeliness 254
Transaction 7, 10, 13, 15, 16, 18, 22, 30, 31, 35, 41, 50, 53, 63, 64, 66, 73, 76, 90, 93, 102, 108, 111, 147, 160, 163, 168–170, 177, 192, 193, 196, 200, 214–216, 221, 222, 226, 252, 271–274, 279, 280, 283, 287, 304, 313, 323, 327, 330, 336–338, 342, 344, 353, 358, 366, 372, 374, 376, 379–382, 385, 387, 389, 390, 393
Transferees. *See* Collectors and Transferees
Transferors. *See* Collectors and Transferees
"Two-stage ABS Contractual Process" 74–79

Unconscionable Contracts 215–220
UN Convention on Contracts for the International Sale of Goods 306, 309–312
UNCLOS 326, 328, 329–332, 343
UNIDROIT 302–304
User Measures 48

Validity 197–198, 199, 200, 206–207

WHO PIP framework 218–220, 326, 346, 368
WIPO 219, 328